CHIDUSHIM ON PARSHA

Sefer Bemidbar

Rabbi Bernard Fox

Edited by

Rabbi Eliezer Barany

Table of Contents

Preface

It is with the help of *HaKadush Baruch Hu* and with tremendous joy that I can present the collected writings of Rabbi Bernie Fox on the *Parsha*. Those familiar with his writings know how invaluable a *melamed* – teacher – he is. He disseminates *Torah* so clearly and helps others develop in learning and a love of *Hashem*. For those unacquainted, I can share with you a glimpse of what you're about to experience.

He articulates complex details in a way that is accessible to even casual students and helps guide them through the mazes of multifaceted issues. These books convey brilliant teachings that provide foundational lessons; allowing the reader to properly learn the *Torah*, delve into the *Talmud*, understand the *Rishonim*, and advance their own *Talmud Torah* abilities. The reader will gain broad knowledge on a myriad of topics while also diving deeply into specifics, thus enabling a substantial understanding of a verse and its surrounding topic. I write this with the idea that the reader will be prepared for how deep and comprehensive these writings are and also to instill the sense of excitement about what is in store, that I always feel when I read the Rabbi's thoughts and ponder his natural prose style. Studying these writings will allow one to truly approach *Kol HaTorah Kulo* – the entirety of Torah.

On a personal note, I am deeply grateful and honored to be able to share these lessons. Rabbi Fox's writings transfixed me from the very first analysis I read of his; a piece he wrote on *Megilat Ruth*. He established an appropriate approach to understanding the *Rishonim* on the text and allowed for a grasp of the text itself. Since then, I have learned answers to longstanding questions, have better understood passages in the *Torah*, have expanded my learning skills and have grown to love *Talmud Torah* even more! Compiling the Rabbi's writings has been a labor of love which has sustained me from start to finish.

It is my hope, in sharing his collected writings, to be able to be *Marbitz Torah* – disseminate *Torah* – and to help others experience the same enhanced love of learning that I did and which so many of Rabbi Fox's *Talmidim* –students, have.

With tremendous gratitude,

Eliezer Barany

Bemidbar

And Hashem spoke to Moshe in the wilderness of Sinai from within the Tent of Meeting on the first day of the second month in the second year from their departure from the Land of Egypt saying: Count all of the assembly of Bnai Yisrael according to their families and the households of their fathers according to the names of every male by their heads. (BeMidbar 1:1-2)

If You Can't Trust Moshe, Who Can You Trust?

1. The censuses of Sefer BeMidbar and Sefer Shemot

Sefer BeMidbar is also referred to as Sefer Pekudim – the Book of the Censuses. This name is assigned to Sefer BeMidbar because it opens with a census of the nation. A second census is described toward the end of the *sefer*. In other words, most of the material in the *sefer* is found between these two censuses.

In the above passages Hashem instructs Moshe regarding the first of the censuses. It is unclear whether this is the first or the second census taken of the nation. Sefer Shemot includes an account of a census taken at the time that the *Mishcan* was created. The Torah tells us that according to that census the nation included 603,550 males over the age of twenty. The census described in the opening passages of Sefer BeMidbar is focused on this identical demographic group – males over the age of twenty. The census yields the same result as the one described in Sefer Shemot. The group includes 603,550 members. This suggests that both accounts describe a single census.[1]

Others dispute this conclusion. They contend that the accounts describe two distinct events. A census was taken prior to the construction of the *Mishcan*. This is the census described in Sefer Shemot. Sefer BeMidbar is opening with the description of a second census. Of course, this poses a problem. It is remarkable that the two events yielded the same outcome. In both the number of individuals tallied is identical.

2. The miracle of the BeMidbar census and its message

Gershonides – Ralbag responds to this criticism. He explains that each census counted the males between the ages of twenty and sixty. In the period between the two censuses, some members of the first census passed the age of sixty. These individuals were replaced by an identical number of young people who attained the age of twenty. Therefore, the totals of the two censuses are identical.

Ralbag acknowledges that this is a remarkable outcome. Under normal circumstances, the number of young people reaching the age of twenty would exceed those passing the age of sixty. This is because the older and age group, the less its members. Mortality rates generally increase in correspondence with age. The mortality rate for older people is higher than the rate for younger people. In a typical population sample, the number of people attaining the age of twenty

---

[1] This interpretation is championed by Rabbaynu Yosef Bechor Shur. (Rabbaynu Yosef Bechor Shur, *Commentary on Sefer BeMidbar* 1:1) It is subject to a number of criticisms. Among these is that the census here described takes place at a later date than the census described in Sefer Shemot. Rabbaynu Yosef Bechor Shur is aware of the objections to his perspective and briefly addresses them in his commentary.

will exceed the number of people who approaching the age sixty. Therefore, we would expect the second census to yield a larger total than the first census. The number of young people entering the census should exceed the number of elderly people leaving the census population.

Gershonides concludes that the result of the census suggest that a miracle, of sorts, took place. The number of older people was significantly larger than normal. This group did not experience the typical mortality rate. Their number was somewhat bloated. Consequently, an adequate number of elders passed the age of sixty to balance the number of young people attaining the age of twenty.[2]

Why would Hashem bring about this miracle? Ralbag suggest that the intention of the miracle was to communicate a message. Hashem would maintain the nation in the wilderness. The people would live their full years. Their travels through a harsh environment would not afflict them and weigh on the elderly. They would not die prematurely because of the stresses posed by their travels and the environment.[3]

From the age of twenty years of age and above, all that go forth in a host, you should count them according to their hosts – you and Aharon. With you should be a man from each tribe. Each man should be the head of the household of his fathers. (BeMidbar 1:3-4)

3. The purposes of the BeMidbar census

The Torah does not explicitly explain the purpose of this census. The above passage suggests that the purpose was to determine how many men were included on the "hosts" of the nation. These hosts are apparently the army of the nation. In other words, the census determined how many warriors were among the people.

This is a reasonable explanation for the census. The nation was leaving Sinai and embarking upon its journey to the Land of Israel. The plan was for Bnai Yisrael to soon enter the land promised to their forefathers and capture it from its inhabitants. This would require Bnai Yisrael to be prepared to battle these nations. This was the appropriate time to organize an army for the forthcoming campaign.

However, in the above passages Moshe is instructed to enlist a leader from each *shevet* – tribe – to join him in the process of taking the census. Why were these representatives required? It seems that this census would have some impact upon the individual *shevatim* – tribes. Therefore, Hashem directed Moshe to include representatives from the *shevatim*. What was this impact?

Malbim explains that this census not only tallied the warriors of the nation. It also would serve as the basis for the divisions of the Land of Israel among the *shevatim*. Each *shevet* would receive a portion of the land corresponding with the size of its population.

Malbim explains that because of this second objective Moshe was required to enlist the assistance of these leaders. They would advise Moshe regarding the assignment of each individual to his proper *shevet*.[4]

---

[2] Ralbag notes that in Sefer BeMidbar Hashem instructs Moshe to not include the tribe of Leyve in the census. This exclusion is not mentioned in Sefer Shemot. Ralbag concludes that, although not noted in the Torah's narrative, Shevet Leyve was not included in the Sefer Shemot census.

[3] Rabbaynu Levi ben Gershon (Ralbag / Gershonides), *Commentary on Sefer Beresheit*, 1:1.

[4] Rav Meir Leibush ben Yechiel Michel (Malbim), *HaTorah VeHaMitzvah – Commentary on*

And they arose from before Moshe with two hundred fifty men – leader of the assembly, those summoned on important occasions, men of reputation. (BeMidbar 16:2)

4. Hashem anticipated that the census would engender suspicion

According to Malbim, the representatives of the *shevatim* serve a practical and essential function. They assigned the individuals in the census to their appropriate tribe. However, there is another plausible reason for requiring Moshe to enlist these leaders into the process of taking the census.

The above passages introduce the Torah's account of Korach's rebellion. Korach enlisted a number of prominent leaders to his cause. Together, they challenged Moshe's authority. Specifically, they contended that Moshe had seized power for himself and his closest family members. This account is both remarkable and instructive.

It is remarkable that the sincerity, objectivity, and motives of Moshe would be challenged.

Moshe had risked everything in opposing Paroh. He had placed his own life in jeopardy in order to demand the liberation of his people. Moshe was the greatest of all prophets. He had ascended Sinai and returned with the tablets of the Decalogue and with the Torah he had received directly from Hashem. How could the Korach enlist two hundred and fifty leaders – individuals of substance – to join him in challenging Moshe?

The account is instructive. It communicates to us that this is human nature. Even Moshe was subject to suspicion and of serving self-interest. Our relationships with our leaders are complex. They are influenced and formed not only be objective observation. They are also the products of our own internal dynamics – our inner psychology. We strive to be objective and fair but sometimes fail and misjudge even the most righteous and selfless leaders.

This suggests that Hashem may have had another good reason for requiring that Moshe enlist these leaders in the conducting of this census. This census would determine the distribution of the Land of Israel among the *shevatim*. The process had the potential for fostering intense discontent. It could engender terrible envy and conflict. In order to avoid these outcomes, it was essential that the people recognize the census as equitable. The outcome must be credible. Moshe – acting alone – could not produce a census result that would be accepted as credible by the entire nation. He could only secure the acquiescence of the nation to his conclusions through including their leaders in the process.

5. We cannot expect to do better than Moshe and his generation

There are messages here for both a community and its leaders. Community members must recognize that their judgments of their leaders may not be completely objective. Moshe was misjudged by his generation. We are not greater people than those lead by Moshe. We should humbly acknowledge that our judgments may be as flawed as those of Moshe's generation.

There is a message here for those who are leaders or aspire to be leaders. A leader must be able to accept criticism. He must be prepared to accept even unreasonable and unjustified criticism. He should not imagine that he will be a more effective or impressive personality than

---

Sefer BeMidbar 1:4.

Moshe. Moshe was subjected to cruel and unfair assessment. Contemporary leaders should not expect to be above such criticism.

There is a second message here for leaders. Moshe was told by Hashem to enlist the nation's leaders in the conducting of the census. He did not protest that the people should trust him and not question the credibility of his conclusions. He understood the wisdom of conducting himself in a manner that would not evoke suspicions – even unreasonable and unfair suspicion. Contemporary leaders can take a lesson from this episode. A leader must conduct himself with honesty and integrity. He must also strive to place himself above suspicion – even unjustified suspicion. Sometimes this requires taking measures like those Hashem directed Moshe to take. He must be proactive. He must take those measures that proactively assure the community of the integrity of his actions and decisions.

And Hashem spoke to Moshe in the wilderness of Sinai in the Ohel Moed in the second month of the second year of their exodus from Egypt saying: Take a tally of the entire congregation of Bnai Yisrael according to their families (and) their household of their father according to the number of names. (Count) every male head. (BeMidbar 1:1-2)

The Order of the Listing of the Shevatim

1. Moshe and the leaders of the shevatim take a census of the nation

The above passages introduce Sefer BeMidbar. In these passages, Hashem instructs Moshe to conduct a census of the males of Bnai Yisrael. This census will not only determine the adult male population of the entire nation but also the adult male population of each shevet – tribe. In the subsequent passages Hashem instructs Moshe to enlist the cooperation of the heads of the tribes. The census is to be conducted under the auspices of this entire group of leaders. In the course of the Torah's account of the census and its results, the tribes are enumerated three times. In each instance the enumeration has its own unique characteristics and apparent quirks.

Before considering and analyzing these enumerations it will be useful to review three basic issues:

- Each of Yaakov's children was the patriarch of his own shevet. However, there is one exception to this rule. Yosef's two sons – Ephraim and Menashe – were each patriarchs of their own shevet. Therefore, although Yaakov had twelve sons, there are thirteen shevatim. Eleven of his sons served as patriarchs for their own shevet. Yosef's sons served as patriarchs for two additional tribes.

- In the census that Moshe is instructed to conduct, one tribe – Leyve – is to be excluded. Hashem instructs Moshe to conduct a separate census of Shevet Leyve. In other words, Moshe was instructed to conduct one census of twelve tribes and a separate census of Shevet Leyve.

- Yaakov's sons were born from four wives. Leyah gave birth to six sons and Rachel gave birth to two. The remaining four sons were the children of "surrogate" wives. During the period that she was childless, Rachel gave her servant Bilhah to Yaakov as a surrogate for herself. Bilhah gave birth to two sons. Leyah also experienced a period during which she could not conceive and she followed her sister Rachel's example. She gave her servant Zilpah to Yaakov as her surrogate and she gave birth to two sons.

And these are the names of men that should stand with you: For Reuven – Elitzur ben Sheteyur.
(BeMidbar 1:5)

2. The first listing of the shevatim

Hashem instructs Moshe to conduct the census with the participation of the heads of the shevatim. Hashem identifies by name the head of each shevet. This is the first time the shevatim are enumerated in the parasha.

The shevatim are divided into three groups each composed of four tribes. This division into groups reflects the Torah's cantilations – the traditional tune to which the passages are read. It is immediately observable that the order in which the shevatim are listed is not the birth order of their patriarchs. What is the basis of the order?

Apparently, the groups are – in part – determined by aesthetic considerations. Each leader and his shevet are identified in their own passage. Rather than listing of the twelve leaders and tribes a continuous series of twelve passages, the twelve passages are divided into three smaller groups – each composed of four passages. The listing begins with the sons of Leyah. These are listed in their birth order. Next the sons of Rachel are listed in their birth order. Finally, the sons of the two surrogates are listed. Among the sons of the surrogates, the oldest son – Dan – is listed first. However, the remaining sons are not listed in birth order or in any apparent order. There are three important elements of this first listing:

- The shevatim descendant from the sons of Leyah and Rachel are given precedence over those of the surrogate wives and the shevatim descendant from Leyah's sons are placed before those from Rachel's sons.

- The order of the shevatim descendant from Leyah and Rachel reflects the birth orders of their patriarchs.

- The order of shevatim descendant from the surrogates is not as strictly determined by birth order. Dan is recognized as eldest but birth order plays no further role in the listing of these tribes.

And it was that the descendants of Reuven the firstborn of Yisrael – their descendants according to their families (and) the household of their father – according to the number of names corresponding with all of the individual males twenty years of age or above, every one (fit) to go forth in legion. The census for the tribe of Reuven was forty-six thousand five hundred.
(BeMidbar 1:20-21)

3. The second listing of the shevatim

The above two passages are difficult to render into conventional English but their message is simple. They are the first passages of the second listing of the shevatim. These passages initiate the report of the census of Bnai Yisrael and reveal that Shevet Reuven – the tribe of Reuven included 46,500 males over age twenty. In the ensuing passages the Torah reports the census for each tribe.

The order in which the censuses of the tribes are reported is virtually identical to the order followed in the first list. The "Leyah shevatim" come first and are listed in birth order of their patriarchs. The "Rachel shevatim" follow. These are also listed according to the birth order of their patriarchs. Finally the tribes descendant from the surrogates are listed. Dan – descendant from the oldest of the surrogates' sons – is listed first. Birth order is ignored in listing the remaining members of this group. However, there is odd deviation from this order. In this list, Gad – descendant from a surrogate – is inserted in the middle of the tribes descendant from Leyah. How can this placement of Gad be explained?

And Hashem spoke to Moshe and to Aharon saying: Each man of Bnai Yisrael should camp according to the banner (with) the sign for the household of their father. (Camp) at a distance surrounding the Ohel Moed." (BeMidbar 2:1-2)

4. The third listing of the shevatim

These passages introduce the third listing of the tribes in the parasha. Hashem explains to Moshe and Aharon that Bnai Yisrael are to encamp according to a specific plan. The shevatim are to assigned positions surrounding the Mishcan. Each shevet must encamp in its specific assigned locations. Three shevatim are assigned to each side of the Mishcan. Within each of these four groups of tribes one tribe is assigned a lead role and the other three are placed under the banner of the lead shevet.

This third listing of the shevatim utilizes the same order as the second listing. Again, Gad is inserted among the shevatim descendant from Leyah. Rabbaynu Avraham ibn Ezra suggests that if the context of this final listing is considered, the order it employs can be easily explained.

As explained above, this listing places each shevet in its assigned position surrounding the Mishcan. Therefore, in order to understand the sequence of shevatim in this list, it is essential to identify the criteria by which the shevatim were assigned positions and placed in groups.

One issue that is immediately evident is that the groupings were not designed to create four equally sized camps or groups. Yehudah's camp was much larger than any other. It included 186,400 men. Ephraim's was the smallest with 108,100 male members. So, if numerical equivalency was not important, on what basis were the groups formed?

Ibn Ezra suggests that the following considerations determined the groups and the order employed in the listing of the tribes:

- All groups include the same number of tribes. Each group consists of the lead tribe and two additional members.

- The groups preserve the fraternal relationship between the tribes. Preserving this fraternal relationship presents two problems. First, there are five "Leyah shevatim". These are too many shevatim for a single group and not enough for two groups. Second, there are four "surrogate shevatim". These also are too many for a single group and too few for two groups. This problem is solved by joining one of the "surrogate shevatim" to the Reuven group. The selected shevet is Gad. Gad was the oldest son of Zilpah – Leyah's surrogate. Therefore, Gad has the strongest fraternal relationship with the "Leyah shevatim". The inclusion of Gad in the Reuven group, leaves three remaining "surrogate shevatim". These form the northern Dan group.

- Leadership of each group is awarded on the basis of a specific characteristic of the leader shevet. Reuven was Yaakov's firstborn son. His shevet is assigned leadership of the southern group. Yaakov blessed his sons before his death. In these blessings he promised Yehudah that the future leadership of Bnai Yisrael would descend from him. Therefore, Yehudah is assigned leadership of the eastern group. Yaakov also blessed Yosef's sons

9

and he assigned greater status to Ephraim. Ephraim is leader of the western group. Dan was the eldest son of the surrogates. Therefore, Dan is assigned leadership of the northern group.

These factors determine the construction of the four groups. The order in which the groups are listed and the order in which the tribes within each group are listed is determined by the same criteria employed in the parasha's initial list. The two "Leyah shevatim" groups are listed first. The members in each group are listed according to birth order – with Gad inserted as the third member of the Reuven group. The "Rachel shevatim" group appears second. The "surrogate shevatim" group appears last. Dan is given precedence but birth order among the remaining members is ignored.

Finally, ibn Ezra explains that the order used in the second list in the parasha is adopted from the third list. The second list reported the censuses for each tribe.[5] Apparently this was a preparatory step to the assignment of the shevatim to their respective groups and positions. The preparatory nature of this report is alluded to through the adoption of the order used in the third list.

In short, the initial listing of the shevatim provides a basic set of principle that is employed in the other listings. This initial listing does not follow the birth order of the patriarchs of the shevatim. Instead the shevatim are listed based upon a matriarchal scheme. Birth order plays only a secondary role.

The second and the third listings employ the same principles as the first listing. However, these listings deviate from the initial listing because of contextual considerations. These listing are associated with the assignment of shevatim to groups and camps surrounding the Mishcan. This requires that Gad be inserted among the "Leyah tribes" after Shimon.

"Take a census of the entire congregation of Bnai Yisrael according to their families, by the households of their fathers, according to the number of names of each male, taken individually." (BeMidbar 1:2)

Parshat Bamidbar: The Census

Sefer BeMidbar begins with a census of Bnai Yisrael. Hashem commands Moshe to count the people. The phrase that Hashem uses to describe the counting of the nation is "*se'uh et rosh*" – lift the head – of the entire congregation of Bnai Yisrael. Our Sages ask why this particular phrase is used to describe the process of counting.

Our text of Rashi's commentary does not include any comments on this question. However, Nachmanides quotes an explanation that he attributes to Rashi. According to Nachmanides' version of Rashi, the phrase "lift the head" alludes to the instructions provided to an executioner. The executioner is instructed to lift the head – off of the shoulders – of the criminal. In other words, execute him.

Nachmanides explains that according to Rashi, this phrase – which alludes to execution – is employed as a foreshadowing. Those who were to be counted would ultimately be punished with death. Indeed this foreshadowing was accurate. Those that Moshe counted in this census died during the travels in the wilderness. This was their punishment to refusing to enter the Land of Israel.

---

[5] Rabbaynu Avraham ibn Ezra, Commentary on Sefer BeMidbar, 1:20-43.

Nachmanides asks what prompted Rashi to attribute this forewarning to the phrase "lift the head." What compelled Rashi to explain the phrase in this manner?

"Count the sons of Leyve according to the households of their fathers, according to their families. Every male one month of age and above you should count of them." (BeMidbar 3:15)

The *shevet* of Leyve was not included in the general census of the nation. Instead, Moshe was commanded to take a separate census of this *shevet*. In this command, Hashem does not use the phrase "lift the head." Instead, Hashem employs the more literal term "count." Why does Hashem use the phrase "lift the head" when commanding Moshe to take a census of the rest of the nation but the term "count" when commanding Moshe to take a census of Leyve?

Nachmanides suggests that Rashi's interpretation is designed to address this question. The *shevet* of Leyve was not included in the decree upon the generation of the wilderness. The members of the *shevet* of Leyve did not die in the wilderness. Therefore, when commanding Moshe to count the rest of the nation, Hashem used the phrase "lift the head." This phrase foreshadowed the eventual fate of the generation. However, this phrase is not used in the command to count the members of the *shevet* of Leyve. They were not destined to be included in the punishment.

Nachmanides rejects Rashi's explanation of the phrase. He points out that there is a second census taken at the end of Sefer BeMidbar. This census preceded the entry into the Land of Israel. In commanding Moshe to take this census, Hashem again uses the phrase "lift the head."[6] However, in this case there is no foreshadowing attached to the phrase!

Despite this objection Nachmanides does not completely reject Rashi's explanation of the phrase. Instead, he suggests that Rashi's comments are not complete. He suggests the Rashi's comments are based upon a midrash and a study of this midrash will reveal the meaning of Rashi's interpretation.

Like Rashi, the midrash is concerned with the meaning to the phrase "lift the head." The midrash explains that the significance of the phrase can be understood when compared to its use in another context. We all recall Yosef's encounter in prison with Paroh's wine butler and baker. Both were troubled by dreams and asked Yosef to provide interpretations. Yosef told the wine butler that his dream foretold that he would be reappointed to his former position in the royal household. Yosef told him that his head would be lifted and he would be restored to his prior position of prestige. Yosef told the baker that also his head would be lifted. However, in this context Yosef was telling the baker that he would be executed.[7] In speaking to the wine butler and the baker, Yosef resorted to the same terminology. Each would have his head lifted. In reference to the wine butler, this indicated reappointment to a position of honor. In the instance of the baker, the phrase referred to his imminent execution.

The midrash explains that in using the phrase "lift the head," Hashem is telling Moshe that Bnai Yisrael are confronted with to possible destinies. The phrase can be understood as an allusion to the destiny of the wine butler. Like the wine butler, Bnai Yisrael are poised to ascend to greatness. However, the phrase was used by Yosef to also allude to the destruction of the baker. Bnai Yisrael may also face destruction if they fail to follow the will of Hashem.[8]

---

[6] Sefer BeMidbar 26:2.
[7] Sefer Beresheit 40:1-19.

11

The explanation of the midrash provides an answer to Nachmanides' objection to Rashi. The phrase "lift the head" consistently implies the possibility of multiple destinies. In our *parasha*, Hashem is telling Moshe that two possible destinies lie before Bnai Yisrael. They may either rise to greatness or be destroyed. So too, later in Sefer BeMidbar this phrase communicates that two possible destinies lie before the generation that will enter the land. They will either be successful in their conquest and possession of the land or – if they fail to follow Hashem – they too will be destroyed.

Nachmanides' text of Rashi seems to present the content of the midrash in an abbreviated form. Rashi is not suggesting that Hashem's command foreshadowed the destruction of the generation he was counting. But Hashem was providing a note of caution. Two possible fates were before the people. Because the people proved to be unworthy to enter the land, this caution turned out to be a foreshadowing. But Rashi is not suggesting that the destiny of the people was predetermined.

In order to more fully understand the midrash's explanation of our *pasuk*, it is important to consider another question. Why did Yosef use the same figure – the lifting of one's head – to describe restoration of honor and execution?

It seems that the image of lifting a person's head indicates that the person is acknowledged and given special attention. This heightened scrutiny can produce positive or negative results. Paroh would give special attention to both of cases. But once this attention was bestowed, the results would vary. In the case of the wine butler, Paroh would decide that his imprisonment had been a harsh and adequate punishment for his failings. Having served his sentence, Paroh would decide that the wine butler should be reinstated. However when Paroh would reexamined the crimes of the baker, he would come to the opposite conclusion. He would decide that the baker should pay with his life for his crimes.

With this understanding, let us now return to the use of this image in our *pasuk*. Hashem is telling Moshe that the nation is faced with two possible and opposite destinies. Why are these the only possible destinies? Why is there no option for some other destiny – one that is less than greatness but not as harsh as absolute destruction?

The counting of Bnai Yisrael represents a special acknowledgment of the people. Bnai Yisrael will be appointed to serve as Hashem's nation. This special relationship with Hashem is the source of all of the blessings described in Torah. But with this appointment comes with an expectation. As Hashem's chosen, the head of the nation will be lifted. The behaviors and attitudes of the people will be closely scrutinized and held to a higher standard. Being chosen and special provides rewards but this status brings with it responsibilities and expectations. Hashem is telling Moshe that if these expectations are met, the people will enjoy the blessings associated with their special status as the chosen of Hashem. But if the people's behaviors and expectations cannot stand the careful scrutiny that comes with their elevated status, then the people will face destruction.

And their entire number was six hundred three thousand five hundred fifty. (BeMidbar 1:46)

---

[8] Rabbaynu Moshe ben Nachman (Ramban), *Commentary on Sefer BeMidbar* 1:3.

The Strange Correspondence between the BeMidbar Census and the Population Reported in Sefer Shemot

Sefer BeMidbar opens with Hashem commanding Moshe to conduct a census of the male population of Bnai Yisrael. The census included all males of age twenty or older. It covered all of the *Shevatim* – the tribes – with the exception of *Shevet Leyve*. Moshe performed Hashem's command. Our *pasuk* relates Moshe's finding. The number of individuals in the census was 603,550. This is the second census of Bnai Yisrael explicitly discussed in the Torah. The first is found in Sefer Shemot. There, Hashem commanded Moshe to collect a coin from every male of age twenty and above.[9] These coins were subsequently melted down and used in the construction of the *Mishcan* –the Tabernacle. The Torah reports that the coins collected numbered 603,550.[10] This is the same number reported in our *parasha*. Rashi points out that it is impossible for these two accounts to refer to a single census. The account in Sefer Shemot refers to a census taken prior to the building of the *Mishcan*. In fact, the coins collected were used in the *Mishcan's* fabrication. The account in our *parasha* takes place after the assembly of the *Mishcan*. This prompts an obvious question. How could these two censuses result in the same number? Both indicated a population of 603,550.

Rashi offers a somewhat complicated answer. In order to be counted in the census, one was required to be of age twenty or older. According to Rashi, this did not mean that one had actually reached his twentieth birthday. Instead, it was required that the person would be age twenty or older that year. The first census was taken in Tishre. Tishre is the first month of the year. Many men did not reach age twenty until later in the year. Nonetheless, these men were included in this census. The second census was taken in Iyar of the same year. By this point, additional men had reached their twentieth birthday. However, these individuals did not affect the outcome of the census. They had been counted in the original census in Tishre.[11]

Nachmanides rejects Rashi's explanation. He raises two objections. First, he does not accept Rashi's basic premise. Rashi posits that the first of the two censuses included all individuals who would become age twenty or older in the twelve months beginning from Tishre. Nachmanides rejects this assumption. He insists that each census included only those who had actually reached their twentieth birthday. Second, it seems that according to Rashi no one died between Tishre and Iyar. If deaths had occurred, the second census would have resulted in a lower number. Nachmanides insists that it is unreasonable to assume that, in a nation of over 600,000, no one died.

Nachmanides offers a completely different explanation for the identical outcomes of the two censuses. He explains that the outcomes were not at all identical! The two censuses did not count the same group. In the census in our *parasha*, Moshe was commanded to exclude *Shevet Leyve*.[12] Hashem's directions to Moshe in Sefer Shemot do not mention the exclusion of *Shevet Leyve*. Rashi assumes that, although their exclusion is not mentioned, *Shevet Leyve* did not participate in the contribution of coins described in Sefer Shemot. Nachmanides disagrees and asserts that *Shevet Leyve* was included in the first census. In other words, the first census resulted

---

[9] Shemot 30:12-13.
[10] Shemot 38:26.

[11] Rabbaynu Shemuel ben Meir (Rashbam) *Commentary on Sefer Shemot* 30:16.
[12] BeMidbar 1:49.

13

in a count of 603,550 including *Shevet Leyve*. The second census produced the same number. But it did not include *Shevet Leyve*.[13]

Gershonides raises an obvious objection against Nachmanides' answer. What has Nachmanides gained? His original objective was to explain the strange stability in population. It is only reasonable for some change to have occurred in the nation's population during the course of the year. Nachmanides explains that the nation did grow. However, this growth was not directly reflected in the censuses. This is because the first census was more inclusive. However, Nachmanides' answer creates a different problem. It results in a bizarre coincidence. The two censuses measured different groups. They were separated by an interval of seven months. Yet, they produced the same outcome!

Based on these considerations, Gershonides suggests an alternative explanation. First, he agrees with Rashi that *Shevet Leyve* was excluded from both censuses. Second, he accepts Nachmanides' assertion that only those who had actually reached their twentieth birthday were counted in either census. Once these premises are accepted, an entirely different approach is required to explain the agreement between the censuses. The Torah is telling us that the population of the nation remained completely stable between these two censuses. The Torah is revealing a miracle. Of course this raises a question. Every miracle has a purpose. What was the purpose of this miracle? Why did Hashem exercise His providence to maintain this remarkable stable population of Bnai Yisrael over a seven month period?

Gershonides answers this question. He observes that in each census the Torah indicates a minimum age of those included. Only those of age twenty or older were counted. He explains that there was also a maximum age for these censuses. Those over sixty were not counted. Nachmanides also agrees with this assertion.[14] Gershonides then makes a simple observation. What would be the normal pattern of population growth for this age group?

In order to answer this question, we must conduct a simple, two-step, analysis. First, we would expect the number of younger members to be greater than the number of older members. The subset of those between twenty and thirty years of age should be far larger than the subset of those between fifty and sixty. This is because the more senior age group will have a higher mortality rate. Second, the relative mortality rates of these two subsets will affect the growth pattern of the entire group. The population of the nation should grow. This is because the number of people entering the group at age twenty should be far greater than the number leaving the group after age sixty.

We are now ready for Gershonides' answer. The Torah states that the population of Bnai Yisrael between the ages of twenty and sixty was stable. Based on the analysis above, we know that this should not occur. Normally, this population should grow. How could stability occur? Stability could only occur if the number of men leaving the group after age sixty was equal to the number entering at age twenty. This would require a remarkably low mortality rate for all men under sixty! The persistently low mortality note would inflate the number of people graduating out of the census group between the first and second census. This is the miracle the Torah is revealing. Hashem protected Bnai Yisrael. He granted them long-life. This blessing is reflected in the two censuses.[15]

---

[13] Rabbaynu Moshe ben Nachman (Ramban), *Commentary on Sefer Shemot* 30:12.
[14] Rabbaynu Moshe ben Nachman (Ramban), *Commentary on Sefer BeMidbar* 26:64.

The Encampment in the Wilderness as a Representation of the Sinai Revelation

And you should appoint the Leveyim over the Mishcan of Testimony and over its utensils and all associated with it. They will carry the Mishcan and its utensils and will minister to its needs. And around the Mishcan they will camp. (BeMidbar 1:50)

The *Mishcan* was located in the center of the camp of Bnai Yisrael. The *Mishcan* was surrounded by the camp of the *Leveyim*. The other tribes were assigned positions around the perimeter of the *Leveyim's* camp.

Nachmanides explains that this pattern reflected the encampment around Mount Sinai. The majority of the nation was not permitted to approach the mountain. The elders could ascend with Moshe to the lower levels of the mountain. Only Moshe could climb to the top of the mountain. The *Mishcan* represented Sinai. The people could not approach the mountain. Neither could the nation camp directly around the *Mishcan*. This area was reserved for the *Leveyim*.

The *Leveyim* were charged with the duty of dedicating themselves to the study and teaching of the Torah. Through committing themselves to this mission, they earned the right to serve in the *Mishcan*. They attained the status of the elders at Sinai. They could not enter the inner sanctuary of the *Mishcan*, but they were permitted to camp directly around the structure.[16]

This pattern represents the Torah's outlook upon our relationship with Hashem. Moshe ascended to the top of the mountain. This was because of Moshe's wisdom and righteousness. These qualities enabled Moshe to come as close to Hashem as humanly possible. The elders did not achieve Moshe's level of human perfection. However, they possessed sufficient wisdom to climb the lower slopes of the mountain and draw closer to the presence of Hashem. Those lacking the wisdom and righteousness of Moshe and the elders were required to distance themselves from the mountain.

Maimonides explains that love of and closeness to the Creator are not derived from religious fervor or asceticism. They develop through a profound understanding of the Torah and Hashem's infinite wisdom. It is only through the Torah and the revelations of His wisdom that we can know Hashem. True love of Hashem corresponds with our knowledge and understanding of Hashem and His Torah.[17]

The encampment symbolized this concept. The various groups were placed around the *Mishcan* in a specific pattern. Each was assigned a position appropriate to the Torah knowledge associated with the group. This served as a constant reminder of the method by which each of us can draw closer to Hashem.

"And Hashem spoke to Moshe and Aharon saying: Do not cause the tribe of the families of Kahat to be cut off from among the Leveyim. Do this for them, so they should live and not

---

[15] Rabbaynu Levi ben Gershon (Ralbag/Gershonides), *Commentary on Sefer BeMidbar*, (Mosad HaRav Kook, 1998), p 1.

[16] Rabbaynu Moshe ben Nachman (Ramban), Commentary on Sefer BeMidbar Introduction.

[17] Rabbaynu Moshe ben Maimon (Rambam) *Mishne Torah*, Hilchot Teshuva 10:6.

die, when they approach the Holy of Holies. Aharon and his sons shall come and appoint each man individually to his task and his load. They shall not come in to see when the holy [vessels] are being wrapped up, lest they die." (BeMidbar 4:17-20)

The Mishcan – Tabernacle – was the central feature of the camp of Bnai Yisrael in the wilderness. When Bnai Yisrael camped, the Mishcan was erected. When the nation traveled to its next encampment, the Mishcan was disassembled and transported by the Leveyim – the Levites – to this new location. Parshat BeMidbar describes the disassembly of the Mishcan. The various families of Leveyim were assigned the responsibility of transporting specific portions of the Mishcan. The family of Kahat was assigned the responsibility of transporting the most sacred elements. These elements included the altars, the Table of the Shewbread, the Menorah, and the Aron – the ark.

Our passages describe the special treatment of these sacred objects. As the Mishcan was disassembled, the Kohanim – the priests – placed each of the items assigned to the family of Kahat in its own individual wrapping. Only after each item was wrapped was it assigned by the Kohanim to members of the family of Kahat for transport. The Kahati – the member of the family of Kahat – was not permitted to unwrap the object or gaze inside the wrapping. The passages indicate that if a Kahati unwraps the object or looks into the wrapping, he is subject to death.

Maimonides does not include the prohibition against unwrapping these objects or looking into their wrappings as one of the six hundred thirteen commandments – Taryag mitzvot. Maimonides outlines the reason for this exclusion in the second principle of his Sefer HaMitzvot. He explains that in order for a commandment to be included within Taryag mitzvot, it must apply for all generations. Any commandment that is only applicable in a specific period of time cannot be included. The injunction against unwrapping these sacred objects or looking within their wrappings only applied in the wilderness. Once the Bait HaMikdash – the Holy Temple – was built this injunction became meaningless. The components of the Mishcan were no longer transported from one encampment to the next. The sacred objects were no longer placed in their special wrappings for transport. So, the injunction no longer had a context.

Maimonides acknowledges that there is a difficulty with his position. The Talmud explains that a person who steals one of the sacred vessels of the Mishcan or Bait HaMikdash is subject to death. The Talmud cites the final passage above as the source for this law. This passage can alternatively be translated to prohibit stealing one of the sacred vessels and as assigning the penalty of death for violation of this prohibition. This alternative translation is not the literal meaning of the passage. The literal meaning is that the Leveyim cannot unwrap the sacred vessels or gaze within their wrappings. However, the alternative translation provides an allusion to the restriction against stealing a sacred vessel and to the penalty of death for the violation of the prohibition.[18]

This prohibition does exist throughout the generations. Therefore, it seems to meet the standard required for inclusion within Taryag mitzvot. Why does Maimonides not include this prohibition?

Before we can consider Maimonides' response to this question, additional information is needed. As previously explained, the penalty for stealing one of the sacred vessels is death.

---

[18] Mesechet Sanhedrin 81b.

However, in this instance, the death penalty is not executed in the typical manner. Generally, the death penalty is administered by the courts. An individual who witnesses a crime or sin punishable by death does not have the authority to execute the penalty. He must bring the violator to courts for judgment. However, there are four instances in which the courts do not and cannot execute the death penalty. Instead, a righteous zealot is authorized to execute the violator. One of the four special instances is the stealing of a sacred vessel. In this instance, the courts do not execute the death penalty. Instead, it is left to the righteous zealot to execute the offender.

Maimonides outlines two considerations that dictate excluding this prohibition for Taryag mitzvot. First, the Talmud explains that our passage is merely an allusion to the prohibition. Maimonides explains that in order for a prohibition to be included in Taryag a more direct reference in the Torah to the prohibition is required. An allusion to the prohibition is not adequate. Second, Maimonides explains that a person who steals a sacred vessel is not subject to the death. This implies that he has not violated one of the 613 commandments.

This second consideration seems bizarre. A person who steals a sacred vessel is subject to execution by any righteous zealot! How can Maimonides contend that he is not subject to the death penalty? Apparently, Maimonides does not equate execution by the righteous zealot with application of the death penalty. In other words, the thief is not subject to the death penalty. Nonetheless, the righteous zealot is permitted and encouraged to execute the violator.

Nachmanides objects to Maimonides' position. He asserts that the prohibition against stealing a sacred vessel is one of the 613 commandments. The source for the commandment is our final passage. Nachmanides also dismisses Maimonides' second consideration. He explains that it is impossible to assume that the Torah allows and encourages the righteous zealot to execute one who steals a sacred vessel if the thief is not in fact subject to the death penalty. If the righteous zealot can execute the thief, he must have violated a commandment that is subject to the death penalty. Therefore, the authority of the righteous zealot to carry out the execution clearly indicates that a commandment associated with the death penalty has been violated.[19]

Nachmanides' argument seems compelling. How is it possible for the righteous zealot to execute a person who steals a sacred vessel if this person has not violated a mitzvah punishable by execution? In order to understand Maimonides' position another issue must be considered.

Maimonides explains in his code of law – Mishne Torah – that there are circumstances in which the courts can execute a person even though the individual has not violated a mitzvah that is punishable by death. Let us consider one of these instances. A person violates a commandment that is punishable by lashes. The lashes are administered. The person then violates the same commandment and lashes are again administered. The person violates the same commandment a third time. The courts do not administer lashes a third time. Instead, the person is subjected to kipah – imprisonment. He is imprisoned and placed on a restricted diet that ultimately results in digestive distress and death.[20]

There are a number of difficulties with Maimonides' treatment of kipah. First, he does not indicate the source for the courts' authority to administer this consequence. In other words, the person has repeatedly violated a commandment punishable by lashes. The courts are

---

[19] Rabbaynu Moshe ben Nachman (Ramban), *Critique on Maimonides' Sefer HaMitzvot, Principle 3.*
[20] Rabbaynu Moshe ben Maimon (Rambam) *Mishne Torah*, Hilchot Sanhedrin 18:4.

authorized by a specific commandment to administer lashes. But the person has not violated a commandment punishable by death. From where do the courts derive the authority to administer the consequence of kipah? Second, Maimonides places his discussion of kipah in the chapter of his Mishne Torah that deals with the commandment that authorizes the courts to administer lashes. What is the connection between the commandment authorizing lashes and this consequence of kipah?

Maimonides provides a hint to his position in the opening of this chapter. He explains that lashes are administered in three instances. The first instance is the violation of a negative commandment associated with karet – forfeiture of the afterlife – and there is no death penalty administered by the court for the violation of this mitzvah. The second instance is the violation of a negative commandment associated with the death penalty, but the penalty is not administered by the courts; instead it is left to the heavenly court to administer. The third instance is the violation of a negative commandment that involves an action but for which no punishment is specified. In all of these instances, the courts are required to administer lashes. This seems to be a cumbersome formulation. Maimonides could have expressed himself far more concisely. He could have explained that lashes are the general -- or default -- punishment for the violation of any negative commandment involving an action. If the violation is not associated with any other punishment carried out by the courts, lashes are administered. This simple principle would cover all of the instances enumerated by Maimonides. Why did Maimonides provide a listing of all of the individual instances in which lashes are administered rather then providing a simple, concise principle?

Maimonides' formulation reflects his fundamental understanding of the punishment of lashes. Lashes are not a typical punishment. It is not engendered as a direct consequence of the violation of a specific commandment. Maimonides seems to contend that the courts are charged with the responsibility of enforcing observance of the commandments. In order to carry out this responsibility they are invested with the authority to administer the punishment of lashes in cases in which a severe violation of the Torah takes place. Maimonides opens the chapter by listing the types of violations that are regarded as adequately severe as to require the courts to administer this punishment. Maimonides adopts this formulation in order to communicate that lashes are not the administered by the courts as a direct result of the violation of the commandment. Instead, lashes are administered in order to enforce overall observance of the Torah. Therefore, the violation of any commandment of adequate severity requires that the courts respond with the administration of the punishment of lashes.

An example will help illustrate this distinction. If a person commits murder, he is subject to the death penalty. This punishment is a direct result of the violation. The violation carries with it the punishment of death. In contrast, if a person eats meat and milk, he receives lashes. It seems that according to Maimonides, this is not a direct result of the violation. It is not completely proper to assert that the violation carries with it the punishment of lashes. Instead, the violation is of sufficient severity as to require a punitive response from the courts. Lashes are the punitive response that the courts are authorized to administer.

This interpretation of the punishment of lashes provides an explanation of Maimonides' treatment of kipah. The consequence of kipah is applied in an instance in which standard tool provided to the courts to respond to violations of the Torah has proven ineffective. The person has received lashes for the violation on multiple occasions without effect. He continues to violate the same mitzvah. The commandment authorizing the courts to administer lashes charges the courts with the responsibility of assuring observance of the Torah. Implicit in this commandment is the responsibility to take more effective measures – such as kipah – in instances in which lashes are ineffective. Maimonides places the law of kipah in this chapter that discusses lashes in order to communicate the source of the courts' authority to utilize kipah. The commandment that authorizes lashes implicitly charges the courts with the responsibility to take this more drastic measure when lashes prove ineffective. This interpretation explains the placement of the law of kipah in the chapter is devoted to the commandment authorizing lashes and identifies the source of the courts' authority to administer this consequence. In short, the commandment authorizing lashes implicitly empowers the courts to resort to measures – such as kipah – in instances in which the typical judicial punishment of lashes is ineffective.

Let us now return to Nachmanides' criticism of Maimonides' position regarding stealing a sacred vessel. Both acknowledge that in this instance the righteous zealot is authorized to take the life of the thief. Nachmanides argues that this authority presumes that a mitzvah has been violated. Maimonides argues that this consequence is unique. It does not imply the violation of a commandment. Nachmanides' criticism is simple. How is it possible for the Torah to authorize an execution if no commandment has been violated?

In order to answer this question, three additional points must be noted. First, Bait HaBechirah, in his comments on this issue notes that the act of stealing a sacred vessel does not meet the technical legal requirements required for the act to be regarded as theft. In halacha, the crime of stealing always involves the violation of the owner's right of possession. The crime presumes the existence of an owner. A sacred vessel does not have an owner in the typical sense. The object is a component or element of the Bait HaMikdash or Mishcan. But its identity as an element of the Holy Sanctuary is not regarded as ownership.

Second, Bait HaBechirah explains that the stealing of the vessel is not prohibited by any commandment that explicitly prohibits this activity. Instead, it is derived from our passage. Bait HaBechirah acknowledges that our passage's fundamental message is that it is prohibited for the Leveyim to glance at the sacred vessels as they are covered by the Kohanim in their wrappings. Nonetheless, he indicates that this passage serves as a derivation for the prohibition against stealing one of these vessels.[21]

Let us consider this second point more carefully. Bait HaBechirah seems to maintain that the stealing of a sacred vessel is clearly prohibited. However, on technical grounds it is not considered a violation of the standard commandment prohibiting stealing. Nonetheless, our passage does communicate that the activity is prohibited. He makes no mention of the Talmud's device for relating the prohibition to the passage though an alternative translation. He seems to imply that this alternative translation is not the fundamental link to our passage. Instead, this device merely brings to our attention a more fundamental link. What is this link?

The covering of the sacred vessels in their wrappings and the prohibition against looking upon them implies that these objects are to be treated with extreme deference. This deference prohibits the Leveyim from directly handling the objects. They can only transport them once they are installed in their wrappings. This deference does not only prohibit the Leveyim from handling the objects. It also prohibits even gazing upon them! It seems that Bait HaBechirah is suggesting that stealing such an object is clearly inconsistent with the attitude of extreme

---

[21] Rabbaynu Menachem Me'eri, *Bait HaBechirah*, Mesechet Sanhedrin 81b.

deference required by the Torah. So, although the Torah does not state an explicit commandment prohibiting stealing one of the sacred vessels, it is quite clear that such behavior is an affront to the sanctity of the object. In short, no specific commandment prohibits stealing the sacred vessel. But the Torah's overall treatment of these objects clearly communicates that this behavior is grossly inappropriate.

The third point that must be noted is Maimonides' placement of this law in his code – Mishne Torah. Maimonides places his discussion of stealing a sacred vessel and the consequences for this act in the same chapter that discusses the commandment authorizing lashes and kipah![22] Why is the discussion placed in this chapter?

As explained earlier, the commandment authorizing lashes fundamentally authorizes the courts and charges them with the responsibility of ensuring observance of the Torah. This responsibility is the basis for the administration of lashes and kipah. But both of these measures can only be taken by the courts. The courts can only act when a specific commandment has been violated. Stealing a sacred vessel presents a unique dilemma. Because of technical considerations, no specific commandment has been violated. The courts are powerless to respond. Nonetheless, an egregious violation of Torah principles has taken place. How can this dilemma be addressed?

Maimonides seems to maintain that the commandment authorizing lashes is not restricted to the courts. The nation is charged with the enforcement of the Torah. The courts are the agent of the nation. But in an instance in which the courts are not empowered to act – when no specific commandment has been violated – then the nation is responsible to respond with extra-judicial measures. The righteous zealot is authorized and expected to redress the violation.

We can now understand Maimonides' position. The key to this understanding is to recognize that Maimonides contends that the actions of the righteous zealot are an extra-judicial measure. It is specifically because no explicit commandment has been violated, that an extra-judicial response is required. There is no question that stealing the sacred vessel is an egregious violation of Torah principle. But the court cannot act as no specific mitzvah is violated. Therefore, the same commandment that authorizes the nation to administer lashes -- or kipah -- through the courts authorizes and urges the righteous zealot to take action.

This interpretation of Maimonides' position resolves another issue. There is a general principle that when a person commits a violation that simultaneously subjects him to two possible punishments, the courts apply the more severe of the two punishments. For example, if a person ignites a fire on Shabbat and this fire burns someone's crops, the violator is executed for the violation of Shabbat. But, he is not required to first make payment for damages.23[6] Based on this principle Rav Eliezer Shach Zt"l raises a simple question. In addition to a person who steals a sacred vessel, there are other instances in which the righteous zealot is permitted and encouraged to execute the violator. One of these involves a violation which the courts can punish with lashes. Rav Shach asks: If the person can be executed by the religious zealot, how can the punishment of lashes ever be administered? The principle discussed above should apply. The person should be left to the zealots to execute and the courts should not be permitted to administer lashes.[24] Similarly, this question can be expanded to include all instances in which

---

[22] Rabbaynu Moshe ben Maimon (Rambam) *Mishne Torah*, Hilchot Sanhedrin 18:6.
[23] Rabbaynu Moshe ben Maimon (Rambam) *Mishne Torah*, Hilchot Genayvah 3:1-2.

lashes are administered. If the violation continues, the more severe punishment of kipah can be administered. How can the courts ever administer lashes, if the violation is ultimately subject to this more severe punishment?

Rav Shach offers a number of insightful answers to his question. However, the above analysis suggests an obvious response. The principle that the potential of a more severe punishment exempts the violator from the less severe punishment only applies when dealing with the typical punishments administered by the courts. According to Maimonides, any punishment executed by the righteous zealot is extra-judicial. It is not court-administered. Therefore, this principle does not apply. This explanation also explains the administration of lashes despite the potential for the more severe punishment of kipah. Kipah is not a typical punishment. It is a completely different class of response. It is only allowed when the standard response of lashes has not been effective. Because it is only permitted in such circumstances, it is not proper to argue that the potential application of this punishment exempts the violator from the standard punishment of lashes.

---

[24] Rav Eliezer Shacah, *Avi Ezri, Commentary on Maimonides Mishne Torah*, volume 4, p 303.

Naso

If there is no relative to whom to return the dishonest gain, it must be returned to Hashem and given to the Kohen. This is in addition to the atonement offering through which he atones for the sin. (BeMidbar 5:8)

The Association of the Convert to the Kohanim

The meaning of our *pasuk* is not readily apparent. Our Sages discuss the passage. They explain that the section in which the passage appears deals with a person who has been accused of owing money to another individual. The accused has taken an oath that he does not owe the money. Based on this oath, the court released the accused of any liability. Subsequently, the accused admits that he does owe the money. He is required to restore the dishonest gain, add an additional 20%, and offer a sacrifice.[1]

Our passage discusses a special application of this law. The law is predicated on the assumption that the wronged party or his heir is available to receive restitution. If the wronged party has died without heirs, how does the accused make restitution? To whom does the accused give the dishonest gain and the 20% fine?

Before we consider our passage's solution to this dilemma, we must consider another issue. How is it possible for a person to die without any heir? Certainly, through tracing the victim's ancestry, we can find some distant heir! Our Sages respond that the passage deals with a victim who is a convert and dies without children.[2] Those non-Jews who were related to the convert prior to conversion are no longer regarded as heirs. Conversion severs the familial tie between the convert and the non-Jewish community. Therefore, the childless convert truly has no heirs!

Now, let us return to our passage's response. Who receives the money? Our *pasuk* answers that both the principle amount of the wrongful gain and the 20% fine are given to the *kohen*.

Why does the *kohen* receive the money? Gershonides offers a very important answer. He explains that the Torah apparently wishes to associate the convert with the *kohen*. In effect, the Torah makes the *kohen* the heir of the convert. The *kohanim* are the most honored group within the nation. Creating an association between the convert and the *kohen* elevates the status of the convert.

Why does the Torah wish to elevate the status of the convert? Gershonides proposes that the Torah is concerned with the welfare of the convert. The convert does not have extensive family ties within Bnai Yisrael. This might mark the convert as an attractive victim for the unscrupulous. In order to protect the convert from such scheming, the Torah assigns to the convert the most respected relatives in the nation. In short, the message communicated by this law is that one who steals from this lonely convert will have to answer to the honorary relatives – the *kohanim*![3]

---

[1] Rabbaynu Shlomo ben Yitzchak (Rashi), *Commentary on Sefer BeMidbar* 5:6.
[2] Rabbaynu Shlomo ben Yitzchak (Rashi), *Commentary on Sefer BeMidbar* 5:8.
[3] Rabbaynu Levi ben Gershon (Ralbag / Gershonides), *Commentary on Sefer BeMidbar*, 5:5.

Hashem spoke to Moshe, saying: Speak to the children of Israel and say to them: Should any man's wife go astray and deal treacherously with him, and a man lie with her carnally, but it was hidden from her husband's eyes, but she was secluded [with the suspected adulterer] and there was no witness against her, and she was not seized. (Bamidbar 5:11-13)

G-d Living Next Door

The unexpected inclusion of the commandment of the wayward wife in Sefer Bamidbar

Nachmanides notes that Sefer Bamidbar focuses on the travels of Bnai Yisrael in the wilderness. Most of the commandments that are included in the *sefer* are directed to that generation and are not intended for future generations. For example, the *sefer* opens with Hashem directing Moshe to take a census of the people. This commandment was intended to be executed at that time. The commandment does not apply to future generations.

There are a few commandments in Sefer BeMidbar that apply for all generations. Some of those commandments are included in Parshat Naso. One of those is the commandment regarding a *sotah*– the wayward wife. A *sotah* is a married woman whose conduct has created a suspicion of adultery. The suspicion cannot be confirmed through judicial means. In other words, no witnesses can testify to an actual act of adultery. The *parasha* describes a means through which the woman can be tested and a determination made of her guilt or innocence. The test is described in the *parsha* and will not be described in detail here. In short, it was conducted in the *Mishkan* – the Tabernacle – by the *kohen* – the priest. It involved requiring the woman to drink a mixture composed of ingredients that would seem to be harmless. Despite the innocuous nature of its ingredients, the mixture responded to and revealed the woman's behavior. If she was guilty, she and her adulterous partner died. If she was innocent, she conceived.

As Nachmanides notes, few commandments intended for future generations are included in Sefer BaMidbar. This raises the question of why this *mitzvah* is one of the few exceptions. There are a number of responses to this issue. One of those will be considered in the following.

Hashem spoke to Moshe and Aharon saying: The children of Israel shall encamp each man by his division with the flag staffs of their fathers' house; some distance from the Tent of Meeting they shall encamp. (BeMidbar 2:1-2)

The design of the wilderness camp corresponds to the Sinai encampment

Let us begin by returning to Nachmanides' comments on Sefer BeMidbar. Nachmanides notes that Sefer BeMidbar deals primarily with the experiences of Bnai Yisrael in the wilderness and the initial stage of the capture of the Land of Israel. The *sefer* begins with the directions that Hashem gave to Moshe regarding the organization of the camp. Each tribe was assigned a specific place surrounding the *Mishcan*. Both when encamped and when traveling, the placement of each member of the nation was prescribed by these directions.

Nachmaides explains that the camp's design corresponded, in a number of respects, to the encampment at Sinai. For example, Sinai – the mountain upon which the presence of Hashem resided – was in the center of the camp. In the wilderness, Hashem's presence resided in the *Mishcan*. The tribes surrounded the *Mishcan*. At Sinai, Moshe was commanded to establish boundary lines surrounding the mountain. The people were forbidden from crossing those boundary lines and coming too close to, or ascending the mountain. In the wilderness, the people were provided with limited access to the precincts of the *Mishcan* and were completely excluded from the inner precincts. At Sinai, the *kohanim* – the priests – were allowed to approach closer to the mountain and even to ascend its lower region. In the wilderness, these priests were given greater access of the *Mishcan* and they and the *Leviyim* – the Levites – camped in an inner circle directly surrounding the *Mishcan*. In short, the wilderness camp was modeled on the Sinai encampment and mimicked many of its aspects.

Nachmanides notes that the directions for the design of the camp were given to Moshe while the nation was encamped at Sinai. Furthermore, the first stage of the nation's journey to the Land of Israel was not undertaken until these directions were implemented. The reason for urgency in implementing these directions emerges from a further comment of Nachmanides.

The cloud of Hashem was above them by day, when they traveled from the camp. So it was, whenever the ark set out, Moshe would say, Arise, Hashem, may Your enemies be scattered and may those who hate You flee from You. And when it came to rest he would say, Repose Hashem, among the myriads of thousands of Israel. (BeMidbar 10:34-36)

In the wilderness, Hashem dwelled within His nation

Why was the wilderness camp modeled after the Sinai encampment? Nachmanides explains that the design was a response to the presence of Hashem within the midst of the nation. The divine presence demands an attitude of awe. Surrounding the palace of a mighty king are his legions. These legions are an expression of respect for the monarch. Similarly, Bnai Yisrael's encampment surrounding Hashem's *Mishcan* could not be haphazard and arbitrary. Instead, its precision and orderliness expressed awareness of the presence of Hashem in the midst of the camp.

Nachmanides notes that Sefer BeMidbar also includes a description of the many miracles that Hashem performed for the people in the wilderness. These culminate with the initial stages of the capture of the Land of Israel. These miracles include the cloud that traveled with the nation and directed its travels. The movement of the cloud signaled the departure of the nation from its encampment. Its relocation to a new place signaled the nation to encamp at that new location.

The miracles are closely related to the presence of Hashem in the midst of the camp. These miracles were expressions of that presence. Now, the reason for urgency in implementing the design of the camp is understood. The nation traveled and camped in the wilderness accompanied by the presence of Hashem. Their existence in the wilderness was dependent upon the many miracles that expressed Hashem's presence. The passage to the Land of Israel and its conquest were not accomplished though Moshe's careful planning and precise management of the nation. The journey through the wilderness was a supernatural experience that was predicated upon Hashem's presence within the nation. Therefore, this journey could not begin until the camp was ordered in a manner reflecting the divine presence.

Hashem spoke to Moshe saying: Command the children of Israel to banish from the camp all those afflicted with tzara'ath or with a male discharge, and all those unclean through [contact with] the dead. (BeMidbar 5:1-2)

The impacts of Hashem's presence in the midst of the nation

In the passages above Moshe is directed to send forth from the camp those who are in a state of severe ritual impurity. Based on the above discussion the placement of this commandment in Parshat Naso is understood. In Parshat BeMidbar and in the opening portion of Parshat Naso the Torah is describing the design of the encampment. Nachmanides explains that the presence of Hashem within the camp endowed it with sanctity and this sanctity required the exclusion from the camp those who were experiencing severe forms of ritual impurity.

Now, let us return to our initial question. Why is the *mitzvah* of the *sotah* placed in our Sefer Bemidbar? Sefer BeMidbar primarily includes commandments intended for the generation that traveled through the wilderness. This commandment applies to all generations and it continued to be observed after the nation entered and captured the Land of Israel. When the Temple is rebuilt, we will resume observing this commandment.

The above discussion suggests a simple response. The examination of the *sotah* and the determination of her guilt or her vindication are not a judicial process. It is a miraculous test. This test is mentioned at this point because it requires and is an expression of the divine presence within the camp.

In summary, Sefer BeMidbar describes the design of the camp as a response to the presence of Hashem in its midst. This description is followed by the requirement to exclude from the camp those who are ritually impure. This commandment is a consequence of the sanctity of the camp. The *sefer* continues with the *mitzvah* of the *sotah*. This *mitzvah* is an expression of divine influence and reflects the presence of Hashem within the nation.

But only to the place which Hashem your L-rd shall choose from all your tribes, to set His Name there; you shall inquire after His dwelling and come there. And there you shall bring your burnt offerings, and your sacrifices, and your tithes, and the separation by your hand, and your vows and your donations, and the firstborn of your cattle and of your sheep. And there you shall eat before Hashem, your L-rd, and you shall rejoice in all your endeavors you and your households, as Hashem, your L-rd, has blessed you. (Devarim 12:5-7)

Our love for the Land of Israel

A problem emerges from this explanation. This *mitzvah* of the examination of the *sotah* was not limited to the wilderness. As noted above, after the nation entered the Land of Israel, this *mitzvah* continued to be observed. In the Land of Israel, the nation was not encamped around the *Mishcan*. *Mun* – manna did not fall from the heaven and water was not provided by a miraculous well that followed the people to their various places of settlement within the Land. Instead, the people worked the land, they cultivated crops, and dug wells. The divine presence was not expressed as it was in the wilderness. Yet, the examination of the *sotah* was conducted and was effective. If this miraculous *mitzvah* is dependent upon the presence of Hashem within the camp of the nation, how was the *mitzvah* observed after the nation emerged from the wilderness and settled the Land of Israel?

The answer to this question emerges from an insight of Rav Yosef Dov Soloveitchik *Zt"l*. Nachmanides explains that the wilderness encampment was modeled after the Sinai encampment. The Rav explains that the wilderness encampment was duplicated in the Land of Israel! The *Bait HaMikdash* – the Sacred Temple – replaced the *Mishcan*. It was the "residence" of Hashem. The city of Jerusalem replaced the wilderness camp of the Levites. Finally, the rest of the Land of Israel replaced the encampment of the tribes surrounding the *Mishcan*. In other words, the model of Sinai and of the wilderness encampment were the template for the settlement of the nation in the Land of Israel. The same fundamental elements of the Sinai encampment were expressed in the encampment of the wilderness and in the settlement of the Land of Israel.

The Rav's comments demonstrate that Hashem did not depart from the midst of the nation with its emergence from the wilderness. Hashem continued to dwell within His nation. However, His presence was expressed in a difference manner. In the wilderness, Hashem's presence was expressed by manifest miracles. Natural law was subdued and overthrown in order to provide for the sustenance and safety of the Jewish people. In the Land of Israel, Hashem continued to dwell in the midst of His nation. Now, His presence was expressed through the orderly passage of the seasons, the abundance of the harvest, the wealth and comfort of the nation, and the triumph of Bnai Yisrael over their enemies. In other words, in the wilderness, Hashem's presence was expressed through the disruption of the natural order – through manifest miracles. In the Land of Israel, the divine presence found its expression in the beauty and wonder of the natural order. His presence remained and the miracle of the *mitzvah* of *sotah* continued.

Our love for and commitment to the Land of Israel is multifaceted. Its many foundations account for its near universality among our people. Even those among us who are its harshest critics, enthusiastically proclaim their support for the State of Israel. For many Jews, Israel is viewed as the refuge for every Jew. Any Jew fleeing from persecution has a home in Israel. For other Jews, Israel is regarded as an opportunity for the Jewish people to renew and develop our own unique culture. However, from the Torah perspective, these issues are not the foundation for our love of the Land of Israel. Our love is intimate. It cannot be explained or described to an outsider. Our love is a religious experience and even has a romantic aspect. It reflects our desire to be closer to Hashem. It expresses our desire to be in the Land that He has chosen as His abode in this world – to not just know Hashem but to be His neighbor.

And Hashem spoke unto Moshe, saying: Speak unto the children of Israel, and say to them, "If any man's wife go aside, and act unfaithfully against him, and a man lie with her carnally, and it be hid from the eyes of her husband, she being defiled secretly, and there be no witness against her, neither she be taken by force in the act;" (BeMidbar 5:11-13)

"Who's Your Daddy?"

Introduction: The Torah's definition of adultery

Some elements of the Torah seem strange and even unreasonable from our contemporary perspective. One of these elements is the Torah's definition of adultery. According to the Torah, adultery only occurs though the sexual intimacy of a married woman and a man other than her husband. A married man who has an affair with a single woman is not regarded as an adulterer. Marriage is a commitment between a man and a woman. They pledge to each other their fidelity and love. Why is a man's disregard for his marriage commitment treated more lightly than the wife's extramarital affair?

This is a multi-faceted issue. One of the difficulties that complicate any discussion of the questions is that it is associated with various aspects of Torah law that suggest gender inequality. In other words, the discussion of adultery becomes entangled with the larger issue of the Torah position on gender.

The following discussion does not deal with the larger issue of the Torah's outlook on gender. It is focused on one specific issue – the Torah's treatment of adultery.

The difficulty in enforcing a prohibition against adultery

Parshat Naso includes the *mitzvah* of *sotah*. The commandment has many unique aspects. The starting point in the study of this commandment is the prohibition against adultery. As noted above, the Torah defines adultery as sexual intimacy between a man and a married woman. When such a liaison takes place both the man and the woman have violated the prohibition and are subject to the same punishment. If the incident occurred in the presence of witnesses, the two participants may be subject to the death penalty.

By its very nature, this behavior is not easily regulated by the courts or even by society. Adultery is a private act. It takes place hidden from the public eye. A husband or wife may suspect a spouse of adultery yet not have definite knowledge that actual adultery has taken place.

The Torah's attitude toward adultery presents a dilemma. It condemns it in the strongest terms. It is one of the prohibitions that is included in the Decalogue. Yet, this behavior is extremely difficult to regulate. The prohibition cannot be enforced through normal judicial procedures.

The passages above explain that this issue is addressed by the *mitzvah* of *sotah*. Essentially, this *mitzvah* acknowledges that this is not a prohibition that can be enforced by the courts. Instead, it enlists Hashem in the enforcement of the prohibition.

And when he has made her drink the water, then it shall come to pass, if she be defiled, and has acted unfaithfully against her husband, that the water that causes the curse shall enter into her and become bitter, and her belly shall swell, and her thigh shall fall away; and the woman shall be a curse among her people. And if the woman be not defiled, but be clean; then she shall be cleared, and shall conceive. (BeMidbar 5:27-28)

The Torah's solution

The *mitzvah* of *sotah* is the only instance in which the judgment of a crime is not performed by the court and punishment is not executed by the court. Instead, both the judgment and the punishment rely upon a miracle.

The parasha provides a description of the process through which the *sotah* and her suspected partner are judged and – if guilty – punished. In summary, it is the husband of the suspected wife who is charged with the duty of initiating the trial. He cannot do this with without warning. He must first express his concerns to his wife and share his suspicions. He can only proceed with acting against his wife if she ignores these concerns and continues to liaison in seclusion with the man with whom the husband suspects the wife is intimate. If these conditions are met, then the husband can place his wife into the hands of the *kohanim* – the priests – to be tried. The *kohanim* are not judges and they do not conduct a judicial proceeding.

The wife is not required to agree to these proceedings. However, at this point, clear evidence does exist that the wife and her suspected partner have at least entered into seclusion together. This seclusion took place after the husband had shared his suspicions with his wife. If the wife is not willing to resolve these suspicions and exonerate herself through these proceedings, then she and her husband must divorce.

The proceedings include elements of *avodah* – sacrificial service – and a non-judicial proceeding that determines the guilt or innocence of the woman and her suspected partner. This element incorporates the miracle that is the most unique element of this *mitzvah*. The *kohen* creates a mixture that combines water from the laver of the Tabernacle – the *Mishcan*, dirt from the floor of the *Mishcan*, and one more ingredient.

This last ingredient is complex. The *kohen* records the Torah portion of the *mitzvah* of *sotah*. He then scrapes the letters of the text into the mixture.

The woman drinks the mixture. If she is guilty, then the mixture is fatal. It is fatal not only for her. Her partner, even though he does not participate directly in the test, also dies.

And Hashem spoke unto Moshe, saying: Speak unto the children of Israel, and say unto them, "I am HaShem your G-d. After the behaviors of the land of Egypt, wherein you dwelt, you shall not follow. And after the doings of the land of Cana'an, to where I bring you, you shall not follow.

Neither shall you follow their statutes. You shall observe My ordinances and My statutes you shall keep, to walk therein. I am Hashem your G-d. You shall therefore keep My statutes, and Mine ordinances, which if a person does, he shall live by them. I am Hashem. None of you shall approach to any that is near of kin to him, to uncover their nakedness. I am Hashem." (VaYikra 18:1-6)

The odd placement of the *mitzvah* of *sotah* within the books of the Torah

The placement of this discussion in the beginning of Sefer BeMidbar is very difficult to understand. Where should this discussion appear in the Torah? The *parshiyot* – Torah sections – of Kedoshim and Acharei Mot both focused on the Torah's sexual prohibitions. The above passages introduce that discussion. The prohibition against adultery is included in the presentation. Those sections would be a perfect context for discussion of the *mitzvah* of *sotah*. Furthermore, those sections are part of Sefer VaYikra. Sefer VaYikra deals extensively with the roles, duties, and responsibilities of the *kohanim*. The entire *sotah* proceeding is conducted by the *kohen*. Sefer VaYikra would be the appropriate context for this *mitzvah*. Why it this *mitzvah* presented at this point?

And Hashem spoke unto Moshe and unto Aharon, saying: The children of Israel shall pitch by their fathers' houses; every man by his own standard, according to the ensigns; a way off shall they pitch around the tent of meeting. (BeMidbar 2:1-2)

The purpose of the Sefer BeMidbar census

Sefer BeMidbar begins with a census of Bnai Yisrael. Based on this census each person was assigned a specific place to set up one's tent and when the nation camped. This census also assigned to each person a specific place within the procession of the nation as it traveled through the wilderness. In other words, the census was the fundamental tool for the planning of Bnai Yisrael's "neighborhoods" and communities.

Through the census, each person was assigned to a *shevet* – a tribe. Each tribe was assigned a place within a *degel* – a group of three tribes. Each *degel* was assigned a position with the camp surrounding the *Mishcan* and within the procession of the nation, when traveling. As a result of this scheme, the members of each tribe camped together in an assigned place. Each tribe camped within a group of three specific tribes. When the camp traveled, the same scheme was implemented. Each person traveled within one's assigned tribe and each tribe traveled with the other tribes of its *degel*.

An important outcome of this design is that it nurtured a strong community. Family members camped together and were surrounded by families from their own *shevet*. Each *shevet* was surrounded or adjacent to set, unchanging partners. The larger a community the more difficult to create a high degree of social cohesion. Bnai Yisrael was a community of over a million individuals. In other words, its population was larger than Seattle's. Creating social cohesion in a group this size is difficult and perhaps impossible. But the Torah divided this multitude into smaller *shevet*-groups. In these groups the "degrees of separation" between families and individuals were reduced. Everyone could know or have a tangible sense of connection with those who surrounded him. The result is a supportive community.

If your brother be impoverished, and he sells some of his legacy, then shall his kinsman that is next unto him come, and shall redeem that which his brother hath sold. (VaYikra 25:25)

A poor person who is one's relative receives priority over all others. The poor of one's household receive priority over the poor of one's city. And the poor of one's city receive priority over the poor of another city, as [implied by Deuteronomy 15:11]: "[You shall surely open your hand to] your brother, the poor, and the destitute in your land." (Maimonides, Mishne Torah, Matanot Aniyim 7:13)

The importance of family and community

The importance of community and family is discussed in the ending sections of Sefer VaYikra. There, the responsibilities of family to come to the rescue of a member who is impoverished is repeatedly mentioned. The above passage is one example of this emphasis. This value is codified in the laws governing *tzedakah* – charity. Maimonides discusses this issue in his laws governing *tzedakah*. We are required to give priority to helping our family members and members of our own community.

In short, the Torah's system of encampment reflects an outlook on social design. Family, *shevet*, and community are reinforced. A strong community is nurtured between these families and individuals. Members of the family and community are encouraged to render assistance to one another.

A person's *shevet* is determined by one patrilineal descent

An important aspect of the system of encampment is the means by which individuals are assigned to their respective *shevet*. This is determined by patrilineal descent. One's *shevet* is determined by one's father. If the father was a member of Shevet Reuven then his children are members of this *shevet*.

Now, let us return to the discussion of *sotah* and the placement of this *mitzvah* in the context of the description of the camp of Bnai Yisrsel. Apparently, the discussion of the camp segues into the *mitzvah* of *sotah*. The organization of the camp is founded upon patrilineal descent. The *mitzvah* of *sotah* is designed to protect patrilineal integrity.

It is not difficult to determine the mother of a child. Determination of the father requires more than an empirical observation. The degree of certainty of fatherhood is a function of the fidelity between mother and husband. If this fidelity is in question, the child cannot be certain of his father's identity. The proper *shevet* of the child is in doubt and one's place within the community is undermined.

The design of the encampment emphasizes the importance of strong family structure. The most basic unit of family is parents and their children. If the certain identity of the father is in doubt, the family unit is undermined. Father and child must struggle with the uncertainty underlying their relationship. The unit that is the very bedrock of the community is damaged.

The *mitzvah* of *sotah* is directly related to the importance of preserving the basic family unit – mother, father, and children.

Understanding the Torah's definition of adultery

It follows that the infidelity of the wife and husband are treated differently. A husband's infidelity is a violation of the trust that is the foundation of marriage. However, it does not give his and his wife's children cause to doubt that he is their father.

The commentators offer a variety of views on the reasoning behind the Torah's severe attitude toward adultery. However, their opinions share a common thread – the importance of clear parental identification. The above analysis indicates that this view is reflected in the Torah's presentation of the *mitzvah* of *sotah*.

"And the man shall bring his wife to the *Kohen*. And he shall bring her sacrifice on her behalf – one tenth of an *efah* of coarse barley flour. He should not pour upon it oil. And he should not put frankincense upon it – for it is a meal offering of jealousy. It is a meal offering of remembrance – recalling iniquity. (BeMidbar 5:15)

Our *parasha* discusses the test performed upon the *Sotah*. The *Sotah* is a woman suspected of adultery. She is brought to the *Mishcan* or *Bait HaMikdash*. There, she is administered the test described in the Torah. This test culminates in the woman drinking a special mixture. This test relies on a miracle. If the woman is guilty of the suspected crime, then she dies. If she is innocent, the mixture does not harm her.

Our *pasuk* describes the meal offering of the *Sotah*. This sacrifice is brought by the woman's husband on her behalf. This meal offering is very unusual. First, most meal offerings are made of wheat flour. The *Sotah*'s is composed of barley flour. Second, normally the flour of the meal offering is finely milled. The *Sotah*'s barley is coarse. Third, meal offerings are generally accompanied by oil and frankincense. The *Sotah*'s offering does not include these components.

Rashi explains that all of these special characteristics of the *Sotah*'s offering express a single message. These aspects of the offering reflect on the promiscuity of the *Sotah*. The *Sotah*, in her adulterous affair, adopted the behavior of a beast. Therefore, her offering is composed of a coarsely milled grain reserved for animal feed. The addition of frankincense and oil enhance the offering. The offering of a sexually immoral individual does not deserve these enhancements.[4]

In the process of testing the *Sotah* other steps are taken that reflect upon her behavior. For example, her hair is uncovered in public. Rashi explains that this is an intentional attempt to disgrace her.[5]

Perhaps, the most interesting element of the process is the actual administration of the test. The Chumash explains that the ingredients are placed in an earthenware vessel. The mixture is then administered from this vessel. Why does the Torah specify the use of an earthenware vessel? Rashi explains that this vessel is chosen to contrast the woman's unglamorous

---

[4] Rabbaynu Shlomo ben Yitzchak (Rashi), *Commentary on Sefer BeMidbar* 5:15.
[5] Rabbaynu Shlomo ben Yitzchak (Rashi), *Commentary on Sefer BeMidbar* 5:18.

predicament with her amorous behavior. She and the adulterer drank fine wines from expensive goblets. She now drinks the bitter mixture from a simple earthenware vessel.[6]

It seems that this entire process reflects an assumption of guilt. Yet, in fact, we do not know whether adultery has been committed! This is the reason the test is performed. The most disturbing aspect of this question is that the very administration of the test reflects an assumption of guilt. The earthenware vessel, used in the test, represents an assumption of guilt. At least the test itself should be free on any prejudgment!

In order to answer this question, we must recognize that the Torah expects us to conduct ourselves with extreme modesty and discretion. The Torah does not regard flirtatious behavior by a married woman as harmless. This does not mean that a married woman must live a sheltered life. However, we must all conduct ourselves with dignity and restraint.

We do not know whether the *Sotah* has committed adultery. The test is administered to resolve this issue. However, in order for the *Sotah* to be subjected to the test, she must be clearly guilty of promiscuous, flirtatious behavior. Without a pattern of such behavior, she cannot be subjected to the ordeal of the test.

We can now begin to answer our question. The assumption of guilt is based upon the actual behavior of the *Sotah*. We know that she is guilty of immorality. The test only determines the degree of her deviation from Torah expectations. This explains the elements of the procedure designed to disgrace the woman. She is being punished for her promiscuity.

However, this does not explain the assumption of guilt implied within the test itself. In other words, it makes sense that the woman should be reprimanded for her behavior. But the test utilizes an earthenware vessel. This vessel implies the commitment of adultery. The test should be free of any prejudgment.

It seems that ordeal of the *Sotah* cannot be defined as the administration of a test. A test would be free of prejudgment. The ordeal of the *Sotah* can more properly be defined as a punishment. It assumes the guilt of the woman and punishes her appropriately. Even the administration of the mixture is part of the punishment. The mixture is a potential poison. It is administered as an appropriate punishment for an adulterer. Various elements, throughout the process, imply or express guilt. This is now understandable. The process is designed as a punishment for adultery.

However, the process is also a test. The effectiveness of the punishment is uncertain. The potentially toxic mixture may not effect the woman. If the woman survives unscathed, she is vindicated from the crime of adultery. In other words, her vindication is not the result of an unbiased test. It is indicated by surviving the punishment.

And the kohen shall stand the woman before Hashem. And he shall uncover the woman's head. And he shall place on her hands the reminder offering, the jealousy offering. And in the hand of the kohen shall be the bitter, curse-bearing water. (BeMidbar 5:18)

The "Bitter" Mixture Given to the Sotah

---

[6] Rabbaynu Shlomo ben Yitzchak (Rashi), *Commentary on Sefer BeMidbar* 5:17.

This *pasuk* discusses the test of the *sotah*. This test culminates in the woman drinking a special mixture. This test is based on a miracle. If the woman is guilty of the suspected crime, then she dies. If she is innocent the mixture does not harm her.

The Torah describes the drink given to the *sotah* as "bitter". There are various explanations for this characterization. The simplest interpretation is offered by the Talmud in Tractate Sotah. The Talmud explains that a bitter ingredient is added to the water. This water actually tastes bitter.[7] The Midrash Sifri offers an alternative interpretation. The water is referred to as bitter because of its effect. If the woman is guilty of adultery, then the mixture will cause the woman to die. This is a "bitter" outcome.[8] Nachmanides offers another interpretation. He explains that the term "bitter" refers to an aspect of the miracle. When the woman drinks the water, it initially tastes sweet. However, if she is guilty, the water's initial sweetness is followed by a bitter taste.[9] The most obvious interpretation of the term "bitter" is offered by the Talmud. Why do Sifri and Nachmanides insist upon alternative explanations?

Let us begin by considering more carefully the position of the Talmud. According to the Talmud, an ingredient is added to the water that provides a bitter taste. Why is this ingredient needed? Why should the water have a bitter taste? The ordeal to which the *sotah* is subjected is not a neutral test. This is because there is no question that the *sotah* acted promiscuously. The test to which she is subjected – the drinking of the special mixture – is designed to determine whether this promiscuous behavior extended to adultery. This presumption of guilt – in regards to promiscuity – extends to specific details of the test. Essentially, the test is actually formulated as a punishment for adultery. The mixture given to the woman is a potential poison. The *sotah* vindicates herself through surviving the ordeal. In other words, the *sotah* subjects herself to an ordeal that is designed as a punishment for adultery. The test has the potential to kill her. She establishes her innocence surviving the ordeal; thus proving that she is not guilty of adultery. This explains the addition of a bitter ingredient to the mixture. This ingredient communicates the message that the drink is not a neutral test. It is a bitter punishment for the adulterous woman.

Sifri and Nachmanides disagree with this simple interpretation of the term "bitter". It seems that both are guided by a shared consideration. The ordeal is designed to stress the miraculous nature of the adjudication. The addition of an extraneous ingredient to the mixture can only detract from this design. If the ingredient is bitter, this is especially true. One might erroneously attribute the lethal effect of the mixture to its ingredients. Therefore, it is important to create the mixture from innocuous ingredients.

We can now understand the dispute between Nachmanides and Sifri. Sifri maintains that the term "bitter" refers to the ultimate fate awaiting a guilty *sotah*. Nachmanides interprets the term in a more literal sense. The guilty *sotah* will feel an actual bitter taste. But this sensation only occurs after ingesting the sweet tasting mixture.

Nachmanides apparently maintains that the guilty woman must know that her death is a result of the mixture. She cannot be allowed to believe that her death is coincidental. In order to communicate this message to the woman, she is immediately affected by the water itself. She

---

[7] Mesechet Sotah 20a.
[8] Sifrei Parshat Naso, Chapter 11.
[9] Rabbaynu Moshe ben Nachman (Ramban), *Commentary on Sefer BeMidbar* 5:18.

now knows that the mixture has tested her and found her guilty. She will know that the water has caused her demise.

And the man shall be free of sin and the woman will bear the consequence of her sin. (BeMidbar 5:31)

The Trial of the Sotah and Our Responsibility to Uphold the Laws of the Torah

The test administered to the *sotah* requires that she drink a mixture prepared by the *kohen*. The woman drinks the mixture. If she is guilty, both she and the adulterer die. If she is innocent, she is rewarded with offspring.

This entire trial is based upon a miracle. Nachmanides observes that this is the only element of the Torah's judicial system in which justice is dependent upon a miracle.[10] The Talmud explains that this miracle was a blessing from Hashem. However, Hashem only performed this miracle during the period in which the prohibitions against adultery and sexual promiscuity were scrupulously observed. Once the nation became lax regarding these laws, Hashem no longer performed this miracle.[11]

At first glance, this statement from the Talmud seems difficult to understand. It would seem that when the people are devoted to the law, the test of the *sotah* is less necessary. If there is general observance, what harm is there to society in the failure to detect an occasional deviation? In contrast, if the law is generally disregarded, every opportunity and tool is needed to assure its enforcement.

The Talmud is teaching us an important concept regarding our responsibilities for enforcement of the law. Hashem will not perform our duties for us. We are responsible for enforcement of the Torah's *mitzvot*. We cannot expect Hashem to assume this responsibility, in our place. However, if we demonstrate devotion to the Torah, through careful observance, then Hashem will help us fulfill our desire to enforce the law.

With this principle, we can understand the comments of the Talmud. At the time that the people were devoted to observance of the *mitzvot*, Hashem assisted the people in enforcing the law. Hashem helped resolve the innocence or guilt of the *sotah* – the suspected adulterer. The *sotah* was not able to escape justice. When the people were not devoted to observance, this miracle could no longer be expected. If the people did not care about adultery, they could not turn to Hashem to assume responsibility for enforcement of this prohibition.

The priest shall prepare one as a Chatat and one as Olah to atone for his inadvertent defilement by the dead. (BeMidbar 6:11)

The Sin Offering by the Nazir

Parshat Naso describes the laws governing the *nazir*. The *nazir* is a person who takes a vow to separate oneself from material pleasures. The *nazir* may not drink wine or cut his hair. The *nazir* is also prohibited from defilement through contact with a dead body.

---

[10] Rabbaynu Moshe ben Nachman (Ramban), *Commentary on Sefer BMidbar* 5:20.
[11] Mesechet Sotah 47a.

A *nazir* who does come in contact with a dead body is defiled. This defiled *nazir* must bring a series of sacrifices as atonement. One of these sacrifices is a *Chatat* – a sin offering. Rashi explains that this sin offering is required because the *nazir* did not exercise adequate care in keeping the vow.[12]

Rashi offers a second interpretation of the *Chatat* offering. He quotes the comments of the Talmud in Tractate Nazir. Rebbe Eliezer HaKafar explains that the sin of the *nazir* is not merely unintentional contact with a dead body. The *nazir* vowed to abandon the pleasure of drinking wine. The sin of the *nazir* is the self-affliction and denial that he has accepted upon himself. The Talmud further comments that we learn an important lesson from this law. The *nazir* is obligated to bring a *Chatat* because of a vow not to drink wine. A person who, as a general practice, abandons the material pleasures is even more guilty.[13]

This explanation of the *Chatat* is clearly supported by another law. A *nazir* who successfully completed the vow must also bring a *Chatat*.[14] In this case, the vow has not been violated. Why is a *Chatat* required? Rebbe Eliezer HaKafar's explanation resolves this issue. Even the successful *nazir* requires atonement. The *nazir* must atone for the self-affliction and deprivation.

According to Rebbe Eliezer HaKafar, the *nazir* has acted improperly. Yet, the Torah created the *mitzvah* of *nazir*! This interpretation raises an obvious question. How can the Torah define an inappropriate behavior as a *mitzvah*?

Maimonides deals with this question in his introduction to Perkai Avot. He explains the Torah is designed to help us achieve moderation in all of our attitudes. But what constitutes moderation? The term "moderation" assumes that the moderate attitude is balanced between extremes. In other words, every attitude occupies a midpoint along a continuum of possible attitudes. An example helps illustrate Maimonides' position. A person who has a moderate attitude towards personal wealth is able to use his wealth in order to secure a meaningful improvement in his condition. This attitude is balanced between the extreme attitudes demonstrated by the spendthrift and the miserly person. The miser cannot part with his wealth even when circumstances dictate that the expenditure is worthwhile. The spendthrift expends his wealth with abandon, unable to consider the true value of the items he purchases. According to Maimonides, we should strive for to conduct ourselves in a manner that is balanced between the two extremes. A person should not be a spendthrift. Neither should one be stingy. Similarly, we are not permitted to act cowardly. We also may not endanger ourselves unnecessarily. Instead, our attitude towards risk should reflect moderation. We should be willing and able to subject ourselves to a reasonable risk if the circumstances so demand. The same pattern applies to all behaviors and attitudes. We must seek the middle road.

Inevitably, we all have attitudes that are not moderate but instead somewhat extreme. Some of us may be overly shy. Others may be egotistical. How does one correct a flaw? Maimonides explains that the Torah suggests that we temporarily force ourselves to adopt the behavior and attitude of the opposite extreme. The stingy person practices being a spendthrift. The glutton adopts a very restricted diet. With time, this practice will enable the person to break

---

[12] Rabbaynu Shlomo ben Yitzchak (Rashi), *Commentary on Sefer BeMidbar* 6:11.
[13] Mesechet Nazir 19a.
[14] Sefer BeMidbar 6:7.

the original attachment. One will be able to adopt the moderate behavior and attitude required by the Torah.

Maimonides explains that the *mitzvah* of the *nazir* should be understood in this context. The *nazir* is a person who was overly attached to the material pleasures. The *nazir* makes a vow to adopt the behavior associated with the opposite extreme. He embraces self-denial for a period of time. The ultimate goal is to free the personality from his inordinate attachment to material pleasures. This will allow him to ultimately achieve an attitude of moderation.

However, the Torah did not want us to mistakenly view the *nazir*'s behavior of self-denial as an ideal. We must recognize that the *nazir*'s vow is intended as a corrective measure for an extreme attitude and behavior. How was this message communicated? This was accomplished through the *Chatat* of the *nazir*. The *Chatat* teaches that the lifestyle of self-denial adopted by the *nazir* is not inherently proper. The measures adopted by the *nazir* are necessary in order to help him achieve moderation. The ultimate goal is balanced conduct, not the extreme behavior of the *nazir*.[15]

Maimonides seemingly contradicts this interpretation of the *nazir* and the *Chatat* in his Moreh Nevuchim. There, Maimonides explains that one of the goals of the Torah is to completely distance oneself from the material desires. Furthermore, Maimonides asserts that the *nazir* is considered a sanctified individual. How does the *nazir* earn this status? Maimonides responds that the *nazir* has given up wine![16]

These comments seem to completely contradict the position Maimonides outlined in his introduction to Perkai Avot. In the Moreh Nevuchim, Maimonides endorses extreme behavior of the *nazir* as an ideal. He also asserts that the *nazir*'s abandonment of wine is laudable! How can these two positions be reconciled?

In these two texts Maimonides is dealing with two completely separate issues. In his introduction to Perkai Avot, he is discussing the basis for a healthy personality. He explains that psychological health requires, and is manifested, in moderation in behavior and attitudes.

However, the objective of the Torah is to guide an individual to truth and spiritual perfection. As a person grows spiritually and embraces truth, the individual begins to re-evaluate the meaning of life. Material pleasures loose their glamour and attraction. This abandonment is not the result of vows of self-denial. The *tzadik* – the righteous person – simply loses interest in material affairs. This *tzadik* is the individual Maimonides describes in the Moreh Nevuchim. The *tzadik* is a truly spiritual person guided solely by his appraisal of reality and is assessment of what is truly important. In other words, the Torah views moderation in one's attitude towards material pleasures as the ideal attitude to most people However, the Torah also acknowledges that as a person grows intellectually and spiritually, his interest with and attachment to material pleasures declines. With this re-orientation, he naturally abandons material pleasures that were previously far more significant to him.

As explained above, the *nazir* is not the *tzadik* described in the Moreh Nevuchim. This *tzadik* does not require a vow to moderate his interaction with the material world. Instead, the *nazir* is a person attempting to move away from an extreme attachment to material pleasure. The

---

[15] R' Moshe ben Maimon (Rambam) *Commentary on the Mishne*, Intro. to Perkai Avot, Chp 4.
[16] Rabbaynu Moshe ben Maimon (Rambam) *Moreh Nevuchim*, Volume 3, Chapter 34.

nazir is striving to achieve the middle road. The Torah constructed a *mitzvah* to help this person – the *mitzvah* of *nazir*. However, this *mitzvah* is not merely a set of arbitrary restrictions. The *nazir* adopts the behaviors of the *tzadik*. He experiments with living the life and adopting the attitudes of a truly spiritual individual. He learns that although he is not nearly ready to be this exalted person, he can live without the material pleasure to which he previously regarded as necessities. In short, the *nazir* is not the perfected individual described in the Moreh Nevuchim. However, he does adopt the behaviors associated with the *tzadik*.

And this is the law of the Nazirite, when the days of his Nazirite vow are fulfilled: He shall bring himself to the door of the Ohel Mo'ed. (BeMidbar 6:13)

Lessons from the Nazirite

The laws of the Nazirite

Parshat Naso describes the *mitzvah* of the *Nazir* – the Nazirite. The *Nazir* is a person who takes a vow to separate oneself from material pleasures. Specifically, the *Nazir* may not drink wine or cut his hair. The purpose of this removal from material affairs is to encourage greater devotion to Hashem and the Torah. This will be much more thoroughly discussed later. His vow endows the *Nazir* with a degree of sanctity. Because of this sanctity, the *Nazir* is prohibited from defiling oneself through contact with a dead body.

The Torah establishes a minimum duration for the *Nazir's* vow. The *Nazir* must commit to a period of abstinence of at least thirty days. The *Nazir* may subscribe to a longer period of abstinence. The length beyond thirty days is discretionary. A person may vow to be a *Nazir* for a number of months or even years.

Upon completion of the period of the vow, the *Nazir* performs a series of activities in the Temple. These include shaving off the long hair that he has grown during the period of the vow and bringing a number of sacrifices.

The *Nazir* brings himself to the Tabernacle

In the above passage, the Torah explains that on the day that the *Nazir* completes his vow "he brings himself to the *Ohel Mo'ed"* – the Tabernacle and initiates the process described above. This translation of the passage is suggested by Rashi. However, Rashi acknowledges that this translation is not literal. The literal translation of the passage is the "he brings him".[17] Unkelus adopts this literal rendering in his translation of the Torah.

The problem with the literal translation is obvious. Who are the "he" and the "him" in the passage? Presumably, the "him" brought to the Tabernacle is the *Nazir*. But who is the "he" who brings the *Nazir* to the Tabernacle? Because of this difficulty Rashi suggests translating passage less rigorously and that it actually means that the *Nazir* brings himself.

Of course, Rashi's translation does not completely solve the problem presented by the passage. The passage remains difficult to understand. Why did the Torah not express itself more simply; leave out the transitive "brings" and in its place use the intransitive "comes"? The Torah could have said that upon completing his vow, the *Nazir* comes to the *Ohel Mo'ed*! Furthermore,

---

[17] Rabbaynu Shlomo ben Yitzchak (Rashi), *Commentary on Sefer BeMidbar* 6:13.

by expressing itself in this straight-forward manner the Torah would have averted the need to interpret the passage in a less than literal manner.

Rav Meir Simcha of Devinsk – Mesech Chachmah – offers an important answer to this question. Before considering his explanation of the passage, more information about the *mitzvah* of *Nazir* is needed.

Moderation and the purpose of the *Nazir*'s vow

Rambam – Maimonides – explains the Torah is designed to help us achieve moderation in all of our attitudes. But what constitutes moderation? The term "moderation" assumes that the moderate attitude is balanced between extremes. In other words, every proper attitude occupies a midpoint along a continuum of possible attitudes. An example helps illustrate Rambam's position. A person who has a moderate attitude toward personal wealth seeks a level of wealth adequate to secure a reasonable degree of material comfort and security. This attitude is balanced between the extreme attitudes of the spendthrift and the miser. The miser cannot part with his wealth even when circumstances dictate that the expenditure is worthwhile. The spendthrift expends his wealth with abandon, unable to consider the true value of the items he purchases. According to Rambam, we should strive to conduct ourselves in a manner that is balanced between the two extremes. A person should not be a spendthrift. Neither should one be stingy.

Similarly, we are not permitted to act cowardly. Neither may we endanger ourselves unnecessarily. Instead, our attitude toward risk should reflect moderation. We should be willing and able to subject ourselves to a reasonable risk if the circumstances so demand. The same pattern applies to all behaviors and attitudes. We must seek the middle road.

Inevitably, we each have attitudes that are not moderate but instead somewhat extreme. For example, some of us are overly shy; others are egotistical. How does one correct a flaw? Rambam explains that the Torah suggests we temporarily force ourselves to adopt those behaviors that are opposite of our initial tendency. The stingy person practices being a spendthrift. The glutton adopts a very restricted diet. With time, this adopted behavior counters the person's initial extreme attitude. Freed from the initial fixation at the extreme, one is able to achieve the moderate behavior and attitude required by the Torah. The once stingy person is able to spend his wealth reasonably. The glutton finds he has developed a heathier attitude toward food.

Rambam explains that the *mitzvah* of the *Nazir* should be understood in this context. The *Nazir* is a person who was overly attached to material indulgence. The *Nazir* makes a vow to adopt the behavior associated with the opposite extreme. He embraces self-denial for a period of time. The ultimate goal is to free the personality from inordinate attachment to material pleasures. This will allow him to ultimately achieve an attitude of moderation.

However, the Torah does not want us to mistakenly view the *Nazir*'s behavior of self-denial as an ideal. We must recognize that the *Nazir*'s vow is intended to correct an extreme attitude and behavior.[18]

The discretionary period of the *Nazir*'s vow

Mesech Chachmah comments that it is notable that the Torah does not suggest an appropriate length of time for the *Nazir's* vow. However, this is completely understandable

---

[18] R' Moshe ben Maimon (Rambam) *Commentary on the Mishne*, Intro to Perkai Avot, chp 4.

based upon the interpretation of the *mitzvah* presented by Rambam. The *Nazir* is undertaking a process of personal abstinence, in order to temper his desires and to achieve a more moderate attitude. The appropriate period for this vow is subjective and will differ from person to person. One individual may be able to achieve the moderation he seeks after a month-long period of abstinence. Another person may require a period of abstinence extending for months or even years. How does the *Nazir* determine the appropriate period for his vow? He must evaluate himself with complete objectivity and determine the intensity of his tendency toward overindulgence. Once he makes an honest judgment of himself, he can determine how long he must engage in abstinence in order to overcome his tendency. In other words, the person contemplating a *Nazir* vow must engage in a process of personal introspection in which he both conducts the investigation and is its object.

Honest and rigorous introspection

How does one engage in objective introspection? Meshech Chachamah continues and explains this process. It requires that the person look upon himself with the same critical attitude that he typically adopts when analyzing the behaviors of peers and neighbors. Generally, we have no difficulty in identifying the flaws, wrongdoings, and failings of others. However, this critical capacity fails us when we consider our own behaviors and attitudes. The person considering the vow of a *Nazir* must subject himself to the same critical scrutiny that he more easily applies to others. This is the meaning of being both the investigator and object of the investigation.

On the basis of this observation, Meshech Chachmah explains the strange expression employed by the Torah in the above passage. The *Nazir* brings him – meaning, he brings himself – to the Tabernacle. This strange phrasing beautifully captures the introspective aspect of the *Nazir*. He, alone, determines the length of his vow and when he will come to the Tabernacle to complete his duties and obligations as a *Nazir*. He makes this determination based upon objective introspection. He treats himself not as "me" but as him. He – the *Nazir* who has evaluated his flaws and embarked upon a path of personal improvement – brings him – the person whom he objectively evaluated – to the Tabernacle.[19]

Applications of the lesson of the *Nazir*

To understand Mesech Chachmah's comments as relevant only to the *Nazir* is to miss his point. Each of us should constantly strive to improve ourselves through introspection. This is not easily accomplished. It is very difficult to adopt the detached attitude required for effective and thorough introspection. Mesech Chachmah acknowledges this difficulty and is advising a strategy. Use as one's standard of rigor the degree of critical scrutiny and ruthless dissection that we commonly apply to our critique of others.

This may prove to be very difficult to achieve and it will certainly be a painful process. Even If the introspection described by Meshech Chachmah is not perfectly achieved, it will yield a very important secondary benefit. Through an honest process of introspection and through recognizing our own shortcomings, we will become more forgiving of others and of their failings. Our introspection does not need to be perfect to instill within us a greater degree of humility. With the recognition of our own many failings comes more empathy for others and their failings. We learn to forgive others for their flaws though recognizing our own.

---

[19] Rav Meir Simcha of Devinsk, *Meshech Chachmah on Sefer BeMidbar* 6:13.

Placing the Hair of the Nazir on the Fire under His Shelamim Sacrifice

And the nazir shall shave his crown of hair from his head. And he shall take the hair of his crown and place it upon the fire that is under the Shelamim sacrifice. (BeMidbar 6:18)

The *nazir* is an individual who takes a vow to separate himself from the material world. The *nazir* may not drink wine, cut his hair or come into contact with a dead body. The ultimate purpose of this abandonment of material affairs is to encourage greater devotion to Hashem and the Torah.

Upon completion of the period of the vow, the *nazir* performs a series of activities in the Temple. These include bringing a number of sacrifices. As part of the process of offering his sacrifices, the *nazir* shaves his head and throws the hair upon the fire under the *Shelamim* sacrifice. What is the meaning of this unusual requirement?

It is possible for a person to undertake the vow of the *nazir* for various reasons. A person may wish to demonstrate religious superiority over others. This is a misuse of the institution of *nazir*. The only acceptable motivation is to improve one's devotion to Hashem. This concept is demonstrated through the throwing of the *nazir*'s hair under the sacrifice. The hair represents the *nazir's* vow and subsequent abstention from the material world. The sacrifice represents service to Hashem. If the *nazir* has undertaken the vow in order to "fuel" service to Hashem, then the vow was proper. However, if the vow was merely an expression of religious elitism, then it did not serve its true purpose.

"Speak to Ahron and his sons saying: This is how you should bless Bnai Yisrael. Say to them..." (BeMidbar 6:23)

This passage introduces the Torah's discussion of *Birkat Kohanim* – the Priestly blessing. The blessing is actually composed of three separate blessings. These blessings are recited by the *Kohanim*. Through their recital of the *Birkat Kohanim*, they express their desire that the Almighty bestow His blessings upon Bnai Yisrael.

The *Birkat Kohanim* has been incorporated into the *chazan's* repetition of the *Amidah*. There are various practices regarding which days the *Birkat Kohanim* is recited. The dominant practice in the land of Israel is to recite the blessings every day. Outside of the land of Israel customs differ.

The format for the recitation of the blessings is very simple. The *Kohanim* begin by reciting a benediction prior to the performance of the *mitzvah*. This benediction acknowledges that the *Kohanim* have been commanded to lovingly bless Bnai Yisrael. Then, the *chazan* leads the *Kohanim* in the recitation of the *Birkat Kohanim*.

There is an interesting dispute in *halacha* concerning *Birkat Kohanim*. In order to understand this dispute a brief introduction is needed. There is a general principle in *halacha* of *shomea ke'oneh* – one who listens is treated as the one pronouncing. The principle dictates that a person can fulfill an obligation to recite a given formula or text though listening to the recitation of another individual. An example will illustrate the application of this principle. We are obligated to recite *Kiddush* on the night of *Shabbat* and festivals. However, in most families the head of the household recites the *Kiddush* on behalf of all those present. How does the recitation of this one individual discharge the obligation of the others present to recite *Kiddush*? The answer is that the principle of *shomea ke'oneh* is applied. The head of the household recites the *Kiddush* and others present fulfill their obligation through attentively listening.

Can the principle of *shomea ke'oneh* be applied to *Birkat Kohanim*? In other words, can one *Kohen* recite these blessings on behalf of all the *Kohanim* present? Can the other *Kohanim* present fulfill their obligation through listening attentively to the one *Kohen* reciting the blessings?

This issue is disputed by the authorities. Some argue that *Birkat Kohanim* is not different from *Kiddush*. *Shomea ke'oneh* is effective. Others offer various reasons for differentiating between the two recitations. Rav Meshulam David Soloveitchik offers a very interesting reason for differentiating. He explains that the benediction recited by the *Kohanim* states that they are commanded to bless the nation with love. He explains that *shomea ke'oneh* is effective in relating the recital of the blessings to the listening *Kohen*. However, *shomea ke'oneh* cannot transmit this element of love to the listener. The love must come from the *Kohen* himself. He cannot express his love through the feelings of the *Kohen* reciting the blessing. In short, through listening, the *Kohen* has not blessed the nation in love![20]

These comments can be understood in two ways. In order to understand these two approaches we must analyze the idea that the *Kohanim* must bless the nation with love. Midrash Rabbah explains that the *Kohanim* cannot recite the blessings in a rote manner. The blessings must be expressed wholeheartedly.[21] The blessings are an expression of the *Kohanim*'s love for the nation. This means that a *Kohen* does not fulfill his obligation through merely reciting the blessings. The blessings must be an expression of the inner feelings of the *Kohen*. *Shomea ke'oneh* can relate the recital of one *Kohen* to another who is listening attentively. However, *shomea ke'oneh* cannot render these blessings into a personal expression of the inner feeling of the listening *Kohen*. Therefore, *shomea ke'oneh* is ineffective in this case.

There is a second way to understand the Midrash Rabbah and Rav Soloveitchik's comments. Perhaps, *Birkat Kohanim* is more than the recital of a formula. Instead, it can be understood as a relationship between the *Kohanim* and the people. With the recital of their blessing, the *Kohanim* are entering into a relationship with the people. The *Kohanim* are the petitioners and the people are the beneficiaries of their petition. This is the reason for requiring the wholehearted expression of the *Kohanim*. The relationship between the *Kohanim* and the people only exists when the blessings are recited with sincerity. As we explained above, *shomea ke'oneh* can only relate the recital of one *Kohen* to another who is listening attentively. *Shomea ke'oneh* cannot create a relationship between the listening *Kohen* and the people. Therefore, in this case *shomea ke'oneh* is ineffective.

"Speak to Ahron and to his sons saying, "In this manner you should bless Bnai Yisrael. Say to them" (BeMidbar 6:23)

This *pasuk* introduces the *mitzvah* for the *Kohanim* to recite a blessing over the congregation. This blessing is incorporated into the *Amidah*. It is recited prior to the final

---

[20] Rav Shimon Yosef Miller, Shai LaTorah (Jerusalem 5751), volume 1, pp. 183-184.
[21] Midrash Rabba, Sefer BeMidbar 11:4.

blessing of the *Amidah – Seem Shalom*. In the *Bait HaMikdash* the blessing was recited every day. In Israel, this remains the practice. Bait Yosef maintains that this practice should also be observed outside of the Land of Israel.[22] However, Rima disagrees. He comments that the prevalent practice outside of the Land of Israel is to recite the blessing only on Yom Tov. On weekdays and Shabbat it is not recited. Rima offers an interesting explanation for this practice. He begins by explaining that it is appropriate for the *Kohanim* to be in a positive state of mind when reciting the blessing. On weekdays and even on Shabbat, people are often distracted by the concerns of daily life. These distractions are an impediment to achieving the requisite level of happiness that is appropriate for reciting the blessing.[23] Although these are the two basic positions regarding the reciting of the blessing outside of the Land of Israel, there are other variations. For example, some congregations do not recite the blessing on weekdays but do recite it on Shabbat.

"Hashem should bless you and watch over you. Hashem should shine His countenance upon you and enlighten you. Hashem should lift His countenance to you and grant you peace." (BeMidbar 6:24-27)

Sefer HaChinuch, in his discussion of this blessing raises a question. His question is based upon the assertion that the *Kohanim* do not actually bestow their blessing upon the congregation. Instead, Hashem bestows the blessing.[24] An analysis of the actual blessing seems to support this assertion. The passages above are the text of the blessings recited by the *Kohanim*. As the text indicates, the *Kohanim* do not actually pronounce a blessing upon the people. Instead, they appeal to Hashem to bless the people. In short, this *mitzvah* does not require that the *Kohanim* bless the people. Instead, it requires that the *Kohanim* ask for Hashem to bless the nation.

Sefer HaChinuch asks: why does the Torah require the *Kohanim* to play a role in this process? If Hashem wishes to bless the people, He certainly will do so without the intervention of the *Kohanim*! Sefer HaChinuch's answer is somewhat cryptic. His response has two components. First, he explains that we sometimes receive Hashem's blessings and sometimes we do not. This is not because Hashem at times withholds His blessings. Hashem never withholds His blessings. Instead, Hashem's blessings are always available to us. Whether we receive them or not is determined by whether we deserve them. Therefore, we were given the Torah. The Torah provides us with the means of attaining righteousness. Through attaining righteousness, we are able to merit the blessings that Hashem is constantly bestowing.

Second, he explains that Hashem wishes for us to request His blessings and that this request should be made through the sacred and pure *Kohanim*. This very act of asking through the *Kohanim* is meritorious and through this merit we receive the blessings of Hashem.[25]

A thorough discussion of the first element of Sefer HaChinuch's answer is beyond the scope of this discussion. Essentially, Sefer HaChinuch wishes to stress that Hashem is perfect, an absolute unity, and never changes. Therefore, although it sometimes seems that the ways in which Hashem relates or acts towards us change, this is merely our perception. In truth, Hashem

---

[22] RavYosef Karo, *Bait Yosef Commentary on Tur, Orach Chayim* 128.

[23] Rav Moshe Isserles, *Comments on Shulchan Aruch, Orech Chayim* 128:44.

[24] Rav Aharon HaLeyve, *Sefer HaChinuch*, Mitzvah 375.

[25] Rav Aharon HaLeyve, *Sefer HaChinuch*, Mitzvah 375.

is unchanging. If it seems to us that He sometimes bestows His blessings upon us and at other times withholds these blessing, this is not actually the case. Hashem does not change. We change. When we deserve, we experience the effect of His blessings. When we do not deserve, these blessings cannot devolve upon us.

A simple analogy may help explain this concept. A pitcher throws a fastball to the catcher. The catcher easily catches the pitch. The pitcher throws a second pitch and the catcher drops the ball. The catcher is disappointed with his performance. But he assumes that the pitcher must have put a little something extra on the second pitch. However, the reality is that the two pitches were identical. The catcher missed the second pitch because he was a little distracted. Like the catcher, we assume that whether we "catch" the blessing or not is determined by Hashem. But in truth, like the pitcher, Hashem is perfectly consistent. We just sometimes do not deserve and we miss the pitch!

Sefer HaChinuch's second point is a little more difficult to understand. Why is it so important that we ask for the blessings before they are bestowed? And why is it important that we ask though the sacred *Kohanim*?

Let us begin with the first question. Chovot HaLevavot discusses a related issue that provides an important insight into this question. Chovot HaLevavot explains that we are surrounded by the benevolence of Hashem. Yet, most of us do not fully appreciate or comprehend this benevolence. What prevents us from recognizing the many blessings that Hashem bestows upon us? Chovot HaLevavot identifies a number of factors. One is relevant to our discussion. He explains this factor through a parable.

A wealthy person adopted a foundling. He raised the foundling from infancy and treated this child as his own. At a later point, he became aware of a person that has been taken captive by a cruel person. This captive was living in complete destitution and treated with extreme brutality. The wealthy person took it upon himself to save this persecuted person and redeemed him from his captor. Chovot HaLevavot asserts that inevitably the former captive will be far more appreciative of the generosity of his benefactor than the child. Why? He explains that the captive experienced his suffering at a time in his development at which he could fully comprehend the experience. He passed from wretchedness to tranquility at a point in his intellectual development that allowed him to fully appreciate the kindness of his benefactor. In contrast, the foundling passed from destitution to comfort during infancy. At that time, he could not begin to comprehend the event of his rescue. By the time he was mature enough to grasp the experience of redemption, he had no memory of his former destitution and suffering. The only life he remembered, and to which he could relate, was the life he experienced as the privileged adopted son of his benefactor.

Chovot HaLevavot explains that our relationship with Hashem is akin to that of the foundling with his benefactor. We are surrounded by Hashem's blessings from birth. As a result, we take these blessings for granted. We do not comprehend or appreciate Hashem's kindness towards us.[26]

In short, by nature we are somewhat blind to Hashem's kindness. How can we overcome this failing? It seems that Sefer HaChinuch is addressing this issue. It is important that we train ourselves to acknowledge Hashem's benevolence. Training requires repetition. In order to

---

[26] Rabbaynu Bachya ibn Paquda, *Chovot HaLevavot* (Feldheim, 1970), pp 125-127.

impact our attitudes and our innate insensitivity to Hashem's kindness we must remind ourselves of this kindness consistently and repeatedly. One of the ways in which we accomplish this is by reciting blessings of thanks to Hashem. For example, each morning we recite a series of blessings that acknowledge a variety of kindnesses that we receive from Hashem. We recite blessings before we eat. These blessings remind us that we cannot take for granted the food that we are about to eat. However, it is also important that we ask Hashem to respond to our needs. By asking for Hashem's blessings we acknowledge that these blessings come from Hashem and should not be taken for granted.

But why are we required to ask specifically through the *Kohanim*? Perhaps Sefer HaChinuch is alluding to his thinking in his description of the *Kohanim*. He describes the *Kohanim* as "the servants (of Hashem) that are constantly camped around the House of Hashem. All their thoughts are directed towards His service and their souls are directed towards awe of Him all day."[27] Certainly, Sefer HaChinuch is not asserting that every Kohen achieves the level of spiritual perfection that he is describing. Instead, he is describing the role or mission assigned to the *Kohanim* by the Torah. In other words, it seems that – according to Sefer HaChinuch – those members of Bnai Yisrael that are assigned the role of achieving the highest level of spiritual perfection are required to request that Hashem bestow His blessing upon the nation.

Sefer HaChinuch's position can be better understood when considered in conjunction with the first element of his answer. He explained that the blessings that we experience from Hashem are proportionate to the degree to which we deserve of these blessings. The role of the *Kohanim* within Bnai Yisrael is to strive for the highest level of spiritual perfection. It follows that in asking Hashem to bestow his blessings upon the people, the appeal should be made by those most deserving of these blessings. However, it should be noted that a full understanding of this position requires a more thorough discussion.

And the messenger of Hashem appeared unto the woman, and said to her: Behold now, you are barren, and have not borne; but you will conceive, and bear a son. Now, beware, I pray thee, and drink no wine or strong drink, and eat not any unclean thing. For it will be that you will conceive, and bear a son. And no razor shall come upon his head. For the child shall be a Nazir unto G-d from the womb. And he shall begin to save Yisrael from of the hand of the Pelishtm. (Shoftim 13:3-5)

The Nazir Status of Shimshon

These passages are taken from the *haftarah* of Parshat Naso. They introduce the birth of the *shofet* – the judge – Shimshon. A messenger appears to Shimshon's mother before his birth. He tells her that she will give birth to a son. This son is destined to save Bnai Yisrael from the oppression of the Pelishtim. However, the messenger also tells her that Shimshon must be raised as a *nazir* and he must observe the *nazir* restrictions for his entire life.

Why was it necessary for Shimshon to conduct himself as a *nazir*? According to Ribbe Eliezer HaKafar, this is not an ideal mode of behavior. It is odd that Shimshon should be required to conduct himself in a manner that seems at odds with the Torah's values.

---

[27] Rav Aharon HaLeyve, *Sefer HaChinuch*, Mitzvah 375.

Gershonides offers an interesting response to this question. He explains that Shimshon was destined for greatness. He was destined to lead Bnai Yisrael and rescue the nation from oppression. However, Shimshon's potential to achieve greatness was coupled with another characteristic that could threaten his development. Shimshon also possessed very intense material desires. These desires eventually proved overwhelming. But Hashem provided Shimshon – through this message to his mother – with a strategy for combating his intense material urges. Hashem commanded Shimshon's mother that her son should be a *nazir*.[28] In other words, for most people, this behavior would not be appropriate. But because of Shimshon's unusually strong urges, special measures were necessary.

---

[28] Rabbaynu Levi ben Gershon (Ralbag / Gershonides), *Commentary on Sefer Shoftim* 13:3.

BeHa'alotekcha

Hashem spoke to Moshe, saying: Speak to Aharon and say to him: When you light the lamps, the seven lamps shall cast their light toward the face of the menorah. (BeMidbar 8:1-2)

An Integrated Community

The delay in recording the commandment of lighting the *menorah*

Our *parasha* opens with a discussion of the kindling of the *menorah* – the candelabra. The *menorah* was one of the most fundamental vessels of the *Mishcan* – the Tabernacle. In the above passages, Hashem commands Moshe to instruct Aharon in the daily igniting and maintenance of the *menorah*. According to our Sages, this commandment was given to Moshe during the first year of the nation's travels in the wilderness. Specifically, it was given on the day that *Mishcan* was fully installed. The date was the first day of the month of Nisan. The events of that day are described in Parshat Shemini. In that description, this commandment is not noted. Instead, the commandment is first mentioned in the above passages. Why was the commandment not mentioned at an earlier point?

And it was that on the day that Moshe finished erecting the Mishcan, he anointed it, sanctified it, and all its vessels, and the altar and all its vessels, and he anointed them and sanctified them. The princes of Israel, the heads of their fathers' houses, presented [their offerings]. They were the leaders of the tribes. They were the ones who were present during the counting. (BeMidbar 7:1-2)

Aharon and his tribe were not included in the inaugural offerings

Rashi explains that the delay in presenting this commandment is intended to connect the commandment to the previous material. At the end of Parshat Naso, the Torah describes the offerings that were brought by the princes of the various tribes as an initiation of the *Mishcan*. The Torah explains that the princes of the tribes of Israel approached Moshe and proposed bringing an inaugural offering. Hashem instructed Moshe to accept the proposed offering. Each prince was assigned a specific day to bring his offering, and over the course of twelve consecutive days, the princes brought their offerings.

Rashi explains that Aharon was disappointed that he and his tribe were not included in these inaugural offerings. In other words, all of the tribes were represented except that of Aharon – the tribe of Leyve. Hashem responded to Aharon's disappointment. He instructed Moshe to relate to Aharon the *mitzvah* of tending to and lighting the *Mishcan*'s *menorah*.

Why did Aharon not participate with the princes? In other words, how did Aharon become excluded from the inaugural offerings? Rashi derives his comments from the midrash. In the version quoted in Midrash Tanhumah, it seems Aharon and the Levites were excluded at the direction of Hashem. Hashem instructed Moshe to accept the offerings of the other princes and their tribes but He did not include Aharon and the tribe of Leyve. Why did Hashem exclude Aharon and the tribe of Leyve?

The one who brought his offering on the first day was Nachshon, the son of Amminadav of the tribe of Yehudah. (BeMidbar 7:12)

The order in which the inaugural offerings were presented

The answer to this question emerges from consideration of the purpose of these inaugural offerings. Why did the princes request to bring them? The *Mishcan* had been consecrated and installed. What was added by this inauguration?

In the above table, the first two columns list the order in which the princes brought their offerings. This order does not correspond to the birth order of the tribes' patriarchs or any other obvious hierarchy. The second two columns are the order in which the tribes camped around the *Mishcan*. A group of three tribes camped on each side of the *Mishcan*. Each group consisted of the lead tribe and two others that accompanied it. In these two right columns, the tribes are listed in the exact order the Torah employs to assign each its position relative to the *Mishcan*. For example, the Torah explains that the tribe of Yehudah led the group that camped to the east of the *Mishcan*. It was accompanied by the tribe of Yisachar and the tribe of Zevulun. By comparing the two left columns to the two right columns, we discover the basis for the order in which the offerings were brought. The order in which the offerings were brought reflected the order in which the tribes encamped surrounding the *Mishcan*.

And they shall make Me a sanctuary and I will dwell in their midst. (Sefer Shemot 25:8)And Hashem spoke to Moshe and Aharon saying: The children of Israel shall encamp each man by his division with the flag staffs of their fathers' house; some distance from the Tent of Meeting they shall encamp. (BeMidbar 2:1-2)

Two functions of the *Mishcan*

Now, the purpose of the inaugural offerings can be identified. The *Mishcan* served two functions. The first of these functions is expressed in the first quotation above. The *Mishcan* was a place in which the presence of Hashem was manifestly evident. In response to His presence, sacrifices were brought there and offered on its altar. However, the *Mishcan* had a second function. This function is described in the second quotation above. The *Mishcan* formed the spiritual and the actual physical center of the camp and nation. The entire nation integrated itself into an encampment focused upon the presence of Hashem in its midst.

The princes were directed to bring their offerings in the order in which their tribes encamped around the *Mishcan*. The order communicated the meaning of these inaugural offerings. They consecrated the *Mishcan* as the center or focus of the encampment. In other words, the *Mishcan* was first consecrated as the "residence of Hashem". However, the integration of the *Mishcan* and encampment as a nation focused upon the presence of Hashem within its midst was not accomplished by the mere erection of the *Mishcan*, its consecration, and its initial sacrifices. The integration of the *Mishcan* within the camp and the focusing of the nation upon the divine presence in its midst required the initiative of the nation. This integration was achieved through the inaugural offering of the princes.

This is [the rule] concerning the Levites: From the age of twenty-five years and upwards, he shall enter the service to work in the Tent of Meeting. From the age of fifty, he shall retire from the work legion, and do no more work. He shall minister with his brethren in the Tent of Meeting to keep the charge, but he shall not perform the service; thus shall you do for the Levites regarding their charge. (BeMidbar 8:24-26)

The Levites are part of the institution of *Mishcan*

Now, we understand why Aharon and the Levites were not included in these inaugural offerings. The Levites were not among the tribes listed in the two right columns of the above

46

table. They were not assigned a position on a side of the *Mishcan*. Because the Levites were not assigned a position among the other tribes, they did not participate in their inaugural sacrifices.

Of course, this raises a question. Why were the Levites not assigned a place among the other tribes of Israel surrounding the *Mishcan*? An indication of the answer to this question is provided by Maimonides in his Mishne Torah. There, he discusses the commandment upon the Levites to serve in the *Bait HaMikdah* and the commandment to consecrate the *kohanim* – the priests. He places his discussion of these two commandments in the section of his work dealing with the vessels of the *Bait HaMikdah*. His treatment of these *mitzvot* indicates that he regards the Levites and the *kohanim* as part of the institution of the *Bait HaMikdah*. They are an essential component of the Temple. This status is also expressed in the above passages.

The unique status of the Levites is reflected in the place of the Levites' camp in the wilderness. They formed an inner circle directly surrounding the *Mishcan*. The other tribes camped at distance from the *Mishcan*, whereas, the Levites camped directly around it. This demonstrated the more intimate relationship of the Levites to the *Mishcan*. They were part of the institution of the *Mishcan*.

Treating synagogue like the *Mishcan*

The centrality of the *Mishcan* to the camp of Bnai Yisrael has a contemporary parallel. Shulchan Aruch explains that the community's synagogue should be built upon the highest ground of the town and its structure should be taller than the surrounding homes and buildings. This requirement is derived from the placement of the *Bait HaMikdah*. It seems that the requirement regarding the *Bait HaMikdah* reflects the same theme of centrality expressed in design of the camp of Bnai Yisrael in the wilderness. Like the *Mishcan* of the wilderness, the synagogue of the community must form its spiritual center and focus. This is ideally expressed in the physical placement of the synagogue at an elevation above the homes and other buildings of the community.

It follows that we are expected to integrate the synagogue into the community as the princes integrated their tribes' encampments with the *Mishcan* in their midst. This integration requires the initiative of the members of the community. The members must make the synagogue part of their lives. The synagogue becomes integrated into the community and becomes its spiritual focus when the members of the community make the synagogue an important part of their lives.

"And Hashem spoke to Moshe saying: "Speak to Aharon, and say to him, "When you light the lamps, the seven lamps shall give light towards the front of the *menorah*."" And Aharon did so. He lit the lamps of it so as to give light towards the front of the *menorah*, as Hashem commanded Moshe. And this was the design of the candlestick: a beaten work of gold; including its base, and including its flowers thereof, it was beaten work; according unto the pattern which Hashem had shown Moshe, so he made the menorah." (BeMidbar 8:1-4)

Parshat Bahalotecha begins with instructions for the lighting of the *menorah*. The *menorah* is the candelabra located in the *Mishcan* – the Tabernacle. The *menorah* is composed of a central candlestick. From the central candlestick extend six branches. Three branches extend from each side. The above translation corresponds with Rashi's understanding of these instructions. Aharon is told that the candles located on the six branches are to shed their light towards the central candlestick.[1]

There are two obvious difficulties with this section. First, the commentaries are troubled by the placement of these instructions at this location in Sefer BeMidbar. Up to this point, the *sefer* has primarily dealt with the organization of the encampment in the wilderness. In the immediately preceding chapters, the *sefer* described the sacrifices offered to initiate the *Mishcan*. Immediately following this section, the Torah will describe the initiation of the Leveyim – the Levites – into their roles in assisting the *Kohanim* – the Priests and transporting the *Mishcan*. What is the connection between the instructions for the lighting of the *menorah* and the preceding of coming material?

Second, after providing instructions for the lighting of the *menorah*, the Torah provides a description of the design of the *menorah*. This description was presented in even more detail in Sefer Shemot. Why does the Torah repeat this description?

Rashi provides a well-known response to the first question. He explains that Aharon was the leader of Shevet Leyve – the tribe of Leyve. The leaders of the other *shevatim* – tribes – had joined together to offer an elaborate set of sacrifices for the dedication of the *Mishcan*. Each prince offered an identical set of sacrifices and each was assigned his own day on which to present his offering. But Aharon – as leader of Shevet Leyve – did not participate in these offerings. Shevet Leyve was not assigned its own day. Aharon did not offer a set of sacrifices on behalf of Shevet Leyve. Aharon was disturbed with his exclusion from the dedication process. As a consolation, Hashem provided Aharon with the instructions for the lighting of the *menorah*. Hashem told Aharon that his *shevet* would have the honor of lighting the *menorah* each day.[2]

Nachmanides asks a number of questions on Rashi's response. We will focus on one of these questions. According to Rashi, Aharon received the instructions for the lighting of the *menorah* as a consolation for not participating in the offerings of the princes. Why was this specific service selected by Hashem to serve as a consolation? He points out that Aharon was entrusted with a variety of responsibilities in the *Mishcan*. He was the only one who was permitted to execute the responsibilities. For example, only Aharon or a future *Kohen Gadol* – the High Priest – can perform the service of Yom HaKippur. Why were these special responsibilities not adequate consolation?[3]

In order to answer Nachmanides' question, we must consider two sets of passages from last week's *parasha*.

"And the princes brought the dedication-offering of the altar on the day that it was anointed. The princes brought their offering before the altar. And Hashem said to Moshe: They shall present their offering, each prince on his day, for the dedication of the altar". (BeMidbar 7:10-11)

"This was the dedication-offering of the altar, on the day when it was anointed, at the hands of the princes of Israel: twelve silver dishes, twelve silver basins, twelve golden pans. Each silver dish weighing a hundred and thirty shekels, and each basin seventy; all the silver of the vessels two thousand and four hundred shekels, after the shekel of the sanctuary." (BeMidbar 7:84-85)

---

[1] Rabbaynu Shlomo ben Yitzchak (Rashi), *Commentary on Sefer BeMidbar* 8:2.

[2] Rabbaynu Shlomo ben Yitzchak (Rashi), *Commentary on Sefer BeMidbar* 8:2.

[3] Rabbaynu Moshe ben Nachman (Ramban), *Commentary on Sefer BeMidbar* 8:2.

The first set of passages introduces the section of the Torah that describes the offerings of the princes. Each prince is assigned his own day on which he will bring his offerings to the *Mishcan*. It seems that the sacrifices and vessels offered by each prince constitute a discrete set of offerings. In other words, over the twelve days that the offerings were brought, twelve separate sets of offerings were presented. However, a careful analysis of these passages communicates a different message. The passages refer to the twelve sets of offerings as "their offering." The implication is obvious. All of the various sacrifices and vessels presented over the twelve days are regarded as a single offering. In other words, the process of bringing this single offering extends over a twelve-day period. All of the various sacrifices and vessels brought over this period merge into a single offering.

This idea is reflected in the second set of passages. After the Torah describes the sacrifices and vessels presented by each prince on his respective day, the Torah provides a summary. In this summary, the Torah totals all of the sacrifices and vessels by types. For example, in the passages above, the Torah tells us that a total of twelve silver basins were brought. Why is this summary needed? This summary emphasizes the relationship between the various components of the offering. The Torah is communicating that all of the individual offerings provided on each day are parts of an entirety. All of the individual sacrifices and vessels are parts of a single offering.

Why is it necessary for the Torah to communicate this information? What difference is there as to whether we view each prince's sacrifices and vessels as an individual offering from that specific *shevet* or as a part of a larger offering?

We can appreciate the importance of this distinction through reviewing the order in which the princes present their offerings. The first prince to provide sacrifices and vessels is the Prince of Shevet Yehudah. He is followed on the next day by the Prince of Yisachar. Once these two princes present their offerings an order is established that guides the remainder of the princes. What is this order?

During their sojourn in the wilderness, Bnai Yisrael's encampment was organized surrounding the *Mishcan*. Each shevet was assigned a specific location. When the nation traveled, this order was preserved. The nation traveled as a procession of *shevatim*. The place of each *shevet* in this procession was based upon and reflected its location relative to the *Mishcan* where the nation was encamped. As a result, the nation camped and traveled as a system of *shevatim*. In other words, the camp of Bnai Yisrael was designed as a system of *shevatim* – with the *shevatim* functioning as component units within the nation of Bnai Yisrael.

The order in which the princes presented their offerings reflected and was based upon this order – the order in which the various *shevatim* camped in and traveled through the wilderness. Shevet Yehudah led the procession of *shevatim* in the wilderness. Accordingly, the first set of offerings was presented by this *shevet*. Shevet Yisachar followed Shevet Yehudah in the procession through the wilderness. As a result, the second set of offerings was presented by Shevet Yisachar. All of the remaining *shevatim* presented their offerings in the order in which they traveled through the wilderness.

The order in which the offerings were presented reflected the relationship between the offerings of the various *shevatim*. In their travels and in the wilderness encampment, the *shevatim* each functioned as a unit within the overall nation. They were components of a greater entirety – the nation. The offerings were presented in this framework. Each *shevet* separately,

49

and on its own day, presented its offerings. But each *shevet* presented its offerings as a component unit within the entirety of the nation of Bnai Yisrael. In other words, the offerings were not presented by the *shevet* as an independent social-political entity. Instead, the offerings were presented by the *shevet* as a component unit within the entirety of the greater unit of the nation.

This answers our earlier question. Why does the Torah emphasize that all of the offerings presented by the individual *shevatim* were parts of an overall offering? The Torah is teaching us that although the offerings were presented by the individual *shevatim*, the offerings merged into a single offering of the nation of Bnai Yisrael.

We can now reconsider Aharon's concern. Rashi is not suggesting that Aharon was disappointed that his *shevet* did not participate in the presentation of offerings. His concern was based upon an understanding of the nature of this offering. In this offering the component *shevatim* of Bnai Yisrael presented an offering on behalf of the entire nation. Shevet Leyve did not participate. This implicitly excluded the *shevet* from functioning as a unit within the nation.

Rashi explains that Aharon received instructions for the lighting of the *menorah* as a consolation for his *shevet's* exclusion from the presentation of offerings. How did these instructions provide consolation?

Rabbaynu Ovadia Sforno's comments regarding these instructions will help us answer this question. Sforno deals with two issues. First, why is it necessary for the branches to spread their light towards the central candlestick? Sforno explains that this requirement is intended to symbolize an important idea. The nation of Bnai Yisrael is made up of a multitude of individuals. The various members of the nation have different talents and abilities. But in order to enjoy the blessings of Hashem, we must join together in a single mission – service to Hashem. All the candles – from the candle on the extreme right to the candle on the extreme left – must all join together in creating one central illumination. (This is not intended as a trite political statement.) So too, the members of the nation cannot allow the disparity of their talents and dispositions to compromise their commitment to the shared mission of serving Hashem.[4]

Second, Sforno explains the significance of the Torah's review of the *menorah's* construction. The passages above describe the *menorah*'s design. It is beaten from a single ingot of gold. The *menorah* is not composed of individual components that are welded together. The *menorah*'s design is intended to reiterate and reinforce the message communicated by the lighting instructions. Like the *menorah*, the nation must function as a single entity. It must be unified in its devotion to Hashem.[5]

Now we can understand how Rashi would respond to Nachmanides' criticism. Why was Aharon consoled by the instructions for the lighting of the *menorah*? The *menorah* does not only represent the unity of Bnai Yisrael. It explains the basis for the unity. We are not unified merely by a shared history or culture. We are unified by a shared mission. We must all join in the mission of creating light – serving Hashem. The service in the *Mishcan* was performed by the *Kohanim* and Shevet Leyve. The efforts of the nation towards the fulfillment of its mission achieved expression through this service. In other words, the most important aspirations of Bnai Yisrael were reflected in the service performed by Shevet Leyve. These services were the

---

[4] Rabbaynu Ovadia Sforno, *Commentary on Sefer BeMidbart*, 8:2.
[5] Rabbaynu Ovadia Sforno, *Commentary on Sefer BeMidbart*, 8:4.

actualization of the mission of the nation. They were the element that unified Bnai Yisrael. Shevet Leyve did not participate in the presentation of offerings. But its service represented the element that unified the various *shevatim* into a single nation.

"Then when they are fifty years old they shall retire from the work force and not serve any more." (BeMidbar 8:25)

The members of *Shevet Leyve* – the *Leveyim* – were assigned to assist the *Kohanim*. They had various responsibilities. These included singing in the *Mishcan* and guarding it from all ritual impurity. Our *pasuk* indicates that the *Leveyim* were required to retire from their responsibilities upon reaching the age of fifty.

What responsibilities could the *Leyve* no longer perform when reaching the age of fifty? In order to answer this question, we must be aware of an important detail in the transport of the *Mishcan*. How was the *Mishcan* transported? Most of the *Mishcan* was transported by wagon. However, the most sacred components were carried directly by the *Leveyim* – specifically, by the member of the family of Kahat. These components included the altars, the *Shulchan*, *Menorah*, and the *Aron*.

Rashi explains that a *Leyve* reaching the age of fifty was only disqualified from direct carrying. He could not participate in the transport of the *Aron* and those components that were carried directly by the *Leveyim*. His age implied declining strength. This rendered him unfit for this physically challenging task. However, he still participated in other tasks performed by the *Leveyim*. He sang in the *Mishcan*, opened and closed the entrances, and assisted in loading the wagons used to transport other portions of the *Mishcan*.[6]

Nachmanides differs with Rashi. He maintains that, upon reaching the age of fifty, the *Leyve* was also disqualified from participating in the songs of the *Mishcan*.[7] Nachmanides, in his commentary on Maimonides' Sefer HaMitzvot, offers an interesting explanation for his position. He explains that, once the *Leyve* reached the age of fifty, he was no longer fit to carry heavy burdens. In order to avoid confusion, he was also disqualified from participating in song. Participation in song would create the impression that the elder *Leyve* was fit for all service – even carrying portions of the *Mishcan*.[8] In other words, age rendered the *Leyve* fundamentally unfit for carrying heavy burdens. His disqualification from participating in the song of the Temple was the result of a secondary consideration. He was restricted from song in order to avoid confusion.

The Torah is composed of 613 – *Taryag* – mitzvot. Should this restriction upon the *Leyve* be included within the 613 *mitzvot*? The answer depends on the criteria for including a command among *Taryag*. *Taryag* is a permanent system. It applies in all generations. Therefore, one of the criteria for inclusion in *Taryag* is that the commandment must not be fixed to a particular historical moment or circumstance. For example, Hashem gave Bnai Yisrael various commandments in preparation for Revelation on Sinai. One of these was that the people could not approach or ascend the mountain. These instructions only applied during the period of

---

6 Rabbaynu Shlomo ben Yitzchak (Rashi), *Commentary on Sefer BeMidbar* 8:25.

7 Rabbaynu Moshe ben Nachman (Ramban), *Commentary on Sefer BeMidbar* 8:25.

8 R' Moshe ben Nachman (Ramban), *Critique on Maimonides' Sefer HaMitzvot,* 3rd Principle.

Revelation. These restrictions cannot be counted as elements of *Taryag*.[9] Therefore, in order to answer our question regarding this restriction on the *Leyve*, we must ask another question. Does this restriction apply in all generations, or was this restriction only relevant during the sojourn in the wilderness?

Halachot Gedolot includes the restriction upon the *Leyve*'s service among the *Taryag* Mitzvot. Apparently, he maintains that this restriction applies in all generations. Maimonides objects. He argues that this restriction only applied during a specific historical period. Therefore, it is not appropriate to include this restriction within *Taryag*.[10]

Nachmanides supports the opinion of Halachot Gedolot. However, before we consider Nachmanides' argument, we must consider two related issues.

First, as we have explained, during the sojourn in the wilderness, the *Mishcan* was transported on a regular basis. Once Bnai Yisrael entered the land of Israel, this changed. At first, the *Mishcan* was placed at a permanent location. Later, the Bait HaMikdash in Yerushalayim replaced the *Mishcan*. In other words, the *Mishcan* was no longer regularly transported in its entirety, or even partially. However, the *Aron* was moved on a few occasions. One of these occasions was the transfer of the *Aron* to Yerushalayim. King David arranged for this operation.

Maimonides acknowledges that there is a *mitzvah* that regulates the transport of the *Aron*. This *mitzvah* is included in *Taryag*. It stipulates that the *Aron* must be carried directly. It cannot be transported by wagon or some other conveyance.[11]

Second, in the wilderness, the *Leveyim* were responsible for the transport of the *Aron*. However, according to Maimonides, this is no longer the case. The *Kohanim* are now responsible for this task. No other member of *Shevet Leyve* can perform this task. Maimonides explains that during the period of the sojourn in the wilderness, there were few *Kohanim*. It was not feasible to charge this small group with this responsibility. Therefore, the task of transporting the *Aron* was assigned to the *Leveyim*. However, when the number of *Kohanim* increased, this task was permanently assigned to the *Kohanim*.[12]

We can now understand Nachmanides' objection to Maimonides' position. Maimonides maintains that the restriction upon the *Leveyim*'s service beyond the age of fifty is not one of the *Taryag* Mitzvot. Nachmanides raises an obvious objection. The restriction upon the *Leyve* who reaches the age of fifty against carrying the *Mishcan* was a commandment during the sojourn in the wilderness. It was, essentially, a parameter. It defined who was fit and who was disqualified from performing this task. This restriction dictated that one over the age of fifty was not permitted to directly carry any component of the *Mishcan* – including the *Aron*. The task of carrying one component of the *Mishcan*, the *Aron*, is a *mitzvah* counted among *Taryag*. It is reasonable that the parameter of who is qualified and who is disqualified from performance of this task should remain in force. True, the restriction should now apply to the *Kohanim* and not the *Leveyim*. Nonetheless, the restriction should continue to be regarded as a *mitzvah* that defines a fundamental parameter regarding the transport of the *Mishcan*.[13] It should also be noted that

---

9   Rabbaynu Moshe ben Maimon (Rambam) *Sefer HaMitzvot*, Third Principle.
10   Rabbaynu Moshe ben Maimon (Rambam / Maimonides) *Sefer HaMitzvot*, Third Principle.
11   Rabbaynu Moshe ben Maimon (Rambam) *Sefer HaMitzvot*, Mitzvat Aseh 34.
12   Rabbaynu Moshe ben Maimon (Rambam) *Sefer HaMitzvot*, Mitzvat Aseh 34.
13   R' Moshe ben Nachman (Ramban), *Critique on Maimonides' Sefer HaMitzvot*, 3rd Principle.

Maimonides does not only refuse to count this parameter as a *mitzvah*. He does not even regard this parameter as in force. It simply no longer applies!

How can we explain this dispute between Maimonides and Nachmanides? It seems that Maimonides and Nachmanides argue over the fundamental nature of the restriction upon the *Leyve*. There are two ways to understand this restriction. One approach is that this restriction is a law governing the transport of the *Aron* or *Mishcan*. The transport of the *Aron* requires physical strength. The job demands a robust person. A person who is over the age of fifty is simply not assumed capable of performing this duty. In other words, this is not a law directly governing the functions of the *Leyve*. It is a law regarding the transport of the *Mishcan*. The second approach is that the *Leveyim* were assigned a number of tasks. One of the most important was the transport of the *Mishcan* or *Aron*. If a person could no longer fulfill this difficult task, he was disqualified from serving as a *Leyve*. In other words, this law governs the qualifications for serving as a *Leyve*.

Nachmanides maintains that this law is merely a restriction in who can carry the *Aron*. Therefore, as long as there is a *mitzvah* to transport the *Aron*, this restriction continues to function. It deserves to be counted among *Taryag*.

Maimonides disagrees. He maintains that the restriction placed upon the *Leyve* in the wilderness was far more than a parameter defining whom could carry the *Mishcan* and *Aron*. The law in the wilderness defined who was included and counted among the *Leveyim*, and who was not completely included. The responsibility for transporting the *Aron* and *Mishcan* was a fundamental aspect of the *Leyve*'s job. A *Leyve* that could no longer perform this task could not be completely counted as a *Leyve*.

We can now respond to Nachmanides' objection to Maimonides' position. The age restriction that applied to the *Leyve* was only reasonable because the task of transporting the *Mishcan* was a fundamental aspect of his job. He could not perform this task. Therefore, he could not be completely counted among his brethren. Maimonides maintains that this responsibility was transferred to the *Kohanim*. Therefore, it is no longer part of the *Leyve*'s job description. It follows that the inability of the *Leyve* to perform this task should no longer disqualify the *Leyve*. This task is no longer his responsibility. His fitness can no longer be evaluated on the basis of his ability to carry heavy burdens.

The responsibility for carrying the *Aron* has been transferred to the *Kohen*. However, this is a very minor aspect of the *Kohen*'s role. It is not reasonable to disqualify a *Kohen* from being counted among his brethren because he cannot perform this task. The task is not fundamental to the role of *Kohen*.

In short, according to Maimonides, a law that disqualifies a *Leyve* of *Kohen* on the basis of advanced age is no longer feasible. It presumes that the person's primary role is impacted by age. This is no longer the case with the *Leyve*. He has been relieved of his responsibility to carry the *Mishcan* or *Aron*. This is also not the case with the *Kohen*. Albeit that he is responsible for transporting the *Aron*, this is a minor aspect of his job.

And Bnai Yisrael should prepare the Pesach offering in its time. (BeMidbar 9:2)

The Pesach Sacrifice Offered the First Year of Bnai Yisrael's Travels in the Wilderness

Bnai Yisrael completed the first year of their travels in the wilderness. Hashem commanded the nation to observe the *Pesach* celebration on the anniversary of the exodus from Egypt. Our Sages explain that during the forty years that Bnai Yisrael traveled in the wilderness they only offered the *Pesach* sacrifice on this occasion. The remaining years the sacrifice was not offered.[14] Why was that commandment to offer the Pesach not observed during the subsequent years of their journey and why was the commandment observed during the first year?

Nachmanides raises an additional question. The commandment to offer the *Pesach* is one of the *mitzvot* of the Torah. These commandments are to be performed in every generation. Why did Hashem command Bnai Yisrael to offer the *Pesach* on the first anniversary of the Exodus? This is one of the *mitzvot* that the people accepted at Sinai. No additional command should be needed!

In response to Nachmanides' above question, he explains that the permanent *mitzvah* of offering the *Pesach* took effect only after Bnai Yisrael entered the Land of Israel. This commandment did not apply during the travels in the wilderness. Therefore, offering of the *Pesach* on this first anniversary required a special commandment.[15] However, Nachmanides' answer raises a new question: Why did the permanent *mitzvah* to offer the *Pesach* not come into effect until the land was entered? Nachmanides does not comment on this issue. However, there is an obvious explanation. The *Pesach* sacrifice commemorates the redemption from Egypt. This redemption was not completed with the departure from Egypt. The process of redemption included the receiving of the Torah and the entry into Israel.[16] At the first anniversary of the Exodus, the Torah had been received at Sinai. However, the people had not yet entered the Land of Israel. The process of redemption was not complete. Therefore, the permanent *mitzvah* of offering the *Pesach* could not take effect. For this reason a special commandment was needed to legislate the offering of the *Pesach*.

We must now return to our original questions. Our questions were: Why was the *Pesach* not offered after the first year of Bani Yisrael's sojourn in wilderness and why was it offered the first year? According to Nachmanides, the first question is easily answered. The nation only became obligated to annually offer the Pesach after entering the land. During the travels in the wilderness they were not subject to this *mitzvah*. However, our second question still requires a response. Why was the first year different from these subsequent years? Why was the nation provided with a special commandment to offer the sacrifice the first year of their journey? In other words, the *Pesach* could only be offered in the wilderness in response to a special commandment. This commandment was issued during the first year in the wilderness. It was not re-issued the remaining forty years. Why did Hashem not re-issue this special command the remaining years of the travels?

In order to answer this question we must consider subsequent events. Originally, Bnai Yisrael was to enter the land of Israel during this second year. The nation was to be in Israel at the third anniversary of the exodus. The permanent *mitzvah* of offering the *Pesach* would then apply. In short, had this original plan been followed the offering of the *Pesach* would have taken place on each anniversary of the Exodus. There would not have been an interruption.

---

[14] Sifrei, Parshat BeHa'alotecha, Chapter 9.

[15] Rabbaynu Moshe ben Nachman (Ramban), *Commentary on Sefer BeMidbar* 9:1.

[16] Sefer Shemot 6:6-8.

Why did Hashem abandon this plan? The nation sent spies to scout the land. They returned with a discouraging report. The spies questioned the ability of Bnai Yisrael to conquer the nations occupying Israel. The people became fearful and refused to proceed. They were punished. The nation was condemned to wander in the wilderness for forty years. Conquest was postponed. The process of redemption was suspended.

Let us return to our question. Why did Hashem not re-issue the command to observe the *Pesach* sacrifice during the forty years of wandering? As we have explained, the *Pesach* offering reflects redemption. During the wandering, redemption was not complete. A special command was required for this period. However, this special command was very similar to the permanent command. In both commands the *Pesach* offering reflected and recognized the redemption. The *Pesach* of the permanent *mitzvah* recognized a redemption that was complete. The special *mitzvah* related to redemption that was an on-going process.

During this period of wandering the process of redemption was suspended. The redemption was not complete. Neither was the process on-going. Therefore, the permanent command and the special command were not appropriate for this period.

"And there were men that were defiled through contact with the dead. They were not able to perform the *Pesach* offering on that day. And they approached Moshe and Ahron." (BeMidbar 9:6)

On the first anniversary of Bnai Yisrael's travels exodus from Egypt the nation celebrated the festival of *Pesach*. This observance included the offering of the *Pesach* sacrifice. This sacrifice cannot be offered on behalf of those that are defiled. A group of individuals had come into contact with a dead body. As a result, they were excluded from the sacrifice.

These individuals regretted that they could not participate in the *Pesach* sacrifice. They explained their concerns to Moshe.

Moshe approached Hashem. The Almighty responded that there is a solution for these people. Hashem revealed the *mitzvah* of *Pesach Sheynee*. This *mitzvah* provides a second opportunity to participate in the *Pesach*. If a person cannot participate in the *Pesach* on the 14th of Nisan, this individual offers the *Pesach* one month latter.

This opportunity is afforded to a variety of individuals. Included are those that are not able to participate in the offering of the *Pesach* on the 14th of Nisan. In the wilderness, this group primarily consisted of individuals that were defiled. After the conquest of the land of Israel, this group also included those that could not reach the Temple by the 14th of Nisan. *Pesach Sheynee* also applies to a person that do not participate in the offering of the 14th of Nisan out of negligence. This person is also obligated to participate in *Pesach Sheynee*.

There is an amazing discussion in Tractate Pesachim regarding the *mitzvah* of *Pesach Sheynee*. The discussion revolves around an interesting question. After the sacrifice, the meat of the *Pesach* is consumed by those bringing the offering. The *Pesach* is not eaten alone. It must be consumed with *matzah* and *marror*. Assume a person is defiled or unable to reach the Temple on the 14th of Nisan. This person's condition prevents participating in the *Pesach* offering on this date. However, nothing prevents this person from eating the *matzah* an *marror* that accompanies the *Pesach*. These can be consumed by a defiled person. They can be eaten outside of area of the Temple. Does this person consume the *matzah* and *marror*, without the *Pesach*?

55

The Talmud responds that the person does eat *matzah* and *marror* on the 14th of Nisan. Inability to participate in the *Pesach* offering does not interfere with the obligation to eat *matzah* and *marror* on the 14th of Nisan. To this point, there is nothing odd in the Talmud's discussion.

Next, the Talmud discusses the source for this law. Where does the Torah tell us that it is required to eat *matzah* and *marror*? The Talmud offers two responses. We will concentrate on one response. The Talmud suggests that the source is the *pasuk* that states, "In the evening you shall eat *matzah*."[17] The Talmud explains that this passage teaches us that the obligation to eat *matzah* and *marror* apply even in a case in which the *Pesach* cannot be consumed.

This brings us to the remarkable portion of the Talmud's discussion. The Talmud explains that the message of this *pasuk* is not at all obvious. One might think that some individuals would not eat *matzah* and *marror* on the 14th of Nisan. One could reason that those obligated in *Pesach Sheynee* do not eat *matzah* and *marror* on the 14th of Nisan. Instead, they fulfill these obligations in conjunction with the *mitzvah* of *Pesach Sheynee*. Therefore, the *pasuk* stating, "In the evening you shall eat *matzah*" is included in the Torah. The passage indicates that everyone eats *matzah* and *marror* on the 14th of Nisan. The passage specifically includes those that will participate in *Pesach Sheynee*.[18]

This discussion presents a major problem. The passage stating, "In the evening you shall eat *matzah*" was revealed to Moshe in Egypt. According to the Talmud, it specifically addresses the person that will celebrate *Pesach Sheynee*. In other words, the passage deals with a possible misunderstanding created by the *mitzvah* of *Pesach Sheynee*. This implies that if the *mitzvah* of *Pesach Sheynee* did not exist, it would be self-evident that everyone eats *matzah* and *marror* on the 14th of Nisan and the passage would not be needed. This does not seem to make sense. In fact, the *mitzvah* of *Pesach Sheynee* did not exist in Egypt. It only was revealed latter, in the wilderness! The Torah is responding to a *mitzvah* that had not yet been revealed!

There is an interesting comment by Rashi that indirectly deals with this issue. Rashi begins with an interesting question. The *mitzvah* of *Pesach Sheynee* was revealed in response to an inquiry. Defiled individuals approached Moshe seeking an opportunity to participate in the *Pesach* sacrifice. Why did the Almighty not reveal the commandment of *Pesach Sheynee* at Sinai? Why did He wait until these individuals approached Moshe? Rashi responds that the *mitzvah* could have been revealed at Sinai. However, the Almighty decided to delay communication of this *mitzvah*. He wished to reward these sincere individuals. He rewarded them through revealing a section of the Torah in response to their inquiry.[19]

It seems, from Rashi's comments, that this section was not an afterthought. It was part of the Torah revealed at Sinai. However, this specific commandment was withheld. This was done in order to communicate the *mitzvah* at the appropriate time. In other words, the Torah is an integrated whole. Each *mitzvah* is recorded as one of the 613 integrated *mitzvot*. Each *mitzvah* is consistent with all of the others.

This answers our question. It is true that the passage stating, "In the evening you shall eat *matzah*" deals with a problem created by *Pesach Sheynee*. It is also true that this passage was revealed before the *mitzvah* of *Pesach Sheynee* was given. However, the passage is designed as

---

17 Sefer Shemot 12:18.
18 Mesechet *Pesach*im 120a with commentary of Rashbam.
19 Rabbaynu Shlomo ben Yitzchak (Rashi), *Commentary on Sefer BeMidbar* 9:7.

part of a complete Torah. The complete Torah includes all 613 *mitzvot*. *Pesach Sheynee* is one of these *mitzvot*. Therefore, it is reasonable for the *mitzvah* of *matzah* and *marror* to be recorded in a manner that is consistent with the command of *Pesach Sheynee*. The passage assumes the existence of *Pesach Sheynee*, even though the *mitzvah* has not yet been revealed.

"Make for yourself two silver trumpets. You should make them of hammered metal. And they will be yours for summoning the assembly and to cause the camps to journey."
(BeMidbar 10:2)

In our pasuk, Hashem commands Moshe to create trumpets. This passage and the following pesukim outline four functions assigned to these trumpets. First, the trumpets would be used to announce that the camp of Bnai Yisrael must begin a new stage of its journey. Second, the trumpets would to be used to assemble the people or the leadership. Third, the trumpets were to be sounded when the Festival sacrifices or the sacrifices for the *Rosh Chodesh* – the new month – would be offered in the *Mishcan*. Fourth, the trumpets were to be sounded at a time of affliction.

Of course, the first function mentioned in these passages no longer applies. We are not traveling through the wilderness. However, the other three functions continued to apply after the people entered the Land of Israel. Maimonides explains that when Bnai Yisrael is confronted with a threat or affliction, we are required to call out to Hashem and to sound these trumpets.[20] Maimonides tells us the trumpets are to be sounded in the *Bait HaMikdash* during the offering of the Festival and *Rosh Chodesh* sacrifices.[21] He also explains that the trumpets are to be sounded to assemble the people to listen to the King read from the Torah on second day of Succot of the year following the Sabbatical Year.[22]

However, there is an interesting problem in Maimonides' treatment of these trumpets. In his Sefer HaMitzvot, Maimonides explains that we are commanded to sound the trumpets when offering the Festival and *Rosh Chodesh* sacrifices. He adds – seemingly as a postscript – that these trumpets are also sounded when we are confronted with a danger or an affliction.[23] It seems clear from this formulation that not all functions of the trumpets are equally central to the *mitzvah*. The primary function of the trumpets is to be sounded when offering the Festival and *Rosh Chodesh* sacrifices. The sounding of the trumpets at a time of affliction is treated as a secondary function. In this description of the *mitzvah*, Maimonides does not mention the sounding of the trumpets to assemble the people.

In his code of law – the Mishne Torah – Maimonides places the *mitzvah* of sounding the trumpets in the opening law in the laws of fasts. He explains that it is a positive commandment to cry out to Hashem and to sound the trumpets whenever an affliction confronts the people. In this treatment of the *mitzvah* Maimonides does not even make mention of the other functions of the trumpets – their sounding when offering the Festival and *Rosh Chodesh* sacrifices and their sounding to assemble the people.[24] In short, in Sefer HaMitzvot, Maimonides seems to assert

---

[20] Rabbaynu Moshe ben Maimon (Rambam) *Mishne Torah*, Hilchot Ta'aniyot 1:1.

[21] Rabbaynu Moshe ben Maimon (Rambam) *Mishne Torah*, Hilchot Kelai Maikdash 3:5.

[22] Rabbaynu Moshe ben Maimon (Rambam) *Mishne Torah*, Hilchot Chagigah 3:4.

[23] Rabbaynu Moshe ben Maimon (Rambam) Sefer HaMitzvot, *Mitzvat Aseh* 59.

[24] Rabbaynu Moshe ben Maimon (Rambam) *Mishne Torah*, Hilchot Ta'aniyot 1:1.

that the primary function of the trumpets is the requirement to sound them with the offering of the Festival and *Rosh Chodesh* sacrifices. But in Mishne Torah, he treats the sounding of the trumpets at a time of affliction as the primary element of the *mitzvah*.

Actually, this is one of numerous instances in which Maimonides treatment of *mitzvah* in Sefer HaMitzvot differs from his treatment of the same *mitzvah* in his Mishne Torah. In order to understand Maimonides' two different treatments of this *mitzvah* it is helpful to consider another example of a similar seeming inconsistency. In his Mishne Torah, Maimonides introduces his laws of repentance by explaining that when a person violates a *mitzvah* one is required to repent and confess the sin. He explains that this confession is a positive commandment.[25] In this characterization of the *mitzvah* of confession – *veyduy* – Maimonides describes it as the essence or as an essential component of the process of repentance. In his Sefer HaMitzvot, Maimonides offers a similar definition of the *mitzvah* of *veyduy*. However, he includes this *mitzvah* among the commandments relating to sacrifices.[26] In other words, in his Mishne Torah Maimonides presents the *mitzvah* of *veyduy* as the fundamental *mitzvah* discussed in the laws of repentance. In his Sefer HaMitzvot, he presents it as one of the many *mitzvot* related to sacrifices.

Maimonides adds an interesting and important comment to his discussion of the *mitzvah* of *veyduy* in his Sefer HaMitzvot. He explains that the Torah discusses the *mitzvah* of *veyduy* in the context of its treatment of sacrifices. This context might mislead a person to assume that the performance of *veyduy* is an element within the offering of sacrifices and that without a sacrifice *veyduy* is not performed. Maimonides explains that this is not the case. The performance of *veyduy* is required whenever a commandment is violated. Even when a sacrifice is not or cannot be brought the performance of *veyduy* is required. Therefore, *veyduy* deserves to be treated as an independent *mitzvah* and not as a mere element within the process of offering a sacrifice.[27]

Maimonides is clearly defending his treatment of *veyduy* as an independent *mitzvah* within the system of *Taryag* – the 613 *mitzvot*. He is arguing that *veyduy* is not an element of the process of offering a sacrifice. But if this is Maimonides position, why does he include this *mitzvah* among the *mitzvot* dealing with sacrifices?

In short, there are two problems with Maimonides' treatment of the *mitzvah* of *veyduy*. First, in his Mishne Torah he describes it as the *mitzvah* that is the basis of the laws of repentance. He does not relate it to sacrifices. In his Sefer HaMitzvot, he places it among the *mitzvot* relating to sacrifices. Second, in his Sefer HaMitzvot, he stresses the *veyduy* is not merely part of the process of offering a sacrifice. It is an independent *mitzvah*. Yet, the places the *mitzvah* among the *mitzvot* related to sacrifices.

It seems from Maimonides' different treatments of this *mitzvah* in these two works that Sefer HaMitzvot and Mishne Torah have very different organizational schemes. In Sefer HaMitzvot, the commandments are organized and formulated in a manner that reflects their treatment in the Torah. Although *veyduy* is an independent *mitzvah*, it is presented in the Torah in conjunction with the Torah's discussion of sacrifices. Sefer HaMitzvot adopts the organizational scheme of the Torah. Therefore, although *veyduy* is an independent *mitzvah*,

---

[25] Rabbaynu Moshe ben Maimon (Rambam) *Mishne Torah*, Hilchot Teshuvah 1:1.
[26] Rabbaynu Moshe ben Maimon (Rambam) Sefer HaMitzvot, *Mitzvat Aseh* 73.
[27] Rabbaynu Moshe ben Maimon (Rambam) Sefer HaMitzvot, *Mitzvat Aseh* 73.

because the Torah presents the *mitzvah* in relation to sacrifices, Maimonides preserves this presentation in his Sefer HaMitzvot.

However, the Torah is not just a system of 613 *mitzvot*. It is also a system of law – of *halacha* – the guides every aspect of our personal and national lives. Mishne Torah is a code of law. It presents the various laws of the Torah as a systematic and comprehensive legal system. In this context, *veyduy* and repentance play a fundamental role. Therefore, Maimonides places *veyduy* in the first book of his Mishne Torah. This placement reflects the fundamental nature of the process of repentance.

A simple analogy will help illustrate the difference between these two organizational schemes. Assume that an author wishes to write a book that graphically describes the human body. The author begins with the toes and describes every body part up to an including the crown of the head. Another author wishes to write a text on anatomy. He begins with a description of the fundamental internal organs. He describes the heart and lungs, the digestive organs. He eventually arrives at the finger and toes. Both authors are describing the body. Is one organizational scheme more correct than the other? Of course not! Both are correct; the authors have different objectives. The first author wishes to present the body as it appears to the observer. His scheme corresponds with this objective. The second author's objective is to describe the body as a system. He begins with the most fundamental elements of the organic system and then continues on to the other elements. Sefer HaMitzvot organizes the *mitzvot* as they appear in the Torah. Mishne Torah is more concerned with exploring and presenting the *mitzvot* as a system of *halacha*. Therefore, Maimonides departs from the observable organizational scheme and presents the *mitzvot* in a manner that expresses their interrelationship within the system of *halacha*.

Let is now return to Maimonides treatment of the *mitzvah* of sounding the trumpets. Our *parasha* begins with a discussion of material primarily related to the *Mishcan*, and sacrifices. In this context, the *mitzvah* of the trumpets is presented. It follows that in Sefer HaMitzvot Maimonides will present the *mitzvah* in this context. Therefore, he characterizes the *mitzvah* as primarily commanding us to sound the trumpets when offering the Festival and *Rosh Chodesh* sacrifices. This description is true to the presentation in the Torah.

However, according to Maimonides, this *mitzvah* is also the fundamental commandment upon which the laws of fasting are constructed. Mishne Torah is designed to present the system of *halacha*. The laws of fasts are fundamental component of this system. They are certainly not merely a postscript to the obligation to sound the trumpets when offering Festival and *Rosh Chodesh* sacrifices. Therefore, Maimonides places the *mitzvah* of sounding the trumpets at a time of affliction at the opening of the section of the laws dealing with fasts and emphasizes the role of the *mitzvah* as the foundation of this section.

And Hashem spoke unto Moshe, saying: Make for you two trumpets of silver; of beaten work shall you make them. And they shall be unto you for the calling of the congregation, and for causing the camps to set forward. (BeMidbar 10:1-2)

Rejoicing on Shabbat

1. **The silver trumpets of the Mishcan**

59

In Parshat Beha'alotecha Moshe is commanded to fabricate two trumpets of silver. The Torah outlines three basic functions served by these trumpets. First, they were to be used during the sojourn in the wilderness to manage the movements of the nations. For example, various series of sounds produced by these trumpets summoned the people to assemble. Other sounds directed the people to break camp and to travel forth to their next encampment. Second, these trumpets were sounded at times of danger and affliction. Maimonides associates the blasts of the trumpets with calling out to Hashem in anguish.[28] This suggests that the sounds of the trumpets were an expression of prayerful petition. Third, the trumpets were sounded in the Mishcan – the Tabernacle – on festive occasions in accompaniment to the offering of the sacrifices.

The sounding of these trumpets on these occasions is one of the commandments of the Torah. After Bnai Yisrael settled the Land of Israel and constructed the Bait HaMikdash – the Sacred Temple, these trumpets continued to be employed. They were no longer used to signal the movements of the nation. However, they continued to be sounded at times of affliction and danger and also on festive occasions. On these festive occasions the sounding of the trumpets accompanied the offering of sacrifices.

Also on the day of your rejoicing, and to your appointed times, and on your new moons, you shall blow with trumpets over your burnt-offerings, and over the sacrifices of your peace-offerings. And they shall be to you for a memorial before your G-d. I am Hashem your G-d. (BeMidbar 10:10)

2. The festive occasions on which the trumpets are sounded

The Torah describes a number of festive occasions upon which the trumpets are sounded in the Mishcan. The identities of some of the occasions noted in the passage are self-evident. The appearance of the new moon determines the initiation of the new month and Rosh Chodesh – the first day of each new month is celebrated with special sacrifices. The passage instructs us to sound the trumpets at the time of the offering of these sacrifices. The term "appointed times" generally refers to the festivals and holidays. On all of these occasions special sacrifices are offered and the passage instructs that the trumpets be sounded in accompaniment to these offerings. However, to what does the passage refer with the term "the day of your rejoicing"?

3. Shabbat as a "day of rejoicing"

The Sifrai offers two possibilities. The first possibility is that the reference is to Shabbat. In other words, according to this opinion Shabbat is a "day of rejoicing". Although this characterization of Shabbat may seem reasonable and even appropriate, it is actually not consistent with normative halachah. In order to understand this inconsistency, some background information is needed.

Maimonides explains that on Shabbat there is a mitzvah of Oneg – enjoyment or delight.[29] In other words, in observance of Shabbat a person is commanded to engage in activities that bring enjoyment or delight. Maimonides explains that this requirement is fulfilled primarily through indulging in fine foods and including within the observance of the day three meals.[30]

---

[28] Rabbaynu Moshe ben Maimon (Rambam) Mishne Torah, Hilchot Ta'aniyot 1:1.
[29] Rabbaynu Moshe ben Maimon (Rambam) Mishne Torah, Hilchot Shabbat 30:1.
[30] Rabbaynu Moshe ben Maimon (Rambam) Mishne Torah, Hilchot Shabbat 30:7.

Maimonides explains that the mitzvah of Oneg also applies to festivals – Yamim Tovim.[31] However, in addition to the mitzvah of Oneg, Yamim Tovim also features a mitzvah of Simchah – happiness.[32]

4. Simchah and Oneg

The mitzvah of Simchah does have some similarities to the mitzvah of Oneg; they do overlap. However, the mitzvah of Simchah on Yom Tov is a far more extensive obligation than the requirement of Oneg. Maimonides asserts that the mitzvah of Simchah is not composed solely of the performance of actions – as is the case of Oneg. Simchah requires the achievement of an actual state of mind. Furthermore, the mitzvah of Oneg is entirely personal. It is expressed as a requirement for a person to engage in activities that are associated with enjoyment and delight. The mitzvah of Simchah requires a person to not only, himself, be happy. He must also endeavor to bring happiness to the other members of the household. For example, buying clothing and jewelry for one's wife in honor of Yom Tov is an expression of the mitzvah of Simchah.[33]

In summary, the mitzvot of Oneg and Simchah have some similarity. However, they are two distinct mitzvot. The mitzvah of Oneg applies to Shabbat and to Yom Tov. The mitzvah of Simchah is exclusive to Yamim Tovim; it does not apply to Shabbat.

5. The mitzvah of Simchah does not apply to Shabbat

Now, the difficulty with the Sifrai can be identified. According to the first opinion in the Sifrai, the term "day of rejoicing" refers to Shabbat. The actual term used in the passage for rejoicing is Simchah. Therefore, according to this opinion in the Sifrai, Shabbat is a day of Simchah. As explained above, this is not actually correct. It is a day on which there is a mitzvah of Oneg. It is not a day that is subject to the mitzvah of Simchah.

6. Every day is a "day of rejoicing"

Before attempting to reconcile this opinion with normative halachah, it will be helpful to consider the other opinion in the Sifrai. According to the second opinion, the term "day of rejoicing" refers to every day. According to this opinion, the Tamid sacrifices – the daily offerings – in the Mishcan are to be accompanied by the trumpet blasts. In other words, the Tamid introduces an element of happiness into every day. What is the nature of this association between the Tamid offerings and Simchah?

It seems that the Tamid offerings are associated with Simchah because the Kohanim – the priests – who perform the offerings are required to be in a state of happiness. The service is only executed in the optimal manner when it is performed with happiness and joy.[34] The Simchah in the performance of the service is an expression of ahavat Hashem – love of Hashem. In other words, the service should be an expression of the Kohens's deep love of Hashem and this love should find expression in his state of happiness.

7. The ideal Shabbat and ideal Yom Tov

---

[31] Rabbaynu Moshe ben Maimon (Rambam) Mishne Torah, Hilchot Yom Tov 6:16.
[32] Rabbaynu Moshe ben Maimon (Rambam) Mishne Torah, Hilchot Yom Tov 6:17.
[33] Rabbaynu Moshe ben Maimon (Rambam) Mishne Torah, Hilchot Yom Tov 6:18.
[34] Rabbaynu Bahya, Commentary on Sefer BeMidbar, Introduction to Parshat Naso.

Maimonides' description of the ideal Shabbat differs significantly from the description of the ideal Yom Tov. The ideal Yom Tov day is divided into two parts. The first half of the day is dominated by prayer and Torah study. The second half of the day is devoted to the Yom Tov meal. Shabbat is described as a day that is entirely devoted to spiritual pursuits with pauses within the day for the Shabbat meals. In other words, Shabbat is a day primarily devoted to the spiritual and to the service of Hashem.

Apparently, both opinions quoted in the Sifrai take a shared approach to interpreting the passage. Both understand the term "day of rejoicing" as referring to a rejoicing that is an expression of service to Hashem and love of Hashem. The second opinion interprets the passage to refer to every day as a "day of rejoicing". Every day features the Tamid offerings and by virtue of the Tamid service an element of joy is introduced into the day. However, the first opinion understands the term "day of rejoicing" to refer specifically to Shabbat. This is because although every day is endowed with an element of joy, Shabbat's very character is that of joy in service to and love of Hashem.

In fact, Simchah does apply to Shabbat. However, it applies in a different manner than it does to Yom Tov. On Yom Tov, the mitzvah of Simchah directs us to perform specific actions in order to foster rejoicing. Shabbat observance does not include a structured mitzvah of Simchah akin to Yom Tov. However, the very objective of Shabbat observance – dedication to the spiritual and service to Hashem – endows the day with a character of joy.[35]

Also in the day of your rejoicing, and in your appointed seasons, and in your new moons, you shall blow with the trumpets over your burnt-offerings, and over the sacrifices of your peace-offerings; and they shall be to you for a memorial before your G-d: I am Hashem your G-d. (BeMidbar 10:10)

Gershwin's Place in the Bait HaMikdash

1. The commandment to create trumpets and their functions

In Parshat BeHa'alotecha, Hashem commands Moshe to fashion two trumpets of beaten silver. The *parasha* explains that these trumpets had a number of functions. They were to be used to signal the nation to assemble. They signaled the camp to commence its journey to its next destination. These trumpets were to be sounded at times of war or affliction. The above passage explains that they were also sounded on festivals, new months and times of rejoicing when the sacrifices for that occasion were offered. In all of these instances the trumpets were sounded to alert the people or to awaken their awareness. Their sounding was a call for action. This action may have been the movement of the camp or its assembly. At a time of war or danger, the trumpets directed the people to call out to Hashem. On the festivals and joyous occasions they summon the people to direct their thoughts to Hashem at the time that their sacrifices were offered.[36]

Trumpets were also used in the *Mishcan* and in the *Bait HaMikdash* on a daily basis. They were among the instruments that accompanied the *leveyim* when they sang songs of praise.

---

[35] See comments of Rav Naftali Tzvi Yehudah Berlin (Netziv), Commentary Emek HaNetziv on Sifrai, Parsaht BeHa'alotecha 19.

[36] Rabbaynu Avraham ibn Ezra, *Commentary on Sefer BeMidbar*, 10:8-10.

When the communal sacrifices were offered, the *leveyim* – the levites – would sing songs of praise to Hashem and their singing was accompanied by instruments. These included trumpets. What does the use of music – vocal and instrumental – in the service of the *Mishcan* and *Bait HaMikdash* indicate about the Torah's attitude toward music and as a source of religious inspiration?

After that you shall come to the hill of G-d, where is the garrison of the Philistines; and it shall come to pass, when you come there to the city, that you shall meet a band of prophets coming down from the high place with a psaltery, and a timbrel, and a pipe, and a harp, before them; and they will be seeking prophesy. (Sefer Shemuel I 10:5)

2. Music and prophecy

Before addressing this issue, it is appropriate to note another context in which music plays an important role. Maimonides explains that prophecy is received only by those who are transcendent in their wisdom, character, and behavior. However, even one who is exceptional in all of these ways is not yet prepared for prophecy. A proper state of mind is also essential to the prophetic experience.

This principle is illustrated by the life of Yaakov. During all of the years that Yaakov believed that his beloved son Yosef was dead, he did not experience prophecy. Maimonides explains that this is because Yaakov was unable to escape his deep sorrow over the loss of Yosef. Only when he learned that Yosef was alive was his sorrow shed and replaced by happiness and contentment. Maimonides explains Yaakov's experience reflects an important principle regarding prophecy. Prophecy requires a specific state of mind. It can be experienced only by a person who is content and happy. One who is burdened with sorrow and torment cannot achieve prophecy.[37]

Maimonides explains that those transcendent individuals who aspired to achieve prophecy, would utilize the influence of music in order to secure their objective. What was the function of the music? It helped them achieve the requisite state of mind. Music helped them achieve the state of contentment and joy that is requisite to achieving prophecy.

Maimonides cites the above passage as an illustration of this principle. Shemuel tells Shaul that during his upcoming journey he will encounter a group of students who are seeking a prophetic experience. The *pasuk* describes the various musical instruments that they will have in their company. Why does the passage mention that these aspirants for prophecy will travel with musical instruments? Maimonides responds that those seeking prophecy used musical instruments as an aid in achieving prophecy.[38]

The message that emerges from this discussion is that the Torah recognizes the capacity of music to impact one's mood and state of mind. It can help us achieve joy and a sense of well-being. Presumably, melodies can evoke other states as well. In the context of the prophetic experience, music is not used as a source of religious inspiration. It is used to create a mood or state of mind.

3. The function of music in Temple service

---

[37] R' Moshe ben Maimon (Rambam) *Commentary on the Mishne*, Mesechet Avot, Intro chp 7.
[38] Rabbaynu Moshe ben Maimon (Rambam) *Mishne Torah*, Hilchot Yesodai HaTorah 7:4.

As noted above, music was a part of the daily service in the *Bait HaMikdash*. The *leveyim* sang songs of praise as the communal sacrifices were offered. They were accompanied by musical instruments. It is notable that the instruments were used during the service only in the accompaniment of the *leveyim*. The *leveyim* sang their songs of praise and they were accompanied by the instruments.[39] This indicates that the instruments were included to supplement and enhance the singing of the *leveyim*.[40] It added an instrumental element to their vocal presentation of their songs of praise. In other words, the essential element of the music in the service was the content of the song of praise. Instruments and melody were used to more effectively communicate the message of the songs.

The use of music in the service in the *Bait HaMikdash* contrasts with its use by the aspiring prophet. The prophet did not use music for religious inspiration. He used it to evoke the mood consistent with the prophetic experience. The music in the Temple service was intended to accomplish much more than create a mood. It was intended to reinforce and better transmit the message vocally communicated by the songs of the *leveyim*. The central element of the music was the ideas expressed in the songs; the music served to communicate these ideas.[41]

It emerges from this discussion of the service in the *Bait HaMikdash*, that music alone was not used as a source of religious inspiration. Inspiration was to be derived from the message of the songs of the *leveyim*. Music was used to facilitate the message of the songs.

4. Synagogue melodies

This observation has a number of practical applications. We do not use musical instruments in our synagogue services but we do use tunes to enhance our prayers. If we assume that the service in the *Bait HaMikdash* is a model for how we should use these melodies, then the tunes selected must be consistent with and reinforce the message of the prayers. The *chazzan* – the cantor – should not select his tunes based solely upon their beauty. He must understand the prayers and select melodies and create compositions that reflect and reinforce the content of the prayers.

Let us consider a simple example. The *Kedushah* of the *Musaf* service on Shabbat is a responsive prayer that is commonly recited to some melody. The *chazzan* and the congregation sing their respective lines using the melody initiated by the *chazzan*. What is the theme of the *Kedushah*? What is its mood? When we recite the *Kedushah* we are emulating the angels who declare the sanctity of Hashem. Earlier in the service – in the blessings preceding

---

[39] For a description of the musical element of the service see Rabbaynu Menachem Me'eri, *Bait HaBechirah*, Mesechet Succah, chapter 5, comments on first mishne.

[40] Rabbaynu Shlomo ben Yitzchak (Rashi), *Commentary on the Talmud,* Mesechet Succah 50b.

[41] As a young teenager, I had the opportunity to participate in the choir of Cantor Phillip Brummer. His only expectation of me was that I not sing and just stand quietly among those who did the singing. Often, I understood the words only vaguely. But his melodies communicated to me, with remarkable accuracy, the theme and mood of each of the prayers. The experience also provided me with the unique opportunity to observe Cantor Brummer as he sang and chanted the liturgy surrounded by his choir. His expression changed from joy to awe, and to that of a humble petitioner as he progressed though the liturgy. As a young person, it was a very special intimate encounter with a soulful prayer experience. It inspired within me a love for music and an appreciation of the power of prayer.

the *Shema* – we describe their mood at the moment that the angels declare His sanctity. They utter their declaration in awe. When we recite the *Kedushah* we, who are not as close to Hashem as His angels, should feel a deep sense of awe and humility. If the melody selected by the *chazzan* is to reinforce the mood and message of the *Kedushah* it cannot be chosen based solely upon its beauty. It should inspire the reverence and humility that is the very essence of the prayer.

Another issue that emerges from this analysis is that our melodies should be scrupulously faithful to the proper pronunciation of the words and the punctuation of the phrases. The melody must be selected and applied with care. Each word must be pronounced with its proper accent. Accent cannot be sacrificed in order to preserve the rhythm of the melody. Each sentence and phrase must be properly punctuated. The punctuation should not be altered to accommodate the melody.

In summary, it is appropriate to enhance our prayers with melodies. Our melodies should reinforce and communicate the message of our prayers. Because this is their purpose, each melody should be consistent with the theme and mood of the prayer it accompanies and it should preserve the proper pronunciation and punctuation of the material.

And it came to pass, when the ark set forward, that Moshe said: Rise up, Hashem, and let Your enemies be scattered; and let them that hate You flee before You. (BeMidbar 10:35)

The Tabernacle: History's Most Bizarre Capital Campaign

1. The initial plan: To quickly occupy the promised land

Parshat BeHa'alotecha opens with a description of the final preparations for Bnai Yisrael's departure from the Sinai wilderness. The *Mishcan* – the Tabernacle – was completed and it was initiated through the sacrifices of the princes of the *shevatim* – the tribes. The trumpets were fashioned that would be used to direct and coordinate the movement of the camp. The cloud of Hashem had taken its position over the *Mishcan*. All was ready for Bnai Yisrael's triumphant march into the promised Land of Cana'an.

The nation departed Sinai. In a single day the camp traveled an enormous distance. Our Sages explain that a typically three-day journey was completed in a single day.[42] The journey to the Land of Cana'an was to be completed in a matter of days.[43] As the passage above explains, the nations of the land would flee from before Hashem's nation and those who dare to resist will be quickly defeated. Of course, all of this would change in response to the sins of the people. But when Bnai Yisrael departed Sinai, they expected to take possession of their promised legacy in short-order.

And on the day that the Tabernacle was assembled the cloud covered the Tabernacle, even the Tent of the Testimony; and at evening there was upon the Tabernacle as it were the appearance of fire, until morning. So it was always: the cloud covered it, and the appearance of fire by night. (BeMidbar 9:15-16)

2. The *Mishcan* was intended to be a very short-lived structure

---

[42] Rabbaynu Shlomo ben Yitzchak (Rashi), *Commentary on Sefer BeMidbar* 10:33.
[43] Rabbaynu Shlomo ben Yitzchak (Rashi), *Commentary on Sefer BeMidbar* 10:29.

Yet, there is one element of the Torah's narrative that seems completely inconsistent with the image of the nation poised to enter and possess the Land of Can'an. The journey could not begin until the *Mishcan* was constructed and fabricated. The Torah describes the *Mishcan* as an ornate structure, designed with enormous detail, composed of the finest fabrics and the most precious metals. When Bnai Yisrael were commanded to create the *Mishcan* they expected to soon take possession of the Land of Cana'an. With the conquest of the land, this wondrous structure would be replaced by the *Bait HaMikdash* – the Sacred Temple. Why was such an elaborate and magnificent structure necessary for a *Mishcan* that would only be in service for a short period of time?

A simple response lies in understanding the significance of the *Mishcan*. The *Mishcan* was the central element of the encampment of Bnai Yisrael. All of the tribes camped around the *Mishcan*. Also, when the nation traveled through the wilderness, the *Mishcan* remained the central component of the camp. The *Mishcan* represented the presence of Hashem's providence. It endowed the encampment with a sanctity that encompassed the entire camp. Therefore, even through the *Mishcan* was conceived as a structure whose function would be of short duration, its significance was enormous. The detailed and beautiful design of the *Mishcan* reflected its significance. However, there is another fundamental reason for the *Mishcan*'s elaborate and beautiful design.

And the people were as murmurers, speaking evil in the ears of Hashem. And when Hashem heard it, His anger was kindled. And the fire of Hashem burnt among them, and devoured in the extreme part of the camp. And the people cried unto Moshe; and Moshe prayed unto Hashem, and the fire abated. (BeMidbar 11:1-2)

3. Appreciating blessings

As noted above, the first portion of the *parasha* describes the completion of the final preparations for the journey to the Land of Can'an. This portion of the *parasha* ends with the initiation of that journey. The later portion of the *parasha* describes a tragic series of incidents that occurred soon thereafter. The people began to complain. They could not endure the austerity of the wilderness. Their complaints focused on their diet. They had only the *mun* – the manna. There was no excitement or variety in their diet. Ultimately, the nation's laments provoked severe punishment. Why was their sin so grievous as to provoke a plague that took to lives of the protesters?

Many of the commentaries explain that the nation's sin was its complete lack of appreciation for the miracles experienced every day in the wilderness. The *mun* did not provide the people with the exciting fare for which they longed. Nonetheless, the manna was a wonderful blessing that fully satisfied their needs. There was another shortcoming implicit in the people's complaints.

And I spoke unto you at that time, saying: I am not able to bear you alone. Hashem your G-d has multiplied you, and, behold, you are this day as the stars of heaven in multitude. May Hashem, the G-d of your fathers, make you a thousand times so many more as you are, and bless you, as He has promised you! How can I alone bear your cumbrance, and your burden, and your strife? Get you, from each one of your tribes, wise men, and understanding, and full of knowledge, and I will make them heads over you. (Devarim 1:9-13)

4. Distinguishing between the important and trivial

Earlier in the Torah, Moshe's appointment of judges is recorded. These judges shared with Moshe the burden of administering justice and maintaining peace among the people. In his final address to the Bnai Yisrael, Moshe reminds the people of the sins that their parents committed in the wilderness. In the context of this address, Moshe reminds the people that in order to administer justice and preserve order, it was necessary to create and implement a system of judges.[44] Why does Moshe include this observation in his rebuke?

Rabbaynu Ovadia Sforno suggests that the establishment of a system of judges provides a penetrating insight into the emotional state of the people. The nation was traveling to the Land of Cana'an. Moshe had told the people that they would soon arrive in the land, conquer it, and take possession of their legacy. He described the fertility and super-abundance of the land. In short, Moshe told the people that they would very soon enjoy lives of prosperity and comfort. With their material needs met, they would be free to pursue spiritual goals and draw close to Hashem.

What response would have been appropriate and what was the actual response of the people to this wonderful news? We would expect the people to be overtaken by excitement and anticipation. They should have been eager to embark upon the march to the promised land and completely focused upon the remarkable era that would soon begin. How did the people respond? They bickered with one another; they quarreled. So many disputes arose among the people that Moshe could not even begin the march before installing a system of judges to maintain the peace. In other words, the expected excitement and anticipation did not fully emerge. Instead, the trivial strife and conflict that is so typical of human society persisted. This was Moshe's rebuke![45]

Sforno's comments are also relevant to the expressions of dissatisfaction and frustration expressed in our *parasha*. In themselves, these complaints were not astounding. They were a very human response to the people's encounter with the austerity of life in the wilderness. However, these complaints become remarkable when viewed in context. These complaints surfaced early in the short journey to the promised land. All of these perceived deprivations would soon be eliminated with the nation's arrival into the Land of Cana'an. Could the people not endure a short ordeal of hardship on the path to their wondrous destiny? The magnitude of their sin lay in their inability to rise above their mundane desires and grasp the enormity of the material and spiritual blessings that they would soon receive. They should have accepted their perceived hardships as a minor price to be paid in exchange for a wondrous and rapidly approaching future. Rather than graciously accepting their perceived hardships, they denounced their austere condition and lamented their suffering.

And they spoke unto Moshe, saying: The people bring much more than enough for the service of the work, which Hashem commanded to make. (Shemot 36:5)

5. Assessing one's true material needs

---

[44] It is not clear from the passages whether Moshe referred to the appointment of judges at Sinai or the appointment of elders described in our *parasha*.

[45] Rabbaynu Ovadia Sforno, *Commentary on Sefer Devarim*, 1:11.

This analysis sheds light upon the design and construction of the *Mishcan*. All of the precious materials from which it was constructed were presented by the people. They eagerly contributed their gold, silver, copper, and their finest yarns and threads. They gave without reservation. As explained in the above passage, their contributions were only halted when they exceeded the requirements for the fabrication of the *Mishcan*.

Their generosity reflected confidence and security. They did not fear for their future. Normal human anxiety over the uncertainty of the future drives us to save and accumulate resources and wealth. We hope to thereby insulate ourselves from some of the misfortunes that may befall us. The contributors to the *Mishcan* did not have this anxiety. They were confident of the future that awaited them. They felt no need to accumulate and preserve their wealth as a resource to sustain them in future hard times. They were confident there would not be hard times in their future.

Now, the elaborate design and magnificence of the *Mishcan* is more meaningful. Although, this *Mishcan* was intended as a very temporary structure, it was constructed of the finest materials. This was not only because of its important function as the central structure to the encampment and the source of the camp's sanctity. The creation of the *Mishcan* from the finest and most valuable materials was an expression of the people's complete confidence in their future. They gave generously and without concern or anxiety over the future. This attitude reflected a remarkable degree of cognitive clarity. Our *parasha* describes the disintegration of that remarkable clarity of perception and its replacement with a more pedestrian view of the world. Accompanying that more common outlook was the reemergence of mundane desires and the corresponding sense of deprivation.

6. The personal dynamic in practicing *tzedakah*

The Torah account of the *Mishcan* captures the fundamental dynamic of charitable giving – *tzedakah*. The individual's practice of *tzedakah* is determined by two factors. First, the individual must determine that the cause to which he is being asked to contribute is worthy. Second, this individual must be capable of assessing his own needs and determining his capacity to practice *tzedakah*. The campaign to build the *Mishcan* reflected the people's successful assessment of both of these factors. They understood that although the *Mishcan* was to function for only a short period, its significance was enormous. Second, they were able to objectively assess their capacity to participate. They concluded that they had no need for the wealth that they had accumulated and they gave of it freely and generously.

This dynamic applies to us every time we are asked to participate in *tzedakah*. First, we must assess the virtue of the cause we are asked to support. Second, we must objectively assess our capacity to participate. If we cannot be objective regarding our capacity, then we will not participate. If we live in fear of impending disaster or delude ourselves into believing that accumulating wealth provides true security, then no matter how much wealth we accumulate, we perceive ourselves as desperately poor.

When we choose to practice *tzedakah*, we support and sustain individuals who need us and causes that are fundamental to our nation. We also liberate ourselves from our fears and anxieties. While aiding others we perform a *chesed* – a kindness – to ourselves.

"And Miryam and Aharon spoke about Moshe regarding the beautiful woman he had married – for he had married a beautiful woman." (BeMidbar 12:1)

The Prohibition against Lashon Ha'ra and a Strategy for Addressing the Behavior

One of the most popular Torah topics is lashon hara – speaking negatively about another person. It seems that it is universally recognized that this behavior is prohibited by the Torah in the strongest terms. Yet, recognition of the fact that the behavior is unequivocally prohibited seems to have little impact on the prevalence of the behavior. This suggests that we may need some guidance in dealing with the urge to speak and participate in lashon hara. In this week's Thoughts we will discuss the nature of the prohibition against lashon hara and hopefully this discussion will provide a useful insight in dealing with this behavior.

The above pasuk tells us that Miryam and Aharon spoke about their brother Moshe. The Torah does not provide many details regarding the specific conversation that took place between Moshe and Aharon. But our Sages provide some details. They explain that Miryam initiated the conversation. Aharon participated by listening. Miryam told Aharon that she understood from Moshe's wife – Tziporah – that Moshe was not longer intimate with her.[46] Miryam and Aharon found this astounding. They too were prophets. Yet, they had not abandoned intimacy with their spouses.[47] By engaging in this conversation, Miryam and Aharon violated the prohibition of lashon hara – speaking in a derogatory manner about another person.

The Torah explains that as a result of this sin, Miryam was stricken with tzara'at. Tzara'at is a skin disease described in Sefer VaYikra. From the account in Sefer VaYikra it is apparent that tzara'at is a punishment. However, it is not clear from that account what sin precipitates this punishment. Based on this incident in our parasha, it is clear that lashon hara is one of the sins that result in tzara'at.

The connection between tzara'at and lashon hara is also indicated by another set of passages. In Sefer Devarim (Devarim 24:8-9) the Torah tells us to carefully follow the directions of the Kohen in the diagnosis and treatment of tzara'at. Then the Torah admonishes us to remember the incident of Miryam.[48] According to our Sages, the message is that to avoid tzara'at we must refrain from the behavior of Miryam. In other words, one must avoid lashon hara.[49]

All behaviors that are prohibited or required by the Torah are included in one of the 613 mitzvot. What mitzvah prohibits speaking lashon hara? In order to answer this question, we must first define our terms.

Maimonides in his code of Halacha – the Mishne Torah – in Hilchot Dey'ot explains that lashon hara is one type of prohibited speech. It is not the only form or speech about others that is prohibited. There are three types of speech that are prohibited. The first is rechilut. This is gossip. It need not be negative. It is merely the act of discussing someone's affairs with a third party. Lashon hara is a special case of rechilut. It is negative gossip – speaking in a disparaging manner about someone. However, there is one interesting qualification that must be met. Lashon hara involves imparting disparaging information that is true. Lashon hara does not include

---

[46] Rabbaynu Shlomo ben Yitzchak (Rashi), *Commentary on Sefer BeMidbar* 12:1.

[47] Rabbaynu Shlomo ben Yitzchak (Rashi), *Commentary on Sefer BeMidbar* 12:2.

[48] Sefer Devarim 24:8-9.

[49] Rabbaynu Shlomo ben Yitzchak (Rashi), *Commentary on Sefer Devarim* 24:9.

making up outright lies. Spreading disparaging, false rumors is motzi shem ra. In short, gossip is rechilut; lashon hara is speaking about someone in a disparaging manner – albeit that the statement is true. Spreading false, disparaging rumors is motzi shem ra.[50]

We can now identify the mitzvah violated by lashon hara. According to Maimonides no mitzvah specifically prohibits lashon hara. Instead, the Torah prohibits rechilut and this includes the special case of lashon hara.

Nachmanides disagrees with Maimonides. He insists that there is a specific mitzvah prohibiting lashon hara. It is derived from our parasha and the Torah's latter admonition – in Sefer Devarim – to guard ourselves from tzara'at and to remember this experience of Miryam.

Nachmanides argues that our Sages regarded lashon hara as a serious sin. They went so far as to compare lashon hara to the spilling of blood.[51] It is incomprehensible that there is no specific command prohibiting the behavior! He adds that the Torah prescribes a very serious punishment to lashon hara – tzara'at. We would expect that this serious consequence would be in response to the violation of a specific commandment. Based on these considerations, Nachmanides argues that lashon hara is prohibited by a specific commandment. It is either a negative commandment communicated in the admonition to avoid tzara'at or a positive command contained in the admonition to remember the experience of Miryam.[52]

In summary, Maimonides and Nachmanides agree that lashon hara is prohibited. However, according to Maimonides, it is included in the general mitzvah prohibiting gossip. Nachmanides insists that there is a separate mitzvah that specifically prohibits lashon hara.

Let us take a moment to understand the basis of this argument. Each position seems to have its merit. It seems that Nachmanides' argument is rather compelling. Lashon hara is a serious sin. Does it not make sense that it deserves its own mitzvah? How might Maimonides respond to this issue? However Maimonides' position is also reasonable. Maimonides maintains that lashon hara is a form of gossip and is included in the general prohibition against gossip. What is so objectionable to including the prohibition against lashon hara in the more general mitzvah prohibiting rechilut?

It is clear that the Nachmanides' basic premise is that lashon hara must be assessed in view of the damage and hurt that it causes. Our Sages compare the lashon hara to the spilling of blood. Clearly, they are evaluating lashon hara from the perspective of the damage it causes. From this perspective it does not make sense to compare lashon hara to innocent gossip. Gossip is inappropriate. But from the perspective of damage it is a very different activity than lashon hara. Unlike gossip, lashon hara is an explicit attack against a person's reputation. It is not appropriate to include the damaging behavior of lashon hara in the general mitzvah prohibiting senseless gossip. Therefore, Nachmanides argues that lashon hara deserves its own mitzvah and should not be included in the general prohibition against rechilut.

So, why does Maimonides include lashon hara within the mitzvah prohibiting rechilut? It is important to note that Maimonides includes the laws of rechilut in the Hilchot Dayot section of the Mishne Torah. What is the subject matter of Hilchot Dayot? In this section of the Mishne

---

[50] Rabbaynu Moshe ben Maimon (Rambam) *Mishne Torah*, Hilchot Dey'ot 7:1-2.
[51] Mesechet Erechim 15b.
[52] Rabbaynu Moshe ben Nachman (Ramban), *Commentary on Sefer Devarim* 24:9.

Torah, Maimonides outlines the perimeters of general emotional and physical health. The inclusion of the mitzvah prohibiting rechilut in this section implies that engaging in gossip represents a personally destructive behavior. The person that engages in gossip is undermining his or her own emotional well being. From this perspective it is appropriate to include lashon hara within the mitzvah prohibiting all forms of gossip. All of these forms of gossip cause harm to one's own emotional well being.

We can now understand the dispute between Nachmanides and Maimonides. According to Nachmanides, the essential aspect of lashon hara is the harm caused to others. Therefore, lashon hara cannot be included in the general mitzvah prohibiting gossip. Maimonides maintains that essential component of lashon hara is the harm caused to oneself. From this perspective it is appropriate to include lashon hara in the general mitzvah prohibiting rechilut.

However, it must be noted that Maimonides does acknowledge that lashon hara is a special case of rechilut. This acknowledgement implies that the harm caused by lashon hara to one's personal well being is somewhat different from the harm associated with general rechilut. However, it is not clear from Maimonides' comments exactly wherein the difference lies.

If we pursue this issue we may discover that Maimonides' position provides an essential insight into the behavior of lashon hara. We notice that despite the widespread desire to curtail our engagement in lashon hara, this determination does not easily translate into an actual change in behavior. Why is this behavior so difficult to modify and correct? Part of the answer may lie in the traditional method used to address the problem. We notice that the most common method for addressing the problem of lashon hara is to read more about the gravity of the sin. Books about lashon hara are Judaic best sellers. But it seems that in the long-run learning more about the specific laws of lashon hara and the gravity of the sin has limited impact on the behavior.

In fact this outcome is not surprising. If a person wants to change ones eating habits does one seriously think that reading diet books will foster this change? One who wishes to be less of a couch potato will probably not meet this challenge simply by reading about exercise. This reading may provide temporary inspiration. But in the long run this approach does not usually lead to permanent results.

Instead one must identify and address the root source of the behavior. In the case of eating one must discover why one overeats. What is the attraction? What function is food serving in the person's life?

It makes sense that the same is required to effectively approach to problem of lashon hara. What causes us to engage in this behavior? Our Sages provide an amazing insight into this issue. They tell us the when we depreciate others we are really reflecting upon our own inadequacies.[53] In other words, we speak about others in order to deflect our attention – or the attention of others – from our own insecurities, failing and faults.

Let us consider this assertion more closely. We can all acknowledge that one of the greatest challenges we face in achieving personal growth is the need to critically evaluate our own attitudes and behaviors. The more deep-set and behavior or attitude, the more difficult it is to recognize and acknowledge. But this does not mean that we are not in some sense aware or our personal faults. We are frustrated with these imperfections and yet, we are unwilling to

---

[53] Mesechet Kedushin 70b.

completely acknowledge them and confront them. How do we deal with this frustration? Our Sages are suggesting that we self-medicate. We escape our frustration by transferring our attention to the shortcoming of others. Rather than focus on ourselves, we change the focus of our attention to the other person. We evaluate that person and dissect the person's behaviors and attitudes with the precision that we should direct towards the more painful and difficult task of introspection.

This is the reason the Maimonides regards rechilut as a behavior that undermines our own personal health. We are diverting our attention from ourselves and attaching it to another person. Lashon hara is an extreme manifestation of this mechanism. Gossip is a simple diversion. In speaking lashon hara we are actually aware – at some level – of a personal deficiency. But rather than acknowledging our personal shortcoming, we focus our attention on this failing as manifested in someone else. In this manner, we actually engage in denial of our own faults.

This insight of our Sages suggests an approach to dealing with the urge to speak and participate in lashon hara and rechilut. The urge is apparently, motivated by the presence of an awareness of some personal failing. But this awareness is evokes an unhealthy response. We transfer our focus from ourselves to the other person. If this is correct, then each time we feel the urge to participate in lashon hara or rechilut, we need to respond with a question. What is bothering me about myself? What and I trying to avoid considering? Rather than allowing our attention to be diverted, we need to sharpen our focus on ourselves and allow for a moment of introspection.

This is not an easy solution to apply. But it seems to respond to the fundamental motivations behind lashon hara and rechilut. Perhaps, if we keep our Sages insight in mind, we will be better able to overcome the urge to participate in lashon hara and rechilut.

"And when the ark went forth Moshe said, "Arise, Hashem and disperse Your enemies. And those that hate You will flee from before You". And when it came to rest he said, "Return, Hashem to the myriads of the thousand of Israel". (BeMidbar 12:35-36)

In a Torah scroll these two *pesukim* are set apart from the preceding and following passages. An inverted Hebrew letter is appears before the passages. The same inverted letter follows the passages. The letter used is the *nun*.

Why are these passages set apart? The Talmud, in Tractate Shabbat, explains that these passages are regarded as a separate book of the Torah. They are set apart to indicate this special status.[54]

This only raises an additional question. Why are these passages given the status of a separate book of the Torah? There are various responses to this issue. One obvious approach is to attribute some special significance to the content of the passages. However, Rav Naftali Tzvi Yehudah Berlin *Ztl* (Netziv) offers another approach.

Netziv bases his explanation upon a discussion in Tractate Shabbat. The Talmud comments that the Torah is not actually composed of five books. It is composed of seven. Beresheit, Shemot VaYikra and Devarim are each counted as a single book. However, BeMidbar must be counted as three books. This is because our *pesukim* compose a separate book. This

---

[54] Mesechet Shabbat 116a.

book divides BeMidbar into two additional books. The section preceding our passages is one book. Our *pesukim* constitute a second book. The section following our passages is a third book.[55]

Netziv explains that our passages are not set apart because of their unique content. They are set apart in order to divide Sefer BeMidbar into two separate parts. This break is designed to contrast the first portion of the *sefer* with the material that will follow. What is this contrast?

The first part of the *sefer* depicts the close relationship between the Almighty and His nation. The *sefer* begins with a detailed description of the encampment in the wilderness. The various tribes camped around the Tabernacle. The influence of Hashem was manifest in the *Mishcan*. The Almighty was among the people. The inauguration of the *Mishcan* is described.

The *mitzvah* of *sotah* that is related in the pervious *parasha* captures this relationship. This test of a suspected adulterous relies on the intervention of the Almighty. The woman is given a mixture to drink. This drought is harmless. However, if the woman is guilty of adultery, Hashem will perform a miracle. The mixture will kill the woman. This entire concept assumes a remarkably close relationship between G-d and Bnai Yisrael.

The later section of the *sefer* depicts a different relationship. The nation begins to complain against the Almighty. They send spies to study the land of Israel. The nations refuses to enter the land. Korach and his followers rebel. As the nation removes itself from the

Almighty, He responds. He distances Himself from His people. He condemns the generation that left Egypt to death in the wilderness. The ultimate exile of the nation from the land of Israel is decreed. Various other punishments are depicted, throughout the later half of the *sefer*.

We can now define the contrast contained in Sefer BeMidbar. The nation entered the wilderness with a unique closeness to the Almighty. The *sefer* contrasts this intimacy with the more distant relationship that developed in the course of the sojourn in the wilderness. Our *pesukim* are the dividing point between these two relationships.

We can now understand the reason Sefer BeMidbar is characterized as a single book and as three separate books. It can be described as three books because our *pesukim* divide the first portion of the *sefer* from the later portion. These two portions tell of very different relationships between the Almighty and His nation. Each relationship can be appropriately described as a separate stage of the development of Bnai Yisrael. On this basis the sections can be regarded as separate books divided by a third intervening book.

BeMidbar can also be described as a single book. It is designed to express contrast. The contrast is created through including the two relationships in a single book. From this perspective, BeMidbar deserves to be regarded as a single book. [56]

---

[55] Mesechet Shabbat 116a.

[56] Rav Naftali Tzvi Yehuda Berlin (Netziv), *Commentary Hamek Davar on Sefer BeMidbar,* Introduction.

Shelach

"Send for you men. And they will scout the land of Canaan that I am giving to Bnai Yisrael. You should send one man from each tribe. Each of them should be a prince." (BeMidbar 13:2)

Hashem commands Moshe to send scouts into the land of Israel. This group will travel through the land and return with a report.

These scouts return and deliver their report. They assert that Bnai Yisrael will not be able to conquer the inhabitants of Canaan. This report causes panic within the nation. Bnai Yisrael refuse to proceed.

Hashem punishes Bnai Yisrael. He decrees that the people will wander in the wilderness for forty years. The current generation will not conquer the land. Their children will posses the land of Israel.

In Sefer Devarim, Moshe reviews this incident. He adds some crucial information. The suggestion of sending this advance party originated from Bnai Yisrael. The people approached Moshe. Moshe received permission from Hashem to authorize the mission.[1]

Nachmanides raises an interesting question. What was the mission of these scouts? In Sefer Devarim, the people address this issue. They explain that the scouts will determine the best approach to the land. They will evaluate which cities should be first attacked first.[2] In other words, these scouts were to act as spies.

However, when Moshe charged the spies he expanded their mission. In addition to military information, they were to report on the fertility and quality of the land.[3] Why did Moshe make this change?

Nachmanides explains that Moshe knew that the spies would discover a rich and fertile land. He expected that they would report this finding to the nation. This would thrill the people. They would be eager to proceed with the conquest.[4]

This insight does not completely explain Moshe's motives. Why did Moshe feel that this additional encouragement was necessary? Moshe had not originally intended to send these scouts. Bnai Yisrael suggested dispatching spies. How did this suggestion convince Moshe that the nation required reassurance?

Nachmanides' comments provide an interesting insight into the entire incident. Moshe apparently, concluded that the request to send spies was motivated by insecurity. He knew that the spies would report that the land was occupied by mighty nations. The inhabitants lived in fortified cities. This information would add to Bnai Yisrael's fears. Moshe sought to counter these concerns. He expanded the spy's mission. This assured that they would also bring back a favorable assessment of the quality of the land of Israel. He hoped that the resultant enthusiasm would help Bnai Yisrael overcome their fears.

---

[1] Rabbaynu Shlomo ben Yitzchak (Rashi), *Commentary on Sefer BeMidbar* 13:2.
[2] Sefer Devarim 1:22.
[3] Sefer BeMidbar 13:19-20.
[4] Rabbaynu Moshe ben Nachman (Ramban), *Commentary on Sefer BeMidbar* 13:2.

And Hashem spoke to Moshe saying: Send for yourself men and they will scout the Land of Cana'an that I give to Bnai Yisrael. Send one man from each of his fathers' tribes. Each should be a leader among them. (BeMidbar 13:1-2)

Parshat Shelach: Two Paths to Redemption

1. The report of the spies and the resultant controversy

Parshat Shelach relates the tragic account of the failed mission of the meraglim – the spies. These spies were sent to the Land of Cana'an in order to gather intelligence to be used in the conquest of the land. The spies returned and delivered their report to Moshe, Aharon and the nation. Initially they acknowledged the fertility of the land. However, they expressed doubt and anxiety regarding its conquest. One of their members – Kalev – challenged their timidity and expressed confidence that with Hashem's support they would easily take possession of the land.

Kalev's opposition only provoked the other spies to become even more strident in their claims. They further described the might of the nations occupying the land and added a new claim. They revised their report of the land's remarkable fertility and now described the land as uninhabitable by any people other than those reared and acclimated to its environment. The intense negativity of the spies raised a general panic among the people. The nation became despondent and a movement emerged to return to Egypt.

Yehoshua stepped forward. He had also participated in the spies' mission. He took Kalev's side and assured the people that the land was indeed a treasure and that with Hashem's assistance it would easily be possessed. Yehoshua's comments only evoked more confusion, panic and ultimately open rebellion.

And Hashem spoke to Moshe: How long will this nation rebel against Me? How long will they not be faithful to me despite all of the signs that I have performed in their midst? I will strike them with pestilence and drive them out. And I will make from you a greater and mightier nation. (BeMidbar 14:11-12)

2. Hashem's changing response to the rebellion and Moshe's pleas

At this point, Hashem speaks with Moshe and announces that the nation will be destroyed and a new more worthy nation will be formed from Moshe and his descendants. Moshe beseeches Hashem to spare the nation. As a result of Moshe's petition on the nation's behalf, Hashem announces that the people are forgiven. However, immediately after announcing that He has forgiven the people, Hashem declares that the current generation that has failed to place its trust in Hashem will die in the wilderness. Their children – the next generation – will enter the Land of Cana'an and conquer it. In short, within a few passages Hashem takes three different positions. Initially, He declares that He will destroy the nation. Next, He announces that the nation has been forgiven. Finally, He decrees that the current generation – that was apparently forgiven – will die in the wilderness and only their children will enter and posses the Land of Cana'an. How can these changes in Hashem's position be explained? Furthermore, why will Hashem destroy the current generation after He has agreed to forgive their sin?

... And the nations that have heard report of You will say: Hashem lacks the ability to bring this nation into the land that he promised to them and He destroyed them in the wilderness. (VaYikra 14:15-15)

3. The meaning of Moshe's petition

In order to understand Hashem's apparently shifting response to the evolving revolt of Bnai Yisrael and Moshe's pleas it is important to carefully analyze Moshe's petition. Moshe's plea is actually composed of two distinct components. It includes an argument on behalf of Bnai Yisrael and an appeal to Hashem's mercy. The argument has two components:

- Moshe argues that the relationship between Hashem and Bnai Yisrael was firmly established through the nation's redemption from Egypt. The nations of the region had heard reports of the destruction of the Egyptians and the journey of Bnai Yisrael through the desolation of the wilderness. These nations now are aware that Bnai Yisrael was rescued from Egypt and preserved in the wilderness by a mighty deity.

- If Bnai Yisrael is destroyed in the wilderness by Hashem, these nations will not assume that this is the result of a rebellion against Hashem. Instead, the nations will conclude that although powerful, Hashem is not omnipotent. He lacks the power to lead Bnai Yisrael in the conquest of the Land of Cana'an. Therefore, rather than allowing them to be defeated in their battle with the nations occupying the land, He Himself destroyed Bnai Yisrael in the wilderness.

In other words, Moshe argued that the redemption from Egypt was more than the fulfillment of a promise to the Patriarchs of Bnai Yisrael. It was a revelation to humanity. It revealed the existence of an omnipotent G-d that interacts with humanity. He enters into relationships with individuals and nations and He fulfills His promises. The destruction of Bnai Yisrael would nullify this revelation. Hashem would no longer be perceived as omnipotent or capable of fulfilling His promises.

This argument combined with Moshe's appeal to Hashem's mercy succeeded in securing forgiveness for the nation. However, this forgiveness had limitations.

And I also will proceed with them harshly. I will bring them into the land of their enemies and then either their uncircumcised heart will be humbled or their sin will be expiated. And I will recall My covenant with Yaakov. Furthermore My covenant with Yitzchak, and furthermore My covenant with Avraham I will recall. And I will recall the Land. (VaYikra 41-43)

4. Exile and the promise of redemption

The above passages are the conclusion of the blessing and curses outlined in Sefer VaYikra. Hashem tells Bnai Yisrael that their destiny in the Land of Israel will be determined entirely by their behaviors. If the nation is faithful to the Torah, then it will be rewarded with remarkable blessings. However, if the people abandon the Torah then they will be punished with increasingly harsh consequences. Ultimately, stubborn refusal to repent and return to the Torah will be punished by dispossession of the Land and exile. Even in exile Bnai Yisrael will not have peace. The nation will be hounded and persecuted by their enemies.

In the above passages Hashem promises that He will not entirely abandon His nation. They will be redeemed from exile and returned to the land that Hashem promised with a covenant to the patriarchs. The first of these passages is translated as suggested by Nachmanides. According to Nachmanides, there are two circumstances under which Bnai Yisrael will be redeemed. One path to redemption is through repentance. The passage describes this as the restoration of humility to the uncircumcised heart. The second path is through expiation of the nation's sins. Expiation does not involve repentance. It simply means that the sin of the nation has been punished and through enduring this punishment the nation's sin is in some way neutralized.[5]

This concept of expiation is not easily understood. It seems strange that redemption can come about through expiation of a sin and without sincere repentance. However, some insight into the concept of expiation is provided in the passages that follow. These passages focus on Hashem's covenant with the Patriarchs. The apparent relevance of the covenant is that it established an eternal relationship between Hashem and His nation. Therefore, the complete destruction of Bnai Yisrael can never occur. Every exile must come to its conclusion. Redemption may be delayed but it is inevitable. Expiation provides a vehicle for forgiveness and redemption when repentance is not present. Suffering and exile can be ended immediately through repentance. However even without repentance, every exile must come to an end with the ultimate redemption of Bnai Yisrael. Without repentance the exile will be prolonged and may even seem interminable. Redemption will arrive only after the people's sins have been completely expiated.

And Hashem said: I have forgiven according to your word. However, by My life and as the glory of Hashem fills all the land, all of the men who see My glory and My wonders that I performed in Egypt and in the wilderness and have tested Me these ten times and not obeyed My voice, they will not see the land that I promised to their father. All that rebel against Me will not see it.
(BeMIdbar 14:20-23)

5. Moshe secures Hashem's pardon but not His forgiveness

The above passages describe Hashem's response to Moshe's entreaties. He tells Moshe that He will forgive the people "according to your word." In other words, Hashem accepted Moshe's argument. When Moshe's argument is considered carefully, it is clear that Moshe did not argue that Bnai Yisrael deserved to be forgiven. He did not argue that the sin was excusable or understandable. Neither did Moshe attempt to minimize the sin. Instead, Moshe argued that despite their sin, the nation should not be destroyed. Too much would be lost were Bnai Yisrael destroyed. The revelation of the redemption from Egypt would be nullified and the nations of the region would return to ignorance and darkness. This is an argument for pardoning Bnai Yisrael not for their forgiveness.

Hashem told Moshe that He is responding to his entreaties. He will pardon the nation. He will not forgive their sin. The people will be punished. The generation that rejected Hashem will perish in the wilderness. They cannot be rescued from their wanderings in the wilderness. They have not repented. However, the nation's ultimate rescue and redemption is inevitable. With the punishment and passing of this flawed generation, the nation's sin will be expiated. The next generation will enter the land and possess it.

And Hashem spoke to Moshe, saying: Send men for yourself, that they may study the land of Cana'an, which I give to Bnai Yisrael. From every tribe of their fathers you should send a man –each a prince among them. (BeMidbar 13:1-2)

Imagining a Different World

---

[5] Rabbaynu Moshe ben Nachman (Ramban), Commentary on Sefer VaYikra 26:41-42.

Behold, Hashem your G-d has set the Land before you. Ascend! Take possession as Hashem, the G-d of your fathers, has spoken to you. Fear not, neither be dismayed. And you came near unto me every one of you, and said: Let us send men before us, that they may spy the land for us, and bring us back word of the way by which we must go up, and the cities unto which we shall come. (Devarim 1:21-22)

1. Two accounts of the incident of the spies

Parshat Shelach provides the Torah's first account of incident of the meraglim – the spies. A second account is provided in Sefer Devarim. In the second account, the incident is reviewed by Moshe in the context of his final address to Bnai Yisrael before they enter the Land of Israel without him. There are a number of differences between the accounts. One of the most fundamental differences is that in the account in Sefer Devarim, the impetus for sending the spies comes from the people. Moshe tells the people that the moment has arrived to conquer the Land of Israel. The nation responds by suggesting to Moshe that the conquest of the Land should be preceded by a scouting mission. The scouts will investigate the Land and discover the weaknesses in its defenses. The intelligence provided by the spies will be used to devise a plan for the Land's conquest. In Parshat Shelach, the account begins with Hashem's direction to Moshe to send the spies. No mention is made of the nation's role in initiating the ill-fated mission.

Rabbaynu Avraham ibn Ezra and others explain that the two accounts are not contradictory. They merely begin their presentations of the events from different points. The account in Sefer Devarim begins from the very beginning of the incident. The account in Parshat Shelach begins from a later point in the incident. The people have come to Moshe with their suggestion and Moshe has asked Hashem to guide him in responding. The account begins with Hashem's response to Moshe. Hashem tells Moshe that he may send the spies.[6]

3. The appropriateness of sending spies

The commentators dispute whether the nation's request was proper. Nachmanides maintains that the request was completely proper. Bnai Yisrael was poised to wage war against the nations living in the Land. A strategy for conquering the Land needed to be developed and this required intelligence regarding the defenses to be overcome and knowledge of any other physical obstacles that might interfere with the campaign. Furthermore, the Land would be conquered through a series of campaigns. Therefore, it was necessary to determine which areas should be first seized. These areas would form the staging ground for further campaigns and the produce of the territory initially captured would be required to sustain the people until the conquest was completed.[7]

Malbim disagrees. He argues that the normal rules of warfare did not apply to Bnai Yisrael. They should have understood that their conquest of the Land of Israel would not be through the strength of their armies or the wisdom of their military strategy. Instead, they would conquer the Land through miraculous means. Hashem would conquer the nations of Cana'an and not the armies of Bnai Yisrael. The suggestion of the nation to send spies represented a failure in the people's trust in Hashem.[8]

---

[6] Rabbaynu Avraham ibn Ezra, Commentary on Sefer BeMidbar, 13:2.

[7] Rabbaynu Moshe ben Nachman (Ramban), Commentary on Sefer BeMidbar 13:2.

[8] Rav Meir Leibush ben Yechiel Michel (Malbim), HaTorah VeHaMitzvah – Commentary on

And it came to pass, when the Ark set forward, that Moshe said: Rise up, Hashem, and let Your enemies be scattered; and let them that hate Thee flee before Thee. And when it rested, he said: Return, Hashem, unto the ten thousands of the families of Israel. (BeMidbar 10:35-36)

6. Moshe's vision of the conquest of the Land of Israel

Malbim's position is supported by the two passages above. These passages, the Torah describes the first stage of the nation's journey from the Wilderness of Sinai toward the Land of Cana'an. Bnai Yisrael left Sinai with the understanding that it would shortly arrive at the frontier of the Land of Cana'an and the conquest would begin. The cloud of Hashem's glory preceded them and led them through the wilderness. Moshe declares that Hashem should rise up and that He should scatter the nation's enemies. Malbim explains that the meaning of these passages is that Bnai Yisrael will not wage a traditional war employing a carefully developed strategy based upon sound intelligence. Instead, the cloud of Hashem's glory will lead the nation into the Land of Cana'an and Hashem will conquer the nations of Cana'an just as He vanquished the mighty armies of Paroh.[9]

However, Malbim's interpretation of the dialogue between Moshe and Bnai Yisrael raises an important question. Why did the people not follow the cloud of Hashem and allow Hashem to scatter their enemies? Why did the people feel that it was necessary for them to send spies, gather intelligence, develop a traditional strategy, and wage a conventional war?

If you walk in My statutes, and keep My commandments, and do them, then I will give your rains in their season, and the land shall yield her produce, and the trees of the field shall yield their fruit. (VaYikra 26:3-4)

4. The Torah's alternative reality

The above passages begin the Torah's description of the blessings that Bnai Yisrael will enjoy in the Land of Israel in response to their observance of the commandments. This section of the Torah expresses a novel idea. The future of Bnai Yisrael in the Land of Israel will be determined by whether the nation observes the mitzvot. This means that prosperity and comfort, or scarcity and affliction will not be determined by natural material causes. Instead, a direct causal relationship will exist between the spiritual excellence of the people and its material wellbeing. In short, natural cause and effect will not apply.

These passages actually demand that Bnai Yisrael adopt a new and radical view of the physical world. They are to abandon the traditional view that material outcomes are determined strictly by material causes. This perspective is to be replaced by the radical alternative that the spiritual excellence of the nation is the fundamental cause affecting the material existence of the nation in the Land of Israel.

In fact, the laws of Shemitah and Yovel – the Sabbatical and Jubilee Years are essentially expressions of this idea. These two mitzvot are completely counterintuitive and even ludicrous from the perspective of a conventional material understanding of the world. Every seventh year is a Sabbatical Year. Every fiftieth year is a Jubilee Year. Observance of the Sabbatical Year differs from the observance of the Jubilee Year. However, both have an important law in

---

Sefer BeMidbar, 13:2.

[9] Rav Meir Leibush ben Yechiel Michel (Malbim), HaTorah VeHaMitzvah – Commentary on Sefer BeMidbar, 10:35.

common. During both it is prohibited to work the land of the Land of Israel. The abstention from working the land is acknowledgment that it is Hashem's land and must be used as He prescribes. The Torah asserts that prosperity and comfort in the Land of Israel will be secured through the observance of Shemitah and Yovel. If these laws are disregarded, then the nation will experience poverty and anguish. In other words, not working the land will result in prosperity and working the land will bring about desolation and poverty!

What is the message of Shemitah and Yovel? It is that the Land of Israel is not governed by conventional cause and effect. It is governed by "a-material" cause and effect. The spiritual cause governs the material effect.

5. Imagining a different world

In order for Bnai Yisrael to accept Moshe's assurance that the Land of Israel will be conquered miraculously and without waging a conventional war, the people needed to first accept the Torah's radical revision of our perception of the material world. They were required to imagine a very different world. They were required to envision and embrace the proposition that material outcomes – conquest of the Land of Cana'an – would not be brought about through the familiar material means. Instead, Hashem would grant them possession of the Land in some miraculous manner that they could not imagine or grasp. In other words, they were required to use their imagination and perceive a deeper more fundamental reality than the familiar material reality. At this point, the people were not prepared to abandon the conventional perspective with the new radical one proposed by Moshe. Their imagination failed them. Therefore, they responded to Moshe's directive, "Ascend, Conquer!" with "Let us send spies".

"These are the names of the people that Moshe sent to scout the land. And Moshe called Hoshea bin Nun Yehoshua." (BeMidbar 13:16)

Moshe realized that the spies he had appointed were not completely suited for their mission. They lacked the confidence and self-assurance essential to conquest. He suspected that they would be intimidated and foresaw their discouraging report. He renamed his student Hoshea. He bestowed upon him the name Yehoshua. This new name contained Moshe's prayer on his behalf. Hashem should rescue Yehoshua from the influence of the spies.

We can easily understand Moshe's prayers on his student's behalf. However, the alteration of Yehoshua's name is more difficult to explain. Why did Moshe change his student's name? What purpose was served by this change?

Maimonides explains in his Laws of Repentance that there are various behaviors that are associated with repentance. One of these is that the repentant individual changes his name. In adopting a new name, the repentant person is making a statement. He is a new person. He is not the one who committed the sins from which he repents.[10] This is not merely some sort of superficial gesture. Repentance requires a recreation of oneself. One must leave previous modes of behavior and thought and adopt a new life-style. The adoption of a new name encourages the development of a fresh self-image. This self-image is an invaluable asset in the attempt to build a new life. The important element of this analysis is that a person's name can communicate a

---

[10] Rabbaynu Moshe ben Maimon (Rambam) *Mishne Torah*, Hilchot Teshuva 2:4.

personal message. It is an effective vehicle for reminding its owner of one's personal mission and identity.

We can apply Maimonides' reasoning to Moshe's change of Hoshea's name. Moshe realized that his prayers might not be sufficient to save his student. His student must be reminded of the danger that surrounds him. He must appreciate this danger. He must also recognize his personal mission. This mission is to resist this influence and remain unsullied by the sins of the other spies. Moshe provided his student with a device designed to communicate all of these messages. This was his new name. This new name was designed to communicate a personal message. The new name recalled to its bearer Moshe's prayers and the reason for these prayers.

"Is the land fertile or barren? Are there trees there or not? And be courageous and take some of the fruit of the land. And it was during the period of the ripening of the first grapes." (BeMidbar 13:20)

Moshe provides the spies with instructions. Our passage is part of these instructions. One of the directives Moshe gives the spies is to bring back a sample of the fruit of the land.

Why did Moshe require the scouts to bring back this sample of the fruit? The most obvious answer is that he wished to provide a concrete sample of the fertility of the land. Hashem had told Moshe that the land was fertile. Moshe was sure that the fruit would demonstrate this fertility. Therefore, he asked the scouts to bring back a sample of the fruit.

There is another possible explanation for Moshe's instruction to bring back a sample of the fruit. This answer requires an introduction. There is an interesting detail in our *parasha* that deserves some analysis. The Torah specifies that the scouts were sent from the wilderness of Paran.[11] This comment seems redundant. At the end of the previous *parasha*, the Torah tells us that the nation was camped in the wilderness of Paran.[12] It is obvious that the spies were sent from this location.

There seems to be a second redundancy in the same passage. The *pasuk* states that the scouts were sent from the wilderness of Paran "at the word of Hashem."[13] The mention of Hashem's acquiescence seems to be a second redundancy. The *parasha* begins with the Almighty granting permission to send the spies!

Rav Yitzchak Zev Soloveitchik *Ztl* suggests that the explanation for these apparent redundancies can be found in the end of the previous *parasha*. There the Torah explains that each journey of the nation and each encampment were undertaken at the word of Hashem.[14] As explained above, the last *parasha* ends with the nation encamped in the wilderness of Paran. In order for the camp to begin a new journey, the Almighty's authorization was required.

Our *parasha* tells us that the spies were sent from the wilderness of Paran at the word of Hashem. This statement contains a message. The spies were beginning a journey from the existing encampment. Therefore, specific authorization was needed to break camp! In other words, the spies needed two separate authorizations. First, Hashem authorized Moshe to send

---

[11] Sefer BeMidbar 13:3.
[12] Sefer BeMidbar 12:16.
[13] Sefer BeMidbar 13:3.
[14] Sefer BeMidbar 9:15-23.

scouts. This was an authorization of the concept. Second, a specific authorization was needed to undertake a journey from the established encampment.[15]

Of course, there is an obvious question. Hashem's authorization is needed in order for the nation to undertake a journey. In our *parasha*, it is not the nation that is undertaking the journey. It is a group of scouts. Why do the scouts require a special authorization to leave camp?

The Gaon of Rogachov -- Rav Yosef Rozin *Ztl* answers that the spies were not a separate entity, distinguished from the rest of the nation. They were not merely an advanced scouting party. They were the beginning of the nation's journey into the land of Israel. The nation began its journey through sending the spies. With these scouts the nation began to leave its camp. Therefore, the specific authorization of Hashem was required.[16]

This explains an interesting comment in the Talmud. The Talmud is discussing the issue of agency. The Talmud is seeking a source for the rule that an agent can act on one's behalf. The Talmud responds that this principle is derived from the incident of the spies. The spies acted on behalf of the nation.[17] Superficially, the discussion is difficult to understand. In what way were the spies the representatives of the nation? The above analysis answers the question. The journey of the spies represented the journey of the nation. Their departure from the wilderness of Paran was deemed the beginning of Bnai Yisrael's departure. In this manner, the spies were the agents of the entire nation.

This also explains another issue. Moshe selected leaders from the tribes to be members of this group. Why did Moshe choose leaders of the tribes? Many answers are offered. However, the above approach offers a very simple explanation. These scouts were required to act as the representatives of the people. In order to fulfill this role, these individuals were required to be leaders within their respective tribes. Without this position, they could not be deemed as representatives of their tribes.[18]

This brings us back to our original question. Why did Moshe instruct the spies to bring back fruit from the land? Based on the above approach, an interesting answer can be suggested. Moshe was not commanding these spies to merely scout the land. He was commanding them to begin the process of possession. They were to represent the nation and assume ownership of the land. Moshe's instructions to collect a portion of the fruit of the land can be understood in this context.

According to Torah law, land can be acquired in three ways. First, it can be acquired through payment. Second, ownership can be transferred through a document. Third, land can be acquired through *chazakah*. *Chazakah* means performing an action that demonstrates ownership. If a person wishes to transfer ownership of land to another person, the recipient can establish possession through demonstrating ownership.[19]

---

[15] Rav Shimon Yosef Miller, Shai LaTorah (Jerusalem 5753), volume 3, pp. 139-140.
[16] Rav Shimon Yosef Miller, Shai LaTorah (Jerusalem 5753), volume 3, p 141.
[17] Mesechet Kiddushin 41a.
[18] Rav Shimon Yosef Miller, Shai LaTorah (Jerusalem 5753), volume 3, p 141.
[19] Rabbaynu Moshe ben Maimon (Rambam) *Mishne Torah*, Hilchot Mechirah 1:3.

How does a person acquire a parcel of land through *chazakah*? What specific actions are regarded as demonstrations of ownership? One of the forms of *chazakah* is harvesting the fruit of the land. Through harvesting the fruit the person demonstrates possession.[20]

We can appreciate Moshe's instructions. The spies were to initiate the process of possessing the land. He commanded them to perform an act of legal acquisition. They were to utilize *chazakah*. The harvesting of the fruit was an expression of this *chazakah*.[21]

However, the nation that dwells in the land is mighty. And the cities are large and fortified. We also saw there the descendants of the giants. (BeMidbar 13:28)

In our *parasha*, Hashem tells Moshe to send spies into the land of Israel. Moshe explains, in Sefer Devarim, that Hashem was responding to the request of Bnai Yisrael. The people had approached Moshe and suggested that these spies be sent. Moshe regarded this as a reasonable plan. Hashem agreed to the request.[22]

The spies returned. They reported that the land was rich and fertile. They also reported that the land was well defended and would be difficult to conquer. Upon hearing this report, Bnai Yisrael panicked. The people refused to proceed into the land. Hashem punished the nation. The generation that refused to conquer the land was forced to wander in the wilderness for forty years. After this generation died, their children conquered the land under the leadership of Yehoshua.

The Torah explains that the spies sinned and caused the rebellion. What was their sin? It is difficult to condemn the spies for reporting that the land was well defended. This was their job. Moshe charged them with the responsibility of gathering intelligence. They were ordered to asses the fortifications and the strength of inhabitants. Surely the spies cannot be condemned for fulfilling their mission!

The Torah describes their sin as propagating negative report on the land.[23] This seems to be a reference to a specific statement made by the spies. They claimed that the land consumed its inhabitants.[24] This was a false assertion. It is reasonable to hold the spies responsible for this lie.

However, this raises an obvious question. The spies initially reported that the land was fertile and rich. They even brought back fruit to support their report. How could they reasonably claim that the land was unwholesome? Why would the people believe a claim that clearly contradicted the spies' own words?

One possible answer is that the initial report was delivered in front of Moshe and Ahron. Moshe was familiar with the land of Canaan from his younger years.[25] He could easily dispute any negative characterization of the land. The spies did not criticize the land of Israel in front of Moshe and Ahron. They acknowledged its richness. Later the assembly broke up. The spies

[20] Rabbaynu Moshe ben Maimon (Rambam) *Mishne Torah*, Hilchot Mechirah 1:16.
[21] Rav Shimon Yosef Miller, Shai LaTorah (Jerusalem 5753), volume 3, p 141.
[22] Sefer Devarim 1:22-23.
[23] Sefer BeMidbar 14:36.
[24] Sefer BeMidbar 13:32.
[25] Rabbaynu Moshe ben Nachman (Ramban), *Commentary on Sefer BeMidbar* 13:2.

followed the people back to their tents. There, outside of the presence of Moshe and Ahron, the spies denigrated the land.

This does not completely answer the question. Still, the people must have realized that the spies were contradicting themselves in their characterization of the land! Perhaps, the spies responded that they were afraid to contradict Moshe's assurances regarding the land. Therefore, in his presence they had been less than completely truthful. Now, in privacy they could reveal the truth.

Nachmanides suggests that the spies never contradicted themselves. They never retracted from their report that the land flowed with milk and honey. Instead, they claimed that the land was too rich. The luscious fruit and produce would sustain an especially robust metabolism. It seemed to be a perfect diet for giants. But a more average specimen would be harmed by the richness of the diet. They claimed that this must be the case. They had only encountered giants. Apparently, normal human beings would not be sustained by these rich fruits.[26]

Nachmanides further comments that the sin of the spies did not begin with this lie. The lie was the culmination. The sin began with the statement contained in our *pasuk*. At first glance this seems odd. In our *pasuk*, the spies are reporting that the land is well defended. This was an accurate and truthful account!

Nachmanides explains that the role of the spies was to provide intelligence. This information was to be used to formulate a plan for conquest. The spies were never authorized to evaluate the chances of succeeding. If we consider our passage carefully, we can see that the spies overstepped their authority.

The spies use an odd word in our *pasuk*. They say, "However, the nation that dwells in the land is mighty". Let us consider the implications of the word "however". This word creates some connection between the preceding and the following statement. It qualifies the prior statement. What was this prior statement? The spies had just reported that the land was rich and fertile. Then they added their "however". What was their message? They were saying, "Yes, the land flows with milk and honey – just as Moshe promised. However, what good is this to us? We cannot conquer the land. It is too well defended". Of course, the spies did not actually say this. Their intent was implied in the "however".[27]

And Kalev silenced the nation's protest against Moshe. And he said: We will surely ascend and posses it. For we certainly have the ability. (BeMidbar 13:30)

Yehoshua's Initial Silence in Response to the Report of the Spies

Our *parasha* relates the incident of the spies –the *meraglim*. Bnai Yisrael requests that spies precede them into the land. Moshe acquiesces. The spies are charged with the responsibility of scouting the land and bringing back a sample of its fruit. Moshe hopes that the report of the spies will encourage the nation and facilitate their conquest of the land. The *meraglim* scout the land. However, they are intimidated by the challenge of possessing the land. The spies report that the land is indeed fertile. However, it is occupied by mighty nations and its cities are fortified. They imply that Bnai Yisrael will not be capable of taking possession of the land.

---

26 Rabbaynu Moshe ben Nachman (Ramban), *Commentary on Sefer BeMidbar* 13:32.
27 Rabbaynu Moshe ben Nachman (Ramban), *Commentary on Sefer BeMidbar* 13:27.

Two of the spies do not participate in this pessimistic report. Yehoshua and Kalev do not agree with the other spies. When the other spies deliver their report, Kalev immediately protests that the spies have come to an unwarranted decision. In fact, the nation *can* conquer the land.

It is interesting that during this debate between Kalev and the other spies Yehoshua remained silent. He did not take Kalev's side. Instead, he allowed Kalev to act alone in his opposition to other spies. Only after Kalev faied to influence the nation and the people succumbed to the undermining pessimism of the other spies did Yehoshua join Kalev and speak out in favor of proceeding with the conquest. Why did Yehoshua not immediately express his support for Kalev's position?

Rabbaynu Yitzchak Karo suggests that Yehoshua was following a carefully-designed plan. He knew that the other scouts would contest Kalev's assertion that Bnai Yisrael could conquer the land. This would initiate a debate between Kalev and the other spies. Yehoshua felt that by immediately siding with Kalev, little would be gained. He and Kalev would be in the minority opposing the shared view of the other ten spies. However, Yehoshua hoped that Kalev's opponents would interpret his silence as tacit approval of their position. This assumption would encourage them to appeal to Yehoshua to present his position to the nation and serve as the arbitrator. This appeal would enhance his credibility with the nation. Yehoshua planned to surprise the ten spies by using the credibility they bestowed upon him to undermine their position and state his support for Kalev's opinion. This would be devastating for the ten spies. The very person whom they called upon to serve as arbitrator of the truth would side with their opponent. He hoped this strategy would provide him the opportunity to truly impact the outcome of the debate.[28]

Unfortunately, Yehoshua's plan did not work. The ten spies never called upon him to express his opinion. He was forced to simply side with Yehoshua. As he expected, his support of Kalev did not impact the outcome of the debate.

And all of the congregation lifted up its voice, and cried; and the people wept that night. (BeMidbar 14:1)

Small Mistakes/Major Consequences or "I Didn't Mean to Do It" Isn't Always Good Enough

1. The sin of the spies shaped Jewish history

Parshat Shelach describes the sin of the spies. In the opening passages of the parasha, Hashem authorizes Moshe to send spies into the land of Israel. These spies will bring back a report on the land.

The spies return and they describe the fertility and abundance of the land. However, they also note that the inhabitants of the land are mighty and their cities are heavily fortified. The people respond with panic. The spies then modify their report on the richness of the land and suggest that perhaps the land is not healthy.

The people decide to abandon their journey to the Land of Cana'an. They wish to replace Moshe with a new leader and return to Egypt. Hashem threatens to destroy the nation and replace

---

[28] Rabbaynu Yitzchak Karo, *Toldot Yitzchak, Commentary on Sefer BeMidbar* 13.

it with a new nation composed of the descendants of Moshe. Moshe intercedes and Hashem agrees to spare the nation. However, this generation that rejected the promised land will not take possession of it. Instead, this generation will wander in the wilderness for another thirty-eight years. Their children will take possession of the land.

Commenting on the above passage, our Sages explain that the sin of the spies had another more significant impact. Not only did the sin condemn the generation to wander in the wilderness, it also altered the course of the nation's history. Before this sin Bnai Yisrael traveled along a historical path that led to permanent possession of the land. The destiny of the nation was to possess the land and never experience exile. The sin altered this destiny. Now, the nation's historical path was redirected toward a future that included eventual dispossession of the land, exile, and suffering.[29] Ultimately, Bnai Yisrsel would take permanent possession of the land. However, this would not be accomplished in the coming days or weeks. It would be postponed for centuries – until the Messianic era.

Remember what Hashem your G-d did to Miryam, by the way as you came forth out of Egypt. (Devarim 24:9)

2. The spies and their generation should have learned a lesson from Miryam

The Midrash notes that the Torah juxtaposes this account to the sin of Miryam and Aharon. Miryam and Aharon spoke against their brother Moshe. Because Miryam initiated this sin she was stricken with leprosy. The nation should have taken notice of this sin and Miryam's punishment and learned from it. Instead, the people, led by the spies, spoke out against the land and disparaged it.[30]

The Midrash is difficult to understand. How was the sin of Miryam and Aharon similar to the sin of the spies and their generation? It seems that Miryam and Aharon violated the prohibition of speaking against another person. We are prohibited from harming another with speech. Presumably, Miryam and Aharon violated this prohibition through their criticism of Moshe. How was this wrongdoing similar to the sin of the spies? Did they harm the land through speaking against it? Is the Land of Israel a person that is harmed by slander?

There are a number of solutions to this problem. Rav Yosef Dov Soloveitchik *Zt"l* suggests that identifying the relationship between these two sins requires a better understanding of the sin of Miryam nd Aharon.

In the above passage, the Torah enjoins us to remember the punishment of Miryam. There are very few events that the Torah commands us to constantly remember. For example, we are required to not forget Revelation.[31] We are required to remember Shabbat as the day on which Hashem rested from recreation.[32] As these examples illustrate, the few events that we are required to constantly remember are fundamental to the Torah perspective. The authenticity of the Torah rests upon Revelation. The foremost *mitzvah* of the Torah is recognition of Hashem as the creator and absolute ruler of the universe. Miryam's sin and her punishment do not seem

---

[29] Midrash Rabbah, Sefer BeMidbar 16:20.
[30] Midrash Tanchuma, Parshat Shelach, Chapter 5.
[31] Sefer Devarim 4:9-10.
[32] Sefer Shemot 20:8.

nearly as fundamental to the Torah as the other material we are enjoined to constantly remember. Why then must we conscientiously remind ourselves of her punishment?

And Miryam and Aharon spoke against Moshe because of the Cushite woman whom he had married; for he had married a Cushite woman. And they said: Has Hashem indeed spoken only with Moshe? Has He not spoken also with us? And Hashem heard it. (BeMidbar 13:1-2)

3. The severity of Miryam and Aharon's sin

The answer lies in considering Miyram and Aharon's comments about their brother Moshe. The Torah is vague on this issue. It tells us that their comments involved Moshe's relationship with his wife Tziporah. Also, it tells us that Miryam and Aharon asserted that they – like Moshe – were prophets. Our Sages provide more details about Miryam and Aharon's comments. They explain that Moshe had separated from Tziporah.[33] Miyram and Aharon understood that this decision was related to Moshe's exalted status as a prophet. They challenged the appropriateness of Moshe's separation from his wife. They were also prophets. Yet, they lived normal family lives surrounded by their spouses and children. Why should Moshe's prophetic stature demand or justify his abandonment of family life?[34]

The issue raised by Miryam and Aharon was based upon an incorrect premise. They understood that Moshe's prophetic status surpassed their own. However, they believed that the difference was quantitative. They were prophets. Moshe was a greater prophet. Miryam and Aharon did not understand that Moshe was qualitatively differentiated from all other prophets. Maimonides' provides a description of the differences between the prophecy of Moshe and other prophets.[35] The differences can be summarized. For all other prophets, prophecy was an unnatural state. Prophecy was achieved through a difficult and temporary transcension from the prophet's normal material state to a barely sustainable spiritual plane. Moshe was a completely different prophet-type. For Moshe the prophetic experience was a natural state. No transcension took place.

This difference between Moshe and other prophets is among the thirteen fundamental principles of the Torah enumerated by Maimonides.[36] It is also the foundation of two other of the thirteen principles.

The first of these is that Hashem communicated the Written and Oral Torah to Moshe at Sinai. Moshe then taught the Torah to Bnai Yisrael.[37] For Moshe to serve in this capacity – as recipient of the Torah – he entered into a prolonged prophetic dialogue with Hashem. The proposition that such an experience can be achieved by a mortal assumes that Moshe was unique among human beings. He could achieve that which is unattainable by any other human being. In short, Revelation assumes the existence of a human being with Moshe's unique prophetic capacity.

The second of these principles is that Revelation was a singular prophetic experience. All other prophecies are qualitatively inferior. In fact, the authenticity of any other prophetic

---

[33] Targum Unkelus Sefer BeMidbar 12:1.

[34] Rabbaynu Shlomo ben Yitzchak (Rashi), *Commentary on Sefer BeMidbar* 12:2.

[35] Rabbaynu Moshe ben Maimon (Rambam) *Mishne Torah*, Hilchot Yesodai HaDat 7:6.

[36] Rabbaynu Moshe ben Maimon (Rambam) *Commentary on the Mishne*, Mes. Sanhedrin 10:1.

[37] Rabbaynu Moshe ben Maimon (Rambam) *Commentary on the Mishne*, Mes. Sanhedrin 10:1.

message is only determined by its consistency with specific criteria outlined in the Torah. One of these is that the message must be consistent with the Torah. If the prophet claims that he has been commanded by Hashem to add to, subtract from, or change any of the *mitzvot* of the Torah the prophecy and its messenger are assumed to be frauds.[38]

Miryam's contention that she and Aharon shared with Moshe a common prophetic status undermined the authenticity and authority of Revelation and the Torah. This is the reason she was stricken with leprosy. This is the reason that we must remember this episode and contemplate its meaning and implications.[39,40]

> *And all the children of Israel murmured against Moshe and against Aharon. And the whole congregation said unto them: Would that we had died in the land of Egypt or would we had died in this wilderness! And why does Hashem bring us unto this land, to fall by the sword? Our wives and our little ones will be a prey. Were it not better for us to return into Egypt? And they said one to another: Let us make a captain, and let us return into Egypt. (BeMidbar 14:2-4)*

4. The severity of the sin of the spies and their generation

Now, we more clearly understand the sin committed by Miryam and Aharon. We must develop a clearer understanding of the sin of the spies and their generation. It is clear from the Torah's narrative and from the impact of this sin upon Jewish destiny that the sin was severe. However, it is not clear why this rebellion was more grave than those that preceded it or followed. The spies returned with a wonderful report on the land they had explored. They spoke of its fertility and abundance. However, their wonderment did not inspire them. It could not overcome their fear of the mighty nations that inhabited Can'an. They communicated this fear to an already timid nation. The ensuing panic is understandable. They were not ready to accept the challenge of conquest. Why was their sin so grave?

The nation viewed the issue from a completely personal perspective. They understood that the land was a wonderful legacy. However, they were willing to forgo the land rather than risk their own destruction. They failed to understand that the events in which they were involved had an enormous meaning – a meaning more important than the impact upon them personally. They had been selected as the generation through which an ancient promise would be fulfilled and through which the fundamental mission of humanity would be advanced.

Hashem had promised to Avraham and the Partiarchs that their descendants would return to the Land of Cana'an and possess it. However, their possession of the land would not be merely the fulfillment of this ancient promise. It would complete a process of overpowering revelation. All humanity would be transformed by the events that would unfold. This collection of oppressed and ignoble slaves had overcome the mightiest nation of the era. The waters of the sea had split for them and fallen upon their pursuers. Now, they would swiftly capture the land promised to their forefathers. The nations of the land would flee before them. They would dare not oppose the nation that had miraculously overpowered their mighty masters, and before whom the waters of the sea had parted. Humanity would witness history's most astounding revelation of Hashem's

---

[38] Rabbaynu Moshe ben Maimon (Rambam) *Mishne Torah*, Hilchot Yesodai HaDat 8:3.

[39] Rav Yosef Dov Soloveitchik, Recorded Lecture on Parshat Shelach.

[40] The preceding analysis of the sin of Miryam and Aharon was developed by Rav Soloveitchik in the referenced lecture. The analysis of the sin of the spies and their generation, which follows, differs somewhat from Rav Soloveitchik's interpretation.

omnipotence. Humanity would be presented with incontrovertible evidence of the existence of a creator who is intimately involved in the affairs of the world. What impact might this revelation have had upon humanity? How might have these events altered the course of human history?

This generation refused to participate in this drama. Instead, they longed to return to Egypt. As a result, the anticipated drama was compromised and its impact blunted. Ultimately, this generation's descendants entered and conquered the Land of Cana'an. The promise to the Patriarchs was fulfilled. However, the vision was not fulfilled. The nations of the world were unmoved. Humanity was condemned to endless years of darkness and folly.

The sin of the spies and their generation is truly comparable to Miryam and Aharon's sin. In both instances the sin undermined a fundamental element of the Torah. Miryam and Aharon's sin called into question the uniqueness of Moshe's prophecy. The spies and their generation compromised the achievement of Hashem's vision for humanity.

5. Small mistakes and major consequences

It is important to understand that in neither of these instances did the sinner appreciate the enormity of the sin. Miryam and Aharon acted out of shock and concern with Moshe's behavior. The spies and their generation were driven by intense fear. Miryam and Aharon did not intend to undermine fundamental principles of the Torah. The spies did not wish to compromise Hashem's plan for humanity.

From the episode of the spies a practical lesson emerges. The spies and their generation did not appreciate the significance of their sin. They may have understood that they lacked courage and that their timidity prevented them from following Hashem's directive. However, they did not comprehend the impact of their decision upon the destiny of their nation and upon humanity. They viewed the challenge facing them on a personal level. On a personal level it was easier to succumb to their fears than to arise and grasp the wondrous legacy awaiting them. They would forgo the legacy rather than battle their terror. They may very well have known that they were sinning. But they regarded the sin as excusable and minor.

The flaw in their thinking was their belief that they fully understood the meaning and purpose of Hashem's commands. They imagined that their vision was Hashem's vision. Therefore, they assumed that they understood the proportions and magnitude of their sin.

We cannot judge the significance of our own sins. We lack the knowledge of our individual place and our potential within the unfolding plans of Hashem. We also lack the objectivity to soberly evaluate the significance of our own wrongdoings.

We cannot be perfect. We inevitably will experience failures and we will disappoint ourselves. However, we can be honest and not minimize our wrongdoing. If we have the courage to be honest with ourselves then at least our failures will be motivators for self improvement.

And Moshe and Ahron fell on their faces before the whole assembled Bnai Yisrael. (BeMidbar 14:5)

The scouts return. They report that the land will impossible to conquer. They also deny that the land is wholesome. They claim that the land seems to consume or destroy its inhabitants. The nation is discouraged by this report. The people question the purpose of traveling through the wilderness to arrive at this hopeless end. They come to a consensus. They will replace Moshe and Ahron. Another leader will be chosen. This leader will take them back to Egypt.

Our *pasuk* records Moshe and Ahron's reaction to the nation's decision. The Torah does not tell us that they argued with the people. The Torah records that they fell upon their faces before the nation.

What was the purpose of this reaction? Nachmanides explains that Moshe and Ahron were beseeching the people not to perform this wicked act.[41] They should not rebel against the Almighty and refuse to posses the land. They must continue forward and not return to Egypt.

This reaction raises an important question. Why did Moshe and Ahron not respond more forcefully? They behaved as supplicants. They begged the people not to act sinfully. Contrast this to Moshe's reaction upon descending from Sinai. Moshe descended from Sinai and encountered the nation worshipping the *Egel* – the Golden Calf. Moshe did not become a supplicant. He did not beg the nation to repent. Instead, he acted decisively and sternly. He rebuked Ahron for his involvement in the sin. He separated the sinners from the faithful. He immediately executed those responsible for the travesty of the *Egel*. How can we explain Moshe's relative passivity in responding to the transgression in our *parasha*?

The first possibility is that the sin of the *Egel* was more isolated than the movement to return to Egypt. In the instance of the *Egel*, Moshe realized that the majority of Bnai Yisrael remained faithful to Hashem. He enlisted the majority to punish the minority of sinners. In our *parasha*, Moshe was confronted with a mass movement. The nation – as a whole – had decided to abandon Moshe and the quest for the land of Israel. Moshe had very few allies. He could not act forcefully. Therefore, he was forced to become a supplicant. He appealed to the nation reconsider.

However, Rav Simcha Zisil Broudy notes another distinction between the two incidents. He explains that the sin of the *Egel* was not directed against Moshe. The nation had defied the law of the Almighty. Moshe vigorously defended the glory of the Creator. In the incident in our *parasha*, the nation's rebellion was not directed solely against Hashem. The people were also rejecting the leadership of Moshe and Ahron. The people sought new leadership. They wanted leaders that would guide them on a more productive and meaningful path.

Moshe and Ahron could not act forcefully in this incident. One who leads through force can be accused of self-aggrandizement. Furthermore, a leader that forces other to follow is not a true leader. If force must be used, the leader has failed to prove his or her worthiness. Moshe realized that this was not a conflict that could be resolved through force.

Nonetheless, Moshe and Ahron did not abandon the conflict. They realized that they could not coerce the nation. Instead, they resorted to petition. They were not concerned with their own position of honor. They only cared for the welfare of Bnai Yisrael. If this required them to become beggars and supplicants, they were willing.[42]

And Hashem said: I have pardoned according to your word. But indeed, as I live – and all the earth shall be filled with the glory of Hashem – surely all those men who have seen My

---

41 Rabbaynu Moshe ben Nachman (Ramban), *Commentary on Sefer BeMidbar* 14:5.
42 Rav Shimon Yosef Miller, Shai LaTorah (Jerusalem 5753), volume 3, pp. 143-144.

glory, and My signs, which I performed in Egypt and in the wilderness, yet have tested Me these ten times, and have not hearkened to My voice surely they shall not see the land which I swore unto their fathers, neither shall any of them that despised Me see it. (BeMidbar 14:20-23)

Dreams of Eternity

Moshe sends spies to report on the Land of Cana'an

Parshat Shelach describes an incident of the *meraglim* – the spies. Hashem tells Moshe that he may send out spies to explore the Land of Cana'an – the land that has been promised to Bnai Yisrael. The missions of the spies is to bring back a report on the land – to confirm that it is indeed a land that flows with milk and honey. However, the spies are also told to consider the land's fortifications and the obstacles that the people may face in its conquest.

The spies go forth on their mission; they return and they deliver their report to Moshe and Aharon and to the nation. They confirm that the land is indeed wonderfully fertile. It does flow with milk and honey. However, they describe with awe the might of its inhabitants and the defenses of its cities.

The spies incite a rebellion and Hashem decrees He will destroy the nation

The people receive the report and are overtaken by fear and panic. They do not believe that they can succeed in conquering the land. They begin to consider abandoning the entire project and returning to Egypt.

Hashem responds. He has demonstrated to Bnai Yisrael His omnipotence. They witnessed the wonders that He performed in redeeming them from Egypt and in sustaining the nation in the wilderness. Yet, they do not trust that He can and will lead them in their conquest of the Land of Cana'an. Hashem tells Moshe that He will destroy this nation. He will create from Moshe a new nation that will be more worthy of the land promised to the Patriarchs.

Moshe intercedes and secures Hashem's forgiveness

Moshe intercedes. He argues with Hashem. Hashem performed unprecedented miracles in Egypt in order to reveal Himself and His omnipotence. If He will now destroy Bnai Yisrael, the impact of that revelation will be compromised. The nations of the world will skeptically suggest that Hashem destroyed His own people rather than allow them to face defeat at the hands of the mighty nations of the Land of Cana'an. His destruction of His own nation will be interpreted as tacit acknowledgment of His inability to win the land for His people. Moshe then appealed to Hashem's mercy and forbearance.

Hashem responded. He told Moshe that He would forgive Bnai Yisrael. However, Hashem told Moshe that He would not spare this generation that had witnessed His wonders and yet not trusted in Him. This generation would perish in the wilderness and their children would take possession of the land promised to the patriarchs.

Hashem's forgiveness is not total

Hashem's response to Moshe is difficult to understand. Hashem told Moshe He would destroy the nation and create a new nation from Moshe. He then told Moshe that He forgave the people. Yet, He condemned the entire generation to perish in the wilderness. In other words, before Moshe's intervention, Hashem's plan was to destroy the nation. After Moshe's intervention and Hashem's pronouncement that He forgave the people, the generation that committed the sin remained condemned to death. How was Hashem's forgiveness expressed?

There is one obvious outcome of Hashem's forbearance. Before Hashem forgave the people, neither they, nor their descendants, would possess the land. A new nation would be created from Moshe and this new nation would be the beneficiaries of the covenant with the Patriarchs. Hashem's forgiveness saved the children and descendants of the generation that had sinned. These children and descendants would possess the Land of Cana'an. In other words, it seems that Moshe's petition did not persuade Hashem to pardon the generation that had sinned. It only impacted the destiny of their children and descendants.

If this analysis is correct, then a serious problem arises. This interpretation simply is not consistent with Hashem's declaration of His forgiveness. According to this interpretation, He only "forgave" those who were children or yet unborn. Is that the meaning of Hashem's declaration that He forgave the people? Those who committed the sin remained condemned to die in the wilderness and only those relatively guiltless were to survive.

And Nadav and Abihu died before Hashem, when they offered strange fire before Hashem, in the wilderness of Sinai, and they had no children; and Eleazar and Ithamar ministered in the priest's office in the presence of Aharon their father. (BeMidbar 3:4)

Nadav and Avihu died because they did not have children

Let us consider an odd comment found in the Talmud that reveals an important and relevant principle. In Parshat BeMidbar the Torah lists the sons of Aharon. It explains that Nadav and Avihu died when they offered an alien – an unauthorized – sacrifice before Hashem. The passage then adds that these two sons of Aharon did not have children. The Talmud comments that this passage seems to relate the death of Nadav and Avihu to not having children. This teaches us that one who does not have children is worthy of death.[43]

This is a very strange interpretation of the passage and an even more shocking conclusion. The passage is explicit in its explanation of the death of Nadav and Avihu. The passage explains that they died because they offered an unacceptable sacrifice. It adds that they did not have children. It is not stating that their failure to procreate was the reason for their death. What motivated the Talmud to attribute the deaths of Nadav and Avihu to not having children and to further conclude that failure to procreate is a sin of such terrible consequence? The Talmud is communicating an important principle of the Torah. In order to identify that principle and understand the Talmud's comments one more step is required.

And when Yaakov completed charging his sons, he gathered up his feet into the bed, and expired, and was gathered unto his people. (Beresheit 49:33)

The Talmud declares that Yaakov did not die

The Talmud comments on the above passage that in fact Yaakov did not die. What does the Talmud mean by this statement? The Torah describes Yaakov's death, his embalming, and burial. In fact, the Talmud raises this very objection and responds that just as Yaakov's children live, so does Yaakov live![44]

---

[43] Mesechet Yevamot 64a.
[44] Mesechet Taanit 5b.

A number of the commentators on this discussion in the Talmud conclude that it is not the Talmud's intention to dispute the meaning of the Torah's passages that describe Yaakov's death. The Talmud accepts that Yaakov was mortal and his life ended as the Torah describes. However, despite this death Yaakov lives, just as his children continue to survive.[45] In other words, Yaakov continues to live through his children.

On the surface this seems to be an overused and exhausted platitude. Yes, of course, we all live-on through our children! But what does this really mean? Is the Talmud interested only in providing its own version of a trite notion?

Illusions of immortality

Understanding the Talmud's message requires that we better understand the more common sentiment expressed by the notion that one continues to live through one's children and descendants. This will allow us to compare this common notion to the principle the Sages of the Talmud are proposing.

We are mortal and finite individuals. Ultimately, we must each deal with our mortality and the inevitability of our own eventual passing. When we are young, our end seems far off. It does not trouble us or demand our attention. As we mature, our mortality becomes more evident. We cannot imagine or accept our ultimate demise; yet, its inevitability cannot be denied. We attempt to somehow defeat death and overcome the inevitable end of all human beings. We do this through our children. We assert that we will continue to live through our children and grandchildren. If we strongly identify with our children and grandchildren, then the idea that we will continue to live through them gives us some solace and relief from our fear of the abyss.

But our consolation is really only an attempt to deny the inevitable. We will not achieve immortality through our children and descendants. Yes, our children will remember and love us. Our grandchildren will recall us fondly. But our great-grandchildren will know of us only through stories they hear about us and their children will know little or nothing of our lives. Our "immortality" will continue to exist only as an ever-diminishing remnant of genetic material passed on to each consecutive generation of descendants.

The Talmud's principle of immortality

This is the common interpretation of the notion that we continue to live through our children. The Torah's interpretation of this notion is very different from the common sentiment and is a fundamental principle of our outlook.

The Sages of the Talmud are explaining that we each exist in two frameworks. Each of us is a unique individual. Each of us is also a link within a chain of the generation of the Jewish people. As an individual, each of us is charged with the responsibility of making the most of the life that has been granted to him or her. As a link within the chain of the Jewish people, each of us is obligated to create the next link. That link is created through having children and through raising one's children to be the next link in the chain. In other words, we each are granted two lives. The life we are granted as an individual is quite finite and it ends with each individual's personal demise. The life that we are each granted as a link in the chain of our people does not

---

45 See Rabbaynu Yaakov ben Shlomo ibn Habib, *Ein Yaakov,* M'sorat HaShas edition, Lekutim, Mesechet Taanit 5b.

end as long as the chain remains. Only when the chain – G-d forbid – is broken does that life come to an end.

Yaakov's life as a unique individual ended with his personal demise. The Talmud is not suggesting that he did not really die. However, Yaakov – like each of us – had another life. That life did not end when he was embalmed and buried. As the Talmud explains, that life continues to this day and will continue as long as Bnai Yisrael – the nation of Yaakov – continues to exist.[46]

The totality of the deaths of Nadav and Avihu

This principle also explains the Talmud's comments regarding Nadav and Avihu. They died in response to offering an inappropriate offering. But when they were stricken down, more than their individual lives came to an end. They had not created families and children. The tragedy of their deaths as individuals was compounded by the catastrophe of the ending of one of the chains that compose our people. No more links would be created from Nadav and Avihu. Two families within the Jewish nation were destroyed.

Hashem did not annihilate the generation of the spies

Now, Hashem's response to Moshe's petition has meaning. Hashem's original decree was that the members of the generation that heeded the counsel of the spies should be destroyed. They were to die as individuals and their families were to be cut- off from the nation of Hashem. Children would either perish with their parents or be left to wander in the wilderness. But these children would not form the next generation of the Jewish people. Instead, Moshe's descendants would become the nation of Hashem and this new Moshe-nation would be the beneficiaries of the covenant with the Patriarchs. The members of the generation of the spies would die as individuals and as links in the chain of our nation.

Moshe won Hashem's forgiveness of the people. He did not save their individual lives but he did save them as links in the chain of our nation. Each would have the opportunity to create a family and their children would possess the land promised to their forefathers. Each had the opportunity to continue to live indefinitely as links in the chain of our people.

"They will not see the land that I promised to their forefathers. All that anger Me will not see it." (BeMidbar 14:23)

Where should we live? Are we obligated to live in Israel? True, there may be legitimate reasons for not picking up tomorrow and moving. But should we have as a personal objective relocating – at some point – to Israel? There is significant popular confusion regarding this question. It is not my purpose to resolve this question conclusively. But hopefully, this discussion will clarify some of the key issues.

Nachmanides wrote a critique of Maimonides *Sefer HaMitzvot*. *Sefer HaMitzvot* is an enumeration and description of the 613 *mitzvot* of the Torah. As part of his critique, Nachmanides provided a list of commandments that Maimonides neglected to count in his enumeration of the 613 *mitzvot*. In his list of positive commandments that Maimonides "missed", Nachmanides includes the *mitzvah* to posses the land of Israel. According to Nachmanides, we

---

[46] Rabbaynu Yaakov ben Shlomo ibn Habib, *Ein Yaakov,* M'sorat HaShas edition, Lekutim, Mesechet Taanit 5b. See also comments of RaSbA for a similar but alternative explanation.

are commanded to posses the land. We are not permitted to leave the land in the control of any other nations. Neither are we permitted to leave the land in a state of desolation. In other words, according to Nachmanides, the conquering, defending, and developing of the land of Israel is a positive commandment.

Nachmanides quotes many passages from the Torah that seems to confirm his contention. One of his proofs is derived from this week's *parasha*. In this week's *parasha*, the spies discourage Bnai Yisrael from conquering the land of Israel. Bnai Yisrael heeds to the advice of the spies and refuses to enter the land. Both the spies and the nation are punished severely for this rebellion against Hashem. As a result of their refusal to conquer the land the nation is condemned to wander in the wilderness for 40 years. The clear implication of the entire incident is that the Bnai Yisrael are commanded to posses the land of Israel and that they rebelled against Hashem and His commandments by refusing to proceed into the land.[47]

So, Nachmanides' position is clear. There is a *mitzvah* to posses and settle the land of Israel. The *mitzvah* – like all *mitzvot* included in the 613 commandments – applies for all generations. According to Nachmanides, it is time to pack our bags! Incidentally, this thesis provides some justification and *halachic* basis for creating a Jewish State. It is unlikely that Nachmanides expects us to posses and control the land and not establish some sort of governmental structure. But this issue requires more extensive discussion.

But Maimonides' position is less easily understood. As Nachmanides observes, Maimonides does not count possessing or living in the land of Israel as a *mitzvah*. Meggilat Esther offers a well-known explanation for Maimonides' position. He explains that according to Maimonides, a commandment can only be included among the 613 *mitzvot* if it applies for all generation. Any commandment that is given to be performed at a specific time in history cannot be included among the 613 *mitzvot*. For example, at the time of the giving of the Torah Bnai Yisrael were instructed to not approach or ascend Sinai. This injunction was related to a specific time – the Revelation. After Revelation, the *mitzvah* no longer operates. There is no prohibition against climbing Sinai today. Therefore, this injunction cannot be counted among the 613 *mitzvot*.[48] Meggilat Esther contends that the command to posses the land of Israel was given to Moshe and Yehoshua to perform. The command continued to be binding and active until the exile from the land of Israel. But with exile, the command was suspended. It will reemerge with the Messianic era. But in the interim, there is no requirement to posses or conquer the land. Therefore, this is not a command that applies for all generations. Like the injunction to not ascend Sinai, the requirement to conquer the land of Israel emerges and reemerges at specific moments in history. As a result, it cannot be counted among the 613 *mitzvot*.[49]

This is an amazing assertion. It seems to be in direct opposition to numerous statements and rulings of Maimonides. One obvious contradiction is found in Maimonides comments in his *Mishne Torah* regarding the significance of the land of Israel. Maimonides states that a person should live in the land of Israel – even in a city dominated by pagans. He explains that it is prohibited to leave the land of Israel even to live in a city that is predominately populated by

---

[47] Rabbaynu Moshe ben Nachman (Ramban), *Critique on Maimonides' Sefer HaMitzvot -
- Positive Commands that Maimonides Neglected to Include.*

[48] Rabbaynu Moshe ben Maimon (Rambam) *Sefer HaMitzvot,* Pinciple 3.

[49] Rabbaynu Yitzchak DeLeon, *Meggilat Esther, Commentary on Maimonides' Sefer Hamitzvot,* Comments on Nachmanides' Critique.

Jews.[50] It seems very unlikely that Maimonides is referring to some past or future point in history but would not apply his comments to his own times or to ours!

Another ruling of Maimonides seems to contradict Meggilat Esther's thesis. Maimonides explains that if a man wishes to resettle in the land of Israel and his wife refuses, the man may divorce his wife and he has no obligation to pay his wife the amount she is promised by her *ketubah* – her marriage contract. Similarly, if a woman wishes to settle in the land of Israel and her husband refuses, she may demand a divorce with full payment of her *ketubah*.[51]

This ruling clearly seems to contradict Meggilat Esther's thesis that there is no commandment in our times to live in the land of Israel. It would be remarkable and completely unlikely for Maimonides to rule that a woman is deprived of her *ketubah* for refusing to settle in Israel if living in Israel is of not a commandment and obligation. It is also unlikely that Maimonides – in his code of law – is stating a law that was irrelevant in his time and remains irrelevant.

However, the contradiction to Meggilat Esther's thesis is even clearer if the Talmudic source for Maimonides' ruling is explored. Maimonides bases his ruling on a discussion in Tractate Ketubot. Tosefot explain that there are some authorities that do indeed contend that there is no obligation to live in Israel in our times. Tosefot maintain that these authorities would contend that the Talmud's ruling – as quoted by Maimonides – does not apply in our times.[52] In other words, the Talmud's discussion and Maimonides' ruling are premised on the assumption that there is a *mitzvah* to live in Israel. If this *mitzvah* were suspended, the ruling would be void. It is clear from Tosefot's analysis that according to Maimonides, there is a *mitzvah* to live in Israel at all times.

Of course, this creates a problem. If Maimonides agrees that there is an obligation at all times to live in the land of Israel, then Nachmanides' criticism of Maimonides seems well-founded. Why does Maimonides not count this obligation among his 613 commandments?

There is an enigmatic comment of the Sages – quoted by Rashi – that may provide an insight into this issue. The Sages comment that even when we are in exile we should continue to practice the *mitzvot*. We must wear *tefillin* and observe the *mitzvah* of *mezuzah*. We should continue to practice the *mitzvot* so that they will not be new to us when we return to the land of Israel.[53]

This is an amazing comment! Some of the *mitzvot* are clearly tied to the land of Israel. For example, we are obligated to abstain from working the land during the Sabbatical year. We must give portion of the annual harvest to the *kohanim* and *leveyim*. These commandments only apply in the land of Israel. But other – indeed most – *mitzvot* are not tied to the land of Israel. Most *mitzvot* – for example, observing *Shabbat*, the laws of *kashrut* – are personal obligations. They must be observed regardless of our place of residence. The *mitzvot* of *tefillin* and *mezuzah* have no apparent connection to the land of Israel. Yet, according to the Sages, our observance of these *mitzvot* in exile is only practice for our return to the land of Israel!

---

[50] Rabbaynu Moshe ben Maimon (Rambam) *Mishne Torah*, Hilchot Melachim 5:9-12.
[51] Rabbaynu Moshe ben Maimon (Rambam) *Mishne Torah*, Hilchot Eyshut 13:20.
[52] Tosefot,Mesechet Ketubot 110b.
[53] Rabbaynu Shlomo ben Yitzchak (Rashi), *Commentary on Sefer Devarim* 11:18.

Nachmanides, in his commentary on the Torah, deals with this question. But his treatment of the issue is almost as mysterious as the very statement of the Sages that he is attempting to explain. Nachmanides explains that the *mitzvot* were primarily commanded to those living in the land of Israel.[54] It seems that Nachmanides is merely confirming that the Sages are positing an intimate relationship between all commandments – even personal ones – and the land of Israel. But he does not seem to communicate any information regarding the nature of this relationship.

However, a more careful consideration of Nachmanides comments may provide an important insight. We tend to regard the 613 *mitzvot* as a number of independent commandments. We observe *Shabbat*, we pray, we place *mezuzot* on our doorposts. We recognize that various *mitzvot* reinforce one another. But nonetheless, we regard each as a separate and independent entity. Nachmanides seems to reject this popular interpretation of the 613 *mitzvot*. Apparently, he maintains that the individual *mitzvot* are all part of a single complex and integrated system. It is true that a specific *mitzvah* can independently function and be significant. If a person prays but does not place a *mezuzah* on his doorpost, the *mitzvah* of prayer has been fulfilled. But any individual *mitzvah* only achieves its full significance in the context of the overall system of *Taryag* – the 613 *mitzvot*.

Consider an analogy. A human heart can be removed from the body. Using modern technology, we can cause the heart to continue to beat outside of the body. Is the heart working? Is it beating? Of course, it is. But does the heart have its full significance outside of the body? No, we are keeping it alive until we can reintegrate it into the body. So too, it is important that we observe the *mitzvot* in exile. But we delude ourselves if we think that these performances have their full significance. Each *mitzvah* is part of a system of *Taryag*. This is a system that regulates the life of the individual Jew, within the nation of Bnai Yisrael, in the land of Israel. If the land of Israel is removed from the system, the individual *mitzvah* is isolated from the body in which it is designed to best function. Now, Nachmanides comment can be understood. The *mitzvot* were primarily commanded to those living in the land of Israel. In other words, the individual *mitzvot* were given to be fulfilled as part of a totality. A fundamental element of this totality is the land of Israel.

We can now return to Maimonides' position. Why does Maimonides not include the requirement to live in the land of Israel among the 613 *mitzvot*? Maimonides explains that he does not include within his list of *mitzvot* admonishments to observe the Torah. In other words, in order for a command to be counted among *Taryag*, it must enjoin us to perform a specific activity or prohibit a specific behavior. Admonishments to observe the Torah do not meet this criterion.[55] This same principle may explain Maimonides' reasoning for not including the obligation to live in the land of Israel among *Taryag*. As Nachmanides explains, the obligation to live in the land of Israel stems from the very nature of *Taryag*. *Taryag* is a system that only functions in its entirety in the land of   Israel. Perhaps, Maimonides agrees with this interpretation of the *mitzvot* of the Torah. We are obligated to observe the Torah in its entirety. Therefore, we must live in the land of Israel so that we can perform the *mitzvot* of the Torah in the context of the entire system of *Taryag*. If this is correct, Maimonides may maintain that although this obligation engenders a specific requirement, it is essentially a general

---

[54] Rabbaynu Moshe ben Nachman (Ramban), *Commentary on Sefer Devarim* 18:25.
[55] Rabbaynu Moshe ben Maimon (Rambam) *Sefer HaMitzvot,* Pinciple 4.

admonishment to observe the Torah in its entirety. In other words, according to Maimonides, there is no specific obligation to live in the land of Israel. Instead, there is a general obligation to observe the Torah in its complete form. This general obligation generates a requirement to live in the land of Israel – only there can the Torah be observed in its complete form and context. But nonetheless, the requirement to live in the land of Israel stems from a general requirement to observe *Taryag* properly. And according to Maimonides, general admonishments are not counted among *Taryag*.

They will not see the land that I promised to their forefathers. All that anger Me will not see it. (BeMidbar 14:23)

Is Israel Worth the Aggravation?

1. The incident of the spies and the commandment to possess the Land of Israel

Our *parasha* relates the incident of the spies – the *meraglim*. Bnai Yisrael request that spies precede them into the land. Moshe acquiesces. The spies are charged with the responsibility of scouting the land and bringing back a sample of its fruit. Moshe hopes that the report of the spies will encourage the nation and facilitate their conquest of the land. The *meraglim* scout the land. However, they are intimidated by the challenge of possessing the land. The spies report that the land is indeed fertile. However, it is occupied by mighty nations and its cities are fortified. They imply that Bnai Yisrael will not be capable of taking possession of the land.

Bnai Yisrael are discouraged by the report of the spies. The people refuse to enter the land. Both the spies and the nation are punished severely for this rebellion against Hashem. As a result of their refusal to conquer the land, the nation is condemned to wander in the wilderness for 40 years.

According to Nachmanides, one of the Torah's 613 *mitzvot* is that we take possession of the Land of Israel. He explains that included in this commandment is an imperative that we not leave the land in the control of any other nations. Neither are we permitted to leave the land in a state of desolation. In other words, according to Nachmanides, this positive commandment requires that we conquer, defend, and develop the Land of Israel.

Nachmanides quotes many passages from the Torah that seems to confirm his contention. One of his proofs is derived from this week's *parasha*. The clear implication of the incident of the *meraglim* is that the Bnai Yisrael are commanded to possess the Land of Israel. The people rebelled against Hashem and His commandments by refusing to proceed into the land.[56]

Incidentally, this thesis provides some justification and *halachic* basis for creating a Jewish State. It is unlikely that Nachmanides expects us to possess and control the land and not establish some sort of governmental structure. But, this issue requires more extensive discussion.

2. Maimonides acknowledges an obligation to live in the Land of Israel

Maimonides' position differs somewhat from that of Nachmanides. He does not include within his accounting of the 613 commandments of the Torah an obligation to live in and to possess the Land of Israel. However, despite his exclusion of this imperative from his list of the 613

---

[56] Rabbaynu Moshe ben Nachman (Ramban), *Critique on Maimonides' Sefer HaMitzvot* — Positive Commands that Maimonides Neglected to Include.

commandments, it is clear from a number of his comments and rulings that he agrees that we are obligated to live in Israel.

Maimonides states that a person should live in the Land of Israel – even in a city dominated by pagans. He explains that it is prohibited to leave the Land of Israel even to live in a city that is predominately populated by Jews.[57]

In addition, Maimonides rules that if a man wishes to resettle in the land of Israel and his wife refuses, the man may divorce his wife, and he has no obligation to pay his wife the amount she is promised by her *ketubah* – her marriage contract. Similarly, if a woman wishes to settle in the land of Israel and her husband refuses, she may demand a divorce with full payment of her *ketubah*.[58]

This ruling clearly confirms that Maimonides acknowledges an obligation to live in the Land of Israel. It would be remarkable and completely unlikely for Maimonides to rule that a woman is deprived of her *ketubah* for refusing to settle in Israel, if living in Israel is not obligatory.

In summary, Maimonides and Nachmanides seem to disagree over the extent of our obligation in regard to the settlement of the Land of Israel. Nachmanides defines the obligation broadly. It includes an obligation to settle the land, develop it, and possess it. According to Maimonides, the obligation is expressed as a personal imperative to live in the land. Furthermore, Nachmanides includes this obligation among the 613 commandments. Maimonides acknowledges the obligation but does not include it in his list of the Torah's commandments.

3. The importance of living in the Land of Israel

Both Maimonides and Nachmanides make amazing statements regarding the importance of this obligation. As indicated above, Maimonides states that it is preferable to live in the Land of Israel – even in a city whose population is predominately pagan – than to live in exile. This applies even if the population of the exile community is predominately Jewish. He adds that one who abandons the Land of Israel in order to take up residence elsewhere is comparable to one who adopts idolatry.[59]

Nachmanides' comments on the importance of this obligation are even more shocking. He begins by quoting an enigmatic comment of the Sages. The Sages comment that even when we are in exile, we should continue to practice the *mitzvot*. We must wear *tefillin* and observe the *mitzvah* of *mezuzah*. We should continue to practice the *mitzvot* so that they will not be new to us when we return to the Land of Israel.

This is an amazing comment! Some of the *mitzvot* are clearly tied to the Land of Israel. For example, we are obligated to abstain from working the land during the Sabbatical year. We must give a portion of the annual harvest to the *kohanim* and *leveyim*. These commandments only apply in the Land of Israel. But, other – indeed most – *mitzvot* are not tied to the Land of Israel. Most *mitzvot* – for example, observing *Shabbat*, the laws of *kashrut* – are personal obligations. They must be observed regardless of our place of residence. The *mitzvot* of *tefillin*

---

[57] Rabbaynu Moshe ben Maimon (Rambam) *Mishne Torah*, Hilchot Melachim 5:9-12.
[58] Rabbaynu Moshe ben Maimon (Rambam) *Mishne Torah*, Hilchot Eyshut 13:20.
[59] Rabbaynu Moshe ben Maimon (Rambam) *Mishne Torah*, Hilchot Melachim 5:9-12.

and *mezuzah* have no apparent connection to the Land of Israel. Yet, according to the Sages, our observance of these *mitzvot* in exile is only practice for our return to the Land of Israel!

Nachmanides, in his commentary on the Torah, deals with this question. He explains that the *mitzvot* were primarily commanded to those living in the Land of Israel.[60]

This is not a completely satisfying response. It seems that Nachmanides is merely confirming that the Sages are positing an intimate relationship between all commandments – even personal ones – and the Land of Israel. But, he does not seem to communicate any information regarding the nature of this relationship.

In summary, both Maimonides and Nachmanides make amazing statements regarding the significance of living in the Land of Israel. Maimonides compares one who abandons the Land to reside elsewhere to one who adopts idolatry. Nachmanides asserts that the commandments of the Torah were designed primarily for one who lives in the Land of Israel. Those of us who live in the Diaspora are substantially compromising our observance. Both of these statements seem extreme and require explanation.

4. Attitudes influence and bias our perceptions

Let us consider another issue. We know that our attitudes and internal feelings, our character and personality influence our perceptions. Our overall character and personality act as a bias in the processing of information. Therefore, two individuals can observe the same phenomenon and interpret their observations differently.

A simple example will illustrate this point. The State of Israel too often finds itself involved in military operations against its perceived enemies. Some perceive the State of Israel as an embattled and small country surrounded by implacable enemies who are completely dedicated to its destruction. Such individuals observe Israel's military actions and interpret them as necessary defensive actions required to protect the country's citizens from terrorism.

Others regard Israel as an interloper. It is a country governed by a foreign people who have been artificially transplanted into the region. This group of aliens has imposed its will upon the native population, displacing it, and oppressing it. When the same military action is viewed from this perspective, it is interpreted as another expression of inhuman oppression.

5. Personality influences a person's capacity to enter into a relationship with Hashem

This example illustrates the degree to which internal feelings influence the manner in which we process information. However, this illustration also suggests an interesting dilemma. The Torah envisions a society in which the members embrace a relationship with Hashem. This requires that the members of the society perceive Hashem as a reality in their lives. Yet, each of us filters the information that we receive through the sieves of our personalities, attitudes, and character. Some members of a society will be endowed with, or develop, personalities and attitudes that allow them to perceive the presence of a Creator. Others establish attitudes that oppose this perception. Furthermore, even if such an individual overcomes the opposition of innate personality, he or she struggles to "relate" to or enter into a relationship with a Creator.

This is the issue that underlies the remarks of Maimonides and Nachmanides. Both recognize that we are entrapped by our attitudes and personalities. These influence our capacity

---

[60] Rabbaynu Moshe ben Nachman (Ramban), *Commentary on Sefer Devarim* 18:25.

to relate to Hashem and His Torah. However, both also assert that we can reform or shape our attitudes. How can this be accomplished?

6. Shaping attitudes through behaviors

The underlying premise of the remarks of Maimonides and Nachmanides is that behavior shapes attitude. In other words, we are not helpless to reshape those elements of our personality that we recognize as deterrents to our growth. We can influence our attitudes through action, through behaviors that we adopt. For example, a person who wishes to develop greater empathy should engage in acts of kindness. Empathy and sensitivity can be acquired through adopting consistent behavior that reinforces empathy and sensitivity.

Maimonides and Nachmanides contend that the Torah provides a behavioral system designed to shape our personalities and attitudes so that we can relate to and enter into a relationship with Hashem. This system is the entirety of its 613 commandments. These commandments collectively compose a comprehensive system that is designed to mold and refine our personalities. The objective of this process is to develop within each of us the attitudes and character that facilitates our relationship with Hashem.

7. Creating a Hashem-supportive environment

Now, let us reconsider the comments of Maimonides and Nachmanides. According to Nachmanides, the Torah Is designed to be observed in the Land of Israel. This assertion provides an important insight. The reformation or nurturing of a "Hashem-friendly" personality is not accomplished by the practice of a few of the Torah's commandments. This nurturing process takes place through the influences exerted by a *comprehensive* environment. The Torah's commandments – taken in their entirety – produce this comprehensive environment. When only a portion of the commandments are in place and practiced – which is the case in the Diaspora – this environment does not emerge and the impact of the *mitzvot* that are observed is compromised.

Maimonides compares one who leaves Israel to dwell elsewhere to an idolater. He is simply asserting that our attitudes and our character are influenced by our environment. These attitudes and our character will inevitably influence our thinking. When we choose to live in a non-Torah environment, we should expect that our thinking and perceptions will be shaped by that environment. If we wish to nurture the attitudes and character that encourages and supports a relationship with Hashem, then we must place ourselves in an environment shaped by the Torah's commandments. This is environment only emerges in its full force in the Land of Israel.

Say to them: As I live, so says Hashem, shall it not be as you have spoken in my ears? So I will do to you. (BeMidbar 14:28)

The Consequences of the Sin of the Spies and Bnai Yisrael

The spies returned. They reported that the land could not be captured. They also criticized the quality of the Land of Israel. The people accepted the report. They became despondent. They believed would never capture the fertile land, promised by Hashem. They concluded that rather than die in the wilderness, they should consider returning to Egypt. Hashem punished Bnai Yisrael for this rebellion. This generation would not enter the Land of Israel. Instead, the children, whom they had predicted would die in the wilderness, would conquer the land.

Rabbaynu Ovadia Sforno explains that this episode altered the future of Bnai Yisrael. Hashem had planned for Moshe to lead the people into the land. The Land of Israel would be easily captured. The conquest would be permanent and there would be no subsequent exile. He further explains that the consequence of the sin of the spies and their generation was not limited to the death of these individuals in the wilderness. Instead, the destiny of Bnai Yisrael was altered. Moshe did not lead the nation into the land. He was be replaced by Yehoshua. Without Moshe, the conquest was far less miraculous than the conquest Hashem had planned to execute through Moshe. An even more important consequence of their sin was that the possession of the land would not be permanent. Instead, it would be followed by exile. Only in the Messianic Era will Bnai Yisrael establish permanent possession of the land.[61]

Our Sages explain that this rebellion occurred on the ninth day of the month of Av. This has been a day of tragedy for Bnai Yisrael. Among the catastrophes occurring on this date is the destruction of both Temples.[62] The tradition that the rebellion occurred on the ninth of Av has a special meaning, according to Sforno. The destruction of the Temples was an outcome of this rebellion. It is, therefore, fitting to identify the date of the rebellion to the ninth of Av.

And they arose in the morning. And they ascended to the top of the mountain. And they said: We will ascend to the place of which Hashem spoke for we have sinned. (BeMidbar 14:40)

The Inadequacy of Bnai Yisrael's Repentance

Bnai Yisrael refuses to proceed to the land. Hashem tells the nation of its punishment. The people realize that they have sinned. They want to correct their error. They are prepared to face their fears. They declare they will travel into Canaan and do battle with the nations. Moshe advises Bnai Yisrael not to proceed with its plan. He tells the people that Hashem will not be with them. If they attempted to conquer the Land of Israel, they will be defeated. The people do not listen. They continue their journey towards Canaan. They are attacked by Amalake and are driven back.

This incident is very difficult to understand. The response of Moshe to Bnai Yisrael's declaration of willingness to proceed and Hashem's abandonment of His nation to Amalake seem almost arbitrary. Bnai Yisrael acknowledged that it had sinned. The people accepted responsibility for their doubts and lack of faith. They eagerly undertook dramatic action to overcome their unfounded fears. This seems to be the model of repentance. Why was the repentance of Bnai Yisrael not accepted?

In order to answer this question, we must analyze the process of atonement. Most sacrifices are brought to atone for a sin. The sacrifice is accompanied by a confession. Maimonides discusses this confession in his Mishne Torah. He explains that the confession contains three elements. First, the person must acknowledge the transgression. Second, the person must indicate he has repented. Last, the person must verbally recognize that the sacrifice is required for atonement.[63] Why is this last step necessary? It is easy to understand that

---

[61] Rabbaynu Ovadia Sforno, *Commentary on Sefer BeMidbar* 14:28
[62] Mesechet Sanhedrin 104b
[63] Rabbaynu Moshe ben Maimon (Rambam) *Mishne Torah*, Hilchot Ma'aseh Karbanot 3:15.

atonement for a sin requires acknowledgement of the transgression and repentance, but why is verbal affirmation of the requirement of the sacrifice essential to the process?

It seems that atonement is not secured until the sinner accepts that his transgression has consequences. In this case, the consequence is the sacrifice. Maimonides further discusses this concept in his description of the death penalty. He explains that one receiving this penalty must confess. Maimonides defines the minimum standard for this confession: the person to be executed must ask Hashem to accept his or her death as atonement for the transgression.[64] In other words, his atonement requires he accept that his death is the consequence of his sin.

We can now respond to our original question. Why was the repentance of Bnai Yisrael inadequate? The nation was truly prepared to proceed with the conquest of the land. The people were willing to confront their anxieties. However, this was not sufficient to secure atonement. Hashem had decreed that this generation would perish in the wilderness. Repentance required that the nation acknowledge that their transgression had a consequence. They were required to accept the justice of Hashem's judgment. In other words, Bnai Yisrael certainly had the option of praying to Hashem to reconsider His judgment and the punishment He had decreed upon His nation. However, they must first accept the justice of the decree. Instead, they attempted to defy the decree and to proceed with the conquest of the land.

And they placed him under guard, for it had not been explained what should be done with him. (BeMidbar 15:34)

Bnai Yisrael's Ethical Dilemma

The Chumash recounts the first violation of the Shabbat. Rashi explains that the people knew that the punishment for violation of the Shabbat was death. However, there are four forms of this punishment in the Torah. They did not know which form of the penalty to apply. The violator was placed under guard until Hashem revealed to Moshe the proper punishment.[65]

Hashem certainly knew that the Shabbat would ultimately be violated. Why did He not reveal the specific punishment until the crisis arose? This problem is even more troublesome according to one opinion in the Talmud. In order for a sinner to be punished for the violation of a commandment, he must first be warned by witnesses. The witnesses must notify the sinner that he is violating the *mitzvah*. They must also indicate the punishment. According to Rebbe Yehudah, the notification must include the specific form of punishment. According to this opinion, adequate warning could not be provided for this first violation of the Shabbat.[66] The specific punishment was not known at the time of the violation! The Talmud addresses this problem. It explains that the legal requirements for execution were, in fact, not met. According to normative practice, this first violator of the Shabbat could not be punished. However, the Torah empowers the courts and a prophet to punish an individual, in extreme cases, without meeting these normative requirements. Moshe and his court used this authority to execute this violator.[67] In other words, this first violation of the Shabbat created a crisis that could not be solved in

---

64 Rabbaynu Moshe ben Maimon (Rambam) *Mishne Torah*, Hilchot Sanhedrin 13:1.
65 Rabbaynu Shlomo ben Yitzchak (Rashi), *Commentary on Sefer BeMidbar* 15:34.
66 Mesechet Sanhedrin 80b.
67 Mesechet Sanhedrin 80b.

accordance with normative law. Only through using the extraordinary power of Moshe and the court was the dilemma solved. What were Hashem's reasons for allowing this preventable crisis to occur?

Hashem has commanded Bnai Yisrael to observe the laws. The responsibility for enforcement rests upon the nation. At times, this requires that the people harshly punish one of their own. This is a difficult task. It is easy to be callous in dealing with an outsider. However, we all feel less comfortable rebuking a friend or peer. It is even more challenging to precipitate the punishment of a friend. An even more excruciating ethical dilemma emerges when the crime committed by our friend is a victimless religious violation. However, the Torah does decree that some religious transgressions – like violation of the Shabbat – are so severe that they are punished with death. This decree of the Torah is only meaningful if we as a nation are willing to support it. We must be willing to confront this challenge and moral dilemma and take this most severe action against a peer or friend.

Hashem created a situation in which the people would be required to demonstrate this devotion to and support for the standards of the Torah. According to Rebbe Yehudah, in order to construct an even more meaningful challenge, they were even provided with a rationalization for overlooking the violation. The people did not yet know the specific form of execution that applied to a person guilty of violating the Shabbat. Without this information they could not adequately warn the violator of the consequences of his actions. They knew that because they did not provide an adequate warning, the violator was exempt from the death penalty. However, despite the tempting opportunity to overlook the violation and the accompanying rationalization for this course of action, the nation realized that this initial rebellion against the Shabbat could not be overlooked. They brought the violator to Moshe and the court and entrusted them with deciding the proper course of action, fully realizing that their friend might be executed. They knew that Moshe and the court might resort to their extraordinary power to execute the violator despite the deficiency in the warning he had received. Through following this path, the people demonstrated their commitment to and support of the Torah.

Any Yehoshua bin Nun sent from Shittim two men – secret spies—saying: Go and see the land and Yericho. And they went and they came to the home of a harlot. And her name was Rachav. And they laid down there. (Yehoshua 2:1)

The Differences between the Missions of Yehosua's Spies and Moshe's Spies

This passage is from the *haftara* of Parshat Shelach and is directly related to its content. The Torah portion discusses the incident of the spies. Moshe sends a group of spies into the Land of Israel. The spies return and report that the land is well-defended. They also question the vitality and health of the land's environment. Only two of the spies – Yehoshua and Kalev – demur. They insist that the land is remarkably fertile and that they would succeed in its conquest. The nation is persuaded by the report provided by the majority of the spies and concludes that it is doomed. They will not succeed in the conquest. The nation decides that it must return to Egypt. Hashem punishes Bnai Yisrael. The people are condemned to wander in the wilderness for forty years – until the members of the generation die. Then, their children will possess the Land of Israel.

The *haftara* is taken from Sefer Yehoshua. Forty years have passed and now Yehoshua leads the nation. Bnai Yisrael has arrived at the border of the land of Israel and is prepared to follow Yehoshua into the land. They will vanquish the nations that now occupy it and take possession of the Land of Israel. But Yehoshua makes an amazing decision. He decides that before initiating his campaign, he will send spies into the land. This seems to be a very strange decision. Moshe had sent spies and this lead to disaster. Yehoshua was one of these spies. No one was more familiar with the incident. Why would Yehoshua risk bringing about a repetition of the same catastrophe that Moshe's spies instigated?

> *And look upon the land – what is it? And regarding the nation that dwells upon it – is it strong or weak? Is it many or few? (BeMidbar 13:18)*

Yehoshua's directions to his spies are not outlined in detail. However, the Torah provides a detailed description of Moshe's instructions. It is difficult to determine the overarching mission of Moshe's spies. Nachmanides argues, that the spies were sent to provide information that would be used in developing a strategy for conquest. He explains that it is inappropriate to rely upon miraculous intervention. Instead, we must make every effort to act responsibly. We cannot conduct ourselves impulsively or recklessly and then rely on Hashem to intervene and save us from our own carelessness.[68]

However, this is not the most obvious interpretation of Moshe's directions. He instructs the spies to bring back a sample of the fruit of the land. He tells them that they should report on the fertility of the land. Rabbaynu Avraham ibn Ezra suggests that the spies had a dual mission. They were not only to provide information to be used in developing a strategy for conquest, but were also to provide information to be used to assess the quality of the land.[69]

We can understand the reason for gathering information relevant to conquest. Nachmanides' comments deal thoroughly with this issue. However, it is more difficult to understand the reason for gathering information relevant to the land's fertility. Moshe had already communicated to the nation Hashem's promise that they would be taken to a land flowing with milk and honey. Why was a confirmation of the land's fertility required?

The composition of Moshe's spies and their strange mission can be explained by a single consideration. In his recounting of this event in Sefer Devarim, Moshe explains that the original impetus to send these spies came from the nation. The nation came to Moshe and requested that he send spies.[70] In Parshat Shelach, the account begins with Hashem's response to this request. He authorizes Moshe to send the spies.[71]

The origin of the suggestion to send the spies explains the composition of the group and its assigned mission. The nation's suggestion apparently reflected uncertainly and fear. They were not confident in their ability to confront and defeat the inhabitants of the land. Neither were they convinced that the land's fertility and richness merited the danger they perceived in its conquest. The spies' mission was designed to address both of these doubts. The composition of the group reflected that these spies were selected in order to address the concerns of the entire nation. Their success in addressing the fears and doubts of the nation would depend upon their credibility. The representative composition of the group would assure its credibility.

---

[68] Rabbaynu Moshe ben Nachman (Ramban), *Commentary on Sefer BeMidbar* 13:3.
[69] Rabbaynu Avraham ibn Ezra, *Commentary on Sefer BeMidbar*, 13:18-20.
[70] Sefer Devarim 1:22.
[71] Rabbaynu Shlomo ben Yitzchak (Rashi), *Commentary on Sefer Devarim* 122.

This explains and interesting nuance in the behavior of the spies. Upon their return, they presented their report. We would have expected them to report to Moshe. Moshe would then decide how to best use the information the spies gleaned. But instead, after reporting to Moshe and Aharon, the spies immediately presented their report to the people.[72] This is understandable given the origin of the suggestion to send the spies. The spies were sent in response to the urgings and anxieties of the nation. They were sent as the nation's representatives. Therefore, when they returned, they reported to the entire nation.

We can now better understand Yehoshua's behavior. He did not send spies in response to a popular request. The spies he sent were not a national delegation. Two individuals were sent. They were sent in secrecy. Rabbaynu David Kimchi – Radak – explains that the nation was unaware of the mission.[73] The spies were selected by Yehoshua; he sent them, and they reported only to him.

But what was Yehoshua's objective in sending these spies? As noted above, the narrative does provide an account of exact instructions provided by Yehoshua. Perhaps, the objective of the mission can be deducted by its outcome. As explained above, Rachav hid the spies and then assisted them in their escape. She did this in exchange for a promise that she and her family would be spared during the conquest. But she also explained that she and all of the inhabitants of the land had heard of the destruction of the Egyptians and the other nations that had opposed Bnai Yisrael in its march towards the Land of Israel. The nations of the land were terrified. She was eager to win the favor of the spies because she was fully confident that Bnai Yisrael would conquer the land. The spies brought back to Yehoshua this message that nations of the land were demoralized and disheartened.

This suggests a new perspective from which we must consider the detection of the spies. This detection was an essential step in their success in gathering the intelligence that they reported. Once they were detected, Rachav was forced to choose between her allegiance to her own king and the opportunity to forge an agreement with these representatives of Bnai Yisrael. She chose to create an agreement. In the process, she explained her reasoning and the fear and desperation of the nations of the land. This was the very intelligence that the spies were sent to gather. In other words, the detection of the spies was not the result of an absence of providence. It was an expression of providence.

Now, we can easily understand why Yehoshua was not concerned with a repeat of the disaster brought about by the first spies. These spies were sent by Yehoshua and reported only to him. They were not a delegation. They were two people. Their absence would not be immediately noticed. But most important, these spies were not sent to perform an evaluation of the land or to gather strategic information. Their sole purpose was to report back on the morale of the nations of the land. Yehoshua could not predict the details of the report but he was confident of its general tone. Radak explains that he knew that the spies would bring back a report that he could share with the people and that this report would build their confidence.[74]

---

[72] Sefer BeMidbar 13:26.

[73] Rabbaynu David Kimchi (Radak), *Commentary on Sefer Yehoshua* 2:1.

[74] Rabbaynu David Kimchi (Radak), *Commentary on Sefer Yehoshua* 2:1.

Korach

"And Korach the son of Yitzhar the son of Kahat the son of Leyve separated himself, together with Datan and Aviram the sons of Ahaliav and Ohn the son of Pelet, the sons of Reuven." (BeMidbar 16:1)

Korach initiated a dispute with Moshe regarding the leadership of Bnai Yisrael. Rashi explains that Korach was motivated by personal ambitions. Moshe had appointed Elisafan the son of Uziel as prince of the family of Kahat. Korach believed that he should have received this honor.[1] Datan, Aviram and Ohn were not involved in this issue. They did not have this personal motivation to join the dispute. Why did they become involved?

Bnai Yisrael camped in the wilderness in accordance with a specific order. The *Shevet* – tribe – of Reuven camped adjacent to the family of Kahat. This proximity encouraged close relations between these neighbors. Korach developed a following among members of the *Shevet* of Reuven. Rashi summarizes this phenomenon with the statement, "Woe to the evil doer and woe to his neighbor".[2]

Rashi seems to maintain that the members of *Shevet* Reuven were not, by nature, evil. They were influenced by the attitudes of their neighbors. It is interesting that the good qualities of *Shevet* Reuven did not have a positive influence upon Korach and his followers among the family of Kahat.

Furthermore, the *Shevet* of Reuven was adjacent to the family of Kahat on one side. On other sides the *Shevet* was next to tribes that were not inclined to join Korach's rebellion. Yet, the positive role models among their other neighbors did not guide these members of Shevet Reuven.

It seems that Rashi maintains that the power of evil to corrupt is greater than the influence of the good to motivate righteous behavior. Every person must struggle to achieve human perfection. Although material instincts pull us toward evil, we can overcome this influence. However, we can never completely eradicate the instinctual component of our personality. We can never assume we are beyond the desire to sin. We can only hope to control our tendency towards evil. The desire remains deep within our personality. The desire to do good is apparently more tentative. It requires the conquest of the intellectual and spiritual over the more basic instinctual. This process is a lifelong struggle. Even in a righteous individual some level of conflict remains.

Rashi's analysis can now be more fully understood. When evil confronts good it is easier for the evil to exert influence over the good. The evildoer has less conflict. The righteous individual lives with conflict. The evil person encourages a return to the instinctual desires. The righteous person is now confronted with a growing internal battle. Sometimes he or she succumbs to the evil desires.

Rashi urges us to choose our neighbors well. We should not assume they will not influence us. Instead we should adopt the premise that we will be influenced and choose neighbors whose influence will be positive.

---

[1] Rabbaynu Shlomo ben Yitzchak (Rashi), *Commentary on Sefer BeMidbar* 16:1.
[2] Rabbaynu Shlomo ben Yitzchak (Rashi), *Commentary on Sefer BeMidbar* 16:1.

And Korach, the son of Yitzhar, the son of Kahat separated himself, along with Datan and Aviram, the sons of Eliav, and Ohn, the son of Pelet – the sons of Reuven. And they arose before Moshe, along with two hundred fifty men of distinction from the Children of Israel – princes of the congregation, those summoned to gatherings, men of fame. (BeMidbar 16:1-2)

Moshe, the Real Deal – part 1

Korach challenges the leadership of Moshe and Aharon

These passages introduce the rebellion led by Korach. The *parasha* is devoted to describing this uprising and its aftermath. The passages explain that Korach recruited an impressive group of co-conspirators. These included representatives from the leadership of the tribe of Reuven, and two hundred fifty members of the nation's leadership. This group joined together to confront Moshe and Aharon and challenge Moshe's authority.

They presented a compelling complaint. They asserted that the entire nation is sacred. Why was one tribe and family selected to perform the service in the *Mishcan* – the Tabernacle? In other words, they questioned the appointment of Aharon and his sons as the *Kohen Gadol* and *Kohanim* – High Priest and priests. They also opposed the selection of the tribe of Leyve – the tribe of Moshe and Aharon – to support and assist the *Kohanim* in their service.

Later, a second criticism emerged. Datan and Aviram asserted that Moshe had not earned the right to be their leader. He redeemed them from Egypt but had not improved their lives. They were in the barren wilderness; they had no comforts or luxuries. What had Moshe accomplished to deserve their loyalty and obedience?[3]

Moshe responded. His response consisted of three elements. He immediately turned to Hashem in prayer.[4] Then, he suggested to his adversaries a test to confirm his appointment of Aharon. Those who believe that they have the right to offer sacrifices should meet with Aharon at the *Mishcan*. Each should offer incense. Hashem will send forth a flame and consume the offerings that He accepts. If their offerings are accepted, then they will have substantiated their claim. Finally, Moshe reasoned with his opponents. He attempted to persuade them to abandon their rebellion.

Moshe failed to dissuade his opponents. The next day, the test was performed. A flame descended and consumed all of those, other than Aharon, who offered incense. At the same time, the earth opened. The other followers of Korach fell into the abys.

Moshe's response begins with prayer

It is noteworthy that Moshe immediately responded to this confrontation with prayer. What was the content of this prayer? The commentators make a number of suggestions. Rashi explains that Moshe prayed on behalf of the nation. He petitioned Hashem to act with mercy.[5] It

---

[3] The criticism of Datan and Aviram is not completely clear from its description in the passages. This interpretation is suggested by Ibn Ezra. See: Rabbaynu Avraham ibn Ezra, *Commentary on Sefer BeMidbar* 16:14.

[4] The Torah describes Moshe falling upon his face. Most commentators understand the phrase as describing Moshe prostrating himself in prayer.

[5] Rabbaynu Shlomo ben Yitzchak (Rashi), *Commentary on Sefer BeMidbar* 16:4.

is apparent from this immediate petition that Moshe viewed this confrontation as a serious sin. His first reaction was not to reason with his opponents. Also, it was not to suggest the test. Instead, his instant response was prayer and supplication. He expected Hashem to swiftly and severely punish the people. In order to avert calamity, Moshe pleaded with Hashem for tolerance. Why was this confrontation so reprehensible? It seems to be far less blasphemous than many of the previous clashes between Moshe and the nation. After all, they were challenging Moshe and not Hashem.[6]

And Moshe said to Korach: Listen to me children of Leyve. Is it a small matter to you that the L-rd of Israel separated you from among the congregation of Israel to draw you close to Him, to perform the service in the Tabernacle of Hashem, and to stand before the congregation to serve them? He drew you close and your brothers, the sons of Leyve, with you. And you seek also the priesthood! (BeMidbar 16:8-11)

Korach's proposal

Moshe's assessment of the seriousness of this confrontation was based upon his understanding of the complaint. This understanding emerges in the above passages. They are a portion of Moshe's response to his adversaries. It does not seem that this reply is consistent with their challenge. Korach and his followers rejected the institutions of leadership. They questioned the legitimacy of a priesthood. They argued that all the people are sanctified. They demanded a more egalitarian system. However, Korach does not describe an alternative to the priesthood. Is he suggesting that the institution should be abolished or is he promoting a more inclusive model? If the latter, what would be the parameters of the new model?

Moshe's reply reveals that he understood that Korach did not wish to eliminate the priesthood. He wished to refashion it into a more inclusive institution. This suggests that the narrative has a "back-story". Knowledge of this background to Korach's criticisms informed his understanding of Korach's designs and shaped Moshe's response. What is this background? Rabbaynu Avraham ibn Ezra provides this information.

And Moshe recorded the words of Hashem. He arose in the morning, he built an altar and twelve monuments corresponding with the twelve tribes of Israel. He sent forth the young men of the Children of Israel and they offered Olah sacrifices and they slaughtered Shelamim sacrifices of bulls to Hashem. (Shemot 24:4-5)

The transfer of the priesthood

These passages describe events that occurred at the Sinai Revelation. These events occurred before the establishment of the *Mishcan*. The tribe of Leyve had not yet been selected to serve in the Tabernacle; Aharon and his sons had not been appointed as *Kohanim*. Who offered the sacrifices described in the passages? Rashi and others explain that these sacrifices were offered by the nation's firstborn sons.[7] The priesthood belonged to the firstborn.[8] How and why was the priesthood transferred from the firstborn to Aharon and his sons?

---

[6] Rashi responds to this issue. He explains that this confrontation was not remarkable. It was not more serious than previous conflicts. However, Moshe was responding to the pattern of behavior that had developed. Each time the nation had sinned it had been punished. Nonetheless, a new confrontation emerged. Moshe feared that with this conflict the nation had exhausted Hashem's indulgence. Ibn Ezra (16:28) suggests that this rebellion was uniquely serious.

The reassignment of the priesthood was one of the outcomes of the sin of the *Egel* – the Golden Calf. Through the nation's retreat into idolatry, its firstborn were disqualified from serving as priests. Priesthood was transferred to the tribe of Leyve – who opposed the worship of the *Egel* – and specifically to Aharon and his sons.

This measure was more than a reassignment of the priesthood from one group to another. The reassignment altered the fundamental nature of the institution of priesthood. The priesthood of the firstborn was inclusive. Every tribe and family participated through its firstborn. The transfer of the priesthood to the tribe of Leyve and the family of Aharon excluded the other tribes and their families from participation.

Moshe understood Korach's vision. He sought to reinstitute the original priesthood of the firstborn. This was the egalitarian and inclusive priesthood he promoted. Korach's argument was that the entire nation is sacred. Therefore, every tribe and family should participate in the priesthood through its firstborn.[9]

And they gathered against Moshe and Aharon and they said to them: It is much for you! For all of the congregation is sacred and Hashem is among them. Why have you elevated yourselves over the assembly of Hashem? (BeMidbar 16:3)

Korach questions Moshe's legitimacy

We will understand Moshe's response of terror and his immediate petition for Hashem's mercy when we appreciate one more aspect of Korach's position. In these passages Korach and is followers articulate their criticism. They argue that the entire nation is sanctified by the presence of Hashem in its midst. They add an accusation. Moshe and Aharon have seized authority over the nation. In other words, Moshe and Aharon were not appointed by Hashem. They have assumed leadership through their own initiative.

Ibn Ezra further describes this criticism. The nation – even Korach and his followers – did not deny Moshe's status as prophet and as Hashem's messenger. They could not. They had witnessed the redemption from Egypt and they had observed Moshe enter into the cloud at Sinai to commune with Hashem. However, they also believed that Moshe was capable of promoting his own interests. They believed that some directives communicated by Moshe were not from Hashem; they were his own innovations. Specifically, they believed that the reassignment of the priesthood from the firstborn to his own tribe and brother's family was Moshe's innovation. They argued that they had not heard Hashem direct this reassignment.[10] In short, the fundamental premise of this rebellion was that the Torah was not entirely the word of Hashem. Some portions were Moshe's own product.

Now, the severity of this rebellion emerges. Korach and his followers denied one of the fundamental principles of the Torah. Rambam – Maimonides – outlines this principle:

The eighth fundamental principle is that the Torah is from Hashem. This principle requires that we believe that this entire Torah that is in our hands today is the Torah that was given to Moshe.

---

[7] Rabbaynu Shlomo ben Yitzchak (Rashi), *Commentary on Sefer Shemot* 24:5.

[8] See *Shemot* 19:22 and comments of Rashi and Ibn Ezra. In this passage the firstborn are described as *Kohanim*.

[9] Rabbaynu Avraham ibn Ezra, *Commentary on Sefer BeMidbar* 16:1-3.

[10] Rabbaynu Avraham ibn Ezra, *Commentary on Sefer BeMidbar* 16:3.

It is in its entirety from Hashem... The Sages said that one who says that the entire Torah is from Hashem except for one passage that was not said by Hashem but by Moshe himself is asserting that the Torah is not from Hashem...

Also, its received interpretation is from Hashem. The succah that we make today, and the lulav, shofar, tzitzit, tefilin, and similar items are those that Hashem communicated to Moshe that he should communicate to us.[11] He was merely acting as a trustworthy messenger in that which he brought (to us) (Rambam, Commentary on the Mishne, Mesechet Sanhedrin 10:1)

Korach's rebellion contested this principle. He and his followers were only willing to acknowledge that those commandments they had heard at Sinai were beyond question. All other commandments were communicated through Moshe. These, they claimed, might be legitimately challenged. In short, they undermined the authenticity of the Torah. They were only interested in challenging the institution of priesthood. However, their argument could be applied to virtually every element of the Torah.

This explains Moshe's terror. It is true that Korach and his followers did not complain against Hashem or challenge Hashem's authority. However, their rebellion was an attack on the legitimacy of the Torah. Moshe recognized the severity of this rebellion and immediately petitioned Hashem for mercy.

And they gathered against Moshe and Aharon and they said to them: You have enough! For all of the nation – every member – are sacred and Hashem is among them. Why have you lifted yourselves above the congregation of Hashem? (BeMidbar 16:3)

Parshat Korach: The Torah's Expectations of its Leaders

1. Korach's true objective

Parshat Korach describes a rebellion initiated and led by Korach against Moshe. The Torah provides conflicting indications as to the issue that was the subject of the dispute. In the above passage Korach protests that every member of the nation is sacred. Therefore, it is not appropriate for Moshe to assume the role of leader. Apparently, Korach was proposing some form of egalitarian, collective leadership in which every member of the nation would participate.

Moshe responds to Korach with a rebuke. However, he does not address Korach's criticism. Instead, he rebukes Korach for pursuing power and authority. He says that, as a member of the Tribe of Leyve, Korach has been provided with a special sanctity and a degree of prestige. Korach should be satisfied with this appointment and not seek further honor and prestige. It is apparent from Moshe's rebuke, that he suspected Korach's democratic pronouncements were designed to enlist the support of the nation. He was hiding his true desire within a message he believed would resonate with the people and secure their sympathy.

---

[11] Rambam explains in the introduction to his commentary on the Mishne that not every detail of the Torah's interpretation was revealed to Moshe. Much of the Oral Law was developed by the Sages. However, Moshe did receive the basic interpretation of the Torah's commandments. In the above, he is not proposing that out *tefilin* are the same as those worn by Moshe. Our Sages dispute many of the design details of *tefilin*. He means that our *tefilin* are basically the same as Moshe's.

Rashi quotes our Sages who explain that Moshe correctly interpreted Korach's motives. Korach observed that Moshe had assumed the position of ruler and Aharon had been appointed by Moshe as Kohen Gadol – High Priest. He expected – based upon his place within the lineage of his family – to be appointed as its leader. Instead, Moshe selected Eli'tzafan for this post. This infuriated Korach and resulted in Korach developing and launching a conspiracy whose aim was to unseat Moshe.[12]

With the assistance of Rashi's comments a clear image emerges of Korach's true objectives and character. Korach combined two qualities. First, he was ambitious and eager to achieve authority, power, and honor. In other words, he wished to dominate others and be glorified. Second, he was an astute, shrewd but cynical student of human nature. He understood the human desire to be free from the demands of authority and the appeal of an egalitarian political system. He used his understanding of human nature to further his own personal ends.

2. Modern parallels to Korach's rebellion

Korach's strategy has many modern parallels. One example is the strategy employed by Lenin and the communist leadership to overthrow the Tzar and seize power. Lenin preached an extreme egalitarian approach to government and economics. He promised that political and economic power and influence would lie with the people. He enlisted the population in his campaign to overthrow a despotic dictator. However, when victorious, Lenin introduced his own version of dictatorship. Although he described it as the dictatorship of the proletariat, it was not markedly different from the dictatorship of the Romanov aristocracy which it replaced. Countless other revolutions have followed the same path. These include the overthrow of the Shah in order to replace him with Iran's current theocracy, and the overthrow of Rhodesia's minority white leadership to be replaced by Robert Mugabe's ruthless dictatorship of Zimbabwe. Korach and these other rulers shared the realization that the fundamental desire for freedom can be manipulated by the unscrupulous leader in order to further his own end and even to ascend to absolute power over his followers.

Raban Gamliel the son of Ribbi Yehudah the Prince says, "…. All that toil on behalf of the community should toil for them for the sake of heaven. Then, the merit of their fathers will support them and their righteousness will stand for eternity." (Tractate Avot 2:2)

3. Two archetypes of leadership

In the above mishne Raban Gamliel extols the virtue of serving one's community. However, he stipulates that one's efforts on behalf of the community must be for the sake of heaven. Raban Gamliel explains that if a person serves the community for the sake of heaven, then the "merits of their fathers" will sustain these efforts and contribute to their success.

The exact meaning of Raban Gamliel's message is not clear. Whose fathers' merits will sustain the community worker and leader? Is it possible to understand how these merits will sustain the worker's efforts?

Rabbaynu Ovadia Bertinoro offers a rather simple and straightforward explanation of Raban Gamliel's comments. He explains that the "fathers" to whom Raban Gamliel refers are the righteous individuals of previous generations. Based on this interpretation, he explains Raban Gamliel's message.

---

[12] Rabbaynu Shlomo ben Yitzchak (Rashi), Commentary on Sefer BeMidbar 16:1.

There are two archetypes of community leaders. One type of community leader is primarily focused on their own self-promotion. The efforts and accomplishments of such leaders have no essential connection to one another. Each leader's main objective is self- glorification. If one continues his predecessor's work this is because he views this strategy as an expedient for securing his own recognition. However, on a more fundamental level each worked solely for the purpose of securing his own legacy. Continuity of leadership only occurs on a fundamental level among the second type of leaders. These are leaders who share a single great purpose and end. This is Raban Gamliel's message. A leader who works for the sake of heaven – in order to advance the community's spiritual life – continues the work of countless generations of righteous ancestors. This leader is linked with a past extending into remote history. He is furthering a mission and vision that was shared by those who preceded him and will be continued by those who will follow.[13]

4. Leadership built upon the merit of previous generations

Because they labored for the sake of heaven, the true leaders of previous generations accrued merit. Raban Gamliel asserts that one of the rewards for their merit is that their efforts will not be fruitless and their zeal for their mission will not be in vain. Other leaders will replace them and continue their work. These new leaders – if authentic in their motives – will be sustained by Hashem. This is a reward to the generations of devoted leaders whose mission the new leader continues.

5. A fundamental difference between serving the community and other mitzvot

Raban Gamliel's exhortation seems to contradict another dictum of the Sages. The Sages assert that, of course, it is best to perform commandments for the proper reason. However, even when the commandment is executed for personal reasons, it has value. By habituating oneself in the performance of the commandment one will hopefully elevate oneself to performing the commandment for its proper purpose.[14] It seems that Raban Gamliel does not apply this reasoning to leadership. A leader should lead and toil on behalf of the community only for the sake of heaven. Raban Gamliel does not seem to believe that even a self-centered leader who toils for the community in order to secure acknowledgment and recognition is acceptable because with time and experience he may evolve into a more ideal leader.

Once he (Avraham) recognized and knew he began to respond to the people of Ur Kasdim and to debate them. He said that you do not travel the road of truth. He broke the idols and began to make known to the nation that it is only appropriate to serve the Lord of the universe. To Him it is appropriate to prostrate oneself, offer sacrifices and libations so that all future generations will recognize him. (Maimonides, Laws of Idolatry 1:3)

6. What commandment does the leader fulfill through his efforts?

One possible explanation for Raban Gamliel's exclusion of leaders and community workers from the principle of the Sages is suggested by the above comments of Maimonides. There is no specific mitzvah in the Torah that commands a person to work on behalf of the community or assume the role of a leader. However in the above excerpt from Maimonides' biographical sketch of Avraham, he describes Avraham's emergence as a leader and teacher of

---

[13] Rabbaynu Ovadia Bertinoro, Commentary the Mishne, Mesechet Avot 2:2.
[14] Mesechet Pesacim 50b.

humanity. This raises an interesting issue. What compelled Avraham to assume this role? Why was Avraham determined to teach the truth to others and reform humanity from its idolatrous practices? If Avraham's motivations can be defined, then perhaps we can identify the mitzvah that latter-era leaders fulfill.

It seems reasonable to assume that Avraham was motivated by his love of Hashem. This love was so intense that he felt compelled to share with others his discovery of Hashem and to draw them toward His service and worship. This conclusion also suggests that the commandment that compels latter-era leaders to assume the burden of community leadership is the commandment to love Hashem.

7. The self-serving leader does not fulfill any commandment

Now Raban Gamliel's position makes sense. When a person performs a typical commandment, even if the person's motives are less than ideal, the commandment is fulfilled. For example, if a person performs the commandment of dwelling in a succah on Succot because he enjoys spending time outdoors, the perimeters of the commandment are met and the mitzvah is fulfilled. In other words, whether the person dwelled in the succah because he wished to fulfill the Torah commandment or because he enjoys the outdoors, he has dwelled in the succah. The act required by the mitzvah has been performed and thereby the commandment fulfilled. It makes sense to encourage the person to perform the commandment for even a personal motive. He will become accustomed to performing the mitzvah and hopefully, in time, his motives will become more ideal.

This reasoning does not apply to the commandment to love Hashem. The mitzvah of love of Hashem is fulfilled consequential to one's encounter with the Creator. It is a response to this encounter. The mitzvah is not, in-essence, a performance. It is an experience of adoration and devotion. Love is – by its very definition – a selfless experience. True love requires selfless devotion to the object of one's adoration. Self-interest and true love are antithetical to one another. Therefore, the mitzvah is not even subject to fulfillment in response to a personal motive.

As Avraham demonstrated, authentic leadership is an expression of and derives its legitimacy from the commandment of love of Hashem. Therefore, leadership is only the fulfillment of this commandment when it is motivated by and is a pure expression of this love. If one leads for personal advantage and gain, no Torah commandment is fulfilled through the leadership.[15]

And Korach, the son of Yitzhar, the son of K'hat, the son of Leyve, with Datan and Aviram, the sons of Eliav, and Ohn, the son of Pelet, sons of Reuven, took men and they rose up before of Moshe, with certain of the children of Israel, two hundred and fifty men. They were princes of the congregation, the elect men of the assembly, men of renown. And they assembled themselves together against Moshe and against Aharon, and said to them: You take too much upon you. For all the congregation are holy, every one of them, and Hashem is among them, why lift up yourselves above the assembly of Hashem? (BeMidbar 16:1-3)

---

[15] Compare to Torat Avot on Pirke Avot 2:2.

Fools Rush In

1. The role of the tribe of Reuven in the Korach rebellion

Parshat Korech discusses the Korech rebellion. Korech was a member of the tribe – the *shevet* – of Leyve. He had aspired to be the *kohen gadol* – the high priest – or to be appointed to some other position of authority. He realized that he would not be appointed to any of these positions. In response, he instigated a rebellion against Moshe and Aharon.[16] He succeeded in attracting followers. A large portion of these were members of the *shevet* of Reuven.

What attracted members of Shevet Reuven to join Korach? Our Sages present a number of suggestions. Rashi explains that in the wilderness the encampment of the clan of Shevet Leyve to which Korach belonged was adjacent to Shevet Reuven. Rashi's comment suggests that this incident should impress upon us the impact of our social environment upon our attitudes and behaviors. The members of Shevet Reuven were exposed to ongoing instigation against Moshe and Aharon. With time, this disgruntlement was incorporated into their own outlook. So, when Korach launched his rebellion, these members of Shevet Reuven fell into line behind Korach. Extended exposure led to their internalization of Korach's values. They believed that he was fighting their own fight.

Others note that Shevet Reuven had its own reasons for feeling excluded from the perceived aristocracy of the nation. Reuven, their ancestor, was the first born of Yaakov. In ancient societies the first born was regarded as the most significant of the father's progeny. Yet, the priesthood had been awarded to Aharon and his descendants.[17] A double portion in the land had been awarded to the descendants of Yosef and not to those of Reuven.[18] These complaints suggest that they might also have been disgruntled over Shevet Yehudah's election to kingship and by the creation of a leadership of elders selected from all of the tribes. Every position of authority or esteem to which Shevet Reuven could aspire had been assigned to some other *shevet* or group.

2. The tribe of Reuven felt sympathetic for Korach

An interesting question arises regarding the members of Shevet Reuven who joined Korach's rebellion. Did they actually assume that their complaints were valid? As Nachmanides observes, it is difficult to believe that they opposed Moshe because a double portion in the Land of Israel was awarded to the descendants of Yosef. Moshe had not transferred this privilege of the firstborn son to Yosef. Yaakov had made this decision.[19] All of the complaints of Shevet Reuven seem to be examples of "sour grapes" rather than actionable complaints.

Although their complaints may not have been actionable, they did influence these members of Shevet Reuven. Because of their various perceived injuries the members of the *shevet* were sympathetically disposed to the protests of Korach. When Korach objected that he and other members of his *shevet* had been passed over for positions of authority or prestige, members from the tribe of Reuven felt deeply their pain and frustration. They harbored similar

---

[16] Midrash Rabbah BeMidbar 18:16.

[17] Rav Menachem Mendel Kasher, *Torah Shelymah* vol 11, p 11.

[18] Rabbaynu Chizkiya ben Manoach (Chizkuni), *Commentary on Sefer BeMidbar*, 16:2.

[19] Rabbaynu Moshe ben Nachman (Ramban), *Commentary on Sefer BeMidbar* 16:1.

feelings of rejection and victimization. They identified with Korach and embraced his crusade. They felt that they were brothers in a just fight to redress a terrible injustice.

3. The challenge of monitoring one's own objectivity

Viewing the incident in this manner, an important lesson regarding human nature and behavior emerges. Shevet Reuven had accepted its place within the nation. It understood that it could not be changed. However, acceptance did not translate into contentment. The intellectual acceptance was accompanied by a hidden resentment. This resentment predisposed these members of Shevet Reuven to being co-opted into Korach's rebellion.

The student of the Torah can have two responses to this incident. The student can view the behaviors of these members of Shevet Reuven as aberrant. This reader assesses the behavior of this group as atypical and motivated by a unique set of circumstances. A strange coincidence arose between Korach's message and resentments harbored in the hearts of these individuals. If interpreted in this manner, the account has little practical significance. It is essentially an account of an unusual event in our ancient history.

Alternatively, the student can realize that the Torah's account speaks to the challenge that every person faces in judging the objectivity of one's own decisions. Every person has hidden passions, resentments, and hurts. We each have feelings that are difficult to acknowledge and reside in that obscured area of our minds barely accessible to our consciousness. Can we be sure that important decisions that we make are not influenced by these feelings?

Yehoshua the son of Perachyah said: Make for yourself a teacher; acquire for yourself a colleague. Be accustomed to judge each person favorably. (Tractate Avot 1:6)

4. Seeking the counsel of the wise

Our Sages questioned the capacity of the individual to judge of one's own objectivity. The mishne in Tractate Avot teaches that a person should appoint for oneself a teacher and acquire a friend or confidant. Commenting on this teaching, Rabbaynu Menachem Me'eri notes that even a scholar who cannot find a colleague whose knowledge and wisdom surpasses his own must appoint for himself a teacher. What is the role of this teacher who is the lesser of the scholars? Me'eri explains that this teacher provides his student with objective feedback. Me'eri points out that even the wisest king needs advisors to critique his decisions and policies.[20]

The comments of the Sages provide us with invaluable advice. We should not trust our own decisions to be objective. We should beware of the possibility that we are guided by hidden passions or resentments. We should learn from the behavior of these members of Shevet Reuven that we too can make important decisions based upon influences of which we are barely aware. But we have recourse. We can consult with a mentor who can objectively critique our decision.

5. Not being hasty

There is a relevant story told about Rav Chaim of Volozhin and his teacher the Gaon of Vilna. Rav Chaim established the famous yeshiva of Volozhin which became one of the most prominent institutions of Torah learning in modern times. His decision to devote himself to his vision of creating this institution was the result of countless hours of careful evaluation.

---

[20] Rabbaynu Menachem Me'eri, *Bait HaBechirah*, Mesechet Avot 1:6.

However, before finalizing his decision and acting on his vision, he consulted his teacher the Gaon. He traveled to Vilna and passionately shared with the Gaon his vision and his plans. The Gaon listened carefully but refused to provide Rav Chaim with feedback.

Rav Chaim departed assuming that his teacher had some hesitancy that prevented him from endorsing the initiative. Rav Chaim reconsidered his plans. He carefully studied his objectives and the suitability of the institution he envisions for meeting these objectives. After carefully reconsidering his plan and confident of its soundness, he again traveled to his teacher. Again, he calmly and systematically explained to the Goan his plan and his reasons for undertaking this initiative.

This time the Gaon immediately agreed with Rav Chaim's plan. This was not the response Rav Chaim expected. Astounded, he asked his teacher what had caused his previous hesitancy to be replaced by eager approval. The Gaon explained that Rav Chaim's original presentation was impassioned. This suggested to him that Rav Chaim – moved by his deep passion – might not have carefully considered his plans, their advisability and feasibility. This time he presented his proposal calmly and systematically. His dispassionate presentation suggested to the Goan that the plan was well formulated and thorough.[21]

The Goan recognized that our passions are part of our wiring. They do influence our thinking and actions. Sometimes we are not aware of this influence. Therefore, his initial unstated message to Rav Chaim was to slow down, calm down, and conduct a dispassionate analysis of his plans. Even Rav Chaim – a world class scholar and intensely righteous person – was human and capable of being subtly misled by hidden motives. The Goan played the role recommended of the teacher in Tractate Avot.

Now Korach, the son of YItzhar, the son of K'hat, the son of Levy, with Datan and Aviram, the sons of Eliav, and Ohn, the son of Pelet, sons of Reuven, took men. And they rose up before Moshe, with certain men of the children of Israel, two hundred and fifty men – princes of the congregation, the elect men of the assembly, men of renown. And they assembled themselves together against Moshe and against Aharon, and said unto them: You take too much upon you, for all the congregation is holy, every one of them, and Hashem is among them. Why do you lift yourselves above the assembly of Hashem? (BeMidbar 16:1-3)

And Moshe said unto Korach: Hear now, you sons of Levy. Is it but a small thing to you, that the G-d of Israel has separated you from the congregation of Israel, to bring you near to Himself, to do the service of the Mishcan of Hashem, and to stand before the congregation to minister unto them, and that He has brought you near, and all your brethren the sons of Levy with you? And will you seek the priesthood also? (BeMidbar 16:8-10)

1. Korach's rebellion

Parshat Korach describes the rebellion against Moshe led by Korach and his lieutenants Datan and Aviram. The above passages describe Korach's complaints against Moshe. Korach challenges Moshe's role as leader of Bnai Yisrael. Korach asserts that the entire nation is sacred.

---

[21] Rav Y. Hershkowitz, *Torat Chaim on Pirke Avot*, pp. 380-381.

Every member partakes of the sanctity conferred upon Bnai Yisrael. Therefore, the proposition that Moshe is somehow superior and entitled to impose his will upon the nation is absurd. In short, Korach proposed political anarchy.

However, this was the sole issue that Korach raised. In his response Moshe criticizes Korach for seeking the role of *Kohen* – priest. Apparently, Korach's preference for anarchy not limited to the realm of the political. He also proposed religious anarchy. Every person should participate equally in the service of Hashem. All should share equal access to the *Mishcan* and to participation in the sacrificial service.

And he spoke unto Korach and unto all his company, saying: In the morning Hashem will show who are His, and who is holy, and will cause him to come near unto Him. Him whom He may choose He will cause to come near unto Him. Do this. Take you censors, Korach, and all his company, and put fire therein, and put incense upon them before Hashem tomorrow. And it shall be that the man whom Hashem chooses, he shall be holy. You take too much upon you, sons of Levy. (BeMidbar 16:5-7)

2. Moshe's response

Moshe suggests to Korach a contest to be conducted the next morning. Korach and his followers should prepare an offering of incense. The exact nature of this contest is not completely clear from the passages. There are a number of disputes among the commentators regarding its details. However, it seems that Moshe suggested that Korach, his followers, and Aharon each prepare incense offerings. This offering can only be presented by a *Kohen*. Furthermore, the people were very aware of the consequences for offering the incense in an inappropriate manner. The nation had recently mourned the deaths of Nadav and Avihu.[22] Nadav and Avihu had been consumed by a fire sent forth by Hashem in response to their unauthorized offering of incense.

According to Korach, all of the people were equal in their sanctity and all were equally entitled to participate in divine service. Therefore, all of the offerings presented by the participants should be accepted by Hashem. Presumably, the acceptance of their offerings would be demonstrated by some sign – apparently a flame that would descend from Hashem and consume the incense. However, if only Aharon is the authentic and legitimate *Kohen*, then only his offering will be accepted. Of course, the other participants will place their lives at risk. When the flame descends and consumes Aharon's offering, these pretenders may experience the fate of Nadav and Avihu. The flame that consumes Aharon's offering may consume them.

Most of the commentators agree that Moshe wished only to motivate Korach and his followers to reconsider their criticisms. He anticipated that they would not wish to risk their lives on behalf of a proposition that they probably realized was unfounded. In other words Moshe did not actually intend to harm Korach and his followers. He suggested this contest merely in order to force the insurgents to reconsider their position.[23]

And Moshe was very angry, and said to Hashem: Do not respect their offering. I have not taken one donkey from them. Neither have I hurt one of them. And Moshe said unto Korach: You and all of your congregation should be before Hashem – you, and they, and Aharon, to-morrow. And

---

[22] Rabbaynu Shlomo ben Yitzchak (Rashi), *Commentary on Sefer BeMidbar* 16:6.
[23] Rabbaynu Shlomo ben Yitzchak (Rashi), *Commentary on Sefer BeMidbar* 16:5.

take every man his fire-pan, and put incense upon them, and bring before Hashem every man his fire-pan, two hundred and fifty fire-pans – you also, and Aharon, each his fire-pan. (BeMidbar 16:15-17)

3. Moshe's anger

Next, Moshe summons Datan and Aviram. There is a difference of opinion between the commentators regarding Moshe's purpose in summoning his adversaries. One opinion is that Moshe summoned them to appear before the *Bait Din* – the court. His intent was to employ the courts to resolve the issue.[24] Rashi suggests that Moshe did not summon Datan and Aviram for the purpose of confronting them. Instead, he wished to make peace with them. He hoped that through a face-to-face meeting he would resolve the conflict. Again, it is clear from Moshe's behavior that he was not interested in harming or punishing his adversaries. Instead, he wished to resolve the conflict and deescalate the tension without recourse to force and without harming his opponents.[25]

Datan and Aviram refused to respond to Moshe's summons. This evokes a change in Moshe's attitude. As the above passages explain, Moshe becomes angry with his opponents. He prays to Hashem to reject their incense offerings. Furthermore, he instructs Korach and his followers to immediately implement the test he had previously described. Moshe is no longer using the prospect of the contest to induce his opponents to reconsider their positions. He is now directing them to proceed with the contest. In other words, Moshe is demanding that the insurgents execute a test that he realizes will result in their death.

This is not the response that would be expected of Moshe. This is not the first time he has been subjected to the criticism and even abuse by the people. While still in Egypt, the people questioned Moshe's effectiveness. At the Reed Sea, they suspected that Moshe would not be able to deliver them from the pursuing Egyptians. In the wilderness, the nation had repeatedly complained to Moshe. Sometimes the people came to Moshe with understandable demands. At other times their demands and complaints were more frivolous and unwarranted. The one constant theme in their complaints is dissatisfaction with Moshe's leadership. Yet, on these many occasions, Moshe did not become angry with the people. Even on those occasions on which Hashem responded with anger, Moshe interceded and pleaded with Hashem to treat the people with mercy and compassion. Why in this instance did Moshe become angry and invite the destruction of his opponents?

And Moshe sent to call Datan and Aviram, the sons of Eliav and they said: We will not come up. Is it a small thing that you have brought us up out of a land flowing with milk and honey, to kill us in the wilderness, but you must also rule over us? Moreover you have not brought us into a land flowing with milk and honey, nor given us inheritance of fields and vineyards. If you will put out the eyes of these men, we will not come up. (BeMidbar 16:12-14)

4. Datan and Aviram's response to Moshe's summons

In order to answer this question, Datan and Aviram's response to Moshe's summons must be considered and analyzed. Datan and Aviram immediately refuse to appear before Moshe.

---

[24] Rabbaynu Yonatan ben Uzial, *Tirgum on Sefer BeMidbar* 16:12.
[25] Rabbaynu Shlomo ben Yitzchak (Rashi), *Commentary on Sefer BeMidbar* 16:12.

However, they then present an extensive list of charges against Moshe. They outline three basic charges. First, they criticize Moshe for taking Bnai Yisrael out of Egypt – a bountiful and resource-rich country. They reiterate that Moshe does not deserve to be leader of the people. Finally, they posit that Moshe has failed in the very mission that he had accepted upon himself. He will not bring them into the Land of Israel and he will not give Bnai Yisrael possession of the Land.

Is there a connection and relationship between these various charges or are Datan and Aviram merely creating a list of every imagined failing? Rav Yitzchak Zev Soloveitchik *Zt"l* suggests that all of these charges express a single theme. What is this theme?

5. Moshe's role as leader

In Moshe's response to Datan and Aviram's rejection of his summons, Moshe makes an interesting assertion. He declares that he has never taken a donkey from anyone. Korach and his lieutenants challenged Moshe's authority and accused him of being a failed leader. They did not accuse him of stealing. To what accusation was Moshe responding when he declared his respect of the people's property?

Maimonides explains that a king has the authority to levy and collect taxes from the people.[26] Also, he asserts that Moshe had the authority of a king.[27] Apparently, Moshe was declaring that rather than imposing his will upon the people and forcing them to submit to his authority, he had ruled very benevolently. He had the right to levy and collect taxes but he had not requisitioned from the people even a single donkey.

Now, Datan and Aviram's charges can be better understood and their underlying theme becomes evident. A king is responsible for the welfare of the nation. He is obligated to nurture the nation's spiritual and material wellbeing. He is the enforcer of moral standards and he leads the nation in battle.[28] Datan and Aviram's charges were not merely that Moshe was a poor leader. They assessed Moshe by the standards appropriate to a king. He took the nation out of Egypt – a rich, fertile country. He seized the authority of a king but he has not and will not provide for the nation's material wellbeing. He will not bring them into the Land of Israel and he will not lead the nation in the campaign against the Land's inhabitants. As a king, he has been a failure!

Still, Moshe's response is not explained. Why was Moshe unwilling to overlook this complaint? Why did he insist on punishing his opponents?

6. The obligations to respect parents, teachers, and the king

The Torah directs us to respect various individuals. These include parents, teachers, and the King of Israel. However, there is a fundamental difference between these three obligations of respect. Maimonides explains that a teacher can excuse his students from this obligation.[29] Also, a parent can forego elements of his right to the respect of his children.[30] However, the king has no authority over the duty of his subjects to treat him with respect. He cannot forego this right

---

[26] Rabbaynu Moshe ben Maimon (Rambam) *Mishne Torah*, Hilchot Melachim 4:1.

[27] Rabbaynu Moshe ben Maimon (Rambam) *Mishne Torah*, Hilchot Bait HaBechirah 6:11.

[28] Rabbaynu Moshe ben Maimon (Rambam) *Mishne Torah*, Hilchot Melachim 4:10.

[29] Rabbaynu Moshe ben Maimon (Rambam) *Mishne Torah*, Hilchot Talmud Torah 5:11.

[30] Rabbaynu Moshe ben Maimon (Rambam) *Mishne Torah*, Hilchot Mamrim 6:8.

and any attempt to do so is ineffective. He does not relieve his subjects of their obligations to treat the king with respect and reverence.

Based on this principle, Rav Soloveitchik explains Moshe's response to Datan and Aviram. In the past Moshe had been subjected to harsh criticism. However, in each instance the people were responding to a real or perceived need. If they questioned Moshe's leadership, they did so as an expression of their frustration with the suffering they believed that they were enduring or the danger that they perceived. It is true that in some of these instances the complaints and criticisms included harsh, even scathing, assessments of Moshe's leadership. However, these challenges to Moshe's authority were not the fundamental element or focus of the people's grievances.

Datan and Aviram's charges were different from these previous criticisms. They directly and intentionally attacked Moshe's leadership. They challenged his authority as king. This was the essence of their attack. Moshe was not permitted to overlook or forgive this behavior. As one appointed by Hashem to serve as king of the nation, he was not authorized to overlook this attack. A king is not permitted to absolve his subjects from the responsibility to treat him with respect.[31]

7. Respect for an individual and respect for an institution

Moshe's anger was not limited to Datan and Aviram. It extended to Korach and his other followers. He directed them to offer the incense. Moshe knew that the execution of this test would result in the death of his opponents. Datan and Aviram had directly attacked his authority as king. He had no alternative to punishing them. He did not have the right to overlook their behavior. Why did Moshe's anger extend to Korach and his other followers?

It is very possible that Moshe determined that there was little or no distinction between Datan and Aviram, Korach, and the other members of the insurgency. True, Datan and Aviram had expressed themselves more explicitly. However, the same message was central to Korach's accusations. He charged Moshe with seizing control of the people and asserting an unjustified and inappropriate authority. However, there is an additional element that was fundamental to Korach's rebellion.

As explained above, a father and teacher can forego aspects of the respect and reverence due to them. A king does not have this authority. This distinction suggests a fundamental difference between the respect paid a parent and teacher compared to the respect due the king. The parent and the teacher are the specific objects of the respect. Because the respect of the child and student is shown to the specific individual parent and teacher respectively, these individuals can forego aspects of the respect. In other words, the parent and teacher have a right to be treated with respect and reverence. As a right, it is subject to the preferences of the person who is endowed with the right. The parent or teacher – the individuals who possess the right – can forgo it.

Apparently, the king lacks the authority to forego the respect due to him because the respect is not rendered to the individual king but to the institution and authority of the position. In other words, the individual king is, in a practical sense, the object of the respect and

---

[31] Rav Yitzchak Zev Soloveitchik, *Chidushai HaGRIZ on T'NaCH and Aggadah*, Parshat Korach #130.

reverence. However, it is not truly the individual king that the subjects are obligated to respect. They are obligated to demonstrate respect and reverence for the institution of kingship and the authority associated with the institution. The king cannot forgo the respect due him, because this respect is not a right with which the individual king is endowed.

8. The unique element of Korach's rebellion

Datan and Aviram rebelled against Moshe as king. Because they attacked the institution of kingship, Moshe was not empowered to forbear or overlook their behavior. The political structure of a society or community is the basis for order and peace. Without political institutions, society cannot function. Therefore, basic and fundamental respect for these institutions is essential and it is not in the power of the person who occupies the position of authority to forego the respect due the institution.

The same reasoning applies to the *Kahunah* – the priesthood. Korach and his followers did not attack Aharon; they decried the legitimacy of the very institution of *Kahunah*. Moshe and Aharon repeatedly overlooked and forgave personal attacks against them. However, they were duty-bound to uphold respect for the institutions they represented. They could not merely forgive Korach and his followers – who attached the institution of *Kahunah*.

"And he (Moshe) spoke to Korach and all of his congregation saying, "In the morning Hashem will make known who is His and who is sanctified He will draw close to Himself. Who He chooses, He will draw close to Himself." (BeMidbar 16:5)

Should we devote time to the study of mussar (moral discipline)? It would be best by defining the term mussar. But the term is not easy to accurately define. Mussar is not so much a subject matter as it is a process of study with a specific objective. It is easiest to understand the term mussar in relation to this objective. At a basic level, mussar is study directed towards motivating the student to conduct himself in everyday life in a manner consistent with the Torah. In other words, mussar responds to a specific problem. Knowing how to behave does not necessarily translate into proper behavior. A student can study Torah and understand halacha and the expectations of the Torah but yet encounter difficulty in converting knowledge into action. Mussar is designed to address this issue. It is designed to provide encouragement and the motivation needed to advance from knowledge to action.

Based on this definition, it seems clear that the study of mussar is invaluable. But there is substantial controversy regarding the study of mussar. In fact, various of the Roshei Yeshiva of the famous Volozhin Yeshiva discouraged students in the Yeshiva from studying mussar. At least one even referred to the study of mussar as a distraction from the study of Torah.[32]

This controversy is difficult to understand. What is the basis for this discord regarding the study of mussar?

There is an interesting account of a debate between Rav Chaim Soloveitchik and Rebbi Yitzchok Belzer regarding the study of mussar that may illuminate the issue. Rav Chaim Soloveitchik was one of the last Roshei Yeshiva of the Volozhin Yeshiva. As mentioned above, the study of mussar was not encouraged by the Yeshiva. Rebbi Yitzchok Belzer appealed to Rav Chaim to reconsider the Yeshiva's stance. He supported his arguments with a comment from the

---

[32] Rav Y. Hershkowitz, *Torat Chaim on Pirke Avot*, p 2, note 3.

Talmud in Tractate Berachot. The Talmud explains that a person should always incite his yetzer ha'tov – his good inclination against his yetzer ha'ra – his evil inclination. If a person cannot overcome his yetzer ha'ra by this means, then he should immerse himself in the study of Torah. If this measure is not effective, he should read the Shema. As a final resort – when all else fails – the person should contemplate his day of death.[33] Rebbi Yitzchok Belzer believed that this final measure represents a mussar approach. Therefore, it is clear that the Sages of the Talmud endorsed the study and methods of mussar.

Rav Chaim pointed out that there is another text from the Talmud in Tractate Succah that seems to contradict the comments of the Sages in Tractate Berachot. The Sages comment that if a person encounters the yetzer ha'ra, the person should take his yetzer ha'ra to the bait midrash.[34] In other words, the best response to the yetzer ha'ra is to change one's focus and concentrate on the study of Torah. Rav Chaim explained that the two texts do not contradict each other. In order to resolve the apparent contradiction between the texts, Rav Chaim offered an analogy. If a person is suffering from digestive problems, a doctor might prescribe castor oil. But for a healthy person, it would not be advisable to take this medication. In fact, use of this medication would make the healthy person ill. Based on this analogy, Rav Chaim explained the two texts. I person who is spiritually ill needs to be treated. The treatment for this ill person may include counseling the person to more carefully consider his mortality – a motivational or mussar approach. But a person who is healthy should instead respond to the impulses of his yetzer ha'ra by focusing on Torah study. For this healthy person, contemplation of mortality – or the study of mussar may very well have a negative psychological impact.[35]

It is not our purpose here to remark on this debate between Rav Chaim and Rebbi Yitzchok Belzer. But the debate does provide an insight into the nature of mussar. Two observations emerge from this debate. First, Rav Chaim understood that there is a clear difference between the study of Torah – in its purist form – and the study of mussar. The objective in pure Torah study is to understand the Torah. Once the student shifts the emphasis of his study from seeking an understanding of the Torah to other more personal objectives, the student is no longer studying Torah in the ideal manner. Second, it is apparent from Rav Chaim's analysis that the very nature of mussar dictates that it cannot be regarded as ideal Torah study. Because the objective of mussar is specifically, the reworking of the personality and the evocation of personal motives to deny the urges of the yetzer ha'ra, it diverges from pure Torah study – devoted to seeking a deeper understanding to the Torah.

Rav Dov Katz, in his study of the mussar movement, objects to the perspective articulated by Rav Chaim. He argues that the Torah is not just a work of law. It includes a lengthy account of the lives of the Avot – the forefathers. Other narratives discuss the redemption of Bnai Yisrael from Egypt and their experiences in the wilderness – including their various shortcomings. These narratives are sources of personal moral instruction. Rav Katz asks, "Is this not mussar?"[36]

Maimonides seems to echo this sentiment. He explains that one of the fundamental principles of Torah Judaism is that the entire Torah was revealed to Moshe at Sinai. He explains

---

[33] Mesechet Berachot 5a.
[34] Mesechet Succah 50b.
[35] Rav Y. Hershkowitz, *Torat Chaim on Pirke Avot*, p 2.
[36] Rav Dov Katz, Tnuat Ha*Mussar*, pp. 22-24.

that this revelation includes not only the laws but also the narrative portion of the Torah. He adds that every element of the Torah – including the narrative sections – is the source of unimaginable wisdom.[37] If we accept the contention that mussar is the essential objective of these narrative section, then Maimonides' comments seem to confirm Rav Katz's contention that Torah and mussar are inseparable.

This week's parasha offers an opportunity to explore more carefully the contention that the Torah itself includes accounts that are akin to mussar in their very nature. The parasha discusses the rebellion of Korach and his followers. The Torah explains that Korach and his followers objected to Moshe's assignment of positions of leadership to himself, Aharon and to others. It seems that Korach and his cohorts coveted these various positions and wished to challenge Moshe's right to appoint the leadership. Moshe attempted to reason with his opponents. The Torah does not explain in detail these conversations or debates. But Rashi provides a description of one of Moshe's responses to this uprising. Moshe explained that Hashem created the universe with boundaries. For example, night is separated from day. It is impossible to convert the day to night or the night to day. Similarly Hashem created boundaries within Bnai Yisrael. He separated Aharon to be the Kohen Gadol. Just as the boundary between day and night cannot be opposed, so too, the status conferred on Aharon cannot be reversed.[38]

Rashi's account of Moshe's appeal is difficult to understand. It seems that Moshe's main point is that he did not appoint Aharon as Kohen Gadol. He was merely following Hashem's directive. He is telling Korach and his followers that there is nothing to be gained by opposing him – Moshe. Hashem is the source of Aharon's appointment. But if this is Moshe's appeal, his reference to the boundaries that Hashem established between night and day is superfluous. Why did Moshe stress the immutable nature of these boundaries?

In order to more fully understand Rashi's comments, let us consider a related issue. The Torah commands us not to covet. We are also commanded to not desire the possessions of another person. These two commandments are included in the Decalogue. Maimonides discusses both of these commandments in his code of law the Mishne Torah. We would expect these two mitzvot to be included in the section of Maimonides' code that deals with midot – character traits. But instead, Maimonides incorporates the discussion of these mitzvot in the laws concerning robbery. Maimondes provides an insight into his reasoning. Before we consider Maimondies' comments on this issue, we must clarify some terms. The prohibition against desiring a friend's property is violated once one begins to contemplate how one might pressure his friend to part with the desired object. The mitzvah prohibiting coveting is violated if this plan is put into action. Based on these definitions, Maimonides explains the desire leads to coveting. If the pressure does not lead to the friend selling or delivering the desired object, the coveting leads to robbery.[39] It seems that this reasoning provides the rational for placing the mitzvot prohibiting desiring and coveting in the laws concerning robbery.

However, Maimonides' assertion that desiring a friend's property may ultimately leads to theft seems to be extreme. It is possible to imagine the unfolding of the scenario that

---

[37] R' Moshe ben Maimon (Rambam) *Commentary on the Mishne*, Mesechet Sanhedrin 10:1.

[38] Rabbaynu Shlomo ben Yitzchak (Rashi), *Commentary on Sefer BeMidbar* 16:5.

[39] R' Moshe ben Maimon (Rambam) *Mishne Torah*, Hilchot Gezaylah Ve'Aveydah 1:9-12.

Maimonides describes. But it does not seem that this scenario is completely probable. What is the point in suggesting a scenario that seems somewhat remote?

Perhaps, Maimonides' point is that the underlying attitude expressing in desiring and coveting someone else's property is the same attitude that underlies robbery. In order to be drawn into violating the prohibitions against desiring and coveting someone else's property two basic elements must at work. First, the object must be something that attracts the person. For example, my friend may have a wonderful set of water skies. But I am not at all interested in water skiing. So, I will not desire or covet the skies. Second, the person must be able to form a fantasy of the object being his. I think the White House is a nice home. But I cannot imagine myself as one of its residents. So, it is not likely that I am in danger of violating the prohibitions against desiring or coveting someone else's property as a result of my interest in the White House. Now, the first of these elements is not really the problem. There is nothing wrong with being attracted to material objects – as long as we don't become overwhelmed by the pursuit of material ends. But the second element is of concern. The fantasy that someone else's property can be mine is a denial of the ownership rights of that person. His property is his property and no one else has any right to it. The moment a person indulges in the fantasy of possessing someone else's property, this person has lost sight of the boundaries that halacha creates through property rights.

Now, we can better understand Maimonides' comments on the relationship between desiring, coveting and robbery. The violation of the prohibition against desiring involves indulging a fantasy that is contrary to the reality of the property rights established by halacha. Coveting is a further indulgence of this fantasy and a further deterioration of the person's grasp of reality. Once coveting occurs the basic attitude underlying robbery has been established and reinforced. The person who desires and then covets is lost in fantasy and has lost sight of the reality of the other person's ownership. This may not result in robbery. The person may be afraid to go this next step or not act out his fantasy for other reasons. But nonetheless, that basic attitude underlying robbery has been firmly established.

This interpretation of Maimonides comments is confirmed by Rashi's account of Moshe's appeal. Although Korach and his followers may not have technically violated the prohibition against desiring and coveting – they were not seeking property – their basic attitude was the same as that underlying these two prohibitions. They were wholly absorbed in the fantasy that the leadership roles that Moshe had assigned could be theirs. Moshe appeal was directed towards this fantasy. He explained that just as day cannot be night, they cannot acquire these roles. Hashem – Who created the boundaries between day and night – also assigned the position of Kohen Gadol to Aharon. Imagining themselves in these leadership roles was as far removed from reality as imaging that day could be night!

Let us consider whether this lesson is mussar – as Rav Chaim understood the term. Moshe was not attempting to evoke a countervailing fear or sense of shame that would suppress the rebellion. He was not telling Korah and his cohorts to contemplate their deaths or to merely consider the guidance of their consciences. Moshe's appeal does not include any type of motivational material. He was appealing to the rational or intellectual faculties of his opponents. He was demonstrating the error in their thinking and indicating that their desires were founded upon a flawed and fantastic view of reality. The approach used by Moshe was very different from Rav Chaim's conception or mussar. In fact, Moshe employed an approach that was the opposite of Rav Chaim's understanding to the mussar approach. He did not attempt to motivate by appealing to an internal fear or impulse. Instead, he asked his opponents to rise above their subjective perceptions and fantasies and look at the issue from a strictly objective – truth seeking – perspective.

Using this example as a model, we can anticipate Rav Chaim's response to Rav Katz's contention that the Torah itself includes mussar. It is true that the Torah includes vast narrative sections. It is also true that these sections are designed to serve as a source of moral instruction. However, it is important to recognize that according to Rav Chaim, not all moral instruction can be defined as mussar. When the instruction is primarily motivational, then the lesson can be regarded as mussar. However, material that is primarily designed to reveal a fundamental truth – even an ethical or moral truth – would not be regarded as mussar. Rav Chaim would argue that the narrative sections of the Torah are not intended to be merely inspirational or motivational. Instead, the Torah demands that we guide our lives by truth and these sections reveal fundamental truths. Therefore, he would not agree with the contention that the Torah is permeated with mussar lessons.

Again, this discussion is not intended to evaluate the value of the study of mussar. However, hopefully this discussion does provide some insight into the nature of the debate.

"This is what you should do. Take for yourself fire-plates – Korach and his assembly." (BeMidbar 16:6)

What was the issue raised by Korach and his followers? As we have explained, they disputed Moshe's right to make appointments to the priesthood. However, at a deeper level Korach and his followers questioned the entire institution of priesthood. Korach argued that the entire nation was sacred. The priesthood should not be bestowed upon a single family. Instead, it should be distributed more evenly within Bnai Yisrael. Moshe rejected this argument. He insisted that the priesthood belongs exclusively to Ahron and his descendants.

What was wrong with Korach's argument? Why does Bnai Yisrael have *Kohanim*? Why cannot any individual assume the role of *Kohen*? Rashi deals with this issue. He explains that there is a fundamental difference between the *Torah* and heathen religions. The heathens have many alternative practices. They have various priests. They worship in numerous temples. In contrast, the *Torah* insists upon a single law. There is one *Mikdash* – Temple. There is a single *Kohen Gadol*.[40]

Rashi's response requires further explanation. Rashi identifies a fundamental difference between the *Torah* and heathen practices. However, he does not explain the reason for this difference. Why does the *Torah* insist on a single *Mikdash* and one *Kohen Gadol*? Why does the *Torah* not allow for the diversity accommodated by other religions?

The answer is that the *Torah* proposes a unique approach to Divine service. Heathen religion is essentially an expression of the worshipper. The mode of service is derived from the personal needs of the worshipper. The worshipper designs the service in a manner that is personally meaningful. This results in remarkable diversity. Different cultures produce their own religious expressions and modes of worship. This is because each culture is unique and seeks to express religious feelings in an individual manner.

---

[40] Rabbaynu Shlomo ben Yitzchak (Rashi), *Commentary on Sefer BeMidbar* 16:1.

The *Torah* does not treat worship as an expression of the needs of the worshiper. Instead, *Torah* worship involves submission to the will of the Almighty. Worship is not designed to respond to the needs of the worshiper. It is a response to the will of Hashem.

The *Torah* approach implies that there must be unity of worship. Diversity in Divine service is inappropriate. All Jews submit to a single G-d. This Deity has a single will. Therefore, all Jews must worship in a single manner. There cannot be multiple Temples expressing various versions of worship. Neither can there be various High Priests each proposing his own form of worship. There is a single *Torah*, one *Mikdash* and one *Kohen Gadol*.

"And Moshe became very angry. He said to Hashem, 'Do not accept their offering. I did not take a single donkey from them! I did not do harm to any of them." (BeMidbar 16:15)

Moshe continues to attempt to make peace with Korach and his followers. He sends a messenger to Datan and Aviram. These are two of the leaders of the rebellion. He wishes to meet with them. Datan and Aviram refuse the offer. Instead, they lash-out at Moshe. They raise new issues. Moshe has failed to fulfill his promise to take them to a land flowing with milk and honey. The generation that Moshe brought out from Egypt has been condemned to die in the wilderness. Furthermore, Moshe has made himself ruler over the nation.

Our *pasuk* describes Moshe's reaction. Moshe becomes angry. He prays to Hashem. He asks Hashem not to accept the offerings of Korach and his followers. Finally, he declares that he has not deprived anyone of his property. He has not wronged anyone.

There are two problems with Moshe's comments. First, Moshe seems to be defending himself. He seems to feel that he needs to prove that he has not been despotic. Why is Moshe defending his integrity? Second, Moshe begins his defense by observing that he has not deprived anyone of personal property. This seems to be an odd defense. Moshe seems to be defending himself by asserting that he is not a thief! This does not prove he has not assumed unwarranted authority.

In order to understand Moshe's comments, some background is needed. In fact, Moshe did have the status of a king. He was the temporal ruler of Bnai Yisrael.[41] As king, Moshe did have the right to confiscate private property for his own use.[42] Now, we can begin to understand Moshe's comments. He was not asserting that he was not a thief. He was declaring that he had not exercised his rights as king. He had not practiced his right of confiscation.

Why did Moshe feel compelled to defend the beneficence of his leadership? Datan and Aviram had challenged Moshe's leadership. Moshe realized that there were two possible causes for this rebellion. The first possibility was that Datan and Aviram could not accept anyone's leadership. They were simply unwilling to submit to any leader. The second possibility was that his own behavior had evoked their response. Perhaps, unintentionally, he had been overbearing.

Moshe decided to test the issue. He humbled himself before Datan and Aviram. He attempted to appease them. If Datan and Aviram rejected this overture, Moshe would know that

---

[41]   Rabbaynu Moshe ben Nachman (Ramban), *Commentary on Sefer   Shemot* 30:13; Rabbaynu Ovadia Sforno, *Commentary on Sefer Beresheit* 36:31; Rabbaynu Avraham ibn Ezra, *Commentary on Sefer Devarim* 33:5.
[42]   Rabbaynu Moshe ben Maimon (Rambam) *Mishne Torah*, Hilchot *Melachim* 4:1.

his actions had not produced this dispute. Such a reaction would indicate that even the most unobtrusive leadership would not be tolerated.

Datan and Aviram immediately rejected Moshe's appeal. Now, Moshe knew with certainty that he had not caused this rebellion. This is the meaning of Moshe's comments. Moshe is asserting that he has been not been an overbearing leader. He has not even exercised the rights of a king. Therefore, he is not responsible for this rebellion. Korach, Datan and Aviram will not accept any leader.

"And Hashem spoke to Moshe saying: Say to Elazar, the son of Aharon, the Kohen, that he should pick up the censers from the burned area and throw the fire away, because they have become sanctified – the censers of these who sinned at the cost of their lives. And they shall make them into flattened out plates as an overlay for the altar, for they brought them before Hashem and have become sanctified. And they shall be a sign for Bnai Yisrael. And Elazar the Kohen took the copper censers which the fire victims had brought, and they hammered them out as an overlay for the altar, as a reminder for Bnai Yisrael, so that no outsider, who is not a descendant of Aharon shall approach to burn incense before Hashem. And one should not be like Korach and his company, as Hashem spoke regarding him through Moshe." (BeMidbar 17:1-5)

Parshat Korach describes the rebellion of Korah, Datan, Aviram and their followers against Moshe. This group challenged Moshe's leadership. The specific issues upon which the rebellion focused are not described in detail. However, it is apparent that Korach and his followers opposed the appointment of a specific family to serve as Kohanim. They believed that the entire nation was endowed with sanctity and that all members of Bnai Yisrael should be equal in their right to serve Hashem in His Mishcan. Moshe's contention was that his appointment of Aharon and his descendents to serve as Kohanim did not represent a personal decision. Moshe followed the commandment of Hashem.

Moshe attempted to resolve the issue through discussion. However, he suggested that if Korach and his followers absolutely insisted on challenging Aharon's appointment, then the issue should be decided through a simple test. Aharon and the other aspirants for the priesthood should each take a censer and offer incense in the courtyard of the Mishcan. Hashem will demonstrate through His response which of these individuals is His chosen Kohen Gadol.

Korach and his followers accepted this challenge. They brought their censers to the Mishcan's courtyard, added coals to their censers, and placed incense of the coals. Aharon's offering was accepted. But a flame descended from the heavens and consumed the pretenders.

Our passages deal with the aftermath of these events. Hashem commands Moshe to communicate a set of instructions to Elazar – Aharon's son. There are two elements to these instructions. Elazar is to proceed to the area of the conflagration. The first element is that he is to dispose of the contents of the pretenders' censers. He to empty the contents to the ground. Second, Hashem tells Moshe that the censers used by Aharon's opponents have been sanctified. Elazar is to take the censers and create from them a covering for the altar. This covering will be a reminder to Bnai Yisrael that no person who is not a descendant of Aharon is authorized to offer incense – or other sacrifices – to Hashem.

On the surface these instructions are easily understood. Elazar is to create a permanent reminder of these events. The censers are perfect for this function. They can be beat into flat sheets and fashioned into a covering for the altar situated in the courtyard of the Mishcan. Bnai Yisrael will see this covering each time they looked upon the altar. The covering will remind them that the service performed through the altar – the offering of sacrifices – is preserved for Aharon and the Kohanim.

However, a closer analysis of these instructions suggests a number of problems. First, Moshe is to instruct Elazar to fling the contents of the censers to the ground. Why is this instruction needed? Apparently, Hashem is communicating to Moshe that the ashes of the offering do not require any special treatment. What is this special treatment? Why would Moshe think that special treatment is required? Why is this treatment not required?

Before considering any further problems, let us answer this question. Each day, sacrifices were offered on the altar. These offerings generated ashes. The ashes had sanctity. This sanctity dictated that the ashes receive special treatment. They were removed from the altar and placed in a predetermined place. Rabbaynu Ovadia Sforno explains that Hashem was communicating to Moshe that the ashes of the offerings of the pretenders have no sanctity. They do not require the special treatment afforded to the remnants of sacrifices. Instead, they should be unceremoniously flung to the ground.[43]

This explanation responds to the first question but it creates a second problem. Hashem explained to Moshe that the censers of Aharon's opponents were sanctified. These were formed into a covering for the altar. This is paradoxical. The offerings of the pretenders had no sanctity and were treated disdainfully. But the censers were sanctified and were used to create a covering for the altar!

In order to resolve this paradox it is important to understand it more fully. Moshe was told that the remnants of the offerings of the pretenders did not have sanctity. This implies that their offerings were not regarded as legitimate acts of avodah – service to Hashem. This status was a result of the very nature of the test. All of the contenders offered incense. Only Aharon's offering was accepted. This demonstrated that his offering was regarded by Hashem as a legitimate act of avodah. The other offerings were rejected. The status of avodah was not conferred upon them. Therefore, the ashes of the offerings of the pretenders had no sanctity. They were the ashes from an activity of pseudo-avodah. However, according to this analysis, it follows that the censers the pretenders selected to use for their offerings should also not have sanctity. They selected these censers for an activity that was not truly avodah. They should not have any special status. However, this is not the case. Hashem instructed Moshe that these censers did have sanctity and should be used to fashion a covering for the altar.

Sforno suggests a response to this paradox. He concedes that the selection of these censers for use in this offering did not confer any sanctity upon them. However, he suggests that since these censers did have sanctity, we must conclude that the pretenders had dedicated them for other service in the Mishcan in addition to this offering. The use of the censers in this offering did not confer upon them sanctity. However, the dedication of the censers for more general use in the Mishcan was effective in conferring upon them sanctity.[44] It must be

---

[43] Rabbaynu Ovadia Sforno, *Commentary on Sefer BeMidbar*, 17:2.
[44] Rabbaynu Ovadia Sforno, *Commentary on Sefer BeMidbar*, 17:3.

acknowledged that it seems odd that these pretenders designated their censers for other service in the Mishcan and not simply for this specific occasion. It seems that Sforno is forced to this conclusion. He reasons that if the censers were only used in the Mishcan on this single occasion and they had not been designated for any other service, they could not have become sanctified. Therefore, it must be deduced that the censers had been designated for other service in the Mishcan.

Rashi does not seem to be bothered by our problem. He seems to indicate that the censers received their sanctity from this offering.[45] This is Nachmanides' understanding of Rashi's position. Nachmanides asks the obvious question on this position. The offering was rejected. This means that the only offering for which censers were designated was an invalid offering. This should not confer sanctity on the censers. Nachmanides provides a response on Rashi's behalf. He explains that although the offering was rejected, the pretenders were responding to Moshe's challenge. They were participating in a challenge commanded by Moshe. They believed that their offerings would be accepted. Therefore, the designation of the censers for use in the challenge imposed by Moshe conferred sanctity upon them.[46]

Ultimately, Nachmanides rejects this explanation and proposes an alternative. He argues that Hashem is not telling Moshe that the censers acquired sanctity through the designation of Aharon's opponents. Instead, Hashem is telling Moshe that He has conferred sanctity upon them in order that they may become a reminder to Bnai Yisrael of the authority of Aharon and his descendents.[47] In other words, any designation that these opponents may have given to the censers was misguided and did not confer sanctity. However, Hashem designated these censers as a memorial. This conferred sanctity upon them.

We can understand Sforno's and Nachmanides' resolution of the paradox. According to both of these opinions, the offerings of the pretenders were not actual avodah. Therefore, the ashes from these offerings had no sanctity and the use of the censers in these offerings did not confer any sanctity upon them. Their sanctity was derived from some other source. Sforno and Nachmanides suggest alternative possibilities for this source. However, even with Nachmanides' clarification, Rashi's resolution of the paradox is not evident. The censers acquired their sanctity when they were selected and designated for use in this contest imposed by Moshe. But if the censers acquired sanctity in this manner, why were the ashes of the offerings not also sanctified?

It seems that Rashi differs from Sforno and Nachmanides in his basic understanding of the challenge imposed by Moshe. Sforno and Nachmanides seem to propose a straightforward and obvious interpretation. Aharon's opponents believed that their authority of offer sacrifices was no less than his own. Moshe suggested that this thesis be put to a test. Let them present their own offerings. If their offerings are accepted, then their thesis will be proven. If their offerings are rejected, their thesis will be disproved. Their offerings were rejected. This disproved their claims and indicated that their offerings were not avodah.

Rashi rejects this understanding. His understanding of the test is somewhat more abstract and requires an illustration: A drug manufacturer wishes to test a new medication for some disease. He assembles a group of volunteers to participate in a test of the drug's efficacy. All

---

[45] Rabbaynu Shlomo ben Yitzchak (Rashi), *Commentary on Sefer BeMidbar* 17:2.

[46] Rabbaynu Moshe ben Nachman (Ramban), *Commentary on Sefer BeMidbar* 17:2.

[47] Rabbaynu Moshe ben Nachman (Ramban), *Commentary on Sefer BeMidbar* 17:2.

members of the group suffer from the complaint the drug is designed to treat. Some members of the group receive the medication. Other members of the group receive a placebo. The members of the group that receive the placebo experience some minor improvement in their conditions. However, the members of the group that receive the medication experience marked improvement in their conditions. Which members of this group participated in the test of the new medication? It would be incorrect to say that only the individuals who received the proposed medication participated. Even those who received the placebo participated. Without the administration of the placebo the test would be meaningless.

Rashi seems to propose a similar interpretation for Moshe's challenge. The challenge was designed to affirm Aharon's unique position and authority. This could not be accomplished through Aharon alone offering a sacrifice. In order for the demonstration to have meaning, Aharon's offering needed to be accompanied by the offerings of other individuals. If Aharon's offering would be accepted and theirs rejected, then Aharon's claim to the priesthood would be established.

According to this understanding of the test, all of the individuals who offered incense participated in Aharon's offering. Their participation affirmed the unique status of Aharon and his offering. Certainly, this was only accomplished through the rejection of their incense. However, the designation of their censers for use in this test was effective in conferring sanctity. These censers were designated for use in a single sacrificial service designed to affirm Aharon's status.

In other words, according to Sforno and Nachmanides, each person who participated in the test offered his own sacrifice. Of all of these sacrifices, one was accepted – Aharon's – and the remainders were rejected. According to Rashi, all of these individuals participated in a single service. Aharon's service was only significant because of, and through, the participation of the others. Therefore, their censers which they designated for use in this service were sanctified through this designation.

"And it was on the following day and Moshe entered the Tent of Testimony. And it was that Ahron's staff representing the house of Leyve had blossomed. And it had brought forth blossoms and then unripe fruit and then almonds." (BeMidbar 17:23)

Hashem commanded Moshe to collect a staff from the prince of each tribe. Ahron's staff represented the *Shevet* of Leyve. These staffs were then placed in the *Mishcan*. The following day Ahron's staff blossomed and bore fruit. This miracle indicated that Ahron was truly the *Kohen* appointed by the Almighty.

Korach's rebellion had already ended. He and his followers had been destroyed through a series of miracles. Why was further proof of Ahron's authenticity needed?

One explanation is that there were two elements in Korach's rebellion. First, Korach and his followers rebelled against Moshe's authority. The manner in which they protested the appointment of the *Kohanim* – the priests – was inappropriate. They did not question Moshe in a respectful manner. They denied his authority and encouraged anarchy. Second, they had questioned the concept of priesthood. The destruction of Korach and his followers indicated that their approach had been sinful. However the question of the legitimacy of the priesthood had not been dealt with fully. The people could mistakenly assume that Korach and his camp were punished for their rebellious attitude. There would remain doubts regarding the position of the *Kohanim*.

The miracle of Ahron's staff responded to this possible doubt. Through this sign, Hashem confirmed the legitimacy of Ahron and the *Kohanim*.

Chukat

This is the statute of the Torah that Hashem commanded saying: Take to you a perfect red cow that is without blemish [and] on it a yoke has not been placed. (BeMidbar 19:2)

Seeking Meaning

1. Obedience to commandments

Parshat Chukat opens with the mitzvah of Parah Adumah – the Red Heifer. This cow is sacrificed outside of the Bait HaMikdash – the Sacred Temple. It is entirely burned. Its ashes are gathered and combined with other ingredients. The mixture is placed in water and used to restore the ritual purity of those who have been defiled through association with a dead human body. Rashi quotes the well-known comment of our Sages:

> *"Because the Accuser (Satan) and the nations of the world criticize Israel saying, 'What is the commandment? What explanation is there for it?' Therefore, [the Torah] wrote about it, '[It is] a statute.' [This means] it is a decree from before Me. You are not permitted to criticize it."*
> *(Rashi, BeMidbar 19:1)*

The Sages explain that Parah Adumah is one of Hashem's commandments. We do not understand it. We cannot provide an adequate explanation for it. Yet, because it is one of the commandments, we must be obedient and observe it.

This is one of many commandments whose reasons are not obvious. In many instances, even though the Torah does not explain a commandment, we can speculate on its rationale. Should we engage in this speculation? If there is a benefit in such explorations, is there a method that should be employed?

2. Who benefits from commandments

Let us begin with the second question. Rabbaynu Aharon HaLeyve in Sefer HaChinuch quotes an important midrash:

> "Rav said: The commandments were given to us only to refine humanity. For what concern is it to the Sacred One, Blessed be He, over one who slaughters an animal at the neck on one who slaughters from the back of the neck. It is only [that] the commandments were given to refine through them humanity." (Midrash Beresheit Rabbah 44:1)

The Torah requires that animals we wish to consume as food be slaughtered in a precise manner. The trachea and esophagus are quickly severed using an extremely sharp knife. Rav explains that it makes no difference to Hashem whether the animal is slaughtered in this manner or whether it is slaughtered from the back of its neck. Why did the Torah command us to slaughter animals only in a specified manner? He responds that the commandment is intended to refine humanity.

What is Rav's message? Sefer HaChinuch explains that Hashem does not benefit from our performance of the commandments. He is perfect. Our performance of the commandments does not confer a benefit upon Him. Instead, He gave us the Torah and its commandments for our benefit. Observance of the commandments refines us. Observance transforms us into better human beings.

3. Benefit vs. reason

This analysis provides the direction for Sefer HaChinch's exploration of the rationale for commandments. His focus is upon how each commandment impacts its performer. He does not speculate on why Hashem commanded us but on how we benefit from observance.[1] Applying this approach to the slaughtering of animals, one can conclude that the Torah is encouraging the development of compassion and is discouraging cruelty. It allows the slaughter of animals for nutrition. However, it requires that the slaughter be performed humanely. Through acting with compassion toward animals, we are encouraged to be even more sensitive toward human-beings.[2] Conversely, if we were permitted to slaughter animals brutally, the experience would desensitize us to the pain of living creatures and this insensitivity would carry-over to our treatment of human beings.

4. Rationale for details

Another consideration is discussed by Rambam – Maimonides. He explains that we can speculate regarding the rationale for a commandment. However, this exploration must focus on the overall commandment. One should not seek a rationale for the commandment's details.[3] For example, the Torah commands us to dwell in a succah during the festival of Succot. This is an instance in which the Torah reveals the rationale for its commandment. The succah reminds us of the experience of our ancestors in the wilderness during their journey from Egypt to the Land of Israel.

One of the laws of the succah is that it must have two complete walls and a partial third wall. Rambam's position is that seeking a rationale for this requirement is pointless.[4]

5. Engaging in speculations

The above discussion focused on our second question. It explored the approach for seeking the rationales for commandments. Let us now return to our first question. Is there a reason to engage in these speculations?

A response often given is that through understanding the benefit of the commandments we are more motivated to observe them. Understanding transforms the commandments from imposed obligations to activities or restrictions that are in one's self-interest. For many people, imposed obligations are burdens, but even restrictions are acceptable if they serve one's self-interest.

Rambam suggests a completely different motive for exploring the reasons for commandments:

"It is fitting for a person to contemplate the laws of the sacred Torah and to know the ultimate meaning according to one's capacity." (Rambam, Mishne Torah, Hilchot Me'ilah 8:8)

---

[1] Rabbaynu Aharon HaLeyve, Sefer HaChinuch, Mitzvah 545.

[2] Some individuals are intensely compassionate toward their pets but have difficulty being empathic toward human-beings. It is not always true that compassion toward animals translates into compassion toward people. However, it seems very likely that cruelty toward animals can lead to mistreatment of human-beings.

[3] Rabbaynu Moshe ben Maimon (Rambam) Moreh Nevuchim, volume 3, chapter 26.

[4] Rambam does not intend to suggest that there is no reason for the requirement. However, the explanation lies in the legal – halachic structure of the commandment. The structure of the requirement is not determined by moral or philosophical considerations.

Rambam merely comments that the exploration of the commandments is appropriate. However, his phrasing provides insight into his reasoning. He explains that in exploring the reasons for commandments, one is seeking knowledge of their ultimate meaning (inyanam). We are commanded to study the Torah. This study includes the analysis of its commandments. What is encompassed in this study? We must analyze the legal requirements and the structure of the commandments. However, the complete understanding of a commandment must include an exploration of its objective or purpose. Only with the inclusion of this element is the study of the commandment complete.

Furthermore, the commandments are not six hundred and thirteen isolated imperatives. They combine to create an integrated system of ideas and behaviors. The comprehensive study and understanding of a commandment must include consideration of the commandment's role within this integrated system. This requires exploration of the commandment's meaning – its objective and purpose.

6. The danger in speculation

Of course, the exploration of the rationale for a commandment invites criticism of that rationale. It is possible that one will not discover a rationale. Sometimes, the rationale is obvious – but also objectionable. Rambam discusses this issue:

> Something for which one does not find a reason and its cause is not known should not be treated dismissively…. One should not contemplate it [the Torah] as one contemplates secular matters… The commandments that the Sacred One, Blessed be He, decreed for us, one should not reject because their reason is not known." (Rambam, Mishne Torah, Hilchot Me'ilah 8:8)

Rambam recognizes that inevitably we will not understand some commandments or we will be unsatisfied with their apparent rationale. How should we respond to this encounter? Rambam cautions against rejecting such commandments. We must remind ourselves of the source of the commandments. Our understanding is limited and Hashem's wisdom is infinite.

Our study of the commandments and the exploration of their meanings are not conducted to judge their virtue and relevance. These are assumed. The commandments were given to us by Hashem. We are exploring the commandments in the pursuit of knowledge and truth. An exploration whose aim is knowledge and truth embraces and marvels over mysteries. These mysteries do not compromise one's commitment to observance; they remind us of the infinite wisdom of Hashem – the source of the commandments.

This is the law of the Torah that Hashem commanded saying: Speak to Bnai Yisrael and they should take for you a completely red cow that has no blemish and has never borne a yoke. (BeMidbar 19:2)

The Characterization of Parah Adumah as a Chok

This *pasuk* introduces the laws of the *Parah Adumah* – the red heifer. This animal is slaughtered and completely burned. The ashes of the heifer, with other ingredients, are required for the purification. Severe forms of *tumah* – spiritual defilement – are treated with these ashes.

The passage describes the *mitzvah* of *Parah Adumah* as a law. There are various Hebrew words for "law'". The term used in our *pasuk* is *chok*. Rashi comments on the selection of this specific term. He explains that the term *chok* means decree. In other words, the *mitzvah* of *Parah Adumah* is a decree from Hashem. It is an expression of His divine will. It must be carefully obeyed and respected. Rashi further explains that the use of this term seems to presuppose that the law of *Parah Adumah* is subject to some criticism. The word *chok* is the response to this reproach. Essentially, the response is that regardless of the questions evoked by this *mitzvah* it must be regarded as a decree of Hashem and observed in all its details. What is the criticism evoked by the *mitzvah* of *Parah Adumah*? Rashi is somewhat vague in his response to this issue. He explains that the heathen nations can criticize the *mitzvah*. They will question its reason and design.[5]

These comments are difficult to understand. Many *mitzvot* are enigmatic. A casual review of the *mitzvot* of the Torah will result in endless questions. Certainly, the heathen nations will find many elements of the Torah that seem completely unintelligible! The Torah's response to these reproaches is that a person must study Torah as one would any field of knowledge. One cannot expect to appreciate the wisdom of the Torah through a superficial review of the *mitzvot*. Why does the commandment of *Parah Adumah* require a special response? According to Rashi, in this case the Torah responds, "This is a *chok*! Observe the *mitzvah* regardless of your criticisms and scruples!"

Nachmanides responds to this question. He explains that we must begin by more clearly understanding the reason the Torah uses the term *chok*. This term is not used simply because the *mitzvah* of *Parah Adumah* is difficult to understand. As explained above, many *mitzvot* seem to defy human understanding. The reason the term *chok* is used in this case is because the *mitzvah* of *Parah Adumah* seems to contradict a basic tenet of the Torah. One of the fundamental themes of the Torah is that we must abstain from heathen practices and forms of worship. We are forbidden to worship any power other than Hashem. We may not serve demons, spirits, forces of nature, or even angels. In order to regulate our worship and assure that our service to Hashem is free of any heathen influence, the institution of the *Bait HaMikdash* was created. All sacrifices are to be offered in the Temple where the services are carefully regulated. Generally, we are not permitted to sacrifice outside of the Temple.

However, *Parah Adumah* is remarkably similar to heathen worship. A cow is burned in an open field. The service is performed outside of the *Bait HaMikdash*. It can easily be misinterpreted as a sacrifice to the heathen deities. The heathens can cynically argue that we are hypocrites: we decry heathen worship and practices, and then legislate a service reminiscent of the very practices we condemn!

This is the criticism to which the Torah responds. The *mitzvah* is a *chok*. It is an expression of the Divine will. It may seem inconsistent with the Torah's strong disavowal of heathen practices. But the law is Hashem's decree. We know that Hashem cannot be inconsistent![6]

"This is the law of the Torah that Hashem commanded saying: Speak to Bnai Yisrael. And they should take for you a perfectly red cow that has no blemish and has never had a yoke placed upon it." (BeMidbar 19:2)

---

5 Rabbaynu Shlomo ben Yitzchak (Rashi), *Commentary on Sefer BeMidbar* 19:2.
6 Rabbaynu Moshe ben Nachman (Ramban), *Commentary on Sefer BeMidbar* 19:2.

Parshat Chukat discusses the laws of the *Parah Adumah* – the Red Cow. This cow is burned. Its ashes are used in the process of purifying a person that has become defiled through contact with a dead body.

The cow that is burned and used in this purification process must meet specific requirements. Our *pasuk* describes these three basic requirements. The cow must be completely red. It must be unblemished. The cow must never have had a yoke placed upon it.

The need for the cow to be unblemished is not surprising. This is a requirement of animals used for sacrifice. It is reasonable for this requirement to be applied to the *Parah Adumah*. However, the restriction against using a cow that has born a yoke is unusual. This restriction does not generally apply to sacrifices. What is the reason for this restriction?

There is one instance of a similar restriction. This is in regard to the *Eglah Arufah*. This calf is slaughtered in the process of atonement for an unsolved murder. The Torah requires that the calf has not been used for labor and has not drawn a load with a yoke.[7]

These restrictions are similar. Both the *Parah Adumah* and the *Eglah Arufah* are disqualified through association with labor. However, the restrictions are not identical. A cow is disqualified from serving as *Parah Adumah* through placing a yoke upon it. It is not necessary for the cow to do any actual labor.[8] In contrast, the mere placement of the yoke on a calf does not disqualify it from serving as an *Eglah Arufah*. The calf is only disqualified if it has actually drawn a load.[9] This raises an additional question. Why is this unique restriction formulated differently in these two instances? Why does the mere placement of the yoke upon the *Parah Adumah* disqualify the animal? Why is the *Eglah Arufah* only disqualified through drawing a burden with the yoke?

Gershonides deals with our first question. Why is an animal associated with labor disqualified from use as a *Parah Adumah* and an *Eglah Arufah*? He explains the basic concept underlying this restriction. There is a fundamental distinction between animals used for sacrifice and the animals chosen for *Parah Adumah* and *Eglah Arufah*. An animal chosen for a sacrifice can have a previous identity or function. An animal that has been designated for work or used for labor can become a sacrifice. Only after the animal is chosen for sacrifice, does it receive a designation. After the animal is designated to be a sacrifice, it can no longer be used for labor. Using the animal for labor contradicts its designation as a sacrifice. In short, in the case of a sacrificial animal a previous identity does not disqualify the animal from receiving a new designation. It can still be designated as a sacrifice.

The cow chosen for the *Parah Adumah* cannot have been previously associated with labor. The use of the cow as a *Parah Adumah* must be the first and only identity of the cow. The placement of a yoke upon the cow confers an identity. With the placement of the yoke upon the cow, it is associated with labor. This is an identity in the animal. This disqualifies the animal. The identity of *Parah Adumah* or *Eglah Arufah* must be the first and only identity in the animal. Gershonides expresses the concept in an interesting manner. It must be as if the animal was created to serve as a *Parah Adumah* or *Eglah Arufah*.[10]

---

[7] Sefer Devarim 21:3.

[8] Rabbaynu Moshe ben Maimon (Rambam) *Mishne Torah*, Hilchot Parah Adumah 1:7.

[9] R' Moshe ben Maimon (Rambam) *Mishne Torah*, Hilchot Rotzeach U'Shmirat Nefesh 10:3.

[10] Rabbaynu Levi ben Gershon (Ralbag / Gershonides), *Commentary on Sefer BeMidbar*,

We will now turn to our second question. Why is the restriction of the *Eglah Arufah* formulated differently than the restriction upon the *Parah Adumah*? Why does the mere placement of the yoke upon a cow disqualify it from use as a *Parah Adumah*? Why is a calf disqualified from serving as an *Eglah Arufah* only after it has pulled a load?

Gershonides contends that the restrictions upon the *Parah Adumah* and the *Eglah Arufah* share the same underlying concept.[11] The animal chosen for either of these functions must be free of a previous identity. He explains that the difference in the restrictions lies in the stringency with which this requirement is applied. In the case of the *Eglah Arufah*, the animal becomes associated with labor through the performance of labor. Therefore, only through the actual performance of labor is the calf disqualified. In contrast, the *Parah Adumah* is associated with labor through designation. Placement of the yoke upon the cow designates it for use in labor. This designation alone creates an association. The cow can no longer be used as a *Parah Adumah*.

In short, the two formulations differ in the degree of association to labor that disqualifies the animal. The restriction in regard to *Eglah Arufah* requires a higher degree of association. Only the actual performance of labor produces this degree of association. The restriction in regard to the *Parah Adumah* requires a lower degree of association. Even designation of the cow for labor creates this lower degree of association and disqualifies the cow.

"This is the law of the Torah that Hashem commanded saying, "Speak to Bnai Yisrael and they should take for you a completely red cow that has no blemish and has never born a yoke" (BeMidbar 19:2)

Rashi is probably the most widely studied commentary on the Chumash. There are many comments of Rashi that are well-know and widely quoted. Unfortunately, in some cases these comments are quoted so frequently that we neglect to consider them carefully. As soon as we hear the beginning of the comment, we finish the quote in our minds and do not even think carefully about Rashi's observation. The first comment of Rashi on this week's parasha is one of those oft quoted texts, which may need more attention than it normally receives.

Before considering Rashi's comments, let us first carefully study the pasuk it is intended to interpet. The pasuk above introduces the laws of the Parah Adumah – the red heifer. This animal is slaughtered and completely burned. The ashes of the heifer, with other ingredients, are required for the purification. Severe forms of spiritual defilement are treated with these ashes.

The passage describes the mitzvah of Parah Adumah as chukat ha'torah. In the translation above, this has been rendered to mean "the law of the Torah." But this translation is an oversimplification. The term chok – as in chukat – is used widely in the Chumash. The term generally has three meanings. In most instances the term is used to identify the permanence of a mitzvah or law. In fact, the Torah clearly makes this connection by frequently using the term chok in the phrase chukat olam – a permanent chok. For example, the Chumash tells us the

(Mosad HaRav Kook, 1998), pp. 94-95.
[11] Rabbaynu Levi ben Gershon (Ralbag / Gershonides), *Commentary on Sefer BeMidbar*, (Mosad HaRav Kook, 1998), pp. 94-95.

observance of Pesach is a chukat olam – a chok for all generations.[12] Here, the term chok communicates this idea of permanence.

In some instances the term chok refers to a right or portion assigned to a person or group by some authority. For example, there was a chok in Yosef's time that the leaders of Egypt were awarded by Paroh a portion of land.[13] Similarly, the Chumash tells us that after the death of Nadav and Avihu, Moshe instructed the remaining kohanim that despite this tragedy they must still eat their chok – their portion – from the sacrifices offered that day.[14]

However, there are some instances in which neither of these translations seems appropriate. In these cases, the term chok seems to communicate that the law is a decree from Hashem. For example, in explaining the laws of Pesach Sheynee – a Pesach sacrifice brought by those who could not offer the sacrifice at its normal time – Moshe explains that the Pesach sacrifice must be offered according to all of its chukotav – according to its chok.[15] In this instance it is clear that the term chok does not mean "portion" and does not seem to be a reference to the permanence of the law for all generations. Therefore, in this instance and in other cases in which the first two translations do not apply, Targum Unkelus renders the term to mean "decree."

So, what is the meaning of the term chok in our passage? Clearly it does not mean "portion" and there is no obvious reason to assume that the term is a reference to permanence. It is not surprising that Targum Unkelus renders the term to mean "decree."

It is now possible to more accurately translate our pasuk as "this is the decree of the torah." However, the meaning – and even the translation – of the pasuk is still somewhat unclear. There is another problem. What does the term torah mean? The term torah is used occasionally in the Chumash to refer to the entire corpus of law contained in the Chumash. However, this not the usual manner in which the term is used. Generally, the term refers to a set of detailed laws regulating a specific process. For example, the Chumash introduces the laws regulating the offering of the Mincha sacrifice with the phrase "this is the torah of the Mincha offering."[16] In fact when the term is used to refer to the entire corpus of law contained in the Chumash it is likely that the term is being employed in a similar manner. The term Torah – used in this context – refers to the entire system of detailed laws regulating the various elements of our personal and national lives.

So, what does the term torah mean in our pasuk? It seems unlikely that the term refers to the entire corpus of law. If that were the reference, then the pasuk would mean this is the decree of the entire Torah – implying that there is only this one single decree in the entire system of law outlined in the Chumash. However, there are many decrees included in the Chumash! Therefore, Rashbam rejects this explanation of the term torah in our passage. He suggests that the term torah refers to the detailed laws presented latter in the parasha concerning the transmission of tumah – spiritual defilement – by a dead body.[17] According to Rashbam it seems that the

---

[12] Sefer Shemot 12:14.

[13] Sefer Beresheit 47:22.

[14] Sefer VaYikra 10:13.

[15] Sefer BeMidbar 9:12

[16] Sefer VaYikra 6:7

[17] Rabbaynu Shemuel ben Meir (Rashbam) *Commentary on Sefer BeMidbar* 19:2.

meaning of our passage is that there is an element within the laws of tumah and taharah – spiritual defilement and purification – that must be regarded as a decree. This element is the mitzvah regarding the Parah Adumah – the red heifer.

This raises an obvious question. Why is the mitzvah of Parah Adumah singled out from the laws regulating tumah and taharah and referred to as a decree? This seems to be the question that prompts Rashi's comments.

Before we can consider Rashi's response, we must consider a preliminary issue. As explained above, the term chok has three alternative meanings. The term often communicates the permanence of a mitzvah. Sometimes the term refers to a portion or right awarded by an authority. In other instances – as in our passage – it means "decree." It is unlikely that the Torah would use one term in three completely different ways. Is there some common denominator between these three usages of the term chok? It seems that the term chok always makes reference to a law that rests on authority. A law is permanent because it comes from Hashem. A portion or right that is awarded by authority derives its significance through the sponsorship of the authority that bestows the right or portion. A decree is – by definition – a law that is based on the authority of the body of king that establishes the decree.

This gives more meaning to our passage. The pasuk is communicating that the mitzvah of Parah Adumah – in some sense – is to be understood as resting on and dependant upon the law-giver. In this case the law-giver is Hashem. In other words, in describing this mitzvah as a decree, the Chumash is communicating that appreciation of the mitzvah of Parah Adumah requires that we recognize the authority – Hashem – who has decreed it. What special characteristic of the mitzvah of Parah Adumah demands this recognition?

Finally, we are ready for Rashi's comments. Rashi explains that the Satan and the nations of the world taunt the Jewish people regarding this commandment. They ask, "What kind of mitzvah is this and what is its reason?" Therefore the Chumash tells us that is a decree from Hashem. We are not permitted to cast suspicion upon it.[18]

It's clear from Rashi's comments that there is some odd element in the mitzvah of Parah Adumah that is destined to evoke ridicule. What is this element? Many commentaries suggest that this ridicule would focus on a specific odd law regarding the Parah. As we have explained, the ashes of this Parah are used in the purification process from severe forms of tumah. However, in their preparation the ashes actually transmit tumah. In other words, one who comes into contact with and handles the ashes during their preparation is himself defiled. So, these ashes which are a source of defilement are somehow able to restore purity![19]

However, this does not seem to be the issue that concerned Rashi. Rashi bases his comments on a text from the Talmud. In his commentary on that text, Rashi explains more fully the difficulty in understanding the mitzvah of Parah Adumah. He explains that Parah Adumah is one of the commandments in the Torah for which there is no apparent explanation or apparent benefit. He explains that this characteristic evokes the criticism of the Satan and the nations of the world. They argue that the Torah cannot possibly be true! How can the Torah be true if it commands us to perform mitzvot that have no apparent benefit? To this criticism the Chumash responds that these mitzvot are decrees from Hashem and rest upon his authority. [20]

---

[18] Rabbaynu Shlomo ben Yitzchak (Rashi), *Commentary on Sefer BeMidbar* 19:2.
[19] Rabbaynu Ovadia Sforno, *Commentary on Sefer Beresheit*, 9:2.

Let us now summarize Rashi's comments. The Torah alerts us that the mitzvah of Parah Adumah is a decree. Rashi explains that this alert is important because this mitzvah is one of a group that have no apparent rational or purpose. This characteristic will expose these commandments to criticism and ridicule. The Satan and the nations of the world will challenge the truth of a system of law that includes commandments that have no apparent purpose. We are to respond that these commandments are decrees from Hashem and therefore, rest on His authority.

Frankly, it seems unlikely that the wily Satan and hostile nations of the world will be much impressed by this argument. These critics obviously do not accept the authenticity of the revelation at Sinai. Yet, we are advised to respond to their disparagement with the reminder that the mitzvot are Hashem's decrees!

Again, Rashi's comments on the Talmud provide a clearer understanding of his intention. Rashi explains that the term "Satan" is a reference to the yetzer harah – our own internal evil inclination.[21] In other words, Rashi is describing an internal dialogue. The response that Rashi and the Talmud are suggesting is not intended for the person that scoffs at revelation. Instead, it is designed to respond to our own internal doubts. When others criticize mitzvot like Parah Adumah that have no apparent reason or when we ourselves are mislead by our own internal desires, we are to remind ourselves that these seemingly arbitrary commandments are decrees from Hashem and rest on His authority.

Still, Rashi's comments are difficult to fully understand. Rashi is describing an internal debate that may take place within us. But the nature of this debate remains unclear. If a person is experiencing doubts about the truth of the Torah, how will one be rescued with a reminder that these troubling mitzvot are Hashem's decrees?

Klee Yakar provides an important insight into this issue. After quoting Rashi's comments, he explains that the criticism described by Rashi is not at all unreasonable. He explains that we have every reason to expect the mitzvot to make sense. The Chumash tells us that if we observe the commandments the nations of the world will admire us. They will praise us as a wise and understanding nation.[22,23] This insight suggests a clearer understanding of the internal dialogue described by Rashi. Klee Yakar suggests that we are to conduct ourselves in a way that demonstrates the deep wisdom of the Torah. However, this very obligation evokes a problem. How are we to conduct ourselves as intelligent and wise individuals if we are required to observe commandments that have no obvious meaning? It is natural to be troubled by this paradox. In fact, to not be concerned with this issue, suggests that one is not committed to the obligation to conduct one's affairs intelligently. It is inevitable that a person who takes this obligation seriously will experience a deep level of confusion. How do we respond to this confusion?

Now, let us reconsider the response discussed by Rashi. There are two important marks of intelligence. First, it is incumbent upon us to try to understand and appreciate the wisdom of

---

[20] Rabbaynu Shlomo ben Yitzchak (Rashi), *Commentary on the Talmud,* Mesechet Yoma 67b.
[21] Rabbaynu Shlomo ben Yitzchak (Rashi), *Commentary on the Talmud,* Mesechet Yoma 67b.
[22] Sefer Devarim 4:6
[23] Rabbaynu Shlomo Ephraim Lontshitz, *Commentary Klee Yakar on Sefer BeMidbar* 19:2.

the mitzvot. We cannot regard ourselves as wise, intelligent individuals if we close our minds to contemplation. But there is a second element of wisdom. We must have humility. True wisdom should generate a sense of humility. Humility demands that we recognize the limits of our own insight. A humble person recognizes that there are some mysteries that he cannot resolve. Just as there are elements of the created universe that defy human understanding, it is reasonable to assume that there may be elements of the revealed law that are not completely within human grasp. Therefore, by recognizing the source of the Torah we can resolve our confusion.

"And Hashem spoke to Moshe and to Aaron, saying: This is the statute of the law which Hashem has commanded, saying, "Speak unto the Bnai Yisrael, that they should take for you a red heifer, faultless, that has no blemish, and upon which never came yoke." (BeMidbar 19:1-2)

Parshat Chukat includes three commandments. All of these commandments deal with impurity through contact with a dead body. The first commandment is the requirement to secure and burn a red heifer – a *parah adumah*. The ashes of the *parah* are then retained for use in the purification process of a person who became defiled through contact with a dead body.[24] The second commandment is the laws regarding defilement through contact with a dead body.[25] The final commandment deals with the unique attribute of the mixture created from the ashes of the *parah*. Although these ashes are used in the process of purification, they also transmit impurity to those who process the *parah*.[26]

In our passages Hashem communicates to Moshe and Aharon the first of the commandments and directs them to instruct Bnai Yisrael in this commandment. The instructions begin with the directive that the nation should take a red heifer that meets the requirements of the Torah. It must be completely red; it must be free of any blemish, and it must not have previously employed in any labor.

Maimonides explains that one of the many laws concerning the *parah* is that it should be purchased from the communal funds of the *Bait HaMikdash*.[27] These communal funds are created through an annual tithe. Every male is required to contribute to the fund.

What if a person contributes a *parah adumah*? Can this contribution be accepted for the purpose of fulfilling the *mitzvah* of *parah adumah*? There is a general rule that would seem to address this issue. There are a number of sacrifices that must be offered by the nation. The animal used for the sacrifice must be collectively owned by Bnai Yisrael. In order to meet this requirement the animals used in these sacrifices are purchased from the *Bait HaMikdash's* communal funds. However, if a person contributes an animal to the *tzibur* – to the national community – it may be accepted for and used as one of these communal sacrifices. Mishne La'Melech suggests that this principle also applies to the *parah adumah*. Maimonides does not intend to imply that there is an absolute requirement to purchase the *parah* with community funds. The *parah* must be owned by the *tzibur*. Purchasing the animal with community funds

---

[24] Rabbaynu Moshe ben Maimon (Rambam) *Sefer HaMitzvot, Mitzvat Aseh* 113.

[25] Rabbaynu Moshe ben Maimon (Rambam) *Sefer HaMitzvot, Mitzvat Aseh* 107.

[26] Rabbaynu Moshe ben Maimon (Rambam) *Sefer HaMitzvot, Mitzvat Aseh* 108.

[27] Rabbaynu Moshe ben Maimon (Rambam) *Mishne Torah*, Hilchot *Parah adumah* 1:1.

meets this requirement. However, the requirement is also met when a person donates the *parah* to the *tzibur*.[28]

Others disagree. Aruch HaShulchan contends that the general principle that an animal donated to the *tzibur* may be used for communal sacrifices does not apply to the *parah adumah*. The *parah adumah* should be purchased from communal funds. An animal donated to the *tzibur* does not meet this requirement.[29] Presumably, he maintains that this is Maimonides' position. Maimonides' ruling that the *parah* should be purchased from community funds is to be understood literally.

We can easily understand the position of Mishne LaMelech. According to his understanding, the requirement regarding the *parah adumah* is identical to the requirement for communal sacrifices. The animal must be owned by the *tzibur*. An animal donated to the *tzibur* is acceptable. But the position of the Aruch HaShulcan requires more careful analysis. Why is the *parah adumah* different from communal sacrifices? Why must the animal be secured through purchase with communal funds?

There is another interesting problem with Maimonides' ruling. Maimonides rules that all communal sacrifices must belong to the *tzibur*. This is an absolute requirement.[30] This requirement would seem to apply to the *parah adumah*. However, Maimonides, in discussing the requirement to purchase the animal from communal funds, does not express this requirement as an absolute requisite. Instead, he states that the animal *should* be purchased from communal funds.[31] According to Aruch HaShulchan, this seems to imply that the animal should be purchased from communal funds but that an animal donated to the *tzibur* can be used. In other words, although the community is required to purchase the animal through the communal fund, if the animal is donated to the community it is acceptable. This raises a second question. Why is the requirement to purchase the animal with communal funds not an absolute requisite? If the animal should be purchased with communal funds, why is a donated animal acceptable?

Rav Naftali Tzvi Yehudah Berlin – Netziv – provides an insight that helps answer these questions. He agrees with Aruch HaShulcan that the *tzibur* is required to purchase the *parah* from communal funds. He explains that the source for this requirement is in the midrash Sifrai. Sifrai explains that Moshe is commanded to instruct Bnai Yisrael to "take" a *parah adumah* from which the required ashes will be created. Sifrai explains that this term is the source for the requirement to purchase the *parah* from communal funds. Netziv comments that this derivation clearly adjoins us to purchase the *parah* with communal funds rather than accepted a donated *parah*. If the *parah* is donated, then the *tzibur* has failed to fulfill the obligation of "taking" a *parah*.[32]

Apparently, according to Netziv, the *mitzvah* of *parah adumah* does not only describe the process for creating the ashes of the *parah adumah*; the *mitzvah* also establishes an obligation

---

[28] Rav Yehuda Rosanes, *Mishne La'Melech*, Hilchot *Parah adumah* 1:1.

[29] Rav Yechiel Michal HaLeyve Epstein, *Aruch HaShulchan HaAtede*, Hilchot *Parah adumah* 52:8-10.

[30] Rabbaynu Moshe ben Maimon (Rambam) *Mishne Torah*, Hilchot Klai Mikdash 8:7.

[31] Rav Yosef Babad, *Minchat Chinuch, Mitzvah* 397, note 2.

[32] Rav Naftali Tzvi Yehuda Berlin (Netziv), *Commentary Emek HaNetziv on Sifrai,* Parshat Chukat, chapter 1.

upon the nation to proactively assure that these ashes are available for those who must purify themselves from defilement through contact with a dead body. The requirement that the nation take a proactive role dictates that the *tzibur* purchase the *parah* from communal funds. In other words, the ashes can be created from a donated *parah* and these ashes can be effectively used in the purification process. However, if the nation does not purchase the *parah*, it has not fulfilled its obligation to proactively assure that this instrument for purification is available.

With this insight, we can understand Aruch HaShulchan's interpretation of Maimonides. According to Aruch HaShulchan, the *parah adumah* cannot be compared to other communal sacrifices. The *mitzvah* of *parah adumah* includes an element that is not relevant to communal sacrifices. The nation does not have an obligation to proactively secure these sacrifices. In contrast, the nation does have an obligation to proactively assure that the means of purification from defilement through contact with a dead body are available.

We can also understand why failure to meet this requirement does not affect the efficacy of the ashes. The ashes of a *parah* donated to the *tzibur* are effective. This *parah* is owned by the *tzibur* and consequently, its ashes are completely effective. However, when the *parah* is donated the *tzibur* has failed to fulfill its obligation to proactively secure and provide the means of purification.

And the children of Israel, even the whole congregation, came into the wilderness of Zin in the first month; and the people abode in Kadesh; and Miryam died there, and was buried there. (BeMidbar 20:1)

If You Aren't Moving Forward, You're Falling Back

1. Speaking with silence

Parshat Chukat discusses events that occurred at the end of Bnai Yisrael's sojourn in the wilderness. The above passage introduces this discussion. A period of thirty-eight years passed between the events last described in the Torah and those described in our *parasha*. The events that took place during those thirty-eight years are not at all discussed by the Torah.

Sometimes silence is itself a form of communication and speaks more eloquently than words. This may be one of those incidents. In order to understand the meaning of this silence, we must return to the incident of the spies and its consequences.

The nation departed from Sinai and traveled toward the promised land. Before confronting the nations of Cana'an, Bnai Yisrael sent a group of spies into the land. They reported that the land was indeed fertile. However, they also described the strength of the nations occupying the land and expressed their fears. Their report evoked panic among the people and they refused to proceed forward. Among the people a movement arose to abandon the march to the promised land and to return to the Land of Egypt.

Hashem threatened to destroy the nation but Moshe pleaded on the people's behalf. He succeeded in saving them from immediate destruction but Hashem condemned that generation to wander in the wilderness for another thirty-eight years. That generation would expire in the wilderness and never see the Land of Cana'an. Instead, the march to Cana'an would be resumed by their children. This next generation would realize the promise that had been made to their patriarchs. They would take possession of the Land of Cana'an.

The people heard the decree and recognized that they had been undermined by their fears. They recovered their courage and they understood that because of their fears they had forsaken the wonderful blessing of the Land of Israel. They declared their intention to bravely proceed into the land and conquer it.

Moshe warned the people that their opportunity had passed. They must now accept Hashem's decree and not proceed. An attempt to now capture the land would not be supported by Hashem. The nations of Cana'an would beat them back. But the people were stubborn and refused to accept Hashem's decree. They marched forward. As Moshe warned, they were overwhelmed by the occupants of the land and brutally repelled.

Speak unto the children of Israel, and say unto them: When you come into the land of your habitations, which I give unto you, and will make an offering by fire unto Hashem, a burnt-offering, or a sacrifice, in fulfillment of a vow clearly uttered, or as a freewill-offering, or in your appointed seasons, to make a sweet savor unto Hashem, of the herd, or of the flock; then he who brings his offering unto Hashem shall bring a meal-offering of a tenth part of an ephah of fine flour mingled with the fourth part of a hin of oil; and wine for the drink-offering, the fourth part of a hin, shall you prepare with the burnt-offering or for the sacrifice, for each lamb. (BeMidbar 15:2-5)

And you returned (repented[33]) and wept before Hashem; but Hashem did not hearken to your voice, nor gave ear unto you. (Devarim 1:45)

2. A message of hope in the incident of the spies

At this point, the Torah's account of the events ends. The impression created by the narrative is of tragedy and disaster. The generation was condemned to wander through a desolate and barren wilderness. It would be unable to regain the opportunity to seize the blessing that had been forsaken in fear. However, this impression of unmitigated disaster and tragedy is not completely justified. In fact, in two respects this impression must be amended.

First, in the immediate aftermath of the incident of the spies, Moshe was directed to communicate to Bnai Yisrael laws that would become effective with the nation's entry into the Land of Israel. These laws included a general requirement to accompany sacrifices with wine libations, and the *mitzvah* of *challah*. This *mitzvah* requires that when a person creates a dough of requisite size a portion be separated and given as a gift to the *kohanim* – the priests.

Rabbaynu Avraham ibn Ezra comments that these laws were taught to the people at this time to provide reassurance. They were devastated by the realization that they would not achieve the dream they had anticipated. They would never escape the wilderness. They would wander until they died. They needed a source of hope. Somehow, the dream had to be kept alive. These laws communicated to the people that they would expire in the wilderness but the dream would survive them. Their children would achieve the dream denied to their own generation.[34] In other words, immediately after the incident of the spies, the nation received a message of consolation from Hashem.

---

[33] Rav Meir Leibush ben Yechiel Michel (Malbim), *HaTorah VeHaMitzvah – Commentary on Sefer Devarim*, 1:45.
[34] Rabbaynu Avraham ibn Ezra, *Commentary on Sefer BeMidbar*, 15:2.

Second, in Moshe's review of the incident of the spies in Sefer Devarim he adds a detail that is not included in the first account of the incident in Sefer BeMidbar. He explains that after their defeat by the nations of Cana'an the people repented[35] and cried over their sin. In other words, although belated, they recognized that they had sinned and undertook to repent. Out of tragedy, some good emerged. The nation recognized its mistake and embarked on a path of change and growth.

But did the nation succeed in reinventing itself? Did Hashem's message of consolation encourage the people to continue to strive for the realization of the precious dream and to labor to make Bnai Yisrael more worthy of its realization?

And the people strove with Moshe, and spoke, saying: Would that we had perished when our brethren perished before Hashem! And why have you brought the assembly of Hashem into this wilderness, to die there, we and our cattle? And why have you made us to come up out of Egypt, to bring us in unto this evil place? It is not a place of seed, or of figs, or of vines, or of pomegranates; neither is there any water to drink. (BeMidbar 20:3-5)

3. The true tragedy of the generation of the wilderness

There are two powerful indications that they did not succeed in converting the realization of their sin into a catalyst for change; their initial repentance was not internalized and was not developed into an ongoing process of spiritual growth.

The first indication is that they did not secure Hashem's forgiveness. Maimonides explains that negative decrees by Hashem are not absolute. Repentance can secure salvation from any punishment.[36] The fact that the generation did expire in the wilderness and did not enter the Land of Israel suggests that their repentance did not proceed beyond the powerful but passing recognition of failure in the aftermath of their defeat.

The second indication is suggested by two incidents in Parshat Chukat. As explained above, the *parasha* describes events that took place thirty-eight years after the incident of the spies. This is the story of the new generation – the generation destined to finally realize the dream.

However, this new generation, in some important respects, is not very different from its predecessor. The above passages describe the nation complaining to Moshe over absence of a water supply. They suggest that Moshe has failed them and not fulfilled the promise to bring them to a rich and fertile land. In sentiment and in phrasing, their complaints mirror those of two of the most wicked individuals of the prior generation – Datan and Aviram.

Later, the people bemoan the austerity of their diet composed primarily of the manna. The very complaints that their parents had expressed thirty-eight years ago, this generation renewed.

Both of these incidents suggest that the thirty-eight years in the wilderness did not produce spiritual growth. If their parents had repented and reinvented themselves spiritually, then their children would have learned from them. They would be the product of their parents' enlightened outlook. They would not return to and reassert the very complaints that obsessed their parents.

---

[35] Translation of Malbim.

[36] Rabbaynu Moshe ben Maimon (Rambam) *Commentary on the Mishne*, Introduction.

In short, the generation of the wilderness achieved its highest level of self awareness after the sin of the spies. But that self awareness represented the pinnacle of their personal development. From that height the generation did not advance. Instead, the moment of realization passed and, with time, that generation resumed its familiar mode of thought. It passed its attitudes on to the next generation.

Then we turned, and took our journey into the wilderness by the way to the Reed Sea, as Hashem spoke unto me; and we compassed Mount Seir many days. (Devarim 2:1)

4. Movement without progress

In his final address to Bnai Yisrael, Moshe describes these thirty-eight years as a period during which the nation circumnavigated Mount Seir. Commenting on Moshe's words, Rav Yosef Dov Soloveitchik *Zt"l* suggests that this description communicates more than the route traveled by the nation. It communicates a message of lost and wasted time – circular motion without forward progress.[37] The above discussion suggests that Moshe's description also communicates the spiritual character of those years. Despite a promising beginning, nothing positive occurred. At the end of thirty-eight years a new generation took the place of a prior generation plagued by many of the same shortcomings and troubled by the same doubts.

Why did Hashem's reassurance of the inevitability of the nation's destiny not inspire the generation? Why did the initial repentance not function as a catalyst for meaningful spiritual growth?

The apparent lesson is that meaningful spiritual advancement is not the result of a sudden realization or epiphany. Instead, it requires sustained effort and a plan of action. The generation of the wilderness did achieve a moment of clarity. At that moment, the members of that generation recognized that they had committed a terrible sin and thereby, condemned themselves to a terrible fate. However, that recognition – although vivid and intense – did not have a lasting effect. In fact, even that lucid realization was forgotten with time.

Spiritual growth occurs through sustained effort. The generation of the wilderness did not translate its clear vision into this sustained effort. Consequently, the vision had no long term impact.

5. A contemporary parallel

A contemporary phenomenon will help us better understand the experience of the generation of the wilderness. It is common for graduates of yeshiva high schools to spend the year following high school graduation in Israel. Many of these students spend the year in a Torah learning program. Many undergo remarkable spiritual growth during this year. Upon return to the United States these students enroll in colleges and universities. They recognize that the campus environment will present spiritual challenges. They feel prepared to confront these challenges and are confident that they will remain devoted to their spiritual values.

Too often these students do not succeed in remaining true to these values. They experience a rapid process of spiritual deterioration that strips them of the values embraced while in Israel. Often, by the time these students complete their degree, they have abandoned their commitment to spiritual values and observance.

---

[37] Rav Yosef Dov Soloveitchik, Recorded Lecture on Parshat Chukat.

The experience of these young people demonstrates that spiritual values are rarely stagnant. In order to retain one's commitment to these values one must actually invest in developing and strengthening them. Without an investment in spiritual growth, spiritual decline is almost inevitable.

6. Move forward or invite defeat

The reasons for this phenomenon are twofold. First, our cultural and social milieu is antagonistic to spiritual values. In order to resist the pressures of this environment, we must positively commit to growing spiritually. If we do not dedicate ourselves to growth and make the corresponding investment of time and energy, we will be overcome by our surroundings and adopt the values promoted by our environment.

Second, we are all complex. The human personality includes both a need for spiritual fulfillment and a strongly established material orientation. Our spiritual vision and commitment competes with and is opposed by our natural material perspective.

Consequently, a person who wishes to have a meaningful spiritual life is like a swimmer who is attempting to proceed upstream against the current. The swimmer must labor to advance just to remain in the same place. This is also true of a spiritually committed person. Because of the environmental influences and the complexity of our own personalities we must strive to advance our spiritual agenda if we are to not compromise or abandon our spiritual values.

Young people entering college campuses spiritually inspired often imagine that the experiences from which they drew inspiration and their existing commitment to spiritual values will sustain them throughout their college experience. Their error is that past experiences and existing values are inadequate to meet this challenge. An ongoing commitment to growth and a corresponding investment of time and energy are the only way to persevere. When one is not advancing spiritually, one is falling back.

In short, the experience of the generation of the wilderness beckons us to learn from their failure. It implores us to not take for granted our spiritual values but to invest in their advancement. If we do not move forward, we fall back.

"And the entire congregation of Bnai Yisrael came to the wilderness of Tzin in the first month. And Miryam died there and she was buried there. And there was no water for the congregation. And they gathered against Moshe and Ahron." (BeMidbar 20:1-2)

Our *parasha* tells of the final episodes of Bnai Yirsrael's wanderings in the wilderness. The Torah tells us that Miryam died. Next, the Torah relates that there the nation did not have water. The people approached Moshe and Ahron to complain about their predicament. Hashem commanded Moshe to provide water from a stone. Moshe and Ahron sinned in the process of following these instructions. Hashem condemned Moshe and Ahron to die in the wilderness. They were not permitted to enter the land of Israel. In short, three incidents are related within a few passages. First, Miryam dies. Second, there is no water. Third, Moshe and Ahron sin and are punished.

The commentaries are concerned with the relationship between these incidents. Many maintain that there is a direct connection between Miryam's death and the failure of the water supply. They explain that Hashem provided water to Bnai Yisrael in the desolate wilderness.

This miracle was a reward for the merit of Miryam. With her death, the nation no longer deserved this miracle. The water supply immediately failed.[38]

Rabbaynu Avraham ibn Ezra rejects this approach. He offers a simple interpretation of the connection between the three events. He begins with the assertion that there is no connection between Miryam's death and the depletion of the water supply. Instead, the Chumash is explaining the deaths of Miryam, Moshe and Ahron in unison. First, the Chumash tells of Miryam's passing. The Torah then explains that there was no water for the nation. This is not to suggest any connection between Miryam's death and the lack of water. The Torah is introducing the events that precipitated the deaths of Moshe and Ahron.[39]

And the entire congregation of Bnai Yisrael came to the wilderness of Tzin in the first month. And the nation dwelled in Kadesh. And Miryam died there and she was buried there. And there was no water for the congregation. And they gathered before Moshe and Ahron. (BeMidbar 20:1-2)

Bnai Yisrael's Response to the Death of Miryam

The Chumash explains that Miryam died. Immediately thereafter, Bnai Yisrael found themselves without water. This implies a connection between the death of Miryam and the exhaustion of the water supply. Rashi discuses this relationship. Our Sages explain that the forty years Bnai Yisrael traveled in the wilderness Hashem provided water. This miracle was performed in response to the merit of Miryam. Therefore, with Miryam's passing, the miracle of the water ended.[40] Don Yitzchak Abravanel explains that our Sages did not intend to indicate that a well followed Bnai Yisrael in the wilderness. Instead, their message is that Bnai Yisrael miraculously found water in each encampment. The people were traveling in an arid and desolate land. Yet, incredibly they always found water.[41]

Klee Yakar offers an alternative explanation of the relationship between Miryam's death and the exhaustion of the water supply. He acknowledges the comments of the Sages that the water supply was a result of Miryam's merit. However, he does not conclude that her death should have resulted in the discontinuation of this wonder. He explains that the suspension of this miracle was caused by Bnai Yisrael's reaction to the loss. The Chumash explains that Miryam died and was buried. There is no mention of mourning. The implication is that the nation did not mourn Miryam adequately. She was not fully appreciated. Her loss was not recognized as a calamity. Hashem wished to demonstrate the righteousness of Miryam. He discontinued the miracle that her merit had made possible.[42]

Klee Yakar's comments raise an important question. Why was Miryam not appreciated? Ahron and Moshe were mourned. Their deaths were seen as tragedies. Why did the people not have a similar response to the loss of Miryam?

---

[38] Rabbaynu Shlomo ben Yitzchak (Rashi), *Commentary on Sefer BeMidbar* 20:2.
[39] Rabbaynu Avraham ibn Ezra, *Commentary on Sefer BeMidbar* 20:2.
[40] Rabbaynu Shlomo ben Yitzchak (Rashi), *Commentary on Sefer BeMidbar* 20:2.
[41] Don Yitzchak Abravanel, *Commentary on Sefer BeMidbar* 20:1.
[42] Rabbaynu Shlomo Ephraim Lontshitz, *Commentary Klee Yakar on Sefer BeMidbar* 20:2.

Moshe and Ahron were providers. They had delivered the nation from bondage. They had cared for the people during their sojourn in the wilderness. Bnai Yisrael recognized their dependence on these two giants. Miryam was not a visible leader. She lived a life of righteousness. But she did not conduct her affairs in a public forum. The nation did not recognize a dependency upon Miryam. Therefore, her death was not immediately recognized as a tragedy.

The nation erred in its assessment of Miryam's significance. A nation is the sum of its individual members. Each member contributes to the spiritual whole of the nation. Miryam was an individual of tremendous spiritual perfection. With the loss of Miryam, the spiritual level of the nation was diminished. Bnai Yisrael failed to recognize the importance of the quiet, private *tzadik*. Loss of the water supply drew their attention to this error.

The congregation had no water; so they assembled against Moshe and Aharon. (BeMidbar 20:2)

Moshe, the Real Deal – part 2

The sin of Moshe and Aharon and their punishment

The above passage introduces one of the most disturbing incidents in the Torah. The nation is in the wilderness of Tzin. The people have no water. They confront Moshe and Aharon. The incident concludes with Moshe and Aharon providing water to the nation but being punished for the manner in which they conduct themselves. They will perish before leading the nation into the Land of Israel.

The commentators deal with two obvious and troubling questions. First, the Torah does not specifically identify the sin committed by Moshe and Aharon. What was their sin? Second, Moshe and Aharon had dedicated themselves to leading the Jewish people from bondage into the Land of Israel. Hashem punished them by depriving them of the opportunity to complete their mission. Why did they deserve such a severe punishment? In order to properly understand this incident and the answers to these questions, we must return to Parshat Korach.

Korach accused Moshe of implementing a personal agenda

Parshat Korach described the revolt of Korach and his followers. The specific issue that provoked this rebellion was the appointment of Aharon and his sons as *Kohen Gadol* and *Kohanim* – as High Priest and priests. Korach and his followers believed that the priesthood belonged to the firstborn. They accused Moshe of acting on his own accord in depriving the firstborn of their prominence and reassigning the priesthood to his brother and family. In other words, their contention was that Moshe was not acting at Hashem's direction and as His agent. Instead, he was implementing a personal agenda.[43]

Moshe responded by challenging his opponents to a test. They would join with Aharon and each would offer a sacrifice of incense. Hashem would indicate the one whom He has selected by accepting his offering. The challenge was accepted. The following day the incense sacrifices were offered. Hashem sent forth a fire that consumed Korach and those of his

---

[43] This characterization of the dispute is developed by Ibn Ezra. See part 1 for a more extensive discussion of the dispute.

followers who participated in the test. At the same moment, the earth opened. The fissure swallowed Korach's other followers.

On the following day the congregation of the Children of Israel complained against Moshe and Aharon saying: You have killed the nation of Hashem. (BeMidbar 17:6)

Hashem responds to the people's continued suspicion of Moshe

These events did not resolve the doubts surrounding Moshe's actions. The people accused Moshe of bringing about the deaths of those who opposed them. Rabbaynu Avraham ibn Ezra explains that the people were not convinced of Moshe's and Aharon's legitimacy. They suspected that somehow Moshe had effectuated the wonders that killed his opponents. And even if these wonders were acts of Hashem, perhaps, He was responding to Moshe's prayers that his adversaries be punished. In other words, those killed died directly or indirectly at the hands of Moshe and not as punishment for their wickedness.[44]

Hashem responded to these accusations by bringing a plague upon the nation. Then, Hashem commanded Moshe to organize an overt demonstration of His selection of Aharon and his sons to serve as His *Kohanim*. He directed Moshe to collect the staffs of the princes of the twelve tribes. Aharon was to inscribe his name on the staff for the tribe of Leyve. All the staffs were to be placed before the Sacred Ark. Hashem would demonstrate whom He wished to serve as His *Kohanim* and *Kohen Gadol* through the blossoming of one of these staffs. Moshe acted as directed. The staff of Aharon blossomed.

The reasonable conclusion for the nation to draw from the blossoming of Aharon's staff was that Moshe had appointed Aharon and his sons as *Kohanim* and *Kohen Gadol* at Hashem's direction. The plague Hashem brought upon the nation in response to the accusations made against Moshe communicated that he acted as Hashem's agent. The commandments that he communicated to the people were given to them by Hashem. Moshe was merely the messenger acting as Hashem's intermediary with the nation. However, in Parshat Chukat, the Torah explains that the doubts regarding Moshe's agency remained unresolved.

And the nation contended with Moshe and they said, saying: If only we had died the death of our brothers, before Hashem! Why did you bring the assembly of Hashem to this wilderness to die there – we and our livestock? Why did you bring us up from Egypt to bring us to this evil place? It is not a place for planting, fig, vine, and pomegranate. And there is no water to drink. (BeMidbar 20:3-5)

Moshe is challenged at Tzin

The nation arrives at the wilderness of Tzin. There is no water. The people fear for their lives. They cannot understand their situation. They conclude that their tragic circumstance is the result of Moshe's failed leadership. He has brought them to this place. He is responsible for their inevitable deaths. Underlying their conclusion is the same doubt voiced by Korach and his followers. It is the doubt expressed by the nation in response to the death of Moshe's opponents. Is Moshe truly Hashem's agent? If he is His agent, then how can the nation now be facing death in this wilderness.

This doubt undermines the foundation of the Torah. If Moshe is not Hashem's agent, then the nation cannot be certain that the commandments he has communicated are from Hashem.

---

[44] Rabbaynu Avraham ibn Ezra, *Commentary on Sefer BeMidbar*, 17:6.

They cannot know with certainty that Moshe has acted solely as Hashem's faithful scribe and communicated to the nation only the word of Hashem.

And Hashem spoke to Moshe saying: Take the staff and assemble the congregation – you and Aharon, your brother. And you should speak to the rock before them. It will give forth its water. And you will bring forth to them water from the rock and give water to drink to the congregation and to its livestock. (BeMidbar 20:7-8)

The sin of Moshe and Aharon

In these passages, Hashem directs Moshe to bring forth water from a rock. Moshe and Aharon assembled the nation and proceeded to fulfill this directive. However, they sinned. In some manner, their actions did not conform to Hashem's directive or wishes. What precisely was their sin?

The most well-known response is provided by Rashi. Hashem directed Moshe and Aharon to speak to the rock. They were to *command* it to give forth water. The Torah describes Moshe striking the rock rather than commanding it. This detracted from the intended miracle.[45]

One of the most interesting explanations of Moshe's and Aharon's sin is provided by Rambam – Maimonides. Before striking the rock, Moshe rebuked the people. He said, "Listen now, those who are rebels." He expressed his anger toward the people. Hashem expected Moshe to model appropriate behavior for the nation. In becoming angry and demonstrating to the people his temper, he failed to fulfill this expectation. Furthermore, in observing Moshe's anger the people reasoned that his reaction reflected Hashem's response to their complaints. They concluded that Hashem was angry with them. Hashem had not communicated to Moshe that He was angry with the people. In demonstrating anger, Moshe misrepresented Hashem.[46]

The simplest interpretation of Moshe's and Aharon's sin is provided by Rabbaynu Chananel. Moshe challenged the people. He said to them, "Will we bring forth for you water from this rock?" This challenge was poorly phrased. Moshe should have said, "Will Hashem bring forth for you water from this rock?" Through his phrasing, Moshe suggested that he and Aharon were more than Hashem's agents. He implied that they were somehow causing the water to emerge.[47]

---

[45] Rabbaynu Shlomo ben Yitzchak (Rashi), *Commentary on Sefer BeMidbar* 20:11-12. Ramban objects to this interpretation. The miracle was that the rock gave forth water. This wonder was not lessened through striking the rock. Rashi responds to this issue enigmatically. Hashem told Moshe to command the rock to give forth water. Hashem intended to teach a lesson to the people. A rock is inanimate. Its obedience to Hashem's commands does not secure a reward and its disobedience does not result in punishment. Nonetheless, it is faithful. Human beings whose obedience and disobedience have consequences should certainly adhere to Hashem's commands. This response does not seem to completely address Ramban's objection. How did striking the rock undermine this lesson? See Moshe ben Avraham of Przemysl (Met), *Hoe'il Moshe*, Parshat Chukat. He explains that Hashem commanded Moshe and Aharon to speak to the rock and to not employ any substantial material action in bringing about the miracle. Any action taken by Moshe or Aharon might be interpreted as having some role in the emergence of the water. Rather than being understood as the rock responding to Hashem's command, the event would be interpreted as somehow caused by their action.

[46] R' Moshe ben Maimon (Rambam) *Commentary on the Mishne*, Mesechet Avot, Intro, Chp 4.

Adding a personal element to the execution of Hashem's command

Let's further consider these interpretations. According to Rashi, Moshe and Aharon were punished because they did not perform Hashem's commandment in the manner He had instructed. According to Rambam, Moshe and Aharon did not actually deviate from their instructions. However, they were expected to model ideal behavior and communicate clearly Hashem's position. In expressing their anger, they failed to meet this expectation. They incorporated personal feelings into their response to the people. According to Rabbaynu Chananel, they did not violate their instructions. However, Moshe expressed himself in a manner suggesting that he and Aharon were more than agents of Hashem; they were active participants in causing the miracle. According to all these interpretations, Moshe's and Aharon's sin was the insertion of a personal element into the execution of Hashem's command. Through this insertion, they actually engaged in or appeared to engage in the very behavior of which they were suspected. They stood accused of being more than agents of Hashem and they indeed sinned by becoming or appearing to be more than His agents.

The message of the punishment

We can now better understand the punishment Moshe and Aharon received. Rashi and Rabbaynu Avraham ibn Ezra explain that their punishment sanctified Hashem.[48] How did their severe punishment accomplish this? This punishment conclusively addressed the accusations of the nation and provided absolute proof of Moshe's authenticity as Hashem's prophet. It demonstrated that Hashem would not tolerate Moshe and Aharon acting as other than His agents or misrepresenting Him. Now, there could be no question that the commandments were Hashem's word and not Moshe's inventions. Hashem's punishment of Moshe and Aharon showed that He demanded perfect fidelity from His prophets and would immediately respond to any attempt to misrepresent His will.

Rambam outlines thirteen principle that are the foundations of the Torah. One of these principles is that the Torah was given to us by Hashem. This means that the Written Torah and the fundamental material in the Oral Tradition were communicated to us by Hashem through Moshe.[49] Parshat Korach and Parshat Chukat both deal with the importance of this principle and the means through which it was firmly established.

All thirteen principles are important. However, the principle that has had the greatest practical impact upon Jewish religious practice is that the Torah is from Hashem. This principle distinguishes Orthodoxy from the other branches of Judaism.

The Jewish people is a political/national and religious entity. As a religious movement, the branches of Judaism have different perspectives. These differences relate to fundamental principles and should not be minimized. However, as a political entity, we must seek unity and fellowship. This creates a tension. Can we work together for the benefit of our people despite real and substantial religious differences?

---

[47] Rabbaynu Chananel, *Commentary of Sefer BeMidbar* 20:12.
[48] Rabbaynu Shlomo ben Yitzchak (Rashi), *Commentary on Sefer BeMidbar* 20:13. Rabbaynu Avraham ibn Ezra, *Commentary on Sefer BeMidbar 20:13*.
[49] R' Moshe ben Maimon (Rambam) *Commentary on the Mishne*, Mesechet Sanhedrin 10:1.

There are two approaches to this challenge. One is to minimize the religious differences. This means reducing differences to a matter of opinion. Opinions are subjective. If religious perspective is just opinion, then all positions have equal claim to legitimacy. Unfortunately, the corollary is that all positions are subjective and have very limited legitimacy. If we adopt this approach, then we compromise the foundations of Judaism.

The other approach is to agree to disagree. In other words, to respect or accept differences without minimizing them. This is much more difficult. It requires that we acknowledge that we do not recognize the legitimacy of each other's religious perspectives. Yet, despite these important differences we seek common-ground and work in unity as a political entity. If our religious views are to remain meaningful, we must find the means of treading on this more difficult path.

And Hashem spoke to Moshe saying: Take the staff and you and your brother Aharon gather the nation. Speak to the rock before their eyes and you will bring forth from the rock water for them. You will give the congregation and their cattle water to drink. (BeMidbar 20:7-8)

Humanity's Role in its Partnership with Hashem

1. Moshe's trespass in striking the rock

Parshat Chukat describes one of the most tragic incidents in the Torah. Bnai Yisrael arrive to the Wilderness of Tzin and they have no water. They complain to Moshe and Aharon; they accuse them of failing to fulfill their promise to bring them to a rich and fertile land. They tell them that they would prefer to have died earlier rather than face the miserable death by thirst that now confronts them. Hashem commands Moshe and Aharon to bring forth water from a rock. Moshe and Aharon assemble the nation; Moshe sternly chastises them for their failure of faith – referring to the people as rebels. Then, Moshe completes the mission. He strikes the rock and brings forth water.

But Hashem criticizes Moshe and Aharon for their conduct. He tells them that because they acted inappropriately, they will not lead the people into the Land of Israel. Indeed, they will perish in the wilderness. However, the Torah does not reveal the exact nature of their transgression.

Rashi suggests that Moshe sinned in striking the rock. Hashem instructed Moshe to speak to the rock and to bring forth its water without exerting physical force upon it.[50] Rashbam essentially agrees with Rashi. However, his comments include a curious and important observation. He acknowledges that Hashem told Moshe to "speak" to the rock. However, Moshe has good cause to misinterpret this command. Moshe assumed that this instruction should not be understood literally. Hashem had also instructed him to take with him his staff. Rocks are not sentient. Moshe understood that "speaking" in this context communicated an instruction to use this staff to strike the rock.[51]

Gershonides adds another important observation. The above passage includes the exact instructions that Hashem communicated to Moshe. The instructions specify that Moshe should

---

[50] Rabbaynu Shlomo ben Yitzchak (Rashi), Commentary on Sefer BeMidbar 20:12.
[51] Rabbaynu Shemuel ben Meir (Rashbam) Commentary on Sefer BeMidbar 20:10.

speak to the rock. However, Gershonides notes that the phrase can be properly understood to mean that Moshe should speak to the people regarding the rock. This was the interpretation that Moshe adopted.

Moshe and Aharon gathered the congregation before the rock. And he said to them: Listen now rebels. Will I bring forth for you water from this rock? (BeMidbar 20:10)

2. Moshe's misinterpretation of Hashem's instructions

Moshe executed Hashem's instructions as he understood them. He gathered the nation at the site of the rock and he addressed the assembly regarding the rock. He observed that the rock before them was a common bolder strewn upon a barren expanse. It could not be a source of water. Yet, he proposed to demonstrate that through Hashem's miracle the rock would indeed be transformed into a spring of fresh water. After delivering this address – as he understood he had been instructed – he lifted the staff he had been directed to bring and brought it down upon the rock. As Moshe had prophesized, water gushed forth from the rock and the people were rescued from their suffering.[52]

Moshe had misinterpreted Hashem's instructions. Hashem had not directed him to take the staff in order to strike the rock. Hashem had not intended for him to speak to the people regarding the rock but to speak to the rock and to instruct the rock to bring forth water. Through his misinterpretation of Hashem's instructions Moshe diminished the magnitude of the miracle and Hashem's glory.[53]

This raises an interesting question: Why did Moshe misinterpret Hashem's instructions? Why did he not even recognize that the instructions required further clarification and seek more specific instructions?

Geshonides suggests that the answer to this question is contained in the above passage. Moshe, in anger, rebuked the nation. In this moment of irritation Moshe acted without fully considering what exactly Hashem required of him. Because he acted in anger and without adequate forethought he misinterpreted Hashem's instructions.[54] Rabbaynu Ovadia Sforno takes this explanation a step further. He explains that Moshe concluded that Hashem had instructed him to perform the lesser miracle of striking the rock because it was inconceivable to him that the people deserved the greater miracle that would occur through speaking to the rock.[55] In short, Moshe was blinded from fully understanding Hashem's instructions by his anger with the people. Instead, he interpreted Hashem's instructions in a manner that corresponded with his disappointment with the nation. What was the source of Moshe's anger and disillusionment?

---

[52] Rabbaynu Levi ben Gershon (Ralbag / Gershonides), Commentary on Sefer BeMidbar, 20:8.
[53] The commentaries who explain that Moshe's sin was that he struck the rock agree that by doing so he diminished the intended miracle. However, it is not self-evident that the rock's production of water was rendered less miraculous, through Moshe's error. Therefore, these commentators also discuss this issue. They present a variety of views regarding the inferiority of the actual miracle – initiated with the striking of the rock – as compared to the intended miracle. Rashi and Rabbaynu Ovadia Sforno are two the commentators who discuss this issue and come to different conclusions.
[54] Rabbaynu Levi ben Gershon (Ralbag / Gershonides), Commentary on Sefer BeMidbar, 20:8.
[55] Rabbaynu Ovadia Sforno, Commentary on Sefer BeMidbar, 20:8.

And Bnai Yisrael – the entire congregation – came to the Wilderness of Tzin, in the first month. The nation was situated in Kadesh and Miryam died there and was buried there. (BeMidbar 20:1)

3. The thirty-eight year gap in the Torah

The twentieth chapter of Sefer BeMidbar begins by announcing that the events that will be described occurred in the first month of the year. The Torah does not clearly state to which year it refers. However, Rashi indicates the year in his comments on a latter phrase in the passage. The passage states that "Bnai Yisrael – the entire congregation" arrived in the Wilderness of Tzin. The phrase "the entire congregation" seems superfluous. However, Rashi suggests that the phrase is intended to communicate an important message. According to Rashi, the phrase communicates that Bnai Yisrael arrived at the Wilderness of Tzin as a complete congregation. It was no longer a mixture of those who would merit to enter the Land of Israel and the members of the generation that had been condemned to die in the wilderness. Those who were condemned to die in the wilderness had died, and now, their children composed a new generation that was destined to possess the Land.[56]

This means that the events described in Parshat Chukat occurred in the fortieth year of the nation's sojourn in the wilderness. Furthermore, the Torah is revealing that it is discussing a new generation. Through Parshat Korach, the Torah discussed the experiences of the generation that was redeemed from Egypt. Parshat Chukat resumes the description of the Bnai Yisrael experiences after a passage of thirty-eight years – in the fortieth year of the nation's journey toward the Land of Israel.

Forty years prior to the events in Parshat Chukat Moshe had led the people out of Egypt. They were destined to shortly enter the land promised to the Patriarchs. However, the generation that was redeemed from Egypt never saw the fulfillment of this promise. They rebelled against Hashem and they were condemned to die in the wilderness. Even this harsh consequence did not reform that generation. Parshat Korach describes the continued lapses of the generation and their contentions with Moshe and Hashem.

Finally, that generation passed. A new generation is now poised to enter the land promised for the Forefathers. The promise to Avraham, Yitzchak, and Yaakov will be fulfilled. The historic moment has arrived. It is at this very moment that this new generation addresses Moshe and Hashem with the same contentious attitude that condemned their parents to forty years of wandering in the wilderness.

In this context, the full meaning of Moshe's rebuke and the feelings it expressed can easily be imagined. Moshe feared that he was seeing the errors and sins of the past take root in this new generation. All of his labor and toil over the past forty years would be wasted. This generation was adopting the same poisonous attitudes that had condemned their parents to banishment in the desolate wilderness. This fear quickly transformed into anger and found expressions in Moshe's judgments, words, and actions.

And Hashem spoke to Moshe and Aharon: Because you did not have faith in Me to glorify Me you will not bring this congregation to the land that I gave to them. (Sefer BeMidbar 20:12)

---

[56] Rabbaynu Shlomo ben Yitzchak (Rashi), Commentary on Sefer BeMidbar 20:1.

He said: It is not your responsibility to complete the work but neither are you free to disregard it. (Avot 2:16)

4. The partnership between humanity and Hashem

Ultimately, this account ends in tragedy. Moshe is punished for his misdeed. He will not be permitted to accompany the people into the Land of Israel. This generation that Moshe so feared would squander its opportunity would take possession of the land. But Moshe, their shepherd, would not be among them. How does this severe consequence correspond with Moshe's sin?

In the above passage, Hashem tells Moshe that he did not have complete faith in Him. Moshe acted in anger. He certainly acted improperly. But wherein was his lack of faith in Hashem? Apparently, Moshe's fear and anger expressed this lack of faith. Hashem promised the Patriarchs that their descendants would possess the Land of Israel. He redeemed these descendants from Egypt. When the redeemed generation did not merit to enter the land, Hashem patiently nurtured a new more courageous generation that would confidently conquer its enemies. Hashem had entered into a covenant with the Forefathers and it would be fulfilled. It was not Moshe's responsibility to bring about the fulfillment of this covenant. It is our responsibility to serve Hashem.

Moshe's fear and anger expressed his deep dread that he would not succeed in leading this generation into the Land of Israel. He would fail in his mission. Again, the conquest of the land and the fulfillment of the covenant would be delayed. Gripped by this fear and anxiety, he acted to save the generation and to move his mission forward to its conclusion. However, Moshe's feelings and actions indicate that he so indentified with Hashem's mission – fulfillment of the promise made to the Forefathers – that he adopted it as his own. In doing so, he confused his role with Hashem's. Hashem would be true to His covenant. We must be true to Hashem.

Moshe's punishment gave eloquent expression to this message. The mission that Moshe had adopted as his own would be fulfilled through another leader. The message communicated is the realization of Hashem's covenantal promise is His responsibility. Each of us is to serve the role to which we are assigned. We are to fulfill our obligations with diligence and wisdom. However, we are members of a partnership with Hashem. In this partnership we are assigned a specific role. We must trust in Hashem that He will fulfill His role. Through Moshe's punishment we are told that Hashem does not require the assistance or agency of a specific human being in order to fulfill His promises. The nation would possess the land without Moshe. Instead, our efforts and toils to accomplish His will are privileges and we must execute our responsibilities with wisdom and understanding.[57]

This concept is beautifully expressed by Ribbi Tarfon in Avot. We are responsible to act as Hashem and the Torah requires of us. We must fulfill the role assigned to us. However, we must also recognize that the outcome of our efforts and toils is never assured. It is Hashem who determines the outcome.

---

[57] This interpretation of Moshe's state of mind and his punishment corresponds with an explanation I recall hearing many years ago from my rebbi, Rav Israel Chait.

And the Canaanite king of Arad who dwelt in the south heard that Yisrael was coming by the way of Atarim. And he fought with Yisrael and he captured captives. (BeMidbar 21:1)

The Importance of Carefully-Formulated Prayer

Bnai Yisrael were traveling in the wilderness to the land of Israel. The people were attacked by the King of Arad. Rashi comments that these "Canaanites" were really the people of Amalake. Amalake had previously battled Bnai Yisrael. In that conflict, the prayers of Moshe and the people had a fundamental role in Amalake's defeat. On this occasion, Amalake sought to protect itself from these prayers. The king of Amalake commanded his people to speak the language of the Canaanites. He hoped that Bnai Yisrael would believe that they were under attack from Canaanites. Bnai Yisrael would pray for delivery from this Canaanite adversary. The prayers would improperly describe the attackers. These pleas would not be answered.

Bnai Yisrael encountered the enemy. They were confused. The attackers were speaking the language of the Canaanites. However, their clothing indicated they were the people of Amalake. The decision was made to formulate the prayers in a general format. The people asked Hashem for salvation from the enemy. They did not specify the identity of the adversary. These prayers were answered and Bnai Yisrael were victorious.[58]

Hashem is omniscient. He knew the true identity of the attackers. Bnai Yisrael might pray for delivery from the Canaanites, but Hashem would know the identity of the actual adversary. Yet, Rashi implies that had the people mistakenly pleaded for rescue from the Canaanites, their prayers would have been useless.

The implications of Rashi's comments are very critical for properly understanding *tefilah* – prayer. It is commonly believed that the essential component of the process of prayer is the sincerity of the petitioner. It is assumed that if one prays with good intention and earnestness, the requirement of *tefilah* has been fulfilled. Rashi's comments indicate that this is not true. There is no question that the prayers of a nation confronted with war are sincere. Recognition of mortal danger assures earnestness. Rashi tells us that nonetheless an inaccurate prayer would not have been answered. Sincerity without accuracy is inadequate. Only when these two elements are combined is the *tefilah* acceptable.

Maimonides explains that this idea guided our Sages in the formulation of the prayers. Our Sages realized that not every person could be expected to design the *tefilah* in an accurate and appropriate manner. Therefore, they designed the prayers for us. Through combining this legacy from our Sages with sincerity we can fulfill the obligation of *tefilah*.[59]

And the Canaanite, the king of Arad, who dwelt in the South, heard that Israel came by the way of Atarim. And he fought against Israel and took some of them captive. And Israel vowed a vow unto Hashem and said: If You will indeed deliver this people into my hand, then I will utterly destroy their cities. And Hashem heard the voice of Israel and delivered the Canaanites. And they utterly destroyed them and their cities. And the name of the place was called Charmah. (BeMidbar 21:1-3)

Appropriate and Inappropriate Vows

---

[58] Rabbaynu Shlomo ben Yitzchak (Rashi), *Commentary on Sefer BeMidbar* 21:1.
[59] Rabbaynu Moshe ben Maimon (Rambam) *Mishne Torah*, Hilchot Teffilah 1:4.

1. Bnai Yisrael's encounter with Arad

Parshat Chukat continues the narrative of Bnai Yisrael's journey through the wilderness to the Land of Israel. Parshat Korach focused on events that occurred in the second year of this journey. Parshat Chukat discusses events that took place in the final year. At this point in their journey, the nation is approaching the borders of the Land of Cana'an. The rulers of the land anticipate that they will soon be confronted with the invasion of Bnai Yisrael. The Kingdom of Arad launched a preemptive attack against Bnai Yisrael and although beaten back, achieves some success and takes captives.

In response to the attack Bnai Yisrael makes a vow to Hashem. The nation vows that if Hashem delivers Arad to them, then they will destroy their enemies and their cities. This interpretation of their vow reflects the literal translation of the passage.[60] However, most commentaries explain that the intent was not to destroy the cities. Instead, the people vowed that they would not take any of the spoils of the campaign for their personal use. All spoils would be contributed to the Mishcan – the Tabernacle – for its support and upkeep.[61]

The account ends by recording that Bnai Yisrael did conduct a successful campaign against Arad and adhered to the conditions of the vow.

In short, Bnai Yisrael recognized that the first encounter had a tragic element. Captives had been taken from among Bnai Yisrael. The people first made a vow to Hashem before launching a campaign against Arad to address this tragedy. What was the purpose of this vow and why did the people regard it as a necessary prerequisite to a campaign against Arad?

And Jacob vowed a vow, saying: If G-d will be with me, and will keep me in this way that I go, and will give me bread to eat, and raiment to put on, so that I come back to my father's house in peace, then Hashem will be my G-d, and this stone, which I have set up for a pillar, shall be G-d's house; and of all that You will give me I will surely give a tenth unto You. (Beresheit 28:20-22)

2. The substance and objective of Bnai Yisrael's vow

It will be helpful to more carefully consider the substance of the vow made by the nation. Essentially, the people were committing to forgoing the opportunity to enrich themselves with the spoils. Instead, they would contribute the spoils to the service of a higher cause – the Mishcan. Malbim discusses the objective of such a vow in the context of a similar incident.

The first city in the Land of Cana'an conquered by Bnai Yisrael was Yericho. Before capturing the city, Yehoshua made a vow that was very similar to the vow made before the campaign against Arad. Yehoshua pledged that all of the spoils would be contributed to the Mishcan. Malbim explains that Yehoshua's vow was intended to communicate an important idea. The conquest of Yericho was not accomplished through the brilliant tactical planning and flawless execution of an effective military campaign. It was a miraculous event and an expression of Hashem's providence. In fact, Hashem had conquered Yericho. Bnai Yisrael were not the true conquerors. Contributing the spoils of the victory to the Mishcan acknowledged that Hashem was the actual victor and the spoils were appropriately His.[62]

---

[60] Targum Unkelus Sefer BeMidbar 21:2.

[61] Rabbaynu Shlomo ben Yitzchak (Rashi), Commentary on Sefer BeMidbar 21:2.

[62] Baalai HaTosafot, Commentary on Sefer Bereshiet 28:20.

The same explanation can be applied to the vow made by Bnai Yisrael in this instance. The nation appealed to Hashem for His help in campaigning against Arad. They acknowledged that they lacked the strength, experience and resources to wage a successful battle against their enemy. They could only succeed with the support of Hashem. Their vow acknowledged that a victory would not be theirs. It would be an expression of Hashem's providence. Therefore, the spoils were rightfully Hashem's.

According to the Commentary of the Baalai HaTosefot, the model from this vow is derived from the vow made by Yaakov in the course of his journey from his father's home to the household of Lavan. Yaakov experienced a prophecy in which Hashem assured Yaakov that He would be with him. Yaakov responded and vowed that in response to the fulfillment of this prophecy he would create a house for Hashem at the site of the prophecy and he would tithe his wealth to Hashem.[63] The midrash explains that a principle is derived from Yaakov's vow. This principle is that it is appropriate to respond to challenges and danger with such vows. In other words, when a person is confronted with danger or a daunting challenge, it is fitting to take a vow to perform a meritorious act or adopt a virtuous behavior in exchange for deliverance from the peril.[64] In other words, the nation applied the principle demonstrated by Yaakov and responded to its sense of danger and peril by committing to a vow similar to the one developed by Yaakov.

Better is it that you should not vow, than that you should vow and not pay. (Kohelet 5:4)

3. The Torah's attitude toward vows

The commentators raise an important question regarding the appropriateness of the vows made by Yaakov and Bnai Yisrael. An introduction is required to understand the question.

The above passage explains that is preferable to refrain from making vows rather than making a vow and not fulfilling it. The Talmud explores this principle and concludes that, in general, vows should be avoided. If a person does make a vow, he should appeal to the court to release him from the vow.[65] This is accomplished by appearing before a court of three judges. The members of the court may be lay-judges. The laws governing the circumstances under which a court can release a person from a vow are somewhat complex. In general, if the court determines that the vow was made in error – without adequate consideration of its consequences – then the court can release the person from the vow.

Maimonides provides a brief summary of the Torah's position regarding vows. He explains that a person is permitted to make a vow in order to restrain himself from a negative behavior or encourage a positive behavior. Of course, this assumes that the additional imperative imposed by the vow is necessary for the proper behavior to be adopted or the negative behavior to be abandoned. For example, if a person is parsimonious and makes a vow to give a percentage of his monthly income to charity, the vow is appropriate. A person who struggles with laziness and makes a vow to walk for twenty minutes every day, has made a proper vow. Again, this assumes that the vow is necessary to establish the change in behavior. Other than under these circumstances, vows should be avoided, and if a vow is made, the person should appeal to the court to release him from the vow. Maimonides explains that the Torah discourages vows

---

[63] Midrash Rabbah Parshat VaYetze 70:1.
[64] Mesechet Hullin 2a.
[65] Mesechet Hullin 2a

because they are a potential "stumbling block". The violation of a vow is a serious sin. The more frequently a person resorts to making vows the more likely he is to violate one or more of his vows.[66]

With this introduction the question posed by the commentators emerges. The Torah discourages making vows. Why, then, was it appropriate for Yaakov and Bnai Yisrael to take vows? Would it not have been more appropriate for Yaakov to make a private commitment without framing it as a vow? Should not Bnai Yisrael have refrained from adopting the formal commitment of a vow? After the conquest they could have contributed the spoils to the Mishcan, even without previously making a vow. In fact, in the case of Yehoshua's vow regarding Yericho, the vow was violated, precipitating a terrible punishment.

One of the commentators on the Midrash Rabbah – Yefat Toar – contends that this question is implicitly acknowledged by the Midrash. As explained above, the model for making vows at times of peril is Yaakov. The Midrash is emphatic asserting that Yaakov's vow serves as a model. Yefat Toar suggests that the reason the Midrash emphasizes Yaakov's role as a model is that the assertion that such a vow is appropriate and even praiseworthy is completely counter-intuitive. In other words, had Yaakov not demonstrated that it is appropriate to make a vow at a time of peril, it would be assumed that even such vows are included in the Torah's general condemnation of making vows and creating potential stumbling blocks. When Bnai Yisrael made their vow in preparation of its campaign against Arad, it relied upon Yaakov's example.[67] However, it remains to be explained why vows are permitted and even encouraged at times of peril. Why are they not discouraged as potential entrapments?

4. Reconciling Bnai Yisrael's and Yaakov's vows with the Torah's attitude

Tosefot and others suggest that vows made in response to danger or at a time of peril do not fall within the Torah's general admonition against taking vows. They do not offer any indication of why such vows are excluded from the general principle. However, there is another unusual halachah regarding such vows that hints to the reason for their exclusion.

Ramah, in his glosses on Shulchan Aruch comments that not only is it fitting to make a vow at a time of peril, but such vows may not be annulled. In other words, it is not appropriate for a person to appeal to the court for release from such a vow.[68] According to Ramah the difference between vows made at a time of peril and a typical vow is extreme. A typical vow is discouraged. If one does take a vow, he is encouraged to appeal to the court for relief rather than risk violating the vow. A vow made at a time of peril is encouraged. If one does make this vow, he is discouraged from appealing to the court for release. He must endure the risk of violating the vow. How can this extreme contrast be explained?

In order to answer these questions, it is necessary to review an important message developed by Maimonides. Maimonides explains that when Bnai Yisrael is confronted with peril and danger it is incumbent upon the nation to call out to Hashem. Turning to Hashem is an acknowledgement that the challenge confronting the people is a consequence of their failings and unacceptable behaviors. This acknowledgement is the first step on the path to repentance. Taking

---

[66] Rabbaynu Moshe ben Maimon (Rambam) Mishne Torah, Hilchot Nedarim 3:23-25.

[67] Rav Shmuel Yaffa Ashkenazi, Yefat Toar Commentary of the Torah, Parshat Veytze (Quoted by Lekutim on Midrash Rabbah, Parshat VaYtze 70:1.)

[68] Rav Moshe Isserles, Comments on Shulchan Aruch, Yoreh De'ah 228:45.

this step will bring about the people's salvation.[69] Maimonides further explains that an individual confronted with danger and peril should also respond by calling out to Hashem.[70] In short, Maimonides maintains that we should respond to danger and peril by looking toward our own actions and behaviors as the cause. With this recognition we should call out to Hashem for His salvation and embark upon a journey of repentance.

In this framework, the Torah's treatment of vows made in response to danger and peril can be understood. Maimonides maintains that by calling out to Hashem one acknowledges personal responsibility for the challenge with which one is confronted and also embarks upon a path of repentance. However, essentially the person is asking Hashem to deliver him even though he has just taken the first step upon this path. Will the person continue on this journey of repentance? If delivered from the peril, will he maintain his commitment to change his behaviors and attitudes? Will the deliverance from the peril eliminate the essential motivation for change?

This is the role of the vow. The vow in response to peril is a firm commitment to change that must be executed. The commitment is made while still in peril but it is unlike a commitment that is made only in one's heart. A private and unarticulated commitment can be abandoned after the peril or danger has passed. A vow must be fulfilled. In fact, as explained above, Ramah rules that it should not be annulled by appeal to the court. Now, this ruling can be fully appreciated. The vow was a commitment to change that was intended to bind the person even after the danger and peril passed. It was intended to respond to and counter the natural tendency to be less motivated to change and repent once the motivator – the danger – has passed. Were it permitted to annul such a vow, then its very purpose and design would be undermined.

Now the exception granted to such vows from the general admonition against vows emerges. Ordinarily, vows are discouraged because they can ensnare a person in sin through their violation. Instead, a person should act properly without relying on a vow as a motivator. In other words, the problem with vows is that a vow is made at a moment during which the person feels that the vow is appropriate and at which he is fully committed to execute it. The fulfillment of the vow takes place at a later time. At that time the commitment and motivation may have passed and even recollection of the vow may have a faded and been lost.

This very characteristic of the vow is the reason that it is an appropriate response to danger. It is true that the vow made in the present is a commitment to act after the peril has passed. There is a real danger that it will be forgotten or ignored at this future time. However, the vow does give expression to the person's sincere commitment to change and repent. It translates a weak and unarticulated vision into a firm commitment.

And Israel sent messengers to Sichon the king of the Amorite saying: Let me pass through your land. We will not deviate into fields or vineyards. We will not drink water from the wells. We will go on the road selected by the King until we pass through your boundary. (BeMidbar 21:21-22)

Moshe's Attempt to Avoid War with Sichon

---

[69] Rabbaynu Moshe ben Maimon (Rambam) Mishne Torah, Hilchot Ta'aniyot 1:1-2.
[70] Rabbaynu Moshe ben Maimon (Rambam) Mishne Torah, Hilchot Ta'aniyot 1:9.

Bnai Yisrael approach the land of Sichon. In order to reach the Jordan, they must first pass through the land of Sichon and his people. Bnai Yisrael send messengers to Sichon and ask for permission to pass though his land in peace. Sichon rejects this request and launches an attack against Bnai Yisrael. Bnai Yisrael defeat Sichon, destroy his nation, and capture the entire territory of his nation. This land is subsequently incorporated into the portions of land awarded to the *shevatim* – the tribes – of Reuven, Gad, and half of Menashe.

It is noteworthy that Bnai Yisrael first attempted to pass through Sichon's territory in peace. The war that ensued was a consequence of Sichon's rejection of Bnai Yisrael's request. In other words, this war was not initiated by Bnai Yisrael. It was initiated by Sichon.

In his comments on these passages, Rashi points out that Bnai Yisrael were not specifically commanded by Hashem to offer peace. Nonetheless, Moshe felt that this offer was appropriate.[71] In these comments, Rashi does not explain Moshe's reason for seeking to avoid war. However, Moshe reviews this incident in Sefer Devarim. There, Rashi does offer further explanation. He explains that although Moshe was not specifically required to ask Sichon for permission to pass through his land in peace, Moshe deduced that such an offer would be appropriate. How did Moshe come to this conclusion?

Rashi's comments can only be appreciated, if we consider their context in Sefer Devarim. Moshe explains that Hashem told him that He would deliver Sichon and his nation into the hands of Bnai Yisrael. He commanded Moshe to wage war with Sichon. Moshe sent messengers to Sichon. Sichon rejected the offer presented by these messengers. Moshe attributes Sichon's rejection of the offer to Hashem's providence. Hashem hardened Sichon's heart – as He did to Paroh. Hashem repeated to Moshe that He will deliver Sichon and his land into the hands of Bani Yisrael. Moshe ends his account by reviewing Bnai Yisrael's remarkable conquest of Sichon and his land.[72]

These passages present a number of problems. Nachmanides summarizes these problems. Let us consider two of the issues he raises. First, Hashem told Moshe that he was to wage war against Sichon. The sequence of events suggested by the passages indicates that after receiving this command, Moshe asked Sichon for permission to pass through his land. How could Moshe offer peace to Sichon if Hashem had already commanded Bnai Yisrael to wage war? Second, Moshe acknowledges that Hashem hardened Sichon's heart. Sichon did not really have the ability to make a choice. Hashem deprived him of his free-will. If Sichon did not have free will, what was the objective in offering peace?

Based on these questions, Nachmanides suggests that the passages are not intended to relate the events in their actual sequence. The actual sequence was that, first, Moshe attempted to pass through the land in peace. Sichon rejected this offer. Moshe realized that Sichon had rejected this offer because Hashem had deprived him of the free will to make a reasonable choice. Then, Hashem commanded Moshe to wage war with Sichon and assured Moshe of Bnai Yisrael's victory.

This approach resolves the issues raised by Nachmandies. At the point that Moshe sent messengers to Sichon, he had not yet been commanded to wage war. He received this command after Sichon rejected the peace offer. Also, Moshe was convinced by Sichon's reaction to his

---

[71] Rabbaynu Shlomo ben Yitzchak (Rashi), *Commentary on Sefer BeMidbar* 21:22.
[72] Sefer Devarim 2:24-36.

peaceful offer that he had been deprived of his free will. But when he made the offer, Moshe assumed that there was a reasonable chance that it would be accepted.[73]

We can now return to Rashi's comments. Of course, Rashi must respond to the same problems in the passages identified by Nachmandies. However, his response is very different from Nachmandies'. Rashi begins with the assumption that the passages accurately relate the sequence of events. Hashem told Moshe to wage war with Sichon. Nonetheless, Moshe first attempted to secure a peaceful resolution.

Rashi's comments are an elaboration of his remarks on our *parasha*. He begins by acknowledging that Moshe was not commanded by Hashem to propose to Sichon a peaceful resolution. He explains that, nonetheless, Moshe concluded that the appropriate course of action – from the perspective of the Torah – was to make such an offer. Next, Rashi offers two possible explanations of Moshe's reasoning.

The first explanation is based upon an interesting comment of the Sages. The Sages explain that before Hashem offered the Torah to Bnai Yisrael, He offered it to the other nations. The Sages add that Hashem knew that His offer would be rejected. Nonetheless, He made the offer. Moshe recognized that Hashem had commanded him to wage war against Sichon and it was a foregone conclusion that Sichon would not accept an offer of peace. Nonetheless, using Hashem's own behavior as a model, Moshe concluded that he should offer Sichon the option of peace. In other words, Hashem had foreknowledge of the other nations' reaction to the offer to receive the Torah. Nonetheless, He made the offer. Moshe also knew that Sichon would reject his offer of peace. Nonetheless, he made the offer.

The second explanation of Moshe's behavior is based on a simple observation. Hashem could have instantaneously destroyed Egypt and redeemed Bnai Yisrael. But instead, He sent Moshe to Paroh. He instructed Moshe to tell Paroh to release Bnai Yisrael from bondage. The plagues that Hashem bought upon Egypt were a result of Paroh's refusal to release Bnai Yisrael. Moshe recognized that it would be possible to destroy Sichon without warning. But he recognized that Hashem had provided Paroh with a warning. Moshe concluded that Sichon should also be provided with a warning.[74]

It is interesting that Rashi proposes two possible explanations of Moshe's reasoning. Superficially, these two explanations seem to be very similar. But a more careful analysis suggests that these two explanations are actually very different from one another.

Rashi's first explanation focuses on the issue of foreknowledge. Hashem has perfect foreknowledge of our behaviors and decisions. Nonetheless, He provides us with options. Moshe concluded that we are obligated to emulate Hashem. Moshe also had perfect foreknowledge of Sichon's response to his offer of peace. He knew it would be rejected. Nonetheless, he emulated Hashem and offered Sichon the option of peace. In other words, Moshe concluded that we must act justly towards other individuals. Our concept of the other individual's likely—or definite—response does not excuse us from this obligation. Our responsibility is to act with justice. We cannot ignore this obligation because we assume— or even know— that our behavior will be ignored or not appreciated.

---

[73] Rabbaynu Moshe ben Nachman (Ramban), *Commentary on Sefer BeMidbar* 2:24.

[74] Rabbaynu Shlomo ben Yitzchak (Rashi), *Commentary on Sefer Devarim* 2:26.

Rashi's second explanation does not make reference to the issue of foreknowledge. Instead, Rashi asserts that we are not permitted to take action against an individual without first providing notice and warning. This notice and warning provides an explanation and rationale for our subsequent actions. In other words, without this warning and notice it would not be possible for the observer to appreciate the rationale for attacking Sichon or for destroying Egypt. The result would be that Hashem and Bnai Yisrael would appear to be the aggressors. Moshe recognized that we must always present the Torah in the most positive light. Sometimes, the Torah requires that we act with aggression, and even cause violence to, another individual. But we must recognize that we cannot embark upon such a path without considering the perceptions that will be generated by our actions. So, we must provide an adequate warning and notice.

Both of these explanations are valid and both inform our relationships with others and the way we must behave. We must treat others fairly. This is difficult when we suspect or realize that our efforts will not be appreciated. Everyone has been confronted with the challenge of acting with kindness or evenhandedness towards an individual that we suspect or know will not appreciate or even acknowledge our efforts. But the message Rashi is communicating is that we must put aside our disappointment and frustration and act appropriately.

Rashi is also telling us that we must always portray the Torah in a positive light. We must recognize the manner in which our actions will be perceived. Doing the right thing is not enough if our behavior will be judged as unreasonably aggressive or hostile. We must provide an adequate explanation for behaviors that others may perceive as unkind or aggressive. Of course, we cannot control whether the observer will take notice of our explanation or accept it. But we are expected to provide a rationale.

Balak

And Balak the son of Tzipor saw all that Yisrael had done to the Emoree. (BeMidbar 22:2)

The Egyptian, the Babylonian and the Persian rose, filled the planet with sound and splendor, then faded to dream-stuff and passed away; the Greek and the Roman followed, and made a vast noise, and they are gone; other people have sprung up and held their torch high for a time, but it burned out and they sit in twilight now, or have vanished. The Jew saw them all, beat them all, and is now what he always was, exhibiting no decadence, no infirmities of age, no weakening of his parts, no slowing of his energies, no dulling of his alert and aggressive mind. All things are mortal but the Jew; all other forces pass, but he remains. What is the secret of his immortality? Mark Twain, "Concerning the Jew"

The above quotation is the closing of Mark Twain's essay "Concerning the Jew". Twain concludes with a question. What is the explanation for the survival of the Jewish people? He does not propose a solution to the mystery.

The paradox of Jewish history

The history of the Jewish people is indeed paradoxical. We have experienced countless tragedies. The Holocaust, rather than being completely unique, is only the most recent calamity.[1] These many disasters challenge one's conviction in Hashem's providential role in the affairs of our people. However, our survival, despite these many calamities, provides compelling proof of the existence of that providential relationship. This paradox suggests that the evidence of providence is persuasive; however, our understanding of its workings is limited. The paradox of Jewish history is one of the themes developed and explored in Parshat Balak.

Bilaam's unusual "powers"

Parshat Balak describes Balak's plan to harm the Jewish people. He observed Bnai Yisrael's conquest of the mighty kingdoms east of the Jordan River. He concluded that he could not prevail against the Jewish people through military means. He turned to Bilaam. He believed that Bilaam had the power to impart curses and blessings. He asked Bilaam to curse Bnai Yisrael. Balak believed that once cursed by Bilaam, Bnai Yisrael would be vulnerable.

Was Balak's assessment of Bilaam's abilities the product of his imagination? Was there some basis to Balak's views? The commentators generally assume that Bilaam had some unusual capacity. However, they disagree on its nature. Rabbaynu Avraham ibn Ezra suggests that Bilaam was a master astrologer. He anticipated the future by reading the heavens. He used this knowledge to curse and bless. He created the impression that he was capable of issuing effective curses and blessings. In reality, he was merely using his knowledge of astrology to foresee the future.[2]

When Ibn Ezra (1087-1167) composed these comments, astrology was viewed as a legitimate science among even the enlightened. Rambam (1135-1204) – Maimonides – rejected astrology as a pseudo-science. Nonetheless, many Jewish and non-Jewish scholars and thinkers

---

[1] The Holocaust should not be trivialized as "just another disaster". Its dimensions were enormous. However, it is the expression of a pattern of persecution and not a unique manifestation of hatred toward the Jewish people.

[2] Rabbaynu Avraham ibn Ezra, *Commentary on Sefer BeMidbar*, 22:28.

continued to regard astrology as an authentic science. Among these is Levi ben Gershon (1288-1344) – Ralbag/Gershonides – who was one of Rambam's most ardent champions.

The significance and relevance of Ibn Ezra's comments

The important aspect of Ibn Ezra's position is not that he attributes Bilaam's effectiveness to his mastery of astrology. Instead, it is his approach to understanding Bilaam's methods that is significant. This approach is to remove any magical element from Bilaam's "powers". Bilaam's efficacy was not a consequence of super-natural powers. He used his knowledge to develop predictions and then promoted himself as someone capable of influencing the destinies of individuals and nations.

We can adopt Ibn Ezra's approach and update his comments to correspond with contemporary science. We would no longer ascribe Bilaam's success to knowledge of astrology. Instead, we would assume that his success was the product of his astute understanding of political forces, human behavior, or perhaps, intimate knowledge of the thinking, plans, and goals of local potentates.

Bilaam used his knowledge self-servingly. He has many imitators in our times. A securities trader with inside knowledge can advise clients based on that knowledge. He can conceal his methods and promote himself as a shrewd stock-picker. This trader is a modern-day version of Bilaam. Of course, the religious world also has its "prophets". One wonders how Ibn Ezra would view these contemporary Bilaams.

Based upon this understanding of Bilaam's "powers", let's consider two difficult sets of passages in the *parasha* that now become more easily understood.

For from the top of mountains I see him and from the heights I gaze upon him. It is a nation that dwells alone and is not counted among the nations. Who can count the dust of Yaakov and the number of a quarter of Yisrael? I should die the death of the righteous and my end should be like him. (BeMidbar 23:9-10)

Bilaam learns of Hashem's providence

Balak takes Bilaam to a place from which they can look upon a portion of the camp of Israel. Bilaam has a prophecy[3] and he reports it to Balak. The passages include three elements that seem unrelated. The first is the separateness of the Jewish people; they dwell alone and are not counted among the nations. Second, Bilaam remarks on the numerical size of the nation. He asks rhetorically, "Who can count the members of this nation? They are as numerous as dust!" Third, he expresses the wish to die as one of the righteous of the Jewish people. How are these elements related? Furthermore, why does Bilaam suddenly wish to die the death of the righteous?

According to Ibn Ezra, this prophecy was an epiphany for Bilaam. Bilaam was an astrologer. In modern terms, he believed in the absolute rule of causality. The destinies of individuals and nations is determined by immutable laws. Everything is predetermined by these laws and destiny is unchangeable. Bilaam's first prophecy addressed these views.

---

[3] According to Ibn Ezra, Bilaam was not a prophet. The prophecies received by Bilaam during this interval were unique events.

In the first element of his prophecy, Hashem revealed to Bilaam the phenomenon of providence. Bilaam's understanding of destiny applies to other nations of the world but the Jewish people are not included among these nations and they are not counted among them.

Second, he learned that this is not because the Jewish people will be insignificant and its destiny will be subsumed within those of other nations. The Jewish people will be a numerically significant and distinct nation. Nonetheless, normal causality will not apply to the descendants of Yaakov. They will enjoy Hashem's providence.

Bilaam suddenly discovers that it is possible for a nation and even an individual to have a relationship with the Creator. He had assumed that the destinies of nations and certainly his own destiny was the product of immutable causality. He has now discovered that one can rise above this norm, enter into a relationship with Hashem, and become the object of His providence. He expresses the wish to experience this relationship – even if only in his death.[4]

The L-rd is not a man that He should deceive or a human being that He should repent His decision. That which He says shall He not do? And which He speaks shall He not fulfill? I have been instructed to deliver a blessing and I will not retract it. He has not seen wrongdoing in Yaakov and not evil in Yisrael. Hashem his L-rd is with him and the blast of the trumpet of the King is in his midst. (BeMidbar 23:19-21)

Two aspects of Hashem's providence

Balak takes Bilaam to another location from which Bnai Yisrael can be observed. Again, he asks Bilaam to curse the nation. Bilaam receives another prophecy. The above passages are the first part of this prophecy. According to Ibn Ezra, this prophecy further develops the ideas communicated in the previous prophecy. Hashem had revealed to Bilaam His relationship and providence over the Jewish people. Now He explains two aspects of this relationship. First, it is not a superficial relationship that changes with circumstances. Hashem has blessed Bnai Yisrael. He has commanded Bilaam to conduct himself according to this blessing. Hashem is not fickle. Bilaam and Balak cannot alter His will.

Second, Hashem reveals to Bilaam an underlying element of His relationship with Bnai Yisrael. He tells Bilaam that He has not observed iniquity or evil among the people. Therefore, the trumpet blast of the King – Hashem – is in their midst. The nation enjoys His providence. In other words, His relationship with the nation is impacted by its behavior. He dwells among the Jewish people because they are free of iniquity and evil. Providence is a response to righteousness. The more closely the nation or individual adheres to the will of Hashem, the more intense the providential relationship.[5]

According to Ibn Ezra, this revelation to Bilaam of the workings of providence was responsible for a terrible outcome.

And Israel dwelled in Shittim. And the nation began to engage in harlotry with the daughters of Moav. (BeMidbar 25:1)

Bilaam's advice to Balak

---

[4] Rabbaynu Avraham ibn Ezra, *Commentary on Sefer BeMidbar*, 23:9-10.
[5] Rabbaynu Avraham ibn Ezra, *Commentary on Sefer BeMidbar*, 23:18-21.

Bilaam returns to his home without cursing the Jewish people. Bnai Yisrael camps in Shittim. There, the men develop relationships with the women of Moav. These relationships are intimate and lead the men to engaging in the idolatry of their paramours. Hashem brings a plague upon the Jewish people that takes twenty-four thousand lives.

Rashi, quoting the Talmud, comments that these liaisons did not arise spontaneously. They were planned by the leadership of Moav with the intent of corrupting Bnai Yisrael. In other words, Moav's leadership did not implement this plan as a means of recruiting Bnai Yisrael into its religious beliefs. Instead, this was a cynical strategy to draw forth the wrath of Hashem and His punishment of the Jewish people. The Talmud further explains that this plan was suggested by Bilaam.[6]

The source of Bilaam's strategy

How did Bilaam develop this strategy? What evidence did he have that such a strategy would be effective? Ibn Ezra explains that Bilaam developed this plan based upon his second prophecy. Hashem revealed two aspects of His providential relationship with the Jewish people. He told Bilaam that it was not a superficial relationship that changed with circumstances or could be easily manipulated. He also revealed that the relationship is responsive to the righteousness of the nation. Bilaam inferred that corruption and iniquity could undermine the fidelity of the providential relationship and evoke Hashem's wrath.[7] This inference was the basis of the counsel he provided to the leadership of Moav.[8]

Bilaam and Twain respond to the same paradox

The historical narrative observed by Twain is the expression of the relationship that so astounded Bilaam. Twain could not understand the phenomenon of Jewish survival and did not attempt to explain it. Hashem revealed to Bilaam the principle underlying the history of the Jewish nation. It is not the product of immutable causality. It is the product of Hashem's providence.

Twain and Bilaam both responded with profound wonder to the paradox of Jewish history. Bilaam was shocked to discover the existence of the providential relationship. Twain was equally amazed at observing it in action through the centuries. Twain knew that our history includes countless disasters. Nonetheless, he was deeply impacted by the survival of the Jewish people – despite our history of persecution. Bilaam understood that Hashem's providence would not rescue us from suffering and tragedy. Our destiny would be guided by providence but predicated upon our faithfulness to the Hashem and His Torah.

---

[6] Rabbaynu Shlomo ben Yitzchak (Rashi), *Commentary on Sefer BeMidbar* 25:1. See also Rashi's comments on 24:14.

[7] It is interesting that Hashem revealed to Bilaam this aspect of the workings of providence. In doing so, He provided Bilaam with the insight upon which he formulated a strategy to harm the Jewish people.

[8] Rabbaynu Avraham ibn Ezra, *Commentary on Sefer BeMidbar*, 23:21. See also Ibn Ezra's comments on 24:14.

And Balak saw all that Yisrael had done to the Emorites. And Moav was very much in fear of the nation because of its multitude. And Moav was distressed because of Bnai Yisrael. (BeMidbar 22:3)

Moav and Midyan – Prototypical Enemies of Bnai Yisrael and their Agendas

1. Two explanations for Moav's aggression

Parshat Balak focuses primarily on the efforts of Balak, the King of Moav, to defeat Bnai Yisrael. The above passages introduce the narrative. The Torah explains that after Bnai Yisrael overcame Sichon, Og and their respective nations, the people of Moav were overtaken by fear and dread. However, the passages do not provide a specific explanation for Moav's intense apprehension. The commentaries offer a number of possibilities. One explanation that is quoted by many of the commentators is suggested by the Talmud. The nation of Moav believed that it was in danger of being conquered. It had observed the ease with which Bnai Yisrael had overpowered its mighty neighbors. It assumed that Moav would be the next target for conquest.[9]

This was a miscalculation. Moav was not in danger. Bnai Yisrael did not intend to wage a war of conquest against Moav. In fact, Moav was among the three nations that Hashem forbade Bnai Yisrael from attacking.[10] Moav had no reason to fear Bnai Yisrael.

Rashbam offers a different explanation. He suggests that Moav was not afraid of attack and understood that it was safe from aggression. However, it feared that the region could not support another populous nation. They were afraid that the replacement of the Sichon and Og's nations with the much larger population of Bnai Yisrael would tax the productive resources of the area beyond its capacity. Moav feared that famine and hunger would soon befall it.[11]

And Yisrael captured all of these cities. And Yisrael dwelled in all of the cities of the Emorites – in Cheshbon and its surrounding communities. (This is) because Cheshbon was the city of Sichon the King of the Emorites. He had waged war against the first king of Moav and taken his land from him – up to Arnon (BeMidbar 21:25-26)

2. The history of the kingdoms on the Jordan's east-bank

Chizkuni offers a very interesting explanation for Moav's fear. It is based on the above passages and Rashi's comments. These passages are from the end of Parshat Chukat. The first passage describes the extent of Bnai Yisrael's conquest of the Kingdom of the Emorites. This passage explains that even the capital of King Sichon was captured. The second passage then explains that Sichon had annexed to his kingdom possessions that were previously part of the Land of Moav. The two passages are related. The second passage is introduced with the word "because". In some manner Bnai Yisrael's conquest of this land was related to its earlier conquest by Sichon. However, the exact connection between Sichon's earlier conquest of the area and Bani Yisrael's subsequent conquest is not specified.

Rashi explains the Torah's intention. According to Rashi, the second passage answers an important question. Chesbon – Sichon's capital – was once part of the Land of Moav. It was part of the territory Sichon had annexed through his successful campaign against Moav. Bnai Yisrael were enjoined against taking possession of the Land of Moav. Yet, the first passage explains that

---

[9] Mesechet Sanhedrin 105a.
[10] Sefer Devarim 9:9.
[11] Rashbam 22:4.

Bnai Yisrael settled in Cheshbon and its surroundings. This suggests a problem. How could Bnai Yisrael settle in territory that was once Moav's? They had been commanded to not enter into conflict with Moav! According to Rashi, the second passage provides the explanation. The land was originally part of the Kingdom of Moav. However, with Sichon's conquest of the territory it passed out of the possession of Moav and was no longer rightfully its land. Therefore, Bnai Yisrael acted properly in settling into all of the territory it had captured from Sichon – regardless of its historical ownership.[12]

3. A third explanation for Moav's aggression

Based upon these passages and Rashi's comments, Chizkuni explains Moav's fears. Moav never reconciled itself to Sichon's annexation of its territory. It continued to regard the land as part of the Kingdom of Moav but occupied by Sichon and his people. Therefore, Bnai Yisrael's conquest of Sichon's kingdom renewed Moav's aspirations to regain its traditional lands. Moav hoped that Bnai Yisrael would acknowledge its ancient claim to the territory and return it to its historical inhabitants. Of course, Bnai Yisrael did not offer to restore Moav to its territories. This led to more than mere disappointment.

Moav misinterpreted Bnai Yisrael's actions. Moav did not understand that halachah treated the land as part of the Kingdom of Sichon and not part of the Kingdom of Moav under occupation. In interpreting Bnai Yisrael's actions, Moav focused on its attachment to its lost territories and evaluated Bnai Yisrael's behaviors from that perspective. Therefore, when Bnai Yisrael did not offer to return to Moav its lost territories, Moav concluded that Bnai Yisrael did not respect Moav's sovereignty. Moav assumed that with the conquest of Sichon and the retention of Moav's traditional territories, Bnai Yisrael was announcing its intentions to take possession of all of the Land of Moav.[13]

And Hashem spoke to Moshe saying: Distress the Midyanites and attack them because they caused you distress through their craftiness through which they deceived you in the matter of Pe'or and regarding the matter of Kazbi daughter of a Prince of Midyan – their sister – who was killed on the day of the plague resultant from the matter of Pe'or. (BeMidbar 25:16-18)

4. Hashem's command to destroy Midyan and spare Moav

Throughout the parasha, Moav is joined in its efforts to overcome Bnai Yisrael by the nation of Midyan. Moav's efforts eventually had some impact. It developed a plan to corrupt Bnai Yisrael and to entice a portion of the people to engage in idolatry. The plan reflected the desperation of Moav. It required sending its young women into the camp of Bnai Yisrael with instruction to seduce the men. They were further instructed to entice their victims to join them in pagan worship. The plan had some success and provoked Hashem to unleash a plague that killed 24,000 people. Midyan joined Moav in this scheme and even one of the nation's princesses joined the young women in their seductions.

Immediately following this episode, Hashem commands Moshe to treat Midyan with enmity and to attack and destroy the nation. Of course this commandment raises an interesting question. Midyan was Moav's partner. However, it seems from the Torah that Midyan was the

---

[12] Rashi Sefer BeMidbar 21:26.
[13] Rabbaynu Ovadia Sforno, Commentary on Sefer BeMidbar, 20:8.

junior partner in the association. It is strange that Hashem commanded Moshe to take vengeance against Midyan but not Moav.

Rashi offers a number of explanations for the different treatment of Moav and Midyan. One explanation actually acknowledges that Moav was equally deserving of Bnai Yisrael's enmity. However, Moav was spared because the nation was destined to produce Ruth.[14] Rashi's second explanation is based upon the previous discussion of Moav's motivations. As explained above, the commentators offer various explanations for Moav's aggression toward Bnai Yisrael. However, all of these explanations share a common thread that is expressed in the opening passages of the parasha. Moav was motivated by fear. The commentators differ over the nature and cause of the fear. However, all accept the simple message of the passages; Moav was acting in perceived self-defense. Rashi explains that Midyan had no similar motivation. It had no reason to fear Bnai Yisrael. Therefore, its partnership with Moav was motivated by elemental hatred.[15]

5. Alternative explanations for the command to destroy Midyan

These two explanations imply very different interpretations of Hashem's command regarding Midyan. According to the second explanation offered by Rashi, Bnai Yisrael is told to destroy the nation of Midyan because it acted out of intense hatred. However, Moav is to be spared because it acted according to its perceived self-interest. These different motivations suggest that Moav was only a very temporary enemy. It would soon come to the realization that it was safe from attack from Bnai Yisrael. Once it recognizes that Bnai Yisrael's presence in the region does not threaten its security, it would come to terms with the new reality and accept it.

However, a détente with Midyan would not be possible. Midyan did not act out of self-interest. It was motivated by a primitive, intense hatred. This hatred would induce continued aggression. Bnai Yisrael's security required the destruction of this rabid enemy.

However, this interpretation of the commandment does not apply to Rashi's first explanation. According to that explanation, Moav and Midyan equally deserved to be punished. Moav was spared in order to produce the righteous Ruth. According to this explanation, the destruction of Midyan is not an act of self-defense. It is intended as a punishment. Moav and Midyan both deserved punishment. Both had preferred war to seeking peace. Both attempted to provoke within Bnai Yisrael sedition against Hashem. However, Moav was spared this harsh punishment because of the good it was destined to produce.[16]

"And Bilaam arose in the morning. And he said to Balak's ministers, "Go to your land for Hashem has refused to allow me to go with you." (BeMidbar 22:13)

Hashem appears to Bilaam in a vision. He tells Bilaam that he should not respond to Balak's summons. Bilaam cannot curse Bnai Yisrael. The nation is blessed.

Hashem's meaning was very clear. Bilaam could not affect destiny. He could merely foretell the future. This ability was the foundation of Bilaam's illusions. Hashem told Bilaam he

---

[14] Rabbaynu Shlomo ben Yitzchak (Rashi), Commentary on Sefer BeMidbar 20:1.
[15] This is not to say that the Torah condones acts of aggression and conquest among nations. However, once the conquest did occur, Sichon's sovereignty over the territories of Moav was established and recognized by halachah.
[16] Chizkuni Sefer BeMidbar 22:3.

could not succeed in this case. Bnai Yisrael was blessed. Bilaam would have no opportunity to curse the nation.

Bilaam told the messengers that he could not return with them to Balak. He did not explain the reason. He did not indicate that he could not help Balak or that Bnai Yisrael could not be cursed. Why did Bilaam conceal this information?

Rashi explains Bilaam's motivations. He comments that Bilaam told the ministers that he could not proceed with them. This implied that Balak should send a more worthy delegation. This delegation would earn Bilaam's cooperation. Clearly, Bilaam was attempting to conceal his limitations.[17]

The effect of Bilaam's response is predictable. Balak understood Bilaam's message. He sent a new delegation. This group was composed of ministers of higher rank. These ministers arrived at Bilaam's home. They assured Bilaam he would be amply rewarded for his services. They assured him of Balak's complete cooperation.

Of course, Bilaam's situation remained unchanged. He knew that only the Almighty shaped destiny. Bilaam could not truly curse or bless anyone. He was forced to reveal this limitation.[18] He told the messengers they must wait with him. He must receive guidance from Hashem.

Bilaam's behavior seems bizarre. He knew that ultimately he must follow Hashem's command. Hashem had told him that Bnai Yisrael was blessed. Bilaam would not be able to satisfy Balak's request. Why did he mislead Balak?

Don Isaac Abarvanel explains that Bilaam was involved in an immense internal conflict. He enjoyed the attention he was receiving from Balak – the king of Moav. Balak's entreaties appealed to Bilaam's vanity. He did not want this attention to end. He needed to provide Balak with encouragement. This required Bilaam to create the impression that he had volition. However, Bilaam had no freedom. He could not act without Hashem. This eventually was revealed.

Bilaam's situation was further complicated by his very claim. He presented himself as the true prophet of the Almighty. This implied that he was subject to the Almighty's authority. This created an absolute contradiction. Bilaam implied freedom and subjugation simultaneously.

Bilaam could not resolve this conflict. This is reflected in his actions. He attempted to continue his charade. But in the end was forced, by his own claims, to admit his limitations.

The most revealing aspect of this entire incident is Bilaam's immediate reaction to the second delegation. Essentially, the delegation asked Bilaam to name his price. This angered Bilaam. He responded that all of Balak's wealth could not force a prophet to violate Hashem's command. Why did Bilaam react so sharply? Bilaam had implied that the proper delegation could enlist his support. Balak rightfully understood this to imply that Bilaam had the ability to make a decision. He challenged Bilaam to exercise his freewill. This angered Bilaam. Balak had implied that Bilaam was not a true prophet. Bilaam immediately responded that he must obey Hashem. He was forced to confess his limitations.[19]

---

[17] Rabbaynu Shlomo ben Yitzchak (Rashi), *Commentary on Sefer BeMidbar* 22:13.
[18] Rabbaynu Shlomo ben Yitzchak (Rashi), *Commentary on Sefer BeMidbar* 22:18.
[19] Don Yitzchak Abravanel, *Commentary on Sefer BeMidbar* 22:7.

"And Hashem came to Bilaam in the night. And He said to him, "If these men have come to call for you, arise and go with them. However, that which I will tell you, you should say". (BeMidbar 22:20)

Balak sends messengers to Bilaam. He asks Bilaam to curse Bnai Yisrael. Bilaam responds that he must follow Hashem's instructions. The Almighty appears to Bilaam. He tells Bilaam that he should not accompany the messengers. He cannot curse Bnai Yisrael. They are a blessed people.

Balak sends a second delegation. Again, Bilaam tells the messengers that he must wait for guidance from Hashem. Our pasuk contains the Almighty's response. He tells Bilaam that he may accompany the messengers.

Bilaam leaves on his journey to join Balak. Immediately, the Torah reports that Hashem is angry with Bilaam for deciding to accompany the messengers. An angel of G-d appears to Bilaam. The angel threatens to kill him. Bilaam recognizes his mistake. He offers to abandon his mission and return home. The angel tells Bilaam to continue on his journey. However, he cautions Bilaam not to deviate from the message he will receive from Hashem.

This series of incidents presents a number of problems. First, the Almighty initially told Bilaam not to accompany the messengers. Then, Hashem apparently relented. He told Bilaam he can travel with the delegation back to Balak. How could the Almighty alter His decision?

Second, Bilaam embarked on his journey. The Torah tells us that Hashem was angry. Why was Hashem angry? He told Bilaam he could accompany the delegation! Bilaam had not disobeyed Hashem!

Third, an angel is sent to Bilaam. The angel persuades him that he had not acted properly. Bilaam understood the message. He confessed his sin. He offered to abandon his mission. We would expect the angel to accept this offer and to tell Bilaam to return home. Instead, the angel told Bilaam to continue on his journey! What was the objective in sending the angel? In the end the angel encouraged Bilaam to continue on his journey!

Nachmanides offers a brilliant but simple answer to these questions. He explains that the Almighty never intended to forbid Bilaam from joining Balak. Hashem actually wanted Bilaam to respond to Balak's summons. Why? The Almighty wanted Bnai Yisrael to be blessed by this non-Jewish prophet. He wanted Balak to witness this event. This insight can be applied to answer all of our questions.

First, the Almighty initially forbade Bilaam from accompanying the messengers. The reason is found in Bilaam's explanation of his mission. He told Hashem that he had been called upon to curse Bnai Yisrael. Hashem responded that this is a mission that Bilaam cannot fulfill. He should not accompany the delegation.

Second, Hashem never altered His position. The second time He spoke to Bilaam He told him that if the delegation has called upon him for assistance and counsel, he may accompany the messengers. He did not tell Bilaam he can curse Bnai Yisrael. Hashem specifically told him he can only repeat His words. This is consistent with Hashem's objective. The Almighty wanted Bilaam to bless Bnai Yisrael in the presence of Balak. This required Bilaam to return with the delegation. However, it was made clear that he could not curse Bnai Yisrael.

Third, Bilaam left on his journey. Hashem become angry. This was because Bilaam did not indicate to the delegation the conditions of his agreement to follow them. The delegates assumed that the Almighty had actually agreed to their request. This created a problem. Ultimately, Bilaam will not be permitted to curse Bnai Yisrael. The G-d of the Jews will appear quite capricious.[20]

Third, the angel did not want Bilaam to return home. He demanded that Bilaam clearly state his limitations. Once the angel was convinced that Bilaam would tell Balak that he can not curse Bnai Yisrael, the angel allowed him to proceed.

We can now understand Bilaam's first words when meeting Balak. He told Balak that although he had responded to his summons, he could not utter any pronouncement that is not authorized by the Almighty. Bilaam was fulfilling the commitment made to the angel.[21]

And Hashem opened the mouth of the donkey. She said to Bilaam: What have I done to you that you have struck me these three times? (BeMidbar 22:28)

Mr. Ed and Related Phenomena

1. The donkey who spoke

Some readers will recall the 1960s television show "Mr. Ed". The show centered upon the adventures of Mr. Ed – a talking horse – and his owner Wilbur Post. Mr. Ed's remarkable gift was known only to Wilbur. Mr. Ed spoke to no one else. The creators of the television series were confronted with the question of how Mr. Ed's special gift should be explained to viewers. They decided to leave this issue to the viewer's imagination. When Wilbur confronted Mr. Ed, he responded that Wibur would not be able to understand the phenomenon; "it's bigger than the both of us."

Our Sages were confronted with a similar dilemma presented by Parshat Balak. The *parasha* relates the story of Bilaam and Balak. Balak, the king of Moav, hires Bilaam to curse Bnai Yisrael. Bilaam receives a prophecy from Hashem instructing him to refuse Balak's request. However, both Balak and Bilaam are persistent. Hashem allows Bilaam to travel to Balak but warns him to not act against Bnai Yisrael.

On his journey to Balak, Bilaam receives a further warning from Hashem to act only as directed by Him. This warning is initiated by Bilaam's donkey suddenly speaking to his master. Our Sages were troubled by the proposition that a donkey should engage in speech.[22]

Our Sages were not concerned with the narrative because it posits an extraordinary miracle. Our Sages readily accepted the reality of the miracles described in the Torah. Their concern actually was not related to this specific miracle. Instead, they felt that the miracles – all and any miracles – pose a troublesome problem begging an explanation.

---

[20] Rabbaynu Moshe ben Nachman (Ramban), *Commentary on Sefer BeMidbar* 22:20.

[21] Rabbaynu Moshe ben Nachman (Ramban), *Commentary on Sefer BeMidbar* 22:35.

[22] There is a dispute among the commentators over whether Bilaam's donkey actually spoke to him. Maimonides and others acknowledge that many sages understand the narrative in its literal sense. The donkey did speak. However, Maimonides and these other authorities contend that Bilaam's donkey spoke to him in a prophetic vision but not in physical reality.

That which was is that which shall be. That which was done is what shall be done. There is nothing new under the sun. (Megilat Kohelet 1:9)

2. The problem with miracles

The nature of this problem is beyond this discussion and will only be very superficially summarized. According to Rabbaynu Avraham ibn Ezra, the above passage describes the unchanging character of the universe.[23] The Sages of the Talmud assume that when the sixth day of creation came to its close the process of creation was complete. From that point forward the created universe operates according to the nature with which it was endowed and the physical laws established to govern it. The reason that the Sages assumed that nature and the laws established at creation are immutable is tied to complex philosophical issues that cannot be discussed here. However, it is not necessary to further explore their reasons for this conclusion to appreciate their dilemma. If the physical universe is immutable, then how can a miracle occur? How can the material world apparently shed the bonds imposed by its very nature and disobey the laws imposed upon it?

And Moshe stretched his hand over the sea. Toward morning, the water returned to its might. The Egyptians fled toward it and Hashem stirred the Egyptians within the sea. (Shemot 14:2)

3. Conditions imposed upon creation

The Sages provide two responses. The first is associated with the above passage. The passage describes the final act of the splitting of the Reed Sea. Moshe stretches his hand over the water of the sea. The solid walls of water that formed a path for Bnai Yisrael's passage, collapse. The waters of the sea crash down upon the Egyptians and drown them.

Commenting on this passage the Sages explain that most miracles where pre-set at the time of creation. In the words of the Sages, when Hashem created the seas, He directed the waters of the sea to part in the future for His chosen people.[24] Miracles are merely the execution of an ancient directive issued at the time of creation.

Not all miracles were pre-set in this manner. The second response of the Sages describes a small number of miracles that are exceptional. They identify ten miraculous objects that were created at dusk of the final day of creation. Among these ten objects are Bilaam's talking donkey, the manna, and the tablets of the Decalogue.[25]

Why did the Sages assign the creation of these ten objects this special status of being created at dusk of the final day of creation? It is very difficult to precisely answer this question. Perhaps, these ten objects or phenomena are regarded as unique aberrations of enormous magnitude and cannot be regarded as the consequence of directives given to objects of nature at the time of creation.[26]

---

[23] Rabbaynu Avraham ibn Ezra, *Commentary on Megilat Kohelet*, 1:9.

[24] Midrash Rabba, Sefer Beresheit 5:5.

[25] Mesechet Avot 5:6.

[26] A difficulty with this explanation is that among the ten noted miracles is the rainbow. Nachmanides asserts that the rainbow is a natural phenomenon and existed from the time of creation. After the Deluge, Hashem assigned to the rainbow a new significance. It communicates His promise to preserve humanity. However, Malbim and others describe the Deluge as a refashioning of the earth and the rainbow as a post-Deluge phenomenon. According to this

The main point of this discussion is that according to the Sages, all miracles are expressions of a plan put into place at creation. Each miracle unfolds at its proper time in history.

Parenthetically, it should be noted that this issue is unrelated to the question of how frequently miracles occur. Commentators who assume that miracles are frequent merely posit that the omniscient Creator planed and scheduled each of these "everyday miracles" in antiquity.[27] Each unfolds at its proper moment.

And Moshe stretched his hand over the sea. And Hashem moved the sea with a strong eastern wind that entire night. He made the sea a dry place. And the waters parted. (Shemot 14:21)

4. Miracles as unusual expressions of nature

There does seem to be an interesting dispute between the commentators on the exact meaning of this interpretation of miracles. Most authorities assume that the Sages are positing that miracles are actually only apparent aberrations from the natural order. Really, miracles are uncommon but quite natural events. The sea parted before Bnai Yisrael because of the coincidence of a number of natural causes at that precise moment. These are alluded to in the above passage. The passage describes a wind of enormous power that parts the waters. Every miracle should be understood in the same fashion. A miracle is remarkable only in its timing and uncommon nature. However, it is an expression of the laws of nature and not a violation of them.[28]

5. Miracles as an expression of a higher order

Rabbaynu David Kimchi – RaDaK – seems to prefer an alternative explanation of the Sages' perspective. He begins by acknowledging the immutable nature of the created universe. However, he posits that nature and its laws are subjugated to an overarching higher order. This higher order is the grand design or function of the universe. The universe is fashioned with and designed to conform to spiritual ends and objectives. The most fundamental objective is the advancement of humanity toward recognition of Hashem. Nature and the laws that govern physical phenomena are tools utilized by a set of principles of a higher order that embody this grand design.[29]

An illustration will help demonstrate RaDak's point. I own a computer that I use for many purposes. I did not buy it as an investment or intend to barter it. I bought it to use for work and for personal projects. However, when this computer becomes obsolete, I will sell it and use the funds to help pay for my next computer.

When I sell my computer, have I altered my life mission or my personal goals in life? Of course not. I have merely found a new and more appropriate manner to employ the computer. My life mission, my goals and objectives in life are unchanged and remain my true guiding principles. However, the role of this tool – my computer – within my overall plan – has changed. When I bought the computer, it served my needs and furthered my mission by functioning as a

---

perspective, the Sages' treatment of the rainbow as a miracle of extraordinary proportions seems to refer to the refashioning of the earth from which the rainbow emerged.

[27] The reference to antiquity treats the scheduling of miracles from a human perspective. Hashem does not exist in time. He is not subject to past, present and future.

[28] Rabbaynu Bachya, *Commentary on Sefer Shemot* 14:27.

[29] Rabbaynu David Kimchi (Radak), *Commentary on Sefer Beresheit* 2:1.

computer. At the point at which I sell it, I have decided that it better serves me as an object of value that can be transformed into cash.

RaDak understands the laws that govern the material world much as I see my computer. Nature and its laws exist within a hierarchy. In this hierarchy they are the servant to a set of principles of a higher order – Hashem's plan for humanity. It is this plan and its principles that are immutable not the laws of the physical world. Most of the time, the laws of nature are a faithful servant to this grand scheme of the universe. Sometimes, the physical laws must yield to the demands of the greater plan. To the observer, it appears that the immutable character of the universe has been compromised. On the contrary, it is this immutable nature that demands that the physical laws yield to its imperatives.[30]

The heavens extol the glory of G-d and the sky tells of the work of His hands. (Tehilim 19:2)

6. A religious scientist?

It is often assumed that scientific and religious outlooks are in conflict. The premise underlying this assumption is that religion seeks its validation through providing an explanation for the inexplicable elements of the universe. The greater the mystery of the universe the more evidence it provides of a Creator and Master. The more we understand the universe the less room there is for religion. From this perspective, the scientist is a rational, objective thinker and the religionist is mystical and subjective in his view of the universe.

This perception of conflict is completely contrary to the Torah's outlook. As evident from the discussion above, our Sages assumed that the universe is generally governed by laws. It is the miracles that require explanation!

The attitude of our Sages is beautifully expressed by King David in the above passage. The heavens extol Hashem's glory! David did not see the physical world as a set of random events governed by caprice and chance. He observed patterns and regularity in the changing of the seasons, the movements of the heavens, and the ebb and flow of organic life. We do not know how he understood the laws governing these phenomena but he declares his awe with the overwhelming wisdom exhibited by the workings of the universe.

Like David, our Sages understood that Hashem's wisdom is infinite. They expected the universe that He created to reflect this immense wisdom. From the perspective of our Sages, the more we understand the universe the greater is our appreciation of this wisdom and the more intense our awe.

"And Pinchas, the son of Elazar, (who was) the son of Aharon, saw. And he arose from among the assembly and he took a spear in his hand." (BeMidbar 25:7)

It is interesting that there are certain practices that are generally taboo among Jews, regardless of the level of their commitment to traditional Torah values. One of these pervasive

---

[30] Maimonides, in his commentary on Avot, discusses the position of the Sages and adopts the explanation of Rabbaynu Bachya. However, in *Moreh Nevuchim* he reviews the position of the Sages and without explanation demurs. It is possible that Maimonides believes that Rabbaynu Bachya has properly interpreted the intention of the Sages but himself prefers the position of RaDak.

taboos is intermarriage between Jews and non-Jews. On occasion, non-Jews have remarked to me that this attitude strikes them as xenophobic. But – in truth – this is not an expression of xenophobia. One of the factors that seem to underlie this inhibition is the association between intermarriage and assimilation. This association is so strong that the statistic most often used to measure the rate of assimilation among Jews is the intermarriage rate. The implied message is that intermarriage and assimilation are somewhat synonymous. In other words, this association is based on the premise that intermarriage, almost inevitably, will lead to the assimilation of the Jewish partner in the marriage. Is there a Torah basis for this association?

Maimonides explains that it is prohibited for a Jew to have sexual relations with a non-Jew. The punishment for violating this negative commandment is lashes.[31] Maimonides adds that the Torah is determined to preserve the commitment of Bnai Yisrael to Torah observance. In order to create a barrier against assimilation, the Torah allows only for intimate relations between Jews. Intimacy between individuals creates strong emotional bonds. These emotional bonds will lead to assimilation of each other's values. If the two individuals share the same religious outlook, then this bond will allow each other to reinforce the other's values. But, if their religious values conflict, then the religious identity of one or both of the partners will be jeopardized.[32]

Maimonides' assessment of the effects of intermarriage is not merely based on psychological and sociological insight. His position is founded upon an incident described in our *parasha*.

Our *parasha* begins by recounting the efforts of Balak, the king of Moav, to defeat Bnai Yisrael. Balak hired Bilaam to curse Bnai Yisrael. Bilaam was believed to have supernatural powers. Balak believed that if Bilaam could be induced to curse Bnai Yisrael, then Moav could successfully defeat Bnai Yisrael in battle. However, rather than cursing Bnai Yisrael, Bilaam blessed them. Balak realized that Bnai Yisrael could not be cursed. Balak and Bilaam separated. Each returned to his home.

The end of the *parasha* discusses a related incident. Bnai Yisrael are camped in Shittim. This placed them in close proximity of Moav. Familiarity developed between the men of Bnai Yisrael and the women of Moav. These relations became intimate and sexual. Soon, these men and women began to share cultures. This led to these men associating with the idol of Moav – Ba'al Peor.

Our Sages concluded that this incident in our *parasha* in which sexual intimacy progressed into assimilation was not an isolated, behavioral aberration. Instead, the incident represents an example of normative human behavior. It can generally be assumed that sexual intimacy will result in emotional bonds, and these bonds promote assimilation.

The account of this incident ends with a violent, and somewhat disturbing turn of events. A member of Bnai Yisrael brought a woman from Midyan into the midst of the people and openly engaged in intimate sexual behavior with her. Pinchas, the son of Elazar and the grandson of Aharon, observed this travesty and reacted. He seized a spear and drove it through the two of them.

---

[31] Rabbaynu Moshe ben Maimon (Rambam) *Mishne Torah*, Hilchot Esurai Be'ah 12:1.
[32] Rabbaynu Moshe ben Maimon (Rambam) *Mishne Torah*, Hilchot Esurai Be'ah 12:7-8.

This incident is codified into *halacha*. But, before we can consider *halacha's* treatment of this incident, some basic background is needed. As we have noted, Maimonides explains that sexual intimacy between Jews and non-Jews is prohibited. He further explains that the Torah only prohibits intimate relations between the Jew and non-Jew in the context of marriage – if the two participants live together. Although casual sexual liaisons are also prohibited, the Torah does not empower the courts to punish this behavior. However, the Sages did institute a punishment of lashes for this activity.[33]

On the surface, these laws seem to contradict the implications of the incident in our *parasha*. The two individuals executed by Pinchas were engaged in sexual relations. But, the context of marriage was missing. No explicit Torah law was violated – the Torah only explicitly prohibits sexual relations in the context of marriage. What basis and authority did Pinchas have for executing these two people? Furthermore, even if these two individuals had violated the law prohibiting relations between Jew and non-Jew, the punishment for violating the commandment is lashes. But, Pinchas executed these two people!

This issue is discussed in the Talmud, and Maimonides codifies the discussion. He explains that if the Jew and non-Jew publicly engage in sexual relations, a zealot – like Pinchas – it is permitted to execute the participants. Furthermore, the zealous behavior is praiseworthy![34] In other words, Pinchas is vindicated. The two people that he responded to had made a point of conducting their liaison in public. He observed this overt, public sexual behavior between a Jew and non-Jew, and he assumed the role of the zealot. Not only was he permitted to do so, his behavior was worthy of praise!

Already, a number of questions emerge. According to Maimonides, the two people executed by Pinchas had not violated an explicit Torah prohibition. Yet, Pinchas was permitted to execute them, and was praised for doing so. How is it possible to endorse the execution of two people that have not violated any explicit law on the Torah level?

Ra'avad raises a second issue. Generally, before a person can be executed, he must be warned that he is violating a commandment. Maimonides makes no reference to this requirement in the case of the zealot. Apparently, the zealot can carry out an execution without providing a prior warning.[35] Of course, these two questions are related. Since – according to Maimonides – no explicit Torah commandment is being violated, it would be impossible to provide a warning. What commandment would serve as the basis for the zealot's warning? However, Ra'avad's question does indicate that Maimonides' position results in a fundamental deviation from normative *halacha* – an execution can take place without prior warning.

If we proceed further in Maimonides' discussion of this area, additional questions emerge. Maimondes explains that the zealot can only act at the moment of the incident. But, once the two partners are no longer engaged in sexual activity, the zealot is not permitted to act.[36] Now, if the zealot is allowed to execute these individuals because of the inappropriateness of their behavior, what difference does it make whether the execution takes place while the two

---

[33] Rabbaynu Moshe ben Maimon (Rambam) *Mishne Torah*, Hilchot Esurai Be'ah 12:2.

[34] Rabbaynu Moshe ben Maimon (Rambam) *Mishne Torah*, Hilchot Esurai Be'ah 12:4.

[35] Rabbaynu Avraham ben David of Posquieres (Ra'avad) *Critique on Maimonides' Mishne Torah*, Hilchot Esurai Be'ah 12:4.

[36] Rabbaynu Moshe ben Maimon (Rambam) *Mishne Torah*, Hilchot Esurai Be'ah 12:5.

people are still sexually engaged, or whether it takes place soon afterwards? If their behavior is so seriously sinful as to deserve execution, the zealot should be permitted to carry out this punishment even after the sexual activity has ended.

Maimonides follows this ruling with another that is, perhaps, the most astounding of his comments. If the zealot asks the court to advise him, the court cannot tell the zealot to carry out the execution. Maimonides adds that, furthermore, if the person the zealot is attempting to execute defends himself and kills his assailant, he is not liable.[37]

Let us consider these two rulings. The court cannot direct the zealot to act, or even confirm that it is proper to do so. How is it possible for Maimonides to maintain that the zealot is acting properly and that his behavior is praiseworthy, and, at the same time, contend that the court cannot direct or even confirm the propriety of this behavior? In addition, if the zealot is acting properly, then what right does the sinner have to kill the zealot?

In order to resolve these questions, we must better understand the Torah's position regarding normative punishments. The courts are charged with the duty of enforcing observance of these commandments. The courts have the authority and responsibility to punish specific violations. Their role is to determine whether a crime or sin has been committed. If their judgment is that this is the case, then the guilty party has a liability to receive the punishment. The court merely responds to this liability. In carrying out a punishment, the courts are completely reactive. A liability to receive punishment has been determined to exist. The court reacts and responds to this liability.

Let us contrast this to the execution carried out by the zealot. A zealot is a person who is deeply committed to his convictions. If these convictions have a firm basis – as in the case of a person who is zealous in regard to the Torah, then a zealous attitude is appropriate. However, the zealot is not reactive. No court has judged the case, and no liability to receive punishment has been created. The zealot is not responding to a liability. Instead, he acts upon a personal commitment to protect the Torah. In the specific case of a Jew engaged in overt, public sexual behavior with a non-Jew, this zealot is permitted to, and commended for, acting on his convictions.

In short, a normative punishment stems from a liability within the convicted sinner or criminal to be punished. The courts merely respond to this liability. In contrast, the zealot acts out of personal conviction and is not responding to a liability created through a court judgment.

Based on this distinction, the questions we have outlined can be resolved. First, how can the zealot execute a person for sexual activity with a non-Jew if the Torah is only explicit in prohibiting this behavior in the context of marriage – and even then, only condemns the sinner to lashes? This question is easily resolved. The zealot is not responding to a liability created by the violation of an explicit Torah *mitzvah*. In fact, the court has not convened and judged the person. The zealot is permitted to take action – in this specific case – as an expression of the intensity of his own convictions. Therefore, the absence of any violation of an explicit *mitzvah,* punishable by death, is not a factor.

Ra'avad's question on Maimonides is also answered. It is true that, in this case, the zealot is not required to warn the violator that he is violating the Torah. But, this requirement of

---

[37] Rabbaynu Moshe ben Maimon (Rambam) *Mishne Torah*, Hilchot Esurai Be'ah 12:5.

providing a warning is designed to determine the culpability of the sinner or criminal. In other words, his guilt can only be established if he has first been warned. But, the zealot is not acting in response to the guilt of the sinner. He is given the authority to express his zealousness. Therefore, no prior warning is needed.

Why can the zealot only act at the moment at which the sexual behavior is taking place? This seems to be the question that is most easily answered. The sinner that the zealot seeks to punish has not been found guilty in a court. The zealot can only act because the Torah allows him to give expression to the depth of his convictions. But, the zealot is not permitted to be an avenger. He is permitted to bring this public desecration to an abrupt and emphatic end. Therefore, his authority is limited to the time at which the sin is occurring. But, once the sexual act has ended, the zealot no longer has a role. Now, only the courts can act.

Why can the courts not direct the zealot? First, the courts decide innocence or guilt on the basis of specific principles of jurisprudence. The sinner has not been judged. So, the court is in no position to issue a statement regarding the guilt of the sinner. But more importantly, a zealot acts out of the strength and depth of his own personal convictions. If this person must first go to the court for approval of his actions, then his claim of zealousness is questionable.

Why is the sinner who defends himself and kills his assailant – the zealot – not held responsible for this killing? Again, the sinner has not been found guilty of a crime by the courts. He does not have a liability to receive a punishment. The zealot acts out of his own convictions, and is not responding to any liability that that been established by the courts. Therefore, the sinner has the authority to defend himself, just as any other person has the right to kill another individual in his own self-defense.

This discussion is rather technical, but, from it, an important point emerges. The Torah does not encourage the unrestrained expression of zealous attitudes. The Torah consists of 613 commandments. It is important for a Jew to have strong conviction in the truth of the Torah. However, regardless of the strength of one's convictions and the intensity of one's zealousness, in most cases, one does not have the right to take the law into one's own hand or violate any percept of the Torah. If the zealot had such authority, society would quickly become lawless and *halacha* would become meaningless. It is impossible in an ordered, just society, governed by a system of *halacha,* to allow one member to harm another or disregard *halacha* and then attribute his behavior to zealousness.

In response to a public display of intimacy between and Jew and non-Jew, the Torah does make an exception and allows the zealot to give expression to his convictions. But, as the discussion above indicates, this does not mean that the zealot is permitted to ignore any and all *halachic* considerations in order to address the wrong he observes. On the contrary, the rights and authority of the zealot are strictly prescribed and defined. If he deviates from these rules – for example, if he kills the sinner after the act has been completed – he is no longer defined by *halacha* as a zealot. Instead, he is an avenger and is himself guilty of murder.

My people, what have I done, and how have I wearied you? Testify against Me. For I brought you up out of the Land of Egypt and redeemed you from the house of slavery, and I sent before you Moshe, Aharon, and Miryam. My people, remember now what Balak king of Moav planned, and what Bilaam the son of Beor answered him. From Shittim to Gilgal, may you recognize the righteous deeds of Hashem. (Sefer Michah 6:3-5)

What Has G-d Done for Me Lately?

1. Michah rebukes the Jewish people

The above passage is from the haftarah of Parshat Balak. In this reading from the Prophets, the prophet Michah is sharing a message from Hashem. He challenges the Jewish people to present their complaints against Hashem. The Jewish people have been unfaithful. Michah demands that they defend their behavior. Then, he reviews the relationship between Hashem and the Jewish people. He enumerates acts of kindness that Hashem performed for the Jewish people. He brought them out of Egypt and restored them to the Land of Israel. He rescued them from bondage. He sent them great prophets – Moshe, Aharon, and Miryam. Then, Micah directs them to recall Balak. He plotted against the Jewish people. He recruited Bilaam to curse Bnai Yisrael. Instead, Hashem forced Bilaam to bestow a blessing. Michah reminds them of their sins and Hashem's forgiveness. He closes referring them to the passage of their ancestors going across the River Jordan upon dry land.[38] Michah's message is that the Jewish people have been the object of Hashem's benevolence. They have repaid His kindness with disloyalty and rebellion.

It is odd that in his list of the wonders and kindnesses that Hashem performed on their behalf, Michah mentions Balak and Bilaam. This incident was an expression of Hashem's benevolence but it is not on par with many others that he could have cited. He could have reminded the people of their conquest of the mighty nations that occupied the Land of Cana'an. He might have referred them to Hashem sustaining their ancestors in the barren wilderness. He provided them with ma'an – manna – and water. Why does Michah make mention of Bilaam and Balak? To answer these questions a review of the Torah's account of Balak and Bilaam is required.

And the angel of Hashem spoke to Bilaam, "Go with the men. However, that which I speak to you, it is what you shall speak." And Bilaam went with the officers of Balak. (BeMidbar 22:35)

2. Balak and Bilaam's plot

Balak was king of Moav. Moav realized that it was not directly threatened by Bnai Yisrael. The Land of Moav was not part of the legacy Hashem promised the Jewish people. Nonetheless, Balak and his people loathed Bnai Yisrael. Balak considered how he might harm the Jewish people. He turned to Bilaam. Bilaam was a heathen soothsayer or pseudo-prophet of some sort. He was perceived as capable of effectively cursing and blessing individuals and nations. Balak asked Bilaam to use his powers to curse Bnai Yisrael.

Bilaam was enticed by Balak's offer. However, Hashem came to Bilaam in a vision and warned him against responding to Balak's summons and against cursing the Jewish people. Eventually, Hashem allowed Bilaam to travel to Balak but with the proviso in the above passage. He must tell Balak that he will act only as directed by Hashem.[39]

Bilaam understands these directions but hopes that he will find a means to curse Bnai Yisrael. Twice Bilaam tries to persuade Hashem to allow him to curse the Jewish nation.[40] Both

---

[38] See Rabbaynu David Kimchi (Radak), Commentary on Sefer Michah 6:3-5.

[39] In the above passage, Bilaam is admonished to speak only as instructed by Hashem. However, Ramban explains that Hashem's intention was for Bilaam to share this restriction with Balak's messengers. See Ramban 22:35.

[40] See Ramban 23:16. He planned to address Hashem focusing on Bnai Yisrael's failings. He was prepared to argue that the Jewish people do not deserve Hashem's providence. They are

times Hashem forces Bilaam to report back to Balak and bless Bnai Yisrael. On a third and final occasion, Bilaam realizes he cannot succeed in cursing the nation. He submits to Hashem.[41] He delivers a final, more extensive blessing. Then, he reports to Balak a prophecy regarding the future of Bnai Yisrael and the surrounding nations.

There is an interesting question to be considered. This incident took place without Bnai Yisrael's knowledge. They became aware of Balak and Bilaam's conspiracy through its inclusion in the Torah. Why was it necessary to include this incident in the Torah? Why was it revealed to Bnai Yisrael?

A fascinating story provides insight into Michah's reference to Balak and Bilaam. Also, it suggests a reason for the inclusion of their conspiracy in the Torah.

Praise Hashem, all nations, laud Him, all peoples. For His kindness has overwhelmed us, and the truth of Hashem is eternal. Hallelu-Yah! (Sefer Tehilim 117:1-2)

3. Knowledge of Hashem's benevolence

Rav Yitzchak Volozhin (Rav Itzela) headed the Volozhin Yeshiva established by his father Rav Chaim. He was also a leader of the Russian Mitnaggid – non-Chasidic – community. In his capacity as a communal leader, he met with ministers of the tsarist government. A minister asked that he explain the above passage. He asked Rav Yitzchak, "Because His kindness overwhelms Israel, should the gentile nations praise Hashem?" In other words, why should non-Jews praise Hashem because of kindnesses done for the Jewish people?

Rav Yitzchak responded, "Bnai Yisrael does not know all the plans that you develop against them. Only you – the gentiles – know the degree of Hashem's kindness to Israel. You know how He overturns your evil counsels and does not allow you to execute your plans. Therefore, it is specifically you who are most fit to extol and praise Hashem for this."[42]

4. Hashem's kindness exceeds our awareness

Rav Yitzchak's comments respond to the above questions. Rabbaynu Yitzchak Abravanel explains that Michah included the plot of Balak and Bilaam among his examples of Hashem's kindnesses because it adds a dimension to his message. He reminded the people of the miracles and wonders that Hashem performed for them surrounding their redemption from bondage in Egypt. Then, he added the incident of Balak and Bilaam. His message was that we are only aware of the observable expressions of Hashem's benevolence. We are not aware of the many unobservable acts of kindness that Hashem performs on our behalf. The incident of Balak and Bilaam exemplifies this idea. When it was occurring, Bnai Yisrael was unaware of the plot. Hashem interfered and defeated Balak and Bilaam without Bnai Yisrael's awareness.[43]

Michah is telling the people, "Beyond all the wonders and kindnesses of which you are aware, there are countless others. Hashem does not reveal them to you. But He is constantly exercising His providence and protecting the Jewish people."

This message is also communicated by the inclusion of the Balak and Bilaam conspiracy in the Torah. Its inclusion communicates to us that we should not think that Hashem's kindness to us is expressed only in the acts we observe. The Torah reveals the incident of Bilaam and Balak saying, "There are other acts of Divine protection of which you are not aware."

---

worthy of punishment.

[41] Rabbaynu Moshe ben Nachman (Ramban), Commentary on Sefer BeMidbar 24:1.

[42] Rav Y. Hershkowitz, Netivot Raboteynu, vol 1, pp. 345-6.

[43] Don Yitzchak Abravanel, Commentary on Sefer Michah, 6:5.

5. A balanced view

This is an important message. We easily recognize tragedy and misfortune. We wonder how a benevolent G-d allows us, those we love, and our people to suffer. We do not know the answer. His ways are a mystery. However, it is important to strive to achieve a balanced view. The tragedies and suffering we observe are real. They cannot be dismissed. But we must take care not to disregard the many blessings that are simultaneously bestowed upon us. This is true of the individual and concerning the Jewish people.

Somehow, despite repeated persecutions and virtually continual antipathy, the Jewish people survive. Something prevents our enemies from utterly destroying us. The prophet Michah is admonishing us to recognize the miracle of Jewish survival, to not take it for granted. This does not remove the pain of our suffering, but it allows us to recognize that our persecution does not represent a complete abandonment by Hashem. In ways we are aware and through acts that are concealed from us, He continues to preserve the Jewish people.

Pinchas

Pinchas, the son of Elazar, the son of Aharon the kohen, turned back my anger from upon Bnai Yisrael by being zealous on My behalf among them. And I did not utterly destroy Bnai Yisrael in My anger. (BeMidbar 25:11)

Lying for Love

1. Parshat Pinchas completes Parshat Balak

Parshat Balak ends with a description of the event of Sheetim. Bnai Yisrael were encamped at this location. Women from Moav came into the camp. Midyan was also represented among these women. The young women came with a mission. Their goal was to corrupt the men of Bnai Yisrael. Their strategy was to first seduce the men and then invite them to join them in idolatrous practices.

Their strategy succeeded on three levels. First, they did achieve their goal of seducing men and involving them in their idolatrous worship. Second, their success was met by tremendous confusion among the leadership. The leadership was uncertain how to respond to this catastrophe. Third, in the absence of a vigorous response, Hashem brought upon the people a terrible plague.

Pinchas, the son of Elazar, and the grandson of Aharon was not confused. He took up his spear and drove it through two of the most prominent participants in this orgiastic episode. His two victims were Zimri, the son of Salu. Zimri was a prince of the *shevet* – the tribe – of Shimon. The woman who liaisoned with Zimri was executed with him. She was Kazbee, the daughter of Tzur. Her father, Tzur, was a chieftain of Midyan.

The passages above are the opening passages of Parshat Pinchas. They refer to this incident. In the passages following those above, Pinchas is rewarded for his initiative. Those passages seem to indicate that Pinchas received two rewards. Hashem awarded him a covenant of peace. He was also rewarded with *kehunah* – priesthood.

2. Pinchas' appointment to priesthood

The appointment of Pinchas as a *kohen* – a priest – requires explanation. He was a descendant of Aharon the *kohen*. Was he not a *kohen* prior to this incident? Rashi explains that Pinchas was not among the original *kohanim* – priests. Initially, only Aharon and his sons were anointed and appointed to the *kehunah*. Once bestowed upon them, *kehunah* would extend to any subsequent offspring. Pinchas was not among these sons of Aharon. He was not anointed. Sons born to his father Elazar after his anointment would be endowed with the status of *kohen*. Pinchas was already an adult son at the time of Elazar's appointment. Therefore, up to this point, he was not a *kohen*. According to Rashi, the above passages describe Pinchas' appointment as a *kohen* in response to his act of zealousness.[1]

Others differ with Rashi. Rabbaynu Avraham Ibn Ezra maintains that Pinchas was included among those originally appointed to the *kehunah*. The above passages are not awarding Pinchas *kehunah*. Instead, Pinchas is assured that the role of *kohen gadol* – high priest – will

---

[1] Rabbaynu Shlomo ben Yitzchak (Rashi), *Commentary on Sefer BeMidbar* 25:13.

belong to him and to his descendants.[2] This promise was fulfilled. Most of the *kohanim* who served as *kohen gadol* were descendants of Pinchas.[3]

In short, Pinchas was rewarded with a legacy related to the *kehunah*. The exact nature of the legacy is disputed. According to Rashi, he was appointed to the *kehunah*. According to others, the position of *kohen gadol* was given to his descendants as a legacy.

3. The covenant of peace

There is a debate among the commentators regarding this covenant of peace. Rashi does not understand this covenant of peace as a second separate blessing or reward. Instead, it introduces the reward of *kehunah*. It explains that the reward of *kehunah* is an expression of Hashem's goodwill toward Pinchas. As an expression of His goodwill, Hashem appointed Pinchas to the *kehunah*.[4]

In summary, the essential reward granted Pinchas was related to *kehunah*. According to Rashi, this was the only reward. Why was *kehunah* the appropriate reward for Pinchas?

Therefore, say to him: Now, I grant him My covenant of peace. And to him and his descendants who follow him will be a covenant of eternal priesthood – because he was zealous for his G-d and atoned for Bnai Yisrael. (BeMidbar 25:12-13)

4. Why a reward of priesthood?

The *pesukim* identify two factors through which Pinchas secured his reward. First, Pinchas was zealous for Hashem. Second, he atoned for Bnai Yisrael. These factors provide a compelling explanation for Pinchas' reward. A *kohen* serves Hashem in the *Bait HaMikdash* – the Temple. His life is dedicated to serve Hashem. Also, a fundamental element of this service is the offering of sacrifices brought in the process of atonement. Who could be more fit for these roles? Pinchas demonstrated his devotion to Hashem. He acted decisively and bravely. He recognized that an egregious desecration of the Torah was unfolding and acted while others were paralyzed by indecision. In taking action, he atoned for the nation's paralysis and ended the plague. In short, Pinchas' behavior uniquely qualified him for the *kohen's* role in the Temple service and in the process of atonement for the nation.

The midrash provides a slightly different perspective on the reward of Pinchas and its appropriateness. The midrash focuses upon another role of the *kohen*.

Before considering the comments of the midrash. Let us return to an issue discussed above. As noted, the passages seem to identify two rewards granted to Pinchas – a covenant of peace and a covenant of priesthood. Rashi demurs from this interpretation and suggests that the two references are to a single reward – priesthood. This reward is referred to as a covenant of peace because it was an expression of Hashem's goodwill toward Pinchas.

May Hashem bless you and guard you. May He shine His countenance upon you and grant you grace. May He lift His countenance upon you and place upon you peace. (BeMidbar 6:24-26)

5. The priest as a representative of peace

---

[2] Rabbaynu Avraham ibn Ezra, *Commentary on Sefer BeMidbar*, 25:12.

[3] Don Yitzchak Abravanel, *Commentary on Sefer BeMidbar*. Parshat Pinchas.

[4] Rabbaynu Shlomo ben Yitzchak (Rashi), *Commentary on Sefer BeMidbar* 25:12-13.

The midrash agrees that the two references apply to a single reward – *kehunah*. However, according to the midrash, the appointment of Pinchas to the priesthood is referred to as a covenant of peace because, peace and *kehunah* are synonymous. What is the connection between *kehunah* and peace?

As explained above, the *kohen's* role is to serve Hashem in the *Bait HaMikdash* and participate in the process of atonement for Bnai Yisrael. However, the *kohen* has another role. He bestows a daily blessing upon the people. This tripartite blessing is described in the above passages. The final element is a blessing of peace. Through his appointment to the *kehunah*, Pinchas secured the right to, each day, bless the nation with peace.

According to the midrash, the reason that *kehunah* was an appropriate reward for Pinchas is because of the *kohen's* role in blessing the people with peace.[5] This reward demonstrated that Pinchas was a person dedicated to peace and who loved Bnai Yisrael.

My covenant was with him – life and peace. I granted these to him because of his awe and that he feared me; and that he trembled before My name. The law of truth was in his mouth. Falsehood was not found upon his lips. With peace and justice he traveled before Me. Many he redeemed from iniquity. For the lips of the kohen guard knowledge. They shall seek Torah from his mouth, for he is an angel of Hashem of the hosts. (Malachi 2:5-7)

6. The priest is associated with peace and truth

As explained above, one of the qualities with which *kehunah* is associated is love of peace. The above passages reference this quality but they focus upon another important characteristic of *kehunah*. In these passages, the *navi* – the prophet – Malachi urges the people to seek the guidance of the *kohanim*. The *navi* explains that the *kohanim* are not only selected to serve in the *Bait HaMikdash*. They are also assigned the task of instructing the people in observance of the Torah. These passages associate the *kehunah* with devotion to truth. In other words, the *kohen* is associated with two traits – love of peace and truthfulness.

7. Lying for the sake of peace

The Sages make reference to the above passages from Malachi in an odd context. They explain that Aharon exemplified the pursuit of peace. They provide an example of Aharon's strategies for securing peace among people.

Two friends became embroiled in a dispute. In their anger, they became alienated from one another. Aharon would individually confront each of the disputants. He would tell each that his former friend and current adversary was deeply pained by their conflict and grieved the loss of his dear friend's love. Each would be moved by Aharon's account of the other's grief. They would run to each other to repair and restore the relationship disrupted by their recent dispute. In this context, the Sages cite the words of Malachi.[6]

The reference to Malachi's comments is difficult to understand. It is true that Malachi notes that the *kohen* is devoted to peace. However, he stresses the *kohen's* commitment to uncompromised truth. In the example provided by the Sages of Aharon's efforts to promote peace, truth is sacrificed for the greater good of repairing a relationship between friends. It seems

---

[5] Rav Menachem Mendel Kasher, *Torah Shelymah* Parshat Naso, p 113.
[6] *Avot D'Rav Natan* 12:3.

that Aharon was not uncompromising in his commitment to the truth. Peace was more important to him.

8. Lying for the sake of truth

A more careful examination of the example of Aharon's strategy suggests a solution to this problem. Aharon understood that these two former friends were now adversaries because of a falsehood that each embraced about his former comrade. In response to their dispute, each had reformulated his perception of his former friend. The former friend was demonized and transformed into an adversary bereft of any positive qualities. The positive aspects of his former friend's personality had been either minimized or dismissed as not genuine. In other words, the enmity between these two former friends was founded upon a lie that each accepted regarding the other.

It is true that Aharon fabricated a tale of remorse that he communicated to each of the adversaries. But this tale was devised to prompt each to see past the demonized image invented of his friend and see again the true person with whom he had felt bonds of fraternity. The tale invented by Aharon was a vehicle for tearing away a veil of distortion and revealing a more fundamental truth.

9. Peace and friendship founded upon truth

The Sages cite Malachi's words because they reflect this lesson. So many shattered relationships and conflicts are based upon falsehood and deception. Each party imagines himself the injured. In his desire to give full vent to the fury of his anger, he demonizes his adversary. It does not satisfy his needs to perceive his adversary as a good person with whom he has a dispute. He cannot resent and detest such a person. He vilifies his adversary in order to justify his own odious desires.

In their praise of Aharon, the Sages suggest to us a therapy for our conflicts with one another. These conflicts may be legitimate. However, we must resist the temptation to convert conflict into hatred through embracing a lie – the demonization of our adversary. We must focus on the simple truth that we each have positive and negative characteristics. Like ourselves, our adversaries are neither all good nor all bad – just complex and imperfect human beings who try to do good but sometimes fall short. If we can remember these truths, then we can forgive our adversary's faults and allow our disagreements to exist within a context of mutual respect and fraternity.

"Therefore, say that I give to him my covenant of peace." (BeMidbar 25:12)

The closing passages of Parshat Balak provide an introduction to our *parasha*. Women from the nations of Moav and Midyan enter the camp of Bnai Yisrael. These women seduce members of Bnai Yisrael. The heathen women use these illicit relationships to lead their partners into idolatrous practices. Discipline and sexual restraint begin to break down. Ultimately, Zimri – a leader of Shevet Shimon – publicly enters into a romantic liaison with a woman from Midyan. The woman – Kazbi – is a princess of Midyan. Hashem strikes Bnai Yisrael with a plague. Pinchas, the son of Elazar the *Kohen*, takes action. He executes Zimri and Kazbi. In response to Pinchas' zealousness, the Almighty ends the plague.

Hashem acknowledges Pinchas' righteous zealousness. Hashem rewards Pinchas. Our *pasuk* relates one of the rewards. Hashem enters into a covenant of peace with Pinchas.

What was this covenant of peace? Rabbaynu Avraham ibn Ezra offers the simplest explanation. He explains that Pinchas placed himself in danger. He executed a leader of Shevet Shimon. Zimri's friends and followers would seek retribution. Hashem promised Pinchas that he would live in peace. Zimri's comrades would not succeed in disturbing Pinchas' life.[7]

Rabbaynu Yonatan ben Uziel offers an alternative interpretation of this covenant of peace. He explains that Hashem promised to transform Pinchas into an angel. As an angel, he will be the harbinger of the Messiah.

This interpretation presents two problems. First, how can this interpretation be reconciled with the simple meaning of the passage? The *pasuk* states that the Almighty is entering into a covenant of peace with Pinchas. It makes no reference to Pinchas' transformation or the Messianic era!

Second, Hashem's rewards are not arbitrary. They correspond to our actions. According to Rabbaynu Yonatan ben Uziel, Pinchas would be transformed into and angel and assigned the distinction of announcing the Messianic era. How does this reward correspond with Pinchas' actions?

In order to answer these questions, we must reevaluate the events described above. The behaviors and experiences of Bnai Yisrael at the end of Parshat Balak mirror or presage the phenomenon of the Jewish people's exile. In exile we have been faced with two great threats – persecution and assimilation. These two threats are related. However, this relationship has sometimes been misunderstood.

It is sometimes assumed that assimilation prevents persecution. This theory maintains that persecution is directed against outsiders. The most effective method for avoiding persecution is assimilation into the host society. Jewish history seems to invalidate this theory. The Jewish people have not succeeded in stemming persecution through melting into its surroundings. In fact, attempts at assimilation have often been greeted with increased persecution.

The events at the end of Parshat Balak suggest an alternative relationship between assimilation and persecution. In this incident, Bnai Yisrael began to assimilate. The people joined in liaisons with the women of Moav and Midyan. They adopted their heathen practices. This behavior evoked Hashem's retribution. The nation was struck with a plague. Assimilation led to punishment. This suggests that persecution is a response to attempts to assimilate. In other words, assimilation does not prevent persecution. It invites persecution!

Now let us consider Pinchas' response. Pinchas recognized that the plague was a consequence of the nation's iniquity. He realized that the plague could only be arrested through a return to Torah. He acted energetically and zealously. He demanded that the nation change direction and return to Hashem.

Pinchas saved Bnai Yisrael. He also provided future generations with a model for responding to national tragedy. We must return to Torah. This is the only way to avoid persecution. This is the only means of survival in exile.

---

[7] Rabbaynu Avraham ibn Ezra, *Commentary on Sefer BeMidbar* 25:12.

Based on this analysis, we can understand the relationship between Pinchas' reward and his behavior. He demonstrated the appropriate response to the national tragedy. He demonstrated the proper response to the experiences of exile. He provided guidance in dealing with the sorrows of our banishment. It is fitting that he should announce the end of exile and the advent of the Messianic era.

This interpretation of our passage is not inconsistent with the plain meaning of the words. Pinchas ended the plague. He negotiated a peace between Hashem and Bnai Yisrael.[8] Exile represents banishment from before Hashem. It is a disruption of the peace between Hashem and Bnai Yisrael. Pinchas is promised a covenant of peace. He will announce the Messianic era. He will proclaim the reestablishment of perfect peace between Hashem and Bnai Yisrael.

"And he and his descendants after him will have a covenant of permanent priesthood. This is because he was zealous for his G-d and atoned for Bnai Yisrael." (BeMidbar 25:13)

The opening passages of our Parshah are based upon the incident described at the conclusion of the previous parasha. The Torah explains that Bnai Yisrael were camped at Shittim. A group of women from Moav entered the camp. They seduced some of the men. Once they established their influence over these men, they encouraged them to practice idolatry. Hashem punished the nation with a plague. Hashem instructed Moshe to direct the courts to respond and punish the transgressors. One of the participants in this promiscuous episode was, Zimri, the son of Salu. He was a leader in the tribe of Shimon. He was attracted to a princess of Midyan. Pinchas observed Zimri's behavior. He reacted. He executed Zimri and his paramour. Pinchas' demonstration of zeal had an immediate effect. The plague was suspended.

The Talmud in Tractate Sanhedrin discusses Pinchas' behavior. Typically, the courts are charged with the responsibility of assessing whether a law has been violated and administering the appropriate punishment. What was the source of Pinchas' authority to execute Zimri and his partner? The Talmud explains that Pinchas acted in accordance with an amazing law. One who witnesses a public display of sexual intimacy between Jew and non-Jew has the right to execute the parties without direct consultation with the courts. Pinchas was aware of this law and acted.

There is an interesting dispute in the Talmud regarding the details of Pinchas' behavior. Rav maintains that before acting, Pinchas consulted Moshe. He asked Moshe to confirm his understanding of the law. Moshe confirmed Pinchas' authority to execute Zimri and his partner. Only after this confirmation, did Pinchas take action. Shemuel disagrees. He contends that Pinchas knew the law and was aware of his authority to act. There was no reason for him to consult Moshe. He did not ask any questions. Instead, he acted immediately. He reasoned that a desecration of the Torah and Hashem's name was taking place. No time should be wasted. An immediate response was required!

What is the basis of Rav and Shemuel's dispute? Obviously, neither can claim knowledge of the actual events. Neither was present at the time of the event. Also, it seems that neither possessed an authentic tradition regarding the issue. If such a tradition existed, the issue could not be debated. Instead, it must be assumed that neither Rav or Shemuel claimed to have direct

---

[8] Rabbaynu Levi ben Gershon (Ralbag / Gershonides), *Commentary on Sefer BeMidbar*, (Mosad HaRav Kook, 1998), p 141.

information regarding the details of Pinchas' behavior. However, each assumed that Pinchas acted according to the requirements of the Torah and that he was aware of specific laws relevant to his situation. Therefore, each infers Pinchas' behavior based upon his own interpretation of the requirements of the law. Rav and Shemuel disagree in their interpretation and therefore they attribute different behaviors to Pinchas. It remains to define these two alternate interpretations.

This law essentially allows a person to act as judge and executioner without appointment by the court. Under normal circumstances, Pinchas' behavior would be a crime. But as a response to this extreme instance of public sexual intimacy, his actions were laudable. In other words, in this unique situation normal legal guidelines are suspended. Specifically, what laws are suspended? First, generally only the court can determine a person's guilt. An individual witness does not have the authority to decide this issue. Here, the zealot is permitted to determine that a crime has been committed. Second, normally it is prohibited to take a person's life. Apparently, in this situation, the violators' lives are in forfeiture. The prohibition against shedding their blood is suspended.

However, there is a third law that must be considered. This is a subtle issue that can easily be overlooked. Pinchas decided the law in the presence of the court. This would be generally prohibited. Even though Pinchas had the authority to decide the issue, here a court was present! In deference to the authority and honor of the court, we would expect Pinchas to consult these judges! It seems that this is the issue disputed by Rav and Shemuel. Both agree that the Torah permits the zealot to determine the guilt of the sinners. He is also permitted to shed blood. In a situation in which no court is present, Rav and Shemuel would be in complete agreement. The zealot is free to act unilaterally. However, in Pinchas' situation a court was present. Rav maintains that the zealot must show deference to this institution. Therefore, he infers that Pinchas must have consulted Moshe before acting. Shemuel disagrees. He maintains that the requirement to respect the authority and honor of the court is nullified by the urgency of the situation. The requirement is suspended. Therefore, he infers that there is no reason to assume that Pinchas first consulted Moshe.

Pinchas' behavior is discussed in the Talmud Yerushalmi. The Yerushalmi makes an amazing comment regarding the authority of the zealot and Pinchas' decision. The Talmud begins by establishing the basic law of the zealot. The zealot has the authority to act in this extreme case. One need not consult the court. However, the Talmud then adds that this behavior is not appropriate and is not completely approved by the Sages. In other words, the Sages would not encourage the zealot to execute this law. Furthermore, the Talmud explains that the Sages of Pinchas' time did not approve of his behavior! Our *pasuk* is Hashem's response to the Sages' disapproval. The Almighty rewards Pinchas for his zeal. He indicates that Pinchas acted properly and deserves praise.[9]

This discussion raises many questions. First, the Torah in this instance permits the zealot to execute the sinner. Why do the Sages discourage the zealot from performing this mission? If the Sages are correct in their policy, why did Hashem commend Pinchas? Finally, after the Torah endorsed Pinchas' decision why did the Sages not change their position?

---

[9] Talmud Yerushalmi, Mesechet Sanhedrin 9:7.

Torah Temimah deals with these questions and offers a brilliant answer. He explains that the Torah only permitted a specific type of individual to act in this case. This is an individual motivated by zeal to protect the Torah. Any other individual is prohibited to act in this case.

This answers our questions. The Torah permits the zealot to execute the sinners. However, the Sages discouraged this behavior. They felt that it is difficult for a person to evaluate one's own motives. A person may confuse some personal motivation with authentic zeal. The Sages are not contradicting the Torah. They are merely recognizing the difficulty of meeting the requirements of the law.

The Sages did not feel that even Pinchas should have relied on his own assessment of his personal motivations. For this reason they did not immediately approve of his behavior. The Almighty rewarded Pinchas. This demonstrated that Pinchas had been motivated by authentic zeal.

The Torah's endorsement of Pinchas' behavior did not alter the Sages' general position. True, Pinchas had acted appropriately. However, this does not mean that a lesser individual can be trusted to perform this personal assessment.

And Hashem spoke to Moshe, saying: Pinchas the son of Elazar the son of Aharon the priest has turned My anger away from Bnai Yisrael by his zealously avenging Me among them, so that I did not destroy the children of Israel because of My zeal. Therefore, say, "I hereby give him My covenant of peace. It shall be for him and for his descendants after him [as] an eternal covenant of priesthood, because he was zealous for his L-rd and atoned for Bnai Yisrael." (BeMidbar 25:10-13)

Fighting the "Good" Fight

Pinchas, his zealotry, and his reward

Parshat Balak closed with a description of Pinchas' heroic act. The men of Bnai Yisrael entered into amorous relationships with the women of Moav. This led to their entanglement in idolatrous practices. In response to the nation's degenerate behavior, Hashem brought a plague upon the nation and instructed Moshe on the steps that must be immediately taken to save the people from destruction. Moshe must mobilize the courts and publicly punish the idolators. Moshe moved to act and was immediately challenged by an agitator. This agitator publicly liaisoned with a princess of Midyan. The act was designed to express derision of Moshe and his courts. Pinchas stepped forward. Without hesitation, he took the lives of the agitator and his mistress. The plague was arrested.

Pinchas acted based upon an unusual law. In this specific case, a zealot is permitted to execute one who acts against the standards of the Torah. He does not need to ask the court for authority to act. In fact, the court cannot authorize the zealot's behavior. Were the zealot to ask the court's permission, it would be denied. The zealot is permitted to act but must do so completely upon his own initiative.

Because the zealot acts without the authorization of the court, he is not protected by its authority. If the person he intends to punish, parries his attack and instead, kills the zealot – in self-defense – he cannot be persecuted for his action.

In short, the zealot acts on his own authority and, he bares the responsibility for the consequences of his actions. He hopes to punish a wrongdoer, but if instead, he is injured or even killed, his attacker bares no responsibility for his injury or death.

Parshat Pinchas opens with Hashem's response to Pinchas' act of zealotry. This response has two aspects. It begins with an analysis of the significance or impact of Pinchas' behavior. Hashem tells Moshe that through his zealotry, Pinchas arrested His anger and saved the Jewish people from destruction. Hashem then describes Pinchas' reward. He is given a covenant of peace, and he and his descendants are given a covenant of priesthood.

One of the interesting issues raised by this incident and Hashem's response to Pinchas' behavior is the nature of zealotry. Clearly, Pinchas' reward demonstrates that he acted properly. This means there is a place for zealotry. But when is zealotry appropriate? Also, what is zealotry? Generally, our Sages condemn anger. Is zealotry an expression of anger but acceptable because it is justified, or is it somehow different from anger and therefore, not included in our Sages' proscription? Before addressing these difficult issues, let us consider a more specific problem which will direct us toward understanding the above issues.

The name of the Israelite man who was killed, who was slain with the Midianite woman was Zimri the son of Salu, the chieftain of the Simeonite paternal house. (BeMidbar 25:14)

The zealot must act within the law

The above passage reveals the specific identity of the agitator who was executed by Pinchas. In providing his identity, the passage notes that he was killed by Pinchas along with his paramour. Rav Yitzchak Zev Soloveitchik *Zt"l* suggests that the passage's focus on this detail reflects an important law regarding the zealot. The zealot may only act while the two sinners are engaged in their activity. Once they have disengaged, the zealot is forbidden from acting. This seems like a strange law. The zealot is provoked to act because of his intense disapproval of the activity in which the sinners are engaged. Certainly, these feelings persist as long as the sinners have not been punished. Then, it should be permissible for the zealot to take action as long as justice has not been carried out. Why can he only act while the two sinners are actually engaged in their vile activity?

This legal detail is very revealing. It suggests that the zealot's strong feeling that the behavior he is observing is loathsome does not provide a legal basis for his actions. He does not have the right to punish the sinners for their despicable behavior. Only the courts have this authority. The zealot may only intervene in order to emphatically and forcefully end the wanton public behavior. Once the behavior has ended and punishment is required, the zealot must defer to the courts. If the zealot did not have the opportunity to end the behavior, although he may still be moved by a visceral loathing of the behavior, he may not take action.

This insight addresses one of the issues raised above. When is zealotry permitted? This law reflects a fundamental principle that underlies the Torah's attitude toward zealotry. It is permitted only within the boundaries of *halachah* – Torah law. In other words, the Torah's treatment of zealotry reflects a paradoxical but undeniable attitude of the Torah. The Torah allows the zealot to take a life without consultation with or approval of the courts. Yet, this does not mean the actions of the zealot are not guided by their own set of specific laws. Zealotry is not an excuse to give expression to one's personal feelings and disregard the limits of *halachah*. The zealot's actions are bound by their own set of laws and the zealot must act within these boundaries.

Zealotry and anger

Let us now return to the question of whether the Torah's license of the zealot is an exception to its general disavowal of anger. Rav Avraham Chaim Shur *Zt"l* suggests that this is indeed the case. The Torah allows and even approves of anger in appropriate instances. However, the Torah does limit its expression and places it within bounds. Rav Shur cites a number of texts to support his position. For example, in Tractate Ta'anit, Raba comments that when a young Torah scholar angers, the Torah is the source of his anger. Rav Shur explains the intent of this passage. The young scholar should not be condemned for his anger. His anger is a justified and even appropriate response to his observation of disregard for the laws of the Torah.

The appropriateness of anger

Maimonides seems to take a different position regarding the appropriateness of anger. Maimonides explains that most behaviors and character traits are appropriate in moderation. For example, the Torah encourages a person to enjoy food but condemns gluttony. However, some desires or traits should not be indulged even in moderation. Among those which are never appropriate is anger. Maimonides comments that even when a show of anger is appropriate in order to add emphasis to a criticism or rebuke, the anger should be feigned and not real. In fact, according to Maimonides, Moshe's sin – for which he was denied entry into the Land of Israel – was his expression of anger toward the people. In other words, whereas Rav Shur maintains that at times anger is justified, Maimonides insists that anger is one of a small number of responses that should never be indulged.

The motives of an authentic zealot

In closing, an observation of Rav Chaim Soloveitchik *Zt'l* is relevant to this discussion.

Rav Soloveitchik offered an analogy to explain an important aspect of the Torah's attitude toward zealotry. He told the story of a homeowner who was troubled by an infestation of mice in his home. In order to combat the mice, he purchased a cat. In short order, the cat rid the homeowner of the troublesome mice. Rav Soloveitchik observed that both the homeowner and the cat shared the objective of eliminating the mice. However, their underlying motives were very different. The homeowner would have been even happier if he had never experienced the mice infestation. However, the cat's happiness stems from his engaging hunt and conquest. The cat's pleasure requires that there be an infestation!

Rav Soloveitchik explained that unfortunately, some individuals delight in confrontation and conflict. They masquerade as zealots for the honor of Torah but really enjoy confrontation and strife. The zealot who is acting on Torah principles wishes that his actions would not be required. He responds to a disaster – a public desecration of the Torah's values. He would prefer that the desecration not occur and his response not be required.

"Because he was zealous for his G-d and he atoned for Bnai Yisrael, he and his descendants after him will have a permanent covenant of priesthood." (BeMidbar 25:13)

Parshat Balak ends with an account of Moav's attempt to corrupt Bnai Yisrael. The nation of Moav recruits the young women of the nation. They are sent into the camp of Bnai

Yisrael with orders to seduce the men. Once the seduction is accomplished, the women entice the men to participate in idolatry.

This plan almost succeeds. The young women are successful in seducing some of the men. A princess of Midyan – Kazbi, the daughter of Tzur – actually succeeds in seducing one of the leaders of the shevet of Shimon – Zimri, the son of Salu.

Pinchas, the grandson of Ahron, intervenes. He executes Zimri and Kazbi while they are in the act of fornication.

Our *parasha* begins with an account of the rewards received by Pinchas. Among these rewards, Hashem promises Pinchas a permanent covenant of priesthood. What is the meaning of this blessing?

Superficially, it seems that this covenant endowed Pinchas and his descendants with the priesthood. They were made *Kohanim*. However, Pinchas was that grandson of Ahron. The descendants of Ahron were already chosen to serve as the *Kohanim*! What is Hashem giving to Pinchas that he does not already possess?

In fact, it is not at all clear that Pinchas and his descendants were already appointed as *Kohanim*. How is this possible? The Talmud in Tractate Zevachim discusses this issue. The Talmud explains that there are two opinions regarding the identity of the original *Kohanim*. The opinions differ on a simple question. Who were the original *Kohanim*? Were the only first *Kohanim* the sons of Ahron? Alternatively, did this group include all of Ahron's descendants alive at that time? What is the difference between these two possibilities? Pinchas was a grandson of Ahron. He was Ahron's descendant. However, he was not Ahron's son. According to the first opinion, only the sons of Ahron were the original *Kohanim*. Their descendants who were born subsequently also became *Kohanim*. However, descendants already born were not included in the *Kehunah* – the Priesthood. This means that Pinchas was not one of the original *Kohanim*. Neither could his descendants serve as *Kohanim*. He was not a son of Ahron. His descendants could not claim descent from a *Kohen*.

According to the second opinion, all the descendants of Ahron were included in the original group of *Kohanim*. Pinchas was a grandson of Ahron. He was a descendant. Therefore, he and his children were already included in the *Kehunah*.[10]

Rashi adopts the first opinion. He indicates that Pinchas was not one of the original *Kohanim*.[11] Maimonides sides with the second opinion. He maintains that Pinchas was included among the original *Kohanim*.[12]

Our *pasuk* must be interpreted according to each of these opinions. According to the first opinion, our passage is easily understood. Pinchas and his children were not originally included in the *Kehunah*. At this point, he and his descendants are granted *Kehunah*. This was part of his reward for acting zealously on behalf of Hashem. In our *pasuk*, the Almighty creates a permanent change in the status of Pinchas and his descendants. They will now be *Kohanim* and have the same status as Ahron's sons and their progeny.[13]

---

10 Mesechet Zevachim 101b.
11 Rabbaynu Shlomo ben Yitzchak (Rashi), *Commentary on Sefer BeMidbar* 25:13.
12 Rabbaynu Moshe ben Maimon (Rambam) *Mishne Torah*, Hilchot Bi'at HaMikdash 5:12.
13 Rabbaynu Shlomo ben Yitzchak (Rashi), *Commentary on Sefer BeMidbar* 25:13.

However, according to the second opinion, our *pasuk* is not as easily understood. According to this opinion, Pinchas and his descendants already possessed the status of *Kehunah*. What new office is given to Pinchas in our passage?

Rabbaynu Avraham ibn Ezra proposes an answer to this question. He explains that the passage does not represent a promise of *Kehunah*. Pinchas and his descendants already had this status. Instead, in our *pasuk*, Hashem awards Pinchas the office *Kohen Gadol*. Pinchas and his descendants will hold this office.[14]

Gershonides observes that most of those who held the office of *Kohen Gadol* were descendants of Pinchas. However, there were exceptions. Some of those who served as *Kohen Gadol* were descendants of Itamar. How can these exceptions be reconciled with Ibn Ezra's interpretation of the *pasuk*?

Gershonides responds that Hashem did not tell Pinchas that every *Kohen Gadol* would be one of his descendants. Instead, Hashem promised that this office would always be associated with the descendants of Pinchas. The office would never be transferred to a different family. At times, there would not be a fitting descendant of Pinchas to hold the office. Under such circumstances, the *Kohen Gadol* would come from the family of Itamar. Nonetheless, this interruption will only be temporary. The office will always return to the descendants of Pinchas.

Gershonides maintains that this is an example of a general principle. Hashem's blessings often involve some element of permanency. For example, kingship is awarded to the shevet of Yehudah. This does not mean that there will never be a king who is not from the shevet of Yehudah. Gershonides points out that such an interpretation is untenable. At times, there may not be an appropriate candidate for kingship from the shevet. Alternatively, sometimes the shevet will deserve to be punished. Under these circumstances, the kingship must temporarily be transferred to another shevet. This is not an abrogation of the blessing. This kingship always returns to Yehudah. Any interruption is temporary. The blessing does not promise that there will never be an interruption. It promises that the kingship will never be permanently removed from the shevet.[15]

"Be an enemy unto the people of Midyan and strike them. For they acted as enemies towards you through their plotting. They plotted against you in the matter of Peor and in the matter of Kazbi the daughter of Tzur, their sister who was killed on the day of the plague for the matter of Peor." (BeMidbar 25:17-18)

Hashem commands Moshe to treat the people of Midyan as enemies. Bnai Yisrael are commanded to make war with them. This is because Midyan allied with Moav. They joined in the plot to corrupt Bnai Yisrael.

The *pasuk* explains that Midyan shared responsibility for the "matter of Peor." This phrase is not difficult to interpret. The women of Midyan and Moav attempted to induce the men of Bnai Yisrael to engage in idolatry. The idolatrous entity they introduced to Bnai Yisrael was Peor. The *pasuk* admonishes the people to strike Midyan in response to this nation's efforts to

---

[14] Rabbaynu Avraham ibn Ezra, *Commentary on Sefer BeMidbar* 25:13.
[15] Rabbaynu Levi ben Gershon (Ralbag / Gershonides), *Commentary on Sefer BeMidbar*, (Mosad HaRav Kook, 1998), p 141.

introduce the worship of Peor among Bnai Yisrael. However, the *pasuk* adds that the people of Midyan should also be treated as enemies because of the "matter of Kazbi the daughter of Tzur."

This phrase is difficult to understand. Kazbi was one of the women recruited to participate in the seduction of the men of Bnai Yisrael. She was one of the specific women who was involved in the matter of Peor. It seems that the "matter of Peor" and the "matter of Kazbi" are two references to the same incident and evil. Why does the *pasuk* refer to the incident with both of these descriptions? Why is the incident described as the matter of Peor and as the matter of Kazbi?

The commentaries offer various answers to this question. According to Rashi, the *pasuk* is not only an admonishment to strike against Midyan. The *pasuk* is also a warning. Hashem commands Bnai Yisrael to wage war with Midyan and explains the urgency of this mission. Midyan is a dangerous adversary. This nation is completely committed to the destruction of Bnai Yisrael. What is the indication of this commitment? The nation sent Kazbi, the daughter of Tzur, into the camp of Bnai Yisrael. They assigned her the role of seductress and harlot. This is remarkable! Kazbi was the daughter of Tzur. Tzur was one of the kings of Midyan. The people of Midyan were willing to defile a princess in order to destroy Bnai Yisrael. This is indicative of extreme, self-destructive hatred.[16] Bnai Yisrael must protect itself from this desperate enemy.

Rabbaynu Avraham ibn Ezra offers a different explanation of the passage. He explains that the *pasuk* is providing an enumeration of reasons for the war Bnai Yisrael is to wage. The first reason is that Bnai Yisrael must respond to the actions already taken by Midyan. Midyan plotted against Bnai Yisrael. Midyan attempted to corrupt Bnai Yisrael. Second, Bnai Yisrael should be mindful of the future. Pinchas had killed Kazbi, the daughter of Tzur. Tzur was a king. His daughter was a princess. Surely, the people of Midyan would wish to avenge the death of their princess! In short, Midyan had attempted to destroy Bnai Yisrael without provocation. Now, Midyan had an additional motivation – the death of their princess.[17] Bnai Yisrael must protect themselves from Midyan. They must strike their enemy before Midyan can again plot against them.

And Hashem spoke unto Moshe and unto Elazar the son of Aharon the priest, saying: Take the sum of all the congregation of the children of Israel, from twenty years old and upward, by their fathers' houses, all that are able to go forth to war in Israel. (BeMidbar 26:1-2)

Loved to Death

1. Sefer BeMidbar is the Book of Censuses

Sefer BeMidbar is also referred to as Chumash HaPikudim – the Book of Censuses. Sefer BeMidbar opens with a census of Bnai Yisrael taken during the second year of their sojourn in the wilderness. That census was taken with the expectation that the nation would proceed to and soon take possession of the Land of Israel. This aspiration was not achieved. The generation that left Egypt, because of its failings, forfeited the opportunity to take possession of the Land of Israel. Instead, the children of that condemned generation were led into the land.

---

[16] Rabbaynu Shlomo ben Yitzchak (Rashi), *Commentary on Sefer BeMidbar* 25:18.

[17] Rabbaynu Avraham ibn Ezra, *Commentary on Sefer BeMidbar* 25:18.

The second census in Sefer BeMidbar is described in Parshat Pinchas. This census took place after the generation of the wilderness had perished. This census was taken of their children and their descendents who had been born during the intervening 38 years.

And the sons of Yehudah after their families were: of Sheylah, the family of the Shelanites; of Peretz, the family of the Perezites; of Zerach, the family of the Zerahites. And the sons of Peretz were: of Chetzron, the family of the Chezronites; of Chamul, the family of the Chamulites. These are the families of Yehudah according to those that were numbered of them, seventy-six thousand and five hundred. (BeMidbar 26:20-22)

2. A significant difference between the two censuses

In many ways, these two censuses are similar. However, in one significant respect they are very different from one another. The first census tallied the members of each tribe. The census identified the population of Shevet Reuven, Shevet Shimon, and each of the other tribes. The census described in Parshat Pinchas is more detailed. Like the first census, it provides a population total for each tribe but it also lists the various families within each *shevet*. For example, it reveals that Shevet Reuven consists of 43,730 members. These members are divided among four families – Chanoch, Phalu, Chetzron, and Karmi. A fixed pattern is followed in the Torah's report on the population of each tribe. The tribe is identified; its families are enumerated, and the total population of the tribe is reported.

How did these families form? In general, the families are the descendants of the sons of the *shevet's* patriarch. Returning to the example of Shevet Reuven, the families are identified as Chanoch, Phalu, Chetzron, and Karmi. Each of these is named for a son of Reuven – the *shevet's* patriarch. In other words, the descendants of each son of Reuven formed a family within the *shevet*.

However, there are a number of exceptions to this principle. Sometimes, families are formed from the descendants of a grandson of the *shevet's* patriarch. For example, Shevet Yehudah is composed of five families. Three of the families are named for the sons of Yehudah – Sheylah, Peretz, and Zerach. Two are named for grandsons – children of Peretz. Presumably, these two families which are named for grandsons are composed of the grandson's descendants. The other descendents of Peretz are members of the family bearing his name. The Sheylah and Zerech families are composed of their respective descendants. Why are families generally composed of the descendants of a son of the *shevet's* patriarch but sometimes from the descendants of a grandson?

The sons of Binyamin after their families: of Bela, the family of the Belaites; of Ashbel, the family of the Ashbelites; of Achiram, the family of the Ahiramites, of Shefufam, the family of the Shufamites; of Chufam, the family of the Chufamites. And the sons of Bela were Ard and Na'aman; of Ard, the family of the Ardites; of Na'aman, the family of the Na'amites. These are the sons of Binyamin after their families; and they that were numbered of them were forty and five thousand and six hundred. (BeMidbar 26:38-41)

3. The midrash's understanding of the unique status of Yaakov's company

This is a complex issue. It will become evident in the course of this discussion that possibly more than one factor determine the formation of families within each *shevet*. However, let us focus on one aspect that is discussed by the commentators. The midrash explains that the two sons of Peretz – Chetzron and Chamul were among the seventy individuals who accompanied Yaakov when he descended from the Land of Cana'an to Egypt. The midrash explains that every grandson of Yaakov among the seventy exiles who entered Egypt had the opportunity to create his own family within his father's *shevet*. However, this opportunity was not limited to them. The opportunity extended to all those who were among this group of seventy. Even great-grandchildren of Yaakov who were among this group had the opportunity – depending upon the number of their descendants – to form a family within the *shevet*. Therefore, the descendants of the sons of Yehudah – Sheylah, Peretz, and Zerach – formed families. Two of Peretz's sons were also among the seventy initial exiles who came to Egypt. The descendants of these sons – Chetzron and Chamul also were numerous and they formed their own families.[18]

This insight offered by the midrash does not seem to explain the families enumerated within Shevet Binyamin. Binyamin descended to Egypt with ten sons. The descendants of five of these sons formed families. One of these sons was Bela. The descendants of Bela's sons – Ard and Na'aman also formed families. However, these sons of Binyamin were not among the seventy individuals who were the initial descendants to Egypt! According to the principle developed by the midrash, their descendants should not have formed independent families within the *shevet*.

And the sons of Binyamin: Bela, and Becher, and Ashbel, Gera, and Na'aman, Echi, and Rosh, Muppim, and Chuppim, and Ard. (Beresheit 46:21)

4. Two sets of Ard and Na'aman

Nachmanides offers a number of responses to this problem. The solution that is perhaps the simplest is based upon an apparent contradiction between this census and the listing of the seventy individuals who accompanied Yaakov into Egypt. In that listing in Sefer Bereseit, Ard and Na'aman are identified as sons of Binyamin and not as his grandsons through Bela.[19] In other words, in our *parasha*, Ard and Na'aman are identified as sons of Bela and grandchildren of Binyamin. In Sefer Bereseheit, they are listed among the sons of Binyamin.

Nachmanides explains that these two accounts do not contradict one another. Binyamin had ten sons. These included Ard and Na'aman. Ard and Na'aman died without children. Bela – who was the oldest of Binyamin's sons did not want his brothers to be forgotten by Bnai Yisrael. He wished to preserve their memory. He accomplished this by naming two of his own sons after his departed brothers. Ard and Na'aman – the sons of Bela – were named after Bela's brothers who bore those names.

Bela acted properly in preserving his brothers' memories through his own sons. These sons succeeded in not only preserving the memory of Bela's brothers but they also were provided the opportunity to form families within the *shevet* that would be regarded as the families of these departed sons of Binyamin. In other words, these departed sons continued to be identified as progenators of Bnai Yisrael through the families that bore their names.[20]

Rashi partially agrees with Nachmanides. He agrees that there were two sets of sons who shared the names Ard and Na'aman. One set was children of Binyamin. Also, Bela had two sons

---

[18] Midrash Agadah, quoted by Rav Menachem Mendel Kasher, *Torah Shelymah on BeMidbar* 26:29.

[19] Sefer Bereseit 46:21.

[20] Rabbaynu Moshe ben Nachman (Ramban), *Commentary on Sefer BeMidbar* 26:13.

whose names were Ard and Na'aman. However, he does not accept Nachmanides' suggestion that the latter Ard and Na'aman assumed the role of their departed uncles and therefore their descendants were permitted to form families within the *shevet*. Rashi argues that these two sons of Bela represent a unique phenomenon that required special treatment in regard to forming families. All of those who descended with Yaakov were able to form families. All those who were "children of Egypt" were not founders of families. Ard and Na'aman did not fit cleanly into either of these categories. They were born in exile. However, they were conceived in the Land of Cana'an. Therefore, they were not counted among those who accompanied Yaakov in his descent into exile. However, because they were conceived in the Land of Cana'an their descendants were permitted to form families within Shevet Binyamin.[21]

The sons of Rachel, Yaakov's wife: Yosef and Binyamin. And unto Yosef in the Land of Egypt were born Menashe and Efraim, whom Asenat the daughter of Poti-phera priest of On bore unto him. (Beresheit 46:19-20)

5. Shevet Efraim and Shevet Menashe and their families

Nachmaindes offers an alternative and final explanation for the Torah's treatment of Ard and Na'aman. He begins by referring us to another strange aspect of the census in our *parasha*. Yosef's sons Efraim and Menashe were each the progenitors of their own *shevet*. Their *shevatim* were also composed of family units. However, in their instances these families were composed of the descendants of individuals born in Egypt. In other words, the midrash's principle cannot be applied to the tribes of Efraim and Menashe. Ephraim and Menashe were themselves born to Yosef in Egypt. Their sons and even some of their grandchildren became the progenitors of the families that make up their respective tribes. Nachmanides argues that according to the midrash, Efraim and Menashe should be unique tribes. Because their children were not among the seventy individuals who accompanied Yaakov into exile, these tribes should not have component families.

Nachmanides concludes that the examples of Efraim and Menashe demonstrate that the principle outlined in the midrash is not intended as an absolute rule. Those who accompanied Yaakov had the opportunity to form families. Those who did not accompany Yaakov, in general, were not afforded this opportunity. However, obviously there were exceptions. There were cases in which those who were not among Yaakov's company of seventy were afforded the opportunity to form families.[22] What was the basis for granting these exceptions?

6. The message of the midrash

Before we consider Nachmanides' response, let us return once more to the midrash. Nachmanides in his earlier answer, and Rashi in his treatment of these issues, regard the midrash's principle as absolute. Only those who accompanied Yaakov were the founders of families. According to Rashi, Ard and Na'aman represent a special case. They were conceived in the Land of Cana'an so their descendants formed families within Shevet Binyamin.

Let us consider this issue more carefully. What is the reason for this special status assigned to those who accompanied Yaakov into Egypt? Furthermore, why was this status

---

[21] Rabbaynu Shlomo ben Yitzchak (Rashi), *Commentary on Sefer BeMidbar* 26:24.
[22] Rabbaynu Moshe ben Nachman (Ramban), *Commentary on Sefer BeMidbar* 26:13.

extended to Ard and Na'aman? They were conceived in the Land of Cana'an but they were not actually among the seventy individuals who composed Yaakov's company.

It seems that the special status assigned to those individuals who accompanied Yaakov was intended to communicate a message. This message was that the nation that would develop in Egypt was a nation in exile. Each family that developed in Egypt was composed of the descendants of an individual who left the Land of Cana'an. Even Ard and Na'aman acquired their special status as progenitors of families because of their association with the Land of Cana'an. They were conceived there and not in Egypt. The fact that only those who were born in the Land of Cana'an, or conceived there, could be the patriarchs of families, constantly reinforced the message that the Land of Israel was the home of the people and in Egypt they were exiles.

Of course, according to this interpretation, Shevet Efraim and Shevet Menashe are exceptions. Their members could not identify with a progenitor of their tribe who was from the Land of Cana'an. Even Efraim and Menashe were born in Egypt. The message of connectedness to the Land of Israel could not be communicated through identification with the progenitors of these two tribes.

The underlying concept that emerges from this strict interpretation of the midrash is that the identities of the families was designed to communicate a message. According to the strict interpretation of the midrash's principle, this message was that they were exilees and the Land of Cana'an was their only true home. According to Nachmanides, the identities communicate an additional message.

7. Challenges of exile

He explains that even some of those who were born in Egypt were afforded the opportunity to form their own families. Who were these individuals provided with this opportunity? He explains that these must have been very special individuals whose memory was to be preserved through the association of their name with their family of descendants. He explains that these were individuals who were role models for the people. Role models were very important in the Land of Egypt. Life in Egypt presented a serious challenge to the continuity of the nation.

Why did the experience in Egypt present such a severe threat to the Jewish people? When Yaakov and his family came to Egypt they were welcomed and invited into their host community. Egyptian society accepted the descendants of Yaakov into its midst. However, the values and religious outlook of Egyptian society were antagonistic to the ideas developed by the patriarchs and taught to their children. How would the nation resist assimilation into the host culture that eagerly welcomed it? Role models would be needed. The creation of families from the descendants of the most outstanding role models preserved the memory of these special individuals and, more importantly, communicated the lesson of resistance against assimilation into the Egyptian culture.[23]

8. The plight of the American Jewish community

Both of these interpretations are valid and both are relevant to us. We are blessed to live in a society that provides us with equal rights and access to all of its privileges. However, the

---

[23] Rabbaynu Moshe ben Nachman (Ramban), *Commentary on Sefer BeMidbar* 26:13.

culture in which we live is hostile to religious values and specifically antagonistic toward Judaism. How do we prevent our children from assimilating into this welcoming society and abandoning meaningful Jewish life? The discussion above suggests that we need to focus on two strategies.

We must remember that we are exilees. This means that when we educate our young people about Israel and we encourage them to support Israel we must carefully explain our objective. Israel is not important because of its immense Jewish community. Its importance is not that it is the refuge for every Jew in need. It is important because it is our home. We live in a country that has been and continues to be a remarkable host for our people. But this is not home. Israel is home.

Second, we must provide our sons and daughters with role models. This is difficult to accomplish in a culture that is dominated by skepticism and cynicism. Our perspective is particularly jaundiced in regard to religious leaders and figures. Maybe this is because too many have disappointed us. Maybe, this is because we tend to more easily notice the faults of others than their positive attributes. But we must provide inspirational examples of individuals who embrace their role as citizens of our host community but remain completely committed to their Jewish lives.

"And the sons of Eliav were Datan and Aviram. These are the same Datan and Aviram that were leaders of the congregation and that strove with Moshe and Aharon among the congregation of Korach, in their strife against Hashem." (BeMidbar 26:9)

In our *parasha*, Hashem directs Moshe and Elazar to take a census of the nation. The Torah recounts the details of this census. In discussing the Shevet of Reuven, the Torah tells us that Phalu the son of Reuven had one son – Eliav. Eliav, in turn had three sons –Nemuel, Datan and Aviram. The Torah then tells us the Datan and Aviram were involved in Korach's conflict with Moshe and Aharon. They were punished for this rebellion. The earth opened and swallowed Datan, Aviram and Korach. The Torah then adds that Korach's children were not killed in this punishment.

It is interesting that the Torah seems to assign a prominent leadership role to Datan and Aviram in this rebellion. This does not seem to accord with Rashi's opinion. Rashi implies that Korach was the true leader of the rebellion and he influenced Datan and Aviram to join his insurgency.[24] Rashi's contention is supported by the opening of Parshat Korach that describes Korach as the ringleader of the rebellion.

However, Gershonides rejects Rashi's position based upon the passages in our *parasha* that seem to attribute the leadership role in the rebellion to Datan and Aviram. Gershonides points to another element of our *parasha*'s account of the rebellion that seems to support his position.

A brief introduction is needed in order to understand Gershonides' position. As we have noted, the account in our *parasha* ends by telling us that Korach was killed by Hashem for his actions but his children were spared. The earth opened and swallowed Korach. It is likely that Korach and his children were situated in proximity of each other. But nonetheless, the children

---

[24] Rashi Sefer BeMidbar 16:1

were not swallowed. Rashi is bothered by a problem. The Torah tells us that the children to Korach were spared. This implies that we would presume that they died like their father. The Torah is compelled to correct us and reveal that our presumption is wrong. Korach was killed but his children were spared. Why would we presume that Korach's children should have been punished?

Rashi explains that Korach's children were deeply involved in the rebellion. Korach's children were among the first to join him. In the formative stage of the rebellion, they offered their father support and advice. However, they subsequently recognized the impact of their actions and reconsidered. They repented their mistake and were spared from death.[25] According to Rashi, the apparent intention of the passage is that although they too had been deeply involved in the rebellion, Korach's children were saved by their repentance. In other words, the *pasuk* intends to demonstrate the efficacy of *teshuva* – repentance.

Gershonides points out that Rashi does offer an explanation for the Torah's statement that the children of Korach did not die. But there is another problem that Rashi's interpretation does not address. This section of the *parasha* is describing the census taken by Moshe and Elazar. Specifically, it is providing details regarding the population of Shevet Reuven. Korach was a *Leyve*. We can understand that he is mentioned as an associate of Datan and Aviram. The Torah is explaining why Datan and Aviram died and tells us that they were involved in the rebellion of Korach. But this is an odd juncture to mention that the sons of Korach were spared. Why mention this point in the midst of an account of the census of Shevet Reuven?

Based on this consideration, Gershonides suggests that the simple message of the passages suggests an alternative to Rashi's interpretation. Gershonides begins by emphasizing that these passages are an account of the fate of Datan, Aviram, and their children. Korach is only mentioned in passing to explain the reason for the death of Datan, Aviram, and their children. The Torah tells us that the children of Korach did not die. The apparent purpose of this comment – given the context – is to establish a contrast. Datan and Aviram's role in the rebellion was so substantial that their punishment extended to their children. Not only were Datan and Aviram punished, their children were also killed. In contrast, Korach's role was apparently less significant. So, although Korach was killed, his children were spared. This interpretation supports Gershonides' contention that Datan and Aviram were the instigators of the rebellion. Korach played a lesser, supporting role.[26]

Before proceeding, let us summarize the positions of Rashi and Gershonides. Rashi maintains that Korach was the initial instigator and leader of the rebellion. His children were among his initial followers and advisors. However, they repented and were spared death. Gershonides argues that Datan and Aviram were the initial instigators. Korach was a supporter of their rebellion. As a result of their role in the rebellion, Datan and Aviram were punished with death and this punishment extended to their children. Korach played a lesser role. Therefore, although he was killed, his children were spared.

Of course, there is one obvious problem with Gershonides' position. The Torah in Parshat Korach describes the rebellion in detail. There, the Torah mentions Korach before

---

[25] Rashi Sefer BeMidbar 26:11
[26] Gershonides, Sefer BeMidbar, p 143.

mentioning Datan and Aviram.[27] The obvious implication is that Korach was the leader and Datan and Aviram were junior partners.

Gershonides does not ignore this problem. He explains that Korach is given prominence in this initial account because of his greater stature – he was a more important person.[28]

This is a difficult statement to understand. Why does Korach's greater stature dictate that he should be given prominence in the initial account? It seems that Gershonides maintains that although Datan and Aviram were the initial instigators, the rebellion would not have gained its tremendous momentum and popular support without the involvement of a leader of stature. Korach's participation lent credibility to the rebellion. As a result of his public support and leadership, the rebellion took hold among the people.

We can now understand the contrast between the two accounts of the rebellion. In the initial account – in Parshat Korach, the Torah's objective is to recount the incident of the rebellion and its impact on Bnai Yisrael. From the perspective of this impact, it is irrelevant who the initial instigator was. Korach's involvement in a leadership role was the crucial factor in converting a personal grievance into a popular cause. Therefore, in discussing the rebellion from the perspective of the impact on Bnai Yisrael, Korach is given prominence.

In contrast, the objective of the Torah in our *parasha* is not to recount the rebellion and its impact on the nation. Here, the intention is to explain the fate of Datan and Aviram. The Torah is telling us why they and their children died. In this context, it is important for the Torah to note that Datan and Aviram were the instigators. It is this role that explains their deaths and the deaths of their children.

Let us contrast the position of Rashi with that of Gershonides. According to Rashi, there is little distinction between leader and follower. Datan and Aviram were killed with their children. Korach and his children were also destined to die. However, Korach's children were spared because they repented. Gershonides disagrees. He argues that the responsibility of the instigator is greater than that of the follower – even a prominent, key follower. Therefore, Datan and Aviram's children were killed but Korach's were spared.

Perhaps, it is possible to extend our understanding of this debate between Gershonides and Rashi one step further. Gershonides argues that Datan and Aviram were the instigators. Korach – because of a flaw in his personality – was drawn into their insurgency. He would not have initiated this rebellion. But once underway, he became involved and assumed a leadership role. It seems that Gershonides maintains that the subsequent punishment corresponded with the internal wickedness of the parties involved. Datan and Aviram were self-motivated in their involvement. They were more corrupt than Korach. Korach was drawn into an insurgency he would not have initiated. His wickedness was less than that of Datan and Aviram. As a result his punishment – although severe – was less that that of Datan and Aviram.

Rashi maintains that the punishment does not correspond to the internal wickedness of the parties. He maintains that Korach was the leader and Datan and Aviram were his followers. Nonetheless, they all deserved the same fate. Korach's children were only spared because of their repentance. It seems that according to Rashi, there is little or no distinction between leader

---

[27] Sefer BeMidbar 16:1.
[28] Gershonides Sefer BeMidbar p 143.

205

and follower. The punishment corresponds with the outcome. All three of these individuals openly confronted and challenged Moshe's authority. Regardless of their roles as leader and followers, they all engaged in identical behavior towards Moshe. This behavior dictated the punishment. All were condemned to a death that included not only themselves but also their children.

Pinchas, the son of Elazar, the son of Aharon, the kohen, turned-back my anger from the Children of Israel with his zealotry on My behalf among them and I did not completely destroy the Children of Israel in My zealotry. (BeMidbar 26:11)

Clarifying Values

1. The daughters of Moav

Parshat Pinchas continues and completes the narrative that began in Parshat Balak. Bnai Yisrael was camped at Shittim. The nation of Moav sent young women into the camp of Bnai Yisrael. The mission of these young women was to seduce the men of Bnai Yisrael. Once they succeeded in their seduction, they were to induce their paramours to engage in idol worship. The strategy was successful. The men were seduced and then, persuaded to engage in idolatry.

Hashem responded by bringing a plague upon the people. He also directed Moshe to assemble the courts and act against the violators. Moshe was engaged in convening the courts when Zimri – a leader of the tribe of Shimon – presented himself with Kazbi – a princess of Midyan – and publicly demonstrated his intention to liaison with her.

Pinchas, the son of Elazar the kohen and the grandson of Aharon, stepped forward and executed Zimri and Kazbi while they were intimately engaged.

Parshat Pinchas continues the narrative. Pinchas is rewarded. Hashem grants him the status of kohen.[29] Hashem also bestows upon him His covenant of peace.

Hashem then commands Moshe to wage war against Midyan. Midyan helped Moav develop their strategy and supported it by sending one of their princesses – Kazbi – to participate in the seduction.[30]

And you will take their daughters for your sons. Their daughters will stray after their gods and lead astray your sons after their gods. (Shemot 34:16)

2. The path to idolatry

What caused the men of Bnai Yisrael to succumb to this ploy? Rav Ovadia Sforno addresses this issue. He explains that the Torah prohibits such liaisons. One would expect that

---

[29] Rashi (26:13) explains that before this incident Pinchas was not a kohen. The status of kohen was previously bestowed upon Aharon and his children. Their subsequent descendants would inherit the status. However, only children born after the appointment of the kohanim would inherit their parents' status. The status did not extend and could not be inherited by children of Aharon's sons who were alive at the time of the appointment. Pinchas was born before the status was granted to Aharon and his sons. Therefore, before receiving the reward for his zealotry, he was not a kohen.

[30] Rabbaynu Moshe ben Nachman (Ramban), Commentary on Sefer BeMidbar 25:18.

this prohibition should have protected the men from responding to the wiles of these seductresses. However, in the above passage, the Torah explains the prohibition. It reveals that these liaisons are prohibited because of their potential to encourage idolatry. The men concluded from the Torah's treatment of the prohibition, that these liaisons are not inherently inappropriate. Their prohibition is intended solely to discourage idolatry. These men were sure of themselves and confident that regardless of the intensity of their relationships with these women, they could never be induced to engage in idolatry. Their confidence was misplaced. They were persuaded to participate in some form of idolatry.[31]

3. Assessing oneself

Why were these men incorrect in their calculations? How did they so seriously misjudge themselves? Rav Yisrael Chait explained this phenomenon. When a person makes an initial assessment of how one will act in an anticipated situation, one considers one's character and values at present – at the time of the decision. The men of Bnai Yisrael evaluated the likelihood that they would engage in idolatry before liaising with their paramours. They knew themselves and the strength of their commitment to the Torah and concluded that they would not involve themselves in any form of idol worship.

There is no reason to doubt the accuracy of their assessment. At the time they made their decision, they were firmly and sincerely committed to the Torah. Based on their self-analyses, they decided to proceed with their liaisons.

Their error was that they did not understand that their decision would be transformative. Once they entered into more intense relationships with their paramours, they were not able to dismiss their suggestions, pleadings, or intimations that they participate in their ceremonies. In other words, the person who made the initial decision to enter into the relationship was transformed. It was the emergent personality that had to resist his partner's overtures concerning idolatry.[32]

4. "Off the derech"

Recently, I was asked to comment on the state of Modern Orthodox youth and the frequency of our yeshiva-educated youth abandoning observance. Do I have any suggestions for how this problem might be addressed?

Before responding, three premises must be put forth.

- My perception – shared by many others – is that we are losing too many of our children. They are abandoning observance, going "off the derech". However, I am not familiar with the actual statistics. A statistical analysis of the phenomenon and more specifically of trends will help develop a more thorough analysis and response.

- Any solution that is proposed to a problem is implemented in a dynamic and complex environment. Even if the solution is successful in addressing the issue it targets, it may have other unanticipated, and unwelcome consequences. Therefore, it is not wise to prescribe fixed solutions. Any proposed solution must be implemented cautiously, monitored, and revised or discarded based upon observed outcomes.[33]

---

[31] Rabbaynu Ovadia Sforno, Commentary on Sefer Devarim 4:2-3.
[32] Rav Yisrael Chait, my notes.

207

- Finally, the development of a solution begins with an analysis of the problem and its causes. If we wish to respond to our children's abandonment of observance, we must understand the causes.

5. Crisis of faith

Two challenges confront our young people when they move on to college and into their careers. First, they move from an environment that encourages observance into one that is hostile toward it. This is true of virtually every secular university. The richness of Jewish life on the campus is not, in itself, a solution to this issue. The overwhelming message of the university campus is negative toward religion. The existence of an island oasis of Jewish life does not counter this powerful influence. Our yeshiva and day-school graduates are not prepared to respond to the questions that will arise. They begin to question. They do not have adequate answers. They enter into a crisis of faith. A year or two in yeshiva or seminary in Israel will not much alter their vulnerability.

Part of any solution must be focused upon the education we provide to our children. It is inadequate for preparing them for the challenges that they will encounter when they leave their day-school or yeshiva for college and enter their careers. Improvements to their education that we should consider require a separate discussion. However, these adjustments will not assure their continued commitment to the Torah. This is because a second challenge confronts our young people.

6. Crisis of identity

Our children are exposed to a culture whose values are antithetical to Torah observance. Contemporary culture has moved away from traditional religious values. The pursuit of pleasure and career advancement are the most evident and emphasized values. These are intensely seductive. Enormous commitment to observance is necessary to resist them. Most of our young people are not prepared to confront this challenge. They become confused, unsure of their values and their very identity.

7. Questions that are excuses

The impact of this second challenge should not be underestimated. We should not be misled by explanations proffered by our children for their abandonment of observance. Very often, they will cite a crisis of faith, issues with the Torah's theology, or even doubt in the existence of Hashem as their reasons for abandoning observance. In some cases, this is an accurate assessment. However, how many of these young people sought answers to their questions, turned to Torah scholars, and intensely studied these issues? Too few. In many cases, the actual motivation behind forsaking observance is the allure of a self-indulgent lifestyle. The questions are an excuse, not the reason, for abandoning observance.[34]

---

[33] An example will help illustrate this consideration. Modern Orthodoxy's embrace of university education was based upon the premise that we must integrate our commitment to Torah with our participation in the contemporary economy and society. University education provided the opportunity to fully achieve this integration. However, as we will discuss, today's university environment presents enormous challenges for our children. These challenges are an unforeseen outcome of the decision to embrace university education.

[34] This phenomenon is illustrated by an interesting story. A student of the Volozhin Yeshiva

Questions can serve two very different functions. They can be the catalyst for a crisis of faith and if unanswered lead to forsaking observance. Questions can also be a response to a crisis of identity. They provide a rationalization for rejecting Torah.

8. The lesson of the incident of Shittim

We must improve the education we provide to our children. We must also acknowledge that we often facilitate our children's crises. How are we doing this? Let's consider one example.

We tell our children that we care about their observance. We send them to day-school and yeshiva. Then we encourage them to strive to get into the finest universities. We are confident that they have the strength to resist the influences of the environment. We know our children and we have given them a strong foundation in Torah learning and observance. We believe that they are intensely committed. Often, we are correct! Our children return from a year or two in yeshiva or seminary unequivocally committed to observance. But that student is also the contemporary expression of the men who succumbed to the daughters of Moav at Shittim! The campus environment is transformative. The student who returns from a year or two of Torah study is not the same person after a year on the campus. In my experience, virtually every one of our children graduates from university somewhat less committed than when entering and too many have completely abandoned Torah. We are sending our children into a hostile environment without a realistic and tested strategy for protecting them from its influences.[35] This suggests that we are either naïve or ambivalent in our values. We must clarify our priorities and live by them.

---

abandoned the Torah. He devoted himself to the study of philosophy and joined the Haskala movement. The student had occasion to visit his former yeshiva. There, he met with Rav Chaim Soloveitchik Zt"l who was serving as Rosh HaYeshiva.

Rav Chaim asked the young man to share his reasons for abandoning the life of Torah and pursuing other endeavors. The young man was shocked by Rav Chaim's confrontational tone. After recovering, he explained that he was troubled by various doubts and questions regarding the Torah. He could not find answers to his questions. So, he abandoned the Torah.

Rav Chaim told the young man that he was willing to answer every one of his questions. However, the young man must first agree to answer a single question. Rav Chaim asked, "When did these various questions occur to you? Was it before you experienced the taste of sin of afterward?"

The young man was embarrassed. He responded that only after committing a serious sin had he begun to be bothered by questions.

Rav Chaim responded, "If that is the case, these are not questions. Rather, they are answers you use to excuse your evil actions."

Rav Chaim continued, "I am sure that if you merit to achieve old age, your desires and yetzer harah will diminish. Then you will realize that you do not have any questions. So, why not repent now?" (Rav Y. Hershkowitz, Torat Chaim, p 64)

[35] On occasion, I discussed this issue with individual students. I asked them to make a bargain with themselves. "Pick an aspect of observance that you regard as absolute and which you will not compromise. I don't care what you pick. Let it be the observance of Shabbat, Kashrut, anything. You decide. Promise yourself that if you find yourself at the verge of violating that observance, you will seriously reconsider your decision to attend the university you have selected." Inevitably, this bargain made sense to the student and he or she agreed. But only in a single instance did a student report back to me that he kept the bargain. The reason many

9. Exposure to the outside

This is an element of a much more encompassing dynamic. The Modern Orthodox world has broken down virtually all barriers between ourselves, our children and contemporary culture. We inundate our homes with contemporary culture and its values. Television, music, and the internet communicate a pervasive message. The message is indulgent, pleasure-seeking, and seductive. Our children are constantly exposed to all these. Can we expect that our children will not be influenced and that their values will not be impacted? But we are reluctant to battle our children over access to media. We are even more threatened by the realization that we – the parents – must model for our children our expectations and restore some of the barriers between ourselves and contemporary culture.

Some elements within the Orthodox community have foresworn the internet. Most Modern Orthodox families regard these people as extremists – our version of fundamentalists. However, we need to acknowledge that they are responding to a real problem. Extreme solutions tend to be unrealistic or counter-productive. However, rejecting an extreme solution does not make the problem disappear. If the extreme solution is unacceptable, then an alternative is required.

In conclusion, the challenges confronting our children reflect our confusion. We must improve the Torah education we provide to our children. However, we must also clarify our priorities. We must translate our commitment to observance into an effective strategy to protect our children from the environmental influences that will inevitably challenge and likely compromise their commitment to Torah.

"These are the children of Efraim according to their census – 32,500. These are the children of Yosef according to their families." (BeMidbar 26:37)

Moshe and Elazar conduct a census of Bnai Yisrael. This census is performed in preparation of dividing the land among the *Shevatim* – the tribes – and their individual members. The Torah provides a detailed report of the census. Some of the results deserve attention.

In order to appreciate one of these results, a brief introduction is necessary. Before his death Yaakov blessed Yosef. He told Yosef that his two sons – Efraim and Menashe – would be as Reuven and Shimon. This blessing has many implications. One of these implications is that the population of the *shevatim* of Efraim and Menashe would equal or exceed that of Reuven and Shimon.

This is the second census recorded in Sefer BeMidbar. The sefer begins with a census. This first census was conducted at the beginning of Bnai Yisrael's sojourn in the wilderness. At the time of the first census in Sefer BeMidbar, this blessing had not yet been fulfilled.

---

students were unable to keep their bargain is because of the "Shittim dynamic." The person who made the bargain was transformed. The new emergent personality did not feel bound to a bargain made by a former self.

Shevet	Population		Shevet	Population
Reuven	46,500		Efraim	40,500
Shimon	59,300		Menashe	32,200
Total	**105,800**		**Total**	**72,700**

Table 1

Table 1 compares the total population of Reuven and Shimon to that of Efraim and Menashe. These population statistics are from the first census in Sefer BeMidbar. As this table reveals, the population of the *shevatim* of Reuven and Shimon was substantially greater than that of Efraim and Menashe.

Let us now consider the population statistics for these *shevatim* reported in our *parasha*. These statistics are shown in Table 2.

Shevet	Population		Shevet	Population
Reuven	43,700		Efraim	32,500
Shimon	22,200		Menashe	52,700
Total	**65,900**		**Total**	**85,200**
Percentage change	**-38%**		**Percentage change**	**17%**

Table 2

Table 2 reveals that at the time of the census in our *parasha*, Yaakov's promise was fulfilled. The combined population of Efraim and Menashe exceeded that of Reuven and Menashe.

This table reveals another important statistic. In the period between the first and second census, the *shevatim* of Efraim and Menashe experienced remarkable population growth. During this period the overall population of the nation was virtually unchanged. These two *shevatim* grew at by 17%. This indicates that the population growth of these two *shevatim* exceeded the natural rate. In other words, the Almighty exercised His providence to assure the fulfillment of Yaakov's promise.[36]

Command Bnai Yisrael and speak to them concerning my sacrifice, my bread, a fire offering of appeasing fragrance. They should take care to offer it to me at its appointed time. (BeMidbar 28:2)

This pasuk introduces the discussion of the Tamid offering. The term Tamid means constant. This name refers to the regularity of the sacrifice. It was offered daily, in the morning, and afternoon. The pasuk refers to the Tamid as Hashem's bread. This might seem strange. No bread was included in these offerings. Rav Yosef Bechor Shur explains the meaning of this term. Bread is regarded, by the Torah, as the most basic food. For this reason, the Torah requires that we say Birkat HaMazon – grace – after eating bread. Furthermore, the eating of bread is considered a meal and not a snack. There are other laws that also reflect the special distinction

---

[36] Rabbaynu Levi ben Gershon (Ralbag / Gershonides), *Commentary on Sefer BeMidbar*, (Mosad HaRav Kook, 1998), pp. 143-144.

given to bread, in the Torah. The Tamid was the most basic sacrifice. All other sacrifices were offered between the morning and afternoon Tamid sacrifice. The special sacrifices offered on Shabbat and holidays are refereed to as Musaf – additional – sacrifices. This is because they are additions to the basic Tamid offering. The Tamid was, therefore the most fundamental of all sacrifices. For this reason, it is referred to as Hashem's bread.

And Hashem spoke unto Moshe, saying: Command Bnai Yisrael, and say unto them, "My food which is presented unto Me for offerings made by fire, of a sweet savour unto Me, shall you observe to offer unto Me in its due season." And you should say unto them, "This is the offering made by fire which you shall bring unto Hashem: male lambs of the first year without blemish, two each day, for a continual Olah offering." (Bemidbar 28:1-3)

The Musaf of Rosh Chodesh

1. The relationship between the Tamid and Musaf

The final section of Parshat Pinchas discusses the Musaf sacrifices offered on Shabbat and festivals. The Musaf offerings are additional sacrifices offered on these occasions. However, the section begins with the above passages. These passages do not discuss the Musaf offerings. Instead, they describe the Tamid – the daily offerings. As the passages explain, each day two male lambs are to be offered. One is offered in the morning and the second is offered in the afternoon. Both are Olah sacrifices which are completely consumed on the altar. Later passages add that each of the Olah sacrifices is to be accompanied by a Minchah – a meal offering – and a wine libation.

Why does this section which essentially outlines the Musaf offerings for Shabbat and festivals, begin with a description of the daily Tamid offerings? As explained above the Musaf offerings are the additional sacrifices that are offered on Shabbat and festivals. In order for them to have this status as additional offerings, they must supplement the Tamid. In other words, the very concept of a Musaf offering is predicated upon the existence of the Tamid. The Musaf can only be explained in conjunction with the Tamid that it supplements. Therefore, it is quite fitting that the section of the Torah that describes the Musaf offerings should be introduced with a discussion of the Tomid. This idea explains an interesting quirk in the Torah's description of the Musaf offerings.

This is the Olah offering of every Sabbat, besides the continual Olah offering, and its drink-offering. (BeMidbar 28:10)

2. The Torah's recurring reference to the Tamid in its description of the Musaf offerings

The above passage completes the Torah's description of the Shabbat Musaf offering. The passage specifies that the Musaf offering that the previous passages have described is offered in addition to the Tamid – the continual Olah offering. It is notable that this statement is repeated throughout the section. The Musaf for each festival is described and then the Torah adds that the Musaf is offered in addition to the Tamid. This seems to be unnecessary. The Tamid is the daily offering. Of course, it is offered on Shabbat and festivals. Its very name – Tamid – communicates this idea. Tamid means constant. Why does the Torah specify that each set of Musaf offerings is in addition to the day's Tamid?

As explained above, the Musaf is fundamentally a supplement to the Tamid. It only exists in the context of the Tamid. Therefore, each time the Torah commands the offering of the Musaf it must specify that it is offered as a supplement to the Tamid. Without this element's inclusion in the command, the identity of the offering as the Musaf offering would be lost.

And on your new months you shall present an Olah offering unto Hashem: two young bullocks, and one ram, seven male lambs of the first year without blemish. (BeMidbar 28:11)

3. The Rosh Chodesh Musaf offering

One of the occasions on which a Musaf offering is required is the advent of the new month – Rosh Chodesh. The above passages explain that on Rosh Chodesh two bullocks, one ram and seven male lambs are offered. The Torah adds that these are accompanied by the relevant meal offerings and libations. In addition, a sin-offering is offered. In short, ten Olah sacrifices are offered with their accompanying meal offerings and libations and a single sin offering.

It is interesting that the components of the Rosh Chodesh Musaf offering are identical to the components of the Musaf offerings of Pesach and Shavuot. This suggests that Rosh Chodesh – in some sense – has the same degree of significance as these festivals. This seems odd. These festivals recall events fundamental to the creation of Bnai Yisrael. Also, they are thanksgiving celebrations that accompany key moments of the harvest process. Pesach corresponds with the beginning of the barley harvest and recalls our redemption from Egypt. Shavuot corresponds with the beginning of the wheat harvest and recalls Revelation. What is the significance of Rosh Chodesh? In what sense is it on par with these festivals? An interesting response to this issue emerges from consideration of another problem in passages describing the Rosh Chodesh Musaf.

And their drink-offerings shall be half a hin of wine for a bullock, and the third part of a hin for the ram, and the fourth part of a hin for a lamb. This is the Olah offering of every new month throughout the months of the year. (BeMidbar 28:14)

4. Ibn Ezra's understanding of the formulation of the Rosh Chodesh directive

Rabbaynu Avraham ibn Ezra is concerned with a problem in the passages regarding the Musaf offering for Rosh Chodesh. The initial pasuk (28:11) introduces these sacrifices as the Musaf offering for "your new months". This means that the Musaf offering applies to all new months. The final passage of this set specifies that the sacrifices are offered on all new months. Why does the Torah again direct us to offer these sacrifices on each new month after introducing the sacrifices as the Musaf offering for every Rosh Chodesh?

Ibn Ezra responds that the translation of the initial passage should be reconsidered. The literal translation of the passage is: And on the first of your months you shall present an Olah offering unto Hashem. What does the phrase "first of your months" mean? The phrase is subject to two interpretations. Generally, it is understood to mean on the first day of each month. The transition above of Sefer Bemidbar 28:11 reflects this interpretation of the passage. Ibn Ezra suggests that this interpretation is incorrect. The proper interpretation is that on the first of your months – the first month of the year – you shall offer the Musaf offering specified in the passages. In other words, the passage directs us to offer the Musaf offering described in subsequent passages on the first of the months.

Which month is the first month of the year? Ibn Ezra explains that this is a reference to the month of Nisan. The Torah consistently describes Nisan as the first month of the year. Other

213

months are not assigned names but instead are identified relative to Nisan as the second month, third month, fourth month and so on.

Based upon this interpretation of the initial passage, Ibn Ezra eliminates the redundancy in the passages. The initial passage only directs that a Musaf offering be presented on the advent of the first month – Nisan. The final passage directs that the Nisan practice be applied to all other new months. Therefore, based solely upon this final passage, the Musaf described in the passages is offered also on other Roshai Chadashim – other new months.[37]

Of course, Ibn Ezra's response raises an even more serious problem. Why does the Torah express itself in this manner? According to Ibn Ezra, first, the Torah singles out Nisan for a special Musaf offering and then extends the directive regarding this Musaf offering to all other months. Why did the Torah not just treat all the months as equivalents and formulate a single step directive to offer the Musaf sacrifices on all Roshai Chadashim?

And Hashem spoke unto Moshe and Aaron in the land of Egypt, saying: This month shall be for you the beginning of months. It shall be the first month of the year for you. (Shemot 12:1-2)

5. The Torah's names for the months

Ibn Ezra's interpretation of the initial passage regarding the Rosh Chodesh Musaf offering is also found in his comments on Parshat Bo. In that context, he discusses an additional issue which provides insight into his position. There, he comments on the manner in which the Torah identifies the months of the year. The Torah does not provide the months with names. The names which are now used were assigned to the months during the period of the first exile and are Babylonian in origin. The Torah identifies the months through a numerical identification system. The month now referred to as Nisan is identified as the first month. Each subsequent month is identified relative to the first month. Thus, Iyar is the second month. Sivan is referred to as the third month, and so on. Why does the Torah prefer this numerical system over assigning a name to each month? Ibn Ezra presents a response that is elaborated upon by Nachmanides. He explains that Redemption from Egypt was a fundamental element of our development as a nation. Various mitzvot are designed to remind us of this event. According to Ibn Ezra, the identification system for the months is one of the measures instituted by the Torah to foster our constant cognizance of the Redemption. On every occasion on which we cite a date, there is a reference to Redemption. This is because the month is identified relative to the first month – the month of Redemption.[38] In short, the numerical names of the months provide an ongoing reference to redemption.

6. Ibn Ezra's understanding of the significance of Rosh Chodesh

Now, Ibn Ezra's understanding of the Torah's treatment of the Rosh Chodesh Musaf offering is explained. The Torah begins by directing us to endow the first month of the months of the year with a Musaf sacrifice. This is because it is the month of Redemption. The Torah then directs us to extend this Musaf offering to other Roshai Chadashim. These occasions are endowed with a Musaf offering because of their relationship to the first month. Every month is identified by its relationship to the month of Redemption. Thereby, every month is identified

---

[37] Rabbaynu Avraham ibn Ezra, Commentary on Sefer BeMidbar, 28:11.
[38] Rabbaynu Avraham ibn Ezra, Commentary on Sefer Shemot, 12:2.

with and recalls Redemption. It is because of its identification with Redemption that each month is endowed with a Musaf offering.

With Ibn Ezra's insight, the original question can be answered. Why does Rosh Chodesh have the same Musaf offering as Pesach and Shavuot? The calendar system of months is devised to recall and remind us of Redemption. Therefore, when each new month is declared, the Redemption is recalled through the very identification of the month. As an occasion on which Redemption is recalled, a Musaf is offered.

Mattot

"And Moshe spoke to the heads of the tribes saying, "This is the matter that Hashem commanded." (BeMidbar 30:2)

This *pasuk* introduces the most comprehensive discussion in the Torah of the laws governing vows. What is a vow? A vow is a means by which a person creates a personal obligation or restriction. One reason a person makes a vow is to obligate oneself to offer a sacrifice. This person would verbalize a commitment to bring an *Olah* sacrifice. Once this commitment is verbalized as a vow, the person is obligated to bring the offering. Failure to bring the offering is a violation of a binding Torah obligation.

A person might also make a vow to donate a certain sum to charity. However, vows can also relate to issues that are more mundane. A person eager to control one's diet might make a vow to eat at least one vegetable each day.

A vow can also take the form of a restriction. A person can vow to refrain from eating ice cream for a specific period of time. This person is not permitted to eat ice cream. In fact, for this person, ice cream is no different than the other foods prohibited by the Torah. Just as we are prohibited from eating forbidden fats, this person is subject to an additional restriction. This individual, because of the vow, cannot consume ice cream.

A vow is a serious commitment. The Torah requires strict adherence to vows. Therefore, the Sages discouraged making frivolous vows. This is because the Sages were concerned that a person may violate a vow. The best way to assure that a vow is not violated is not to make the vow in the first instance.

Our *parasha* focuses on a specific aspect of the laws governing vows. The Torah explains that the vows of certain individuals are subject to reversal. In other words, if one of these individuals makes a vow, this vow can be reversed by another party. Who are these individuals? Who is empowered with the authority to overturn their vows? Under what circumstances can this authority be exercised?

The Torah explains that a father can reverse his unwed daughter's vow. A husband can overturn the vow of his wife. This authority does not extend to all vows. The husband can only overturn vows that affect him. However, if the wife makes a vow that affects no person other than herself, the husband cannot reverse the vow. He does not have authority over such vows.[1]

Our *parasha* delineates various perimeters of this authority. For example, the father or husband can only overturn a vow by acting on the same day that he becomes aware of the vow. Another restriction on this authority is that a father can only nullify the vow of a daughter that has not completely reached her majority. However, once the daughter is a complete adult, the father's authority lapses.

Our *pasuk* indicates that Moshe explained these laws to the heads of the tribes – the *shevatim*. Why did Moshe address the heads of the *shevatim* and not all the nation? There are various responses to this question. Rashi rejects the very premise of the question. He explains that Moshe actually announced the material concerning vows to the entire nation. The intent of

---

[1] Rabbaynu Moshe ben Maimon (Rambam) *Mishne Torah*, Hilchot Nedarim 12:1. (See Radvaz for other opinions).

the *pasuk* is to indicate that Moshe first taught the material to the princes of the *shevatim*. After instructing the leaders, he taught the material to the nation. Rashi also contends that this process was not specific to this material. Moshe followed this process in teaching all portions of the Torah. First, he addressed the princes and, afterwards, he again taught the material to the nation.[2] This does leave one question. Why does the Torah, in this instance, mention the preferential treatment afforded the princes? According to Rashi, these leaders were consistently provided with the initial communication of the laws. However, specifically in this instance the Torah reveals this process!

Nachmanides disagrees with Rashi. He maintains that the Torah is describing a unique event. In general, Moshe taught the *mitzvot* to the entire nation. However, this *mitzvah* was revealed to the princes. It was not initially revealed to the entire nation. Why is this *mitzvah* special? Nachmanides offers a number of possibilities. One is that the princes have a unique role in regard to vows. The laws of vows were revealed to the princes as an indication of their special role and responsibility in this regard. What is this singular role and responsibility?

As has been explained, the Torah requires that we adhere to our vows. A person cannot make a vow, then decide that it was ill considered, and disregard it. Perhaps this person should not have made the vow. Nonetheless, the vow must be respected. However, there is a means of release from a vow. An expert scholar or a court can release a person from a vow. The person must show cause. *Halacha* delineates the criteria for such a release.

Nachmanides explains that this unique role and responsibility afforded the scholars and courts is not explicitly stated anywhere in the Torah. However, it is alluded to in our *pasuk*. The princes represented the scholars and judges. In speaking to the princes, Moshe communicated that these princes, and the scholars and courts that would exist in the future, have responsibility for vows. What is this responsibility? They are empowered to release a person from a vow.[3]

Rashi utilizes this same concept to resolve the difficulty engendered by his explanation of our passage. Rashi explains that Moshe regularly revealed the commandments to the princes prior to the nation. This detail is mentioned in our *parasha* as an allusion to the unique role of the judges and scholars in regard to vows. They are endowed with the right to release a person from a vow.

In summary, there are two means by which the binding power of a vow can be nullified. A husband or father can reverse the vow. The court can release the person from the vow.

There are many differences between these two processes. However, there is one distinction that the commentaries note is particularly significant. The father or husband does not require the consent of the wife or daughter. He can act unilaterally. In other words, even if the daughter wishes the vow to be binding, the father may reverse it. The same is true of the husband's authority in regard to his wife's vow. The courts do not have this ability. The court cannot act unilaterally. The court does not even initiate the process. Instead, a person wishing release from a vow must petition the court. The court can only act in response to the request of the person seeking release.

---

[2] Rabbaynu Shlomo ben Yitzchak (Rashi), *Commentary on Sefer BeMidbar* 30:2.
[3] Rabbaynu Moshe ben Nachman (Ramban), *Commentary on Sefer BeMidbar* 30:2.

This seems to be an odd arrangement. We would expect the opposite. We would expect a court of law to have greater authority than a lay person would. Yet, the opposite is true. A father or husband has greater authority over vows than the most elevated court of the nation! What is the reason for this paradoxical arrangement? More importantly, what does this arrangement reveal about the natures of these processes?

The commentaries suggest an important concept that explains this distinction. What is the legal basis for the authority of the father and husband? Sforno contends that the Torah actually endows the father and husband with authority over the vows of a daughter or wife. As head of the household, the father or husband has the authority to reverse these vows.[4]

What is the legal basis for the license of the courts? Nachmanides addresses this issue. His comments are not completely clear. He seems to maintain that the Torah does not require our unqualified adherence to our vows. However, we are required to treat a vow as a serious commitment. It cannot be regarded lightly. This means that, given sufficient grounds, a vow can be rescinded. If these grounds exist and the vow is rescinded after careful analysis of these grounds, then the vow has not been disregarded. It has not been treated lightly. The role of the court is to conduct this analysis. The court validates the cause presented by the petitioner for nullification of the vow.[5]

This distinction explains the paradox outlined above. Why does the father or husband have greater authority over vows than the courts? The father or husband actually has authority over a daughter or wife's vow. As a result, he can unilaterally overturn these vows. The courts do not have actual authority. They cannot unilaterally release a person from a vow. Instead, the court merely evaluates the credibility of the reasons provided by the petitioner for release from a vow. The person who made the vow presents an argument for release from the vow. The court analyzes this argument and validates its credibility. This process can only take place through the person who made the vow petitioning the court. It is impossible for the court to act without the initiation of the person who made the vow.

And Moshe spoke to the leaders of the tribes of Bnai Yisrael saying: This is the matter that Hashem commanded. (BeMidbar 30:2)

Speaking the Word of Hashem

1. Only Moshe said: This is the matter

This *pasuk* introduces a discussion of laws governing vows. Rashi, based upon the midrash, makes an enigmatic comment on this passage. He explains that Moshe sometimes prefaced a communcation with the phrase, *khoe* – "thus said Hashem." This introduction was also used by other prophets. In our *pasuk,* Moshe begins with the phrase, *zeh* – "this is the matter that Hashem commanded." The preface *zeh* – this – was *not* used by other prophets.[6]

What is the message of Rashi? Rashi apparently maintains that these two phrases are very different. "This is the matter that Hashem commanded" is uniquely appropriate for Moshe. Other

---

[4] Rabbaynu Ovadia Sforno, *Commentary on Sefer BeMidbar* 30:2
[5] See Rabbaynu Moshe ben Nachman (Ramban), *Commentary on Sefer BeMidbar* 30:2.
[6] Rabbaynu Shlomo ben Yitzchak (Rashi), *Commentary on Sefer BeMidbar* 30:2.

prophets could not use this introduction. However, the two phrases seem very similar! What is the difference between these two statements?

Rav Eliyahu Mizrachi explains that these two phrases are actually very different from one another. When a prophet uses the preface "thus said Hashem", he indicates that he is attributing the substance of his message to Hashem. He is not suggesting that the words with which he will present the message are the words of Hashem. The content of his message is from Hashem. The specific form or wording that the prophet uses to present the content is his own.

The preface "this is the matter that Hashem commanded" communicates the words that Moshe will use, are the exact words provided by Hashem. Both the substance and the form of the message that will be communicated are from Hashem.

2. The unique character of Moshe's prophecy

Mizrachi explains that Moshe achieved a higher level of prophecy than any other prophet. One of the special aspects of Moshe's prophecy was its absolute clarity. He communicated with Hashem as clearly as two mortal individuals communicate with one other. He perceived the communication as the words of Hashem. Therefore, he transmitted his prophecy to the nation with the preface "this is the matter that Hashem commanded". In other words, these are Hashem's own words.

Other prophets did not communicate with Hashem on this level. The message that they perceived through prophecy was not expressed in specific words. They received visions and the visions were accompanied by understanding of the visions' meanings. However, part of the role of the prophets was to put into words their understanding of the visions. They prefaced their communications to the people with "thus said Hashem". They were telling the people that their message came from Hashem. The words in which they expressed the message were their own.[7]

Rav Yaakov Kaminetsky Zt"l supports and expands this interpretation. His comments are based upon a difficult text in the Talmud. The Talmud explains each prophet expressed his or her prophecy with a unique language and expression. It is impossible for two prophets to express the same prophecy employing identical wording. Should this occur, we can be sure that one is a false prophet.[8]

This is a difficult concept. Genuine prophecy is received from Hashem. If Hashem delivered the identical prophecy to a number of prophets, should not each provide exactly the same report of the prophecy? Why is this very consistency indicative of falsehood and subterfuge?

Rav Kaminetsky suggests that prophecy involves a personal element. The prophet receives a message from Hashem. The prophet is charged with the duty of communicating the message to the people. It is the responsibility of the prophet to choose the wording and phrasing for this communication. Each will naturally construct a unique presentation. It is impossible that different individuals will independently construct identical presentations. If all the prophets communicate the message in identical language, then it is evident that some collusion has taken place.[9]

---

[7] Rav Eliyahu Mizrahi, *Commentary on Rashi*, BeMidbar 30:2.

[8] Mesechet Sanhedrin 89a.

[9] Rav Yaakov Kaminetsky, *Emet LeYaakov* (RJJ School Press, 1990), Sefer BeMidbar 30:2.

In summary, the distinction between these phrases reflects a basic difference between Moshe's prophecy and other prophets' prophecy. Only Moshe could communicate Hashem's exact words. Other prophets could only communicate the substance of the message and were required to express the message in their own words. Therefore, they were enjoined against introducing their prophecy with the word "this". This word was reserved for Moshe alone.

3. Early in his career, Moshe introduced messages with "thus"

Rashi acknowledges that Moshe sometimes did introduce his communications with "thus said Hashem". We understand that other prophets used this introduction because it reflected their level of prophecy. However, Moshe was on a higher level of prophecy. Why did he ever use this introduction?

Mizrachi suggests that Moshe was not initially qualitatively distinguished from other prophets. The Torah describes Moshe's first prophecy. He observed a bush that had a fire in its midst, but yet, was not consumed. This was a vision. At this stage, Moshe had not yet achieved the level of prophecy that would distinguish him from all prophets who proceeded or would follow him. He received a vision – much like other prophets. Most of the instances in which Moshe introduced his communications with "thus" are from this early period in his prophetic career. He had not yet achieved the unique greatness that distinguished him from other prophets. He did not yet communicate with Hashem with the clarity requisite for use of the introduction "this is the matter".[10]

4. Moshe received two types of prophecy

Gur Aryeh does not accept Mizrachi's explanation for Moshe's use of "thus". Mizrachi insists that Moshe used this phrase only before he achieved his full prophetic stature. Gur Aryeh notes that there is one instance in which Moshe used "thus" after he had fully attained his special status.

After the people heard the Decalogue at Sinai, Moshe ascended the mountain in order to receive the Torah. Hashem communicated to Moshe the exact words of the text. Only because Moshe had achieved his unique level of prophecy was he capable of receiving from Hashem the precise words of the Torah. Essentially, Moshe's prophetic attainment made it possible for him to act as Hashem's stenographer.

Before Moshe could descend from the mountain, the nation committed the sin of the *egel* – the golden calf. Moshe was expelled from the presence of Hashem and ordered to quickly descend from the mountain. He descended, entered the camp, and observed the people participating in the worship of the *egel*. Moshe summoned those loyal to Hashem. The tribe of Leyve rallied to him. He communicated to them a directive from Hashem. They must pass through the camp of the Bnai Yisrael and execute those guilty of idolatry. He introduced this directive with "thus said Hashem".

Gur Aryeh notes that this incident occurred after Moshe had achieved his distinct prophetic greatness. Why did he introduce his message with "thus"? He should have said "this is the matter that Hashem has commanded".

Gur Aryeh responds that Moshe received two types of prophecy. Some of his prophecies were instructions or messages relevant for the specific moment. These instructions or messages

---

[10] Rav Eliyahu Mizrahi, *Commentary on Rashi*, BeMidbar 30:2.

are not part of the Torah's 613 commandments. Because the relevance of the messages and instructions was related to the time at which they were communicated, their exact wording and text was not important. Content was important but not the exact words. In these instances, Moshe was required to communicate the substance of the message. He was not required to express himself with the same words used by Hashem. In these instances, Moshe prefaced his remarks with "thus". He was suggesting that the substance of the message was from Hashem but he was using his own words.

The commandments of the Torah and the Torah's actual text are intended for all generations. Each word is important. The text communicates an overt message. Other messages are communicated by the words selected and the phrasing used. The many laws which are to be followed to fulfill the commandments are imbedded in the nuances of the language and phrasing of the passages. In the communication of the commandments and in the text of the Torah, the exact words are essential. The distinction between form and substance is not valid in regard to the commandments and the text of the Torah. The exact text is an inseparable element of the substance of the prophecy.

Gur Aryeh explains that when Moshe spoke to the tribe of Leyve, in real time, he was providing them with instructions for that moment. He was not communicating a commandment for future generations. In that instance, the exact wording Hashem had used was not important. Moshe needed to communicate, to those who would follow him, the substance of Hashem's commandment but not His exact words. Therefore, he used the phrase "thus". However, Moshe never used the phrase "thus" when communicating commandments.[11]

5. The Torah is the word of Hashem

Gur Aryeh's comments are a reminder to us of the remarkable character of the Torah. The Torah is not composed of Moshe's personal directives. It is not his presentation of the communications that he had with Hashem. It is the exact words that Hashem dictated to Moshe. When we read and study the Torah, we are contemplating the actual words of Hashem.

"Take vengeance for Bnai Yisrael against the Midianites and afterward you will be gathered to your people." (BeMidbar 31:2)

The Parshat Shelach edition of Thoughts *discussed the obligation to take possession of and live in Israel. This week's edition continues that discussion.*

Maimonides does not include within his list of the 613 *mitzvot* an obligation to possess or live in the land of Israel. However, Maimonides does maintain that we are obligated to possess and live in the land of Israel.[12] His exclusion of this obligation from his list of the 613 *mitzvot* is based on technical considerations and does not reflect a disregard for the centrality of the land of Israel within the Torah.

However, Maimonides' position regarding the land of Israel does present a problem. In order to understand this problem, an introduction is needed. The Torah urges us to always pursue peace. Nonetheless, the Torah recognizes that sometimes the Jewish nation must engage in war. Even in war, the laws and ethics of the Torah cannot be disregarded. The Torah mandates

---

[11] Rav Yehuda Loew of Prague (Maharal), *Gur Aryeh Commentary on Sefer BeMidbar* 30:2.
[12] Rabbaynu Moshe ben Maimon (Rambam) *Mishne Torah*, Hilchot Melachim 5:9-12.

various laws for the conduct of war. In general, the Torah outlines two categories of war – *milchemet mitzvah* and *milchemet reshut*. *Milchemet mitzvah* is a war which is a *mitzvah*. *Milchemet reshut* is a war which is not a *mitzvah*. It is optional.

Obviously, these terms need some clarification. Under what circumstances is a war regarded as a *mitzvah*? Maimonides does not include in his codification of the *mitzvot* a specific *mitzvah* to wage war. Instead, Maimonides records two *mitzvot* regarding specific wars – war to destroy Amalek and war to destroy the seven nations of Cana'an.[13] This indicates that according to Maimonides, a *milchemet mitzvah* is a war authorized by some specific obligation in the Torah. In other words, a war waged to destroy Amalek is a *milchemet mitzvah* because it fulfills the *mitzvah* to destroy Amalek. A war against the seven nations is a *milchemet mitzvah* because it fulfills the *mitzvah* to destroy the seven nations. Maimonides adds that *milchemet mitzvah* includes a third case. A war to rescue the nation from an attacking adversary is also regarded as a *milchemet mitzvah*. Although, there is some controversy regarding the identity of the specific *mitzvah* that is fulfilled in this last case, it is reasonable to assume that we are obligated to defend our fellow Jew. Therefore, a war waged to defend and save other Jews meets the criterion for being defined as a *milchemet mitzvah*. In contrast, a war which is not required by a specific Torah obligation is not a *milchemet mitzvah*. It is a *milchemet reshut*.

There are various differences between a *milchemet mitzvah* and a *milchemet reshut*. For example, all members of Bnai Yisrael are obligated to participate in a *milchemet mitzvah*. However, there are various exemptions for a *milchemet reshut*.[14] Because a *milchemet mitzvah* is waged in response to a Torah obligation, no further authorization is required for this war to be waged. However, because a *milchemet reshut* is not waged in response to a specific Torah obligation, it must be authorized by *Bait Din* – the court.[15]

As explained above, Maimonides agrees that we are obligated by the Torah to possess the land of Israel and to live in the land. Therefore, we would expect that a war waged in order to seize control of the land would be a *milchemet mitzvah*. However, as indicated above, Maimonides only identifies three forms of *milchemet mitzvah* – a war to destroy Amalek, a war to destroy the seven nations of Cana'an, and a war to save other Jews. He does not include in this list a war waged in order to take possession of the land of Israel. Yet, it would seem that such a conflict would meet Maimonides' criterion for a *milchemet mitzvah*.

In order to answer this question, we must return to an issue mentioned earlier. According to Maimonides, a war waged in order to save members of Bnai Yisrael is a *milchemet mitzvah*. It is reasonable to regard such a war as obligatory. However, as mentioned earlier, there is some controversy regarding the exact identity of the *mitzvah* that obligates such conduct. Let us consider this issue more closely.

In the above passage, Moshe is instructed to wage war against Midyan. This war fulfills a commandment outlined in last week's *parasha*. There, Hashem reminds Moshe that Midyan had attempted to destroy Bnai Yisrael. Therefore, Bnai Yisrael must eliminate Midyan.[16] In our *parsha*, Hashem tells Moshe that the time has come to fulfill this obligation. The midrash

---

[13] Rabbaynu Moshe ben Maimon (Rambam) *Mishne Torah*, Hilchot Melachim 5:1.
[14] Rabbaynu Moshe ben Maimon (Rambam) *Mishne Torah*, Hilchot Melachim 7:4.
[15] Rabbaynu Moshe ben Maimon (Rambam) *Mishne Torah*, Hilchot Melachim 5:2.
[16] Sefer BeMidbar 25:17-18.

comments that one is permitted to take another's life in order to defend oneself. In other words, if a person is aware that another individual is preparing to attack him, he may take the measures needed to save himself. He may even take the life of this person that plans to assail him. The midrash explains that this law is derived from Hashem's instructions to Moshe regarding Midyan. Midyan had proven through previous behavior that it was determined to destroy Bnai Yisrael. In instructing Moshe to annihilate Midyan, Hashem specifically noted Midyan's previous attempts to destroy Bnai Yisrael. The midrash asserts that the message of the Torah is clear. If one plans to kill you, you may protect yourself by killing this would-be assailant before he can attack you.[17]

This midrash would seem to contradict a well-known teaching of our Sages. The Torah informs us that if we discover a burglar in our home, we are permitted to kill him.[18] The Sages explain that this is an act of self-defense. It is assumed that if the homeowner opposes the burglar, the thief is prepared to kill his opponent. Therefore, the homeowner's actions against the burglar are regarded as self-defense. Rashi suggests that this law is the source for the dictum that one is permitted to kill someone in order to defend oneself.[19] In other words, it is agreed that one may kill another person as a preemptive measure to save oneself. However, the source for this law is disputed. The midrash suggests that the source is Hashem's instructions to Moshe to destroy Midyan. Rashi seems to disagree with the midrash and suggests an alternative source. According to Rashi, the source is the law permitting the homeowner to kill a burglar.

Rav Aharon Soloveitchik suggests that there is not contradiction between Rashi and the midrash. Rashi is identifying the source for an individual's right to take preemptive measures against an attacker. However, the midrash is extending this rule to the nation. In other words, the midrash is explaining that just as the individual is permitted and encouraged to defend himself and preempt an attack, so too the nation of Bnai Yisrael is authorized and expected to take the same action.

Rav Aharon explains that this midrash is the source for Maimonides' ruling that a war waged to save fellow Jews is a *milchemet mitzvah*. Even if one is not under personal attack, the midrash rules that we are obligated to take preemptive action on a national level. In other words, the midrash extends to the nation as a whole the right of the homeowner to protect himself.

Rav Aharon further explains that his thesis has important implications. According to his explanation of Maimonides, the obligation of the nation to defend itself is an extension of the prerogative of the homeowner. He notes that the homeowner may exercise this prerogative in order to protect his property. In other words, the homeowner is not expected to step aside and allow the thief to rob him. He is permitted and encouraged to oppose the robber. Rav Aharon points out that if the thief succeeded in ejecting the homeowner from his property, the homeowner would not be deprived of his prerogative. He would have every right to forcibly reclaim his property even at the expense of the thief's life.

Rav Aharon suggests that the same reasoning applies to the national prerogative or obligation to defend itself. This obligation includes the right and obligation to protect its property – the land of Israel – from all those who seek to steal it. Furthermore, if we are removed from the

---

[17] Midrash Tanchuma, Parshat Pinchas, Chapter 3.
[18] Sefer Shemot 22:1.
[19] Rabbaynu Shlomo ben Yitzchak (Rashi), *Commentary on Sefer Shemot* 22:1.

land, we have the right to reclaim it – just as the homeowner may reclaim his property. In short, according to Rav Aharon, the obligation of the Jewish nation to defend itself implies a right and obligation to defend the land of Israel.

Based on this reasoning, Rav Aharon answers our question on Maimonides. Why does Maimonides not include within his list of conflicts that are *milchemet mitzvah* a war waged to possess the land of Israel. Rav Aharon answers that Maimonides does include this war in his list. This war is regarded as a war of self-defense. Just as the homeowner is regarded as acting is self-defense when he protects his property, so too Bnai Yisrael is acting in its own self-defense when it protects its land from those who would take it from the Jewish people.[20]

"Take vengeance against the people of Midyan and afterwards you will be gathered to your nation." (BeMidbar 31:2)

The closing passages of Parshat Balak provide an introduction to our passage. Women from the nations of Moav and Midyan enter the camp of Bnai Yisrael. These women seduce members of Bnai Yisrael. The heathen women use these illicit relationships to lead their partners into idolatrous practices. Discipline and sexual restraint begin to break down. Ultimately, Zimri – a leader of Shevet Shimon – publicly enters into a romantic liaison with a woman from Midyan. The woman – Kazbi – is a princess of Midyan. Hashem strikes Bnai Yisrael with a plague. Pinchas, the son of Elazar the *Kohen*, takes action. He executes Zimri and Kazbi. In response to Pinchas' zealousness, the Almighty ends the plague.

In Parshat Pinchas, Hashem commands Moshe to avenge the evil done by the people of Midyan. Moshe is told to "afflict" Midyan. Now, Hashem seems to repeat this command. He tells Moshe to take vengeance against the people of Midyan. This raises an obvious question. Why did Hashem repeat the command? Why is the command first stated in Parshat Pinchas and then repeated in our *parasha*?

It seems that each command is unique. The command in Parshat Pinchas does not indicate any specific action. It establishes a relationship. Bnai Yisrael is to view the nation of Midyan as an adversary. Our relationship with Midyan should be predicated upon this assumption. We should assume that the people of Midyan feel animosity towards Bnai Yisrael. We should act aggressively to protect ourselves. However, this command does not include a specific obligation to wage war.

The command in our *parasha* is more specific. It requires engaging Midyan in war. Moshe is commanded to seek out the people of Midyan and wage war against them.

Our *pasuk* makes an interesting connection. Hashem tells Moshe that he will die only after completing this task. This implies that Moshe's involvement is essential. Why is Moshe's participation important?

In order to answer this question, we must review the Torah's comments concerning Moshe's special status. In the final passages of the Torah, Moshe's uniqueness is described. The Torah writes that no other individual can achieve Moshe's prophetic level. The Torah also explains that the wonders performed through Moshe exceed those executed through other

---

[20] Rav Aharon Soloveitchik, *Settling the Land of Israel and Milchemet Mitzvah in Current Times*, Or HaMizrach, October 2003.

prophets. These passages teach another important lesson. The *pesuk*im link Moshe's prophecy to the wonders he performed. Moshe was the greatest prophet. His closeness to the Almighty was reflected in the profound level of his prophecy. This same intimacy allowed Moshe to perform wonders beyond the ability of other prophets.

Based upon the above analysis, Gershonides answers our question. He explains that Moshe could not die until Midyan was destroyed. This is because this war would be fought through the Almighty. Hashem would destroy Midyan through His wonders. Moshe's participation allowed for the performance of the greatest miracles. No other prophet could destroy Midyan as totally and wondrously.[21]

"And Moshe sent one thousand men from each tribe as an army. And with them was Pinchas the son of Elazar the *Kohen* as part of the army. And in his hand was the sacred vessels and the trumpets of the *teruah*." (BeMidbar 31:6)

This passage presents a problem. Hashem commanded Moshe to destroy Midyan. As we have explained, Moshe's involvement was crucial. Yet, Moshe did not lead the nation into war. Instead, he sent Pinchas. Why did Moshe, himself, not lead the nation into battle?

Da'at Zekaynim offers two answers to this question. Let us consider each answer. We will begin with the second explanation. Da'at Zekaynim explains that Pinchas had previously executed Kazbi – a princess of Midyan. He had begun to fulfill a *mitzvah*. Punishing the people of Midyan completed this *mitzvah*. It is appropriate for the person that initiates a *mitzvah* to complete it. Therefore, Moshe charged Pinchas with the duty of completing this *mitzvah*.[22]

This answer presents a problem. According to this interpretation, this war completed a *mitzvah* initiated by Pinchas. Therefore, Pinchas was chosen to complete the *mitzvah* he had begun. However, the exact identity of this *mitzvah* is not clear. Pinchas executed Kazbi because she was publicly engaged in sexual activity with Zimri. The war against Midyan was a response to Hashem's command to destroy a dangerous enemy. These seem to be two separate commands.

Rav Yitzchak Zev Soloveitchik Zt"l deals with this problem. He explains that a more careful analysis does indicate that a single *mitzvah* underlies Pinchas' pervious actions and the war against Midyan. Let us reconsider Rav Soloveitchik's analysis.

Pinchas acted within the law in executing Zimri and Kazbi. The Torah prohibits sexual relations between Jews and non-Jews. Primarily, this prohibition restricts relations in the context of marriage. However, even casual sexual relations are prohibited. If a liaison is flaunted publicly, a zealot is permitted to execute the parties involved. Pinchas acted within the authority granted by this law. He was such a zealot.[23]

Maimonides points out that the Jew and the non-Jew are not executed for the same reason. The Jew is executed for violating the laws of the Torah. Obviously the non-Jewish partner cannot be punished for this reason. The non-Jew is not obligated to observe the laws of

[21]   Rabbaynu Levi ben Gershon (Ralbag / Gershonides), *Commentary on Sefer VaYikra*, (Mosad HaRav Kook, 1997), p 142.

[22]   *Da'at Zekaynim, Commentary on Sefer BeMidbar* 31:6.

[23]   Rabbaynu Moshe ben Maimon (Rambam) *Mishne Torah*, Hilchot Esurai Beyah 12:4.

the Torah. Maimonides seems to maintain that the non-Jewish woman is executed because she served as the vehicle of the Jews abandonment of sexual morals.

Maimonides compares the status of this woman to another case. This is the case of an animal involved in an act of bestiality. The animal is destroyed. Clearly, the animal is not responsible to observe the Torah's laws. It is destroyed because it was involved in an act of sexual depravity. In our case as well, the woman is executed because of her association with immorality.

Maimonides adds another point. In order to understand this comment, a brief introduction is required. Bnai Yisrael defeated Midyan. They executed the men. However, initially they spared the women. Moshe was angered. He observed that these women had corrupted the men of Bnai Yisrael. Maimonides explains Moshe's objection. Moshe maintained that it was inappropriate to spare these individuals. They were associated with corrupting the sexual morality of Bnai Yisrael.

Based on Maimonides' comments, Rav Soloveitchik explains that a single *mitzvah* underlies Pinchas' initial actions and the war against Midyan. Pinchas executed Kazbi because of her association with Zimri's corruption. In order to complete this *mitzvah*, he led Bnai Yisrael in battle against Midyan. The commandment was completed with the execution of the women of Midyan. These women – like Kazbi—were put to death because they were associated with the corruption of Bnai Yisrael.[24]

Now let us consider Da'at Zekaynim's first answer. The first answer is that Moshe had received a kindness from Midyan. Moshe killed an Egyptian taskmaster. Moshe knew his life was in danger. He fled to Midyan. He remained there until Hashem commanded him to return to Egypt and rescue Bnai Yisrael. Da'at Zekaynim explains that it was inappropriate for Moshe to lead a campaign against Midyan. Midyan had provided him sanctuary. Moshe was obligated in *hakarat hatov* – acknowledging the benefit that he had received from Midyan.[25]

This answer presents a problem. Hashem commanded Moshe to wage war against Midyan. The Almighty wanted Moshe to be involved. This involvement was necessary to assure that Midyan would be devastated. This seems to mean that Pinchas was merely Moshe's proxy. Moshe was the true leader that destroyed Midyan. In short, Moshe did not spare Midyan in any way. How did Moshe demonstrate his *hakarat hatov*? He destroyed Midyan thoroughly! Where was Moshe's show of appreciation?

It seems that this answer is based upon a novel understanding of *hakarat hatov*. We usually, understand *hakarat hatov* as an obligation to repay a debt. An individual who receives a kindness is obligated to repay the kindness. This interpretation of *hakarat hatov* confounds us in attempting to understand the position of the Da'at Zekaynim. We can now better define our question. In order to repay a debt, some significant benefit must be proffered. Moshe did not show any mercy towards Midyan. He did not repay his debt through providing a substantial kindness in return.

Apparently, Da'at Zekaynim understands *hakarat hatov* in a more literal sense. *Hakarat hatov* means that we are obligated to demonstrate that we recognize receiving a benefit.

---

24 Rav Shimon Yosef Miller, Shai LaTorah (Jerusalem 5755), volume 3, pp. 214-215.
25 *Da'at Zekaynim, Commentary on Sefer BeMidbar* 31:6.

Generally, the most meaningful act of recognition is to return the kindness. However, sometimes this is not appropriate. Moshe faced this situation. He was commanded to completely destroy Midyan. He could not show mercy. Hashem's commandment prevented him from returning the kindness he had received.

Nonetheless, the obligation of *hakarat hatov* applies. Even when we cannot return the kindness we must acknowledge its receipt. Moshe provided this acknowledgement. He refused to personally lead Bnai Yisrael into battle. This was not an act of kindness. However, it was an acknowledgement of the kindness received.

The descendants of Gad and the descendants of Reuben came, and they spoke to Moshe and to Elazar the kohen and to the princes of the community, saying: Atarot, Divon, Yazer, and Nimrah, Cheshbon, Elaleh, Sebam, Nevo, and Beon, the land that Hashem struck down before the congregation of Israel is a land for livestock, and your servants have livestock. They said: If it pleases you, let this land be given to your servants as a heritage; do not take us across the Jordan. (BeMidbar 32:2-5)

The problem posed by the request of the tribes of Reuven and Gad

Parshat Mattot opens with a discussion of the laws regarding vows and oaths. The commentators provide a number of explanations for the placement of these laws at this juncture of the Torah's narrative. One of the most interesting explanations is provided by Rabbaynu Avraham ibn Ezra. Before considering his explanation, we must review another portion of the *parasha*.

The *parasha* closes with an account of a negotiation that took place between Moshe and the tribes of Reuven and Gad. Moshe and Bnai Yisrael had approached the Land of Israel from the east. Their path into the land required passing through the kingdoms of Sichon and Og. Both of these rulers opposed this passage. Bnai Yisrael engaged Sichon and his legions and then Og and his armies. Both were defeated and their lands were occupied by Bnai Yisrael.

Moshe did not plan to permanently occupy these lands. Instead, Yehoshua – Moshe's successor – was to lead the nation in the conquest of the lands west of the Jordan. These lands would be divided among the tribes. The Jordan would be the eastern border of the Land of Israel.

In the above passages, the tribes of Reuven and Gad ask that Moshe allow them to settle in the lands captured from Sichon and Og – the lands east of the Jordan. Moshe initially rejects their request with a stern rebuke. He explains that their brethren would interpret their request as abandonment. This would undermine the nation's courage and its commitment to the Land of Israel. Moshe reminds the tribes of Reuven and Gad that thirty-eight years earlier the nation had turned away from the challenge of conquering the land. In response to their rebellion against His will, Hashem condemned that generation to wander for its remaining years in the wilderness. Moshe declares to these tribes that they are risking precipitating a repeat of that terrible crisis.

We will then arm ourselves quickly [and go] before Bnai Yisrael until we have brought them to their place. Our children will reside in the fortified cities on account of the inhabitants of the land. We shall not return to our homes until each of the children of Israel has taken possession of his inheritance. (BeMidbar 32:17-18)

So build yourselves cities for your children and enclosures for your sheep, and what has proceeded from your mouth you shall do. (BeMidbar 32:24)

The tribes of Reuven and Gad vow to lead the nation into the Land of Israel

The tribes of Reuven and Gad take to heart Moshe's concern and suggest the solution described in the first set of above passages. They will build fortified settlements for their families and cattle. After settling their families, the men will lead the nation in conquering the lands west of the Jordan. Only after conquering these lands and settling the other tribes in their homelands will they return to their own homes east of the Jordan. Moshe accepts this arrangement.

Ibn Ezra explains that the opening discussion in the *parasha* regarding vows and oaths is directly related to this narrative. As indicated in the final passage above, Moshe accepted the arrangement offered by the tribes of Reuven and Gad only after they presented their arrangement as a vow. Moshe was confident that the terms of the agreement would be fully observed because the tribes of Reuven and Gad expressed them as a vow. Moshe knew that the tribes would not violate their words.

The opening section of the *parasha* describes Moshe teaching to the nation the laws regarding vows. Moshe impressed upon the people the importance of adhering to such commitments. Because he concluded that the nation understood this lesson, he accepted the arrangement offered by the tribes of Reuven and Gad. He was confident that an arrangement expressed as a vow would be observed.

According to Ibn Ezra, the opening and closing sections of the *parasha* deal with a single theme. We are expected to adhere to our vows, promises, and verbal commitments. The *parasha* opens with laws regarding vows and it ends by describing a specific agreement that Moshe accepted based upon his conclusion that the nation understood the lesson taught in this opening section.

If a woman makes a vow to Hashem, or imposes a prohibition [upon herself] while in her father's house, in her youth, if her father heard her vow or her prohibition which she has prohibited upon herself, yet her father remains silent, all her vows shall stand, and any prohibition that she has imposed upon herself shall stand. But if her father hinders her on the day he hears it, all her vows and her prohibitions that she has imposed upon herself shall not stand. Hashem will forgive her because her father hindered her. (BeMidbar 30:4-6)

Vows may be annulled

In the context of the above discussion, it is notable that the opening section of the *parasha* focuses upon the circumstances under which a vow may be annulled. The Torah explicitly outlines specific circumstances but also provides for a more general mechanism that is fully developed only in the Oral Law. This is the principle of *hatarat nedarim* – the nullification of vows. According to this principle, an expert sage or a court composed of three lay people may nullify a person's vow. The person must present the sage or the lay court with a valid basis for the nullification. In general, one must identify a circumstance or consideration that was known or knowable to the person when he or she made the vow but was not properly considered and weighed before entering into the commitment.

An example will be helpful in illustrating the principle of *hatarat nedarim*. Assume I made an oath to not eat cookies or cake for a month. Now, at the time I made the vow, I knew that I would be attending a wedding at the end of the month. The celebration would include an extensive buffet of unusual and remarkably enticing desserts. Despite this foreknowledge, I did not take the wedding into account when making my vow. As the wedding is approaching, I realize that my vow will ruin my experience at the wedding. I have recourse to the principle of *hatarat nedarim*. I can annul my vow and enjoy the wedding.

From this discussion it seems that the attitude of the Torah toward vows and oaths is paradoxical. Ibn Ezra explained that the theme uniting the opening and closing portions of the *parasha* is the importance of being true to one's word and adhering to one's verbal commitments. In contrast to the importance of keeping these commitments, the opening portion of the *parasha* also explains that vows can be annulled and our Oral Torah grants to the courts broad authority over vows and verbal commitments. How can the Torah's emphasis upon being true to one's words be reconciled with the various avenues it provides for annulling vows and verbal commitments?

Moshe spoke to the heads of the tribes of Bnai Yisrael, saying: This is the thing Hashem has commanded. If a man makes a vow to Hashem or makes an oath to prohibit himself, he shall not make hollow his word; according to whatever came out of his mouth, he shall do. (BeMidbar 30:2-3)

Vows may be annulled, but they are serious verbal commitments

Maimonides and others suggest a solution to this problem. Their insight is based upon a careful analysis of the Torah's specific phrasing. In discussing our obligation to observe our verbal commitments, the Torah commands, "One should not make his word hollow or profane". Maimonides explains that the Torah uses this specific phrasing rather than an unequivocal statement prohibiting acting contrary to one's word. He explains that the Torah is admonishing us to treat our verbal commitments seriously. We should not regard them as casual statements which can be lightly dismissed.

Maimonides explains that this phrasing provides a rationale for the authority granted by the Oral Law to the courts or an expert sage to annul vows and verbal commitments. One may not treat vows and verbal commitments lightly. These are serious commitments. However, the Torah provides a means through which a person can gain relief from an ill-considered vow. The person must seek the intercession of a sage or court. Because one cannot on one's own accord dismiss a verbal obligation but requires the intercession of a sage or court, the seriousness of these commitments is reinforced.

Sefer HaChinuch expands on Maimonides' insight. He explains that the Torah's treatment of vows and verbal commitments is designed to balance two conflicting considerations. The Torah seeks to teach us that vows and verbal commitments are serious and should not be made or treated casually. Also, the Torah recognizes that we sometimes make such commitments without fully considering their impact. In order to reconcile these concerns, the Torah creates a means through which a person may gain relief from a vow or verbal commitment – the intercession of the sage or court. This arrangement preserves the message that these commitments are significant but provides one who makes an ill-considered vow a means of extrication.

Moshe addressed himself to only the elders

Nachmanides suggests that the above discussion provides a solution to another problem in the *parasha*. In the above passages introducing the discussion of vows, Moshe addresses himself to the leaders of the tribes. He teaches them the laws of vows and instructs them in the means by which vows and verbal commitments can be annulled. Usually, when Moshe teaches a commandment, he addresses the nation. Why are these remarks addressed to the leaders of the tribes?

Nachmanides suggests a novel response. In this instance, Moshe did not deliver his instruction to the entire nation. He communicated the laws regarding the annulment of vows to only the leaders. Why did Moshe teach these laws to the elders and not to the entire nation? Nachmanides suggests that the unusual transmission of these laws was required because of the issues outlined above. Vows and verbal commitments are serious. Yet, these commitments can be annulled. Above, the resolution of this apparent paradox is discussed. Also, the reason the Torah created this paradoxical arrangement is explored. However, these ideas are not simple and require careful and focused consideration. Moshe's primary objective was that the people appreciate the significance of verbal commitments. In his instruction to the people, he stressed this lesson. He could not undermine that message by revealing that these commitments are not absolute and may be annulled. This information is important and Moshe communicated it to the elders of the nation. He empowered them to teach the people the laws regarding the annulment of vows as circumstances required. Through his circumscription, he preserved the nation's commitment to observing their verbal commitments and also provided the means through which relief might be secured.

Nachmanides adds that this same consideration is reflected in the absence of any mention in the *parasha* of the authority of a sage or court to annul vows. The laws regarding this authority and how it may be used are included in the Oral Law and not the Written Torah. Nachmanides explains the absence from the Written Torah of any mention of this authority is designed to reinforce the message that our verbal commitments are serious. Mention of the authority of a sage or court to annul such commitments, would undermine this message.

An interesting lesson emerges from this discussion. The laws of the Torah are not simple and their meaning cannot be grasped through superficial study. The *mitzvot* are not banal platitudes or a set of easily understood instructions. For example, the laws regarding vows are paradoxical. Hashem instructed Moshe to communicate these laws to the nation with care and discretion. Moshe was even directed to conceal from the people aspects of the laws in order to not undermine the people's understanding of the seriousness of verbal commitments or invite their incredulity.

There is a lesson here for the teacher and for the student. The teacher must recognize that questions and puzzlement are to be expected. Moshe anticipated bewilderment and put in place a strategy to respond. He decided that some of the laws he wished to transmit should not be immediately shared with the entire nation. Instead, the nation would learn these laws in installments. The teacher also must anticipate questions, welcome them, but prepare for them. As in the instance described above, it is sometimes best for the teacher to forego or postpone teaching a lesson, rather than confuse one's students. A teacher's enthusiasm very much impacts the effectiveness of his or her instruction. But this enthusiasm cannot alone decide whether material should be taught to the students. Instead, the teacher's passion must be balanced with the needs and preparedness of the students. Material should be selected for instruction that will deepen and broaden the students' understanding rather than create confusion and frustration.

The student also learns an important lesson from this discussion. The student should expect to sometimes be troubled by the meaning or message of a commandment. We should react to our perplexity with humility. Our confusion is a result of the profoundness of Torah. We must recognize that often the answers to our questions can only emerge after extended and intense study. Rather than responding to our perplexity with judgment and condescension, we should renew our search for understanding and insight.

And Moshe said to them: If you do this and arm yourself for war before Hashem and you pass over the Jordan – each of you armed – before Hashem, until His enemies have been driven out before Him, and the land is captured before Hashem, and (only) afterwards you return, then you will be innocent before Hashem and Yisrael and this land will be yours as a possession before Hashem. (BeMidbar 32:20-22)

The Relationship between the Torah and the Navi

1. Moshe's agreement with the tribes of Reuven and Gad

In the previous parasha, Hashem told Moshe that his time had come to a close. Yehoshua was identified as the next leader. In Parshat Mattot, the Torah continues its description of Moshe's final acts as leader of Bnai Yisrael. The nation was encamped on the eastern bank of the Jordan. This territory was recently captured by Bnai Yisrael in its conquest over the kingdoms of Sichon and Og. The people were poised to cross the Jordan under Yehoshua's leadership and take possession of the Land of Israel. The Torah relates that Moshe was approached by two of the shevatim – the tribes. These shevatim had a controversial request. They told Moshe that they judged the land that the nation currently occupied as ideal for their settlement. These tribes possessed immense flocks and this land was perfect for grazing. They suggested to Moshe that they forfeit their portion in the territory west of the Jordan in exchange for the land they currently occupied.

Upon hearing this request, Moshe sternly chastised these shevatim. He reminded them how the timidity of the previous generation had led to its demise. That generation lacked the courage to follow Hashem into the land and conquer it. The generation was condemned to wander in the wilderness for forty years and denied entry into the promised land. Now, a more courageous and confident generation was beckoned to enter and conquer its legacy beyond the Jordan. However, the suggestion that these tribes now presented was sure to undermine this courage and confidence. When the nation learned that two of its shevatim were not prepared to cross the Jordan and conquer the nations of Cana'an, their confidence would be severely shaken. They might repeat the sin of their fathers and refuse to proceed – thereby condemning yet another generation to death and destruction.

These shevatim understood Moshe's concern and responded responsibly. They suggested that they lead the nation across the Jordan and form the vanguard of the conquering army. They would battle alongside their brothers. Only after the other tribes possessed their own portions in the land west of the Jordan would they return to the eastern bank and settle the territory they now sought.

And Moshe commanded Elazar the Kohen and Yehoshua bin Nun and the leadership of the tribes of Bnai Yisrael in their regard. And Moshe said to them: If the children of Gad and Reuven pass over the Jordan with you – all armed for war – before Hashem, and the land is captured before you, then you should give to them the Land of Gilad as a possession. (BeMidbar 32:28-29)

And to the people of Reuven, Gad and half of the tribe of Menashe Yehoshua said: Remember that which Moshe the servant of Hashem commanded you saying, "Hashem your G-d has relieved you and given you this land. Your wives, children, and cattle should dwell in the land that Moshe gave you across the Jordan. And you will pass over armed before your brothers – every mighty warrior – and assist them. (Sefer Yehoshua 1:12-14)

2. Moshe's charge to the next generation to observe and enforce the agreement

Moshe accepted this offer. However, he would not pass over the Jordan with the nation and could not expect to enforce the terms of the agreement. He convened the nation's leadership – Yehoshua, Elazar the Kohen and the heads of the shevatim. He communicated to them the agreement that had been reached and charged all parties to observe the terms of the agreement and its conditions.

This leadership was scrupulous in its observance of the agreement reached between Moshe and the shevatim of Reuven and Gad. Sefer Yehoshua, the first of the books of the Prophets, continues the account of the conquest of the Land of Israel. It opens with a description of Yehoshua's first measures as the leader of the nation. Virtually his first act was to reaffirm with Reuven and Gad the agreement reached between them and Moshe. However, the inclusion of the account of this reaffirmation in the Navi is a little odd.

Sefer Yehoshua deals with the conquest of the Land of Israel by the nation led by Yehoshua. The Navi describes the miracles that accompanied this conquest, and the challenges that were faced by the nation and its leadership in fulfilling their destiny. The Navi opens with Yehoshua's assumption of leadership responsibility and Hashem's charge to him. It continues with Yehoshua's instructions to the people to prepare themselves to cross the Jordan and initiate the conquest. Then suddenly, the Navi describes Yehoshua's discussion with the shevatim of Reuven and Gad. Insertion of this discussion breaks the rhythm and tempo of the text. The text is describing a moment of enormous historical import. Moshe's successor is charged by Hashem to take over leadership of the nation. He prepares the nation to meet its destiny and then suddenly the text interrupts to describe Yehoshua's review of a recent agreement between Moshe and the shevatim of Reuven and Gad – in all its details.

3. The relationship between Moshe and Yehoshua

One simple explanation is that the Navi is communicating that Yehoshua was not a new leader who redirected the nation along a path that he selected. Instead, Yehoshua continued the mission that Moshe initiated. The inclusion of Yehoshua's review of Moshe's agreement with the shevatim of Reuven and Gad – one of Moshe's final acts – demonstrates and announces that Yehoshua is Moshe's successor both as leader and as guardian of the mission assigned to Moshe by Hashem.

An alternative explanation for the composition of Sefer Yehoshua's opening passages is suggested by a fascinating comment of Malbim. In order to undertand Malbim's insight, an introduction is required.

Do not be like your fathers to whom the ancient prophets called saying: Thus says Hashem, Lord of Hosts, "Repent now from your evil ways and from your evil actions." "And they did not listen or pay attention to me" says Hashem. Where are your fathers? And will the prophets live forever? (Sefer Zecharya 1:4-5)

4. The close of the era of the prophets

Zecharya was one of the final prophets. He lived during the period of the nation's restoration to the Land of Israel that followed the first exile and the destruction of the first Bait HaMikdash. Zecharya was charged with the difficult task of encouraging the exiles to return to the Land of Israel and to repent from the behaviors that had occasioned their parents' exile and suffering. In the opening chapter of Sefer Zecharya, he urges the people to consider the experiences of their parents and the lesson expressed in those experiences. They had rejected the repeated messages of the prophets. They had stubbornly refused to repent. Their obstinate attitude led to their downfall, exile, and terrible suffering. He admonishes the people to consider, "Where are your fathers?" In other words, consider their ill-chosen actions and the consequences. However, Zecharya then adds another admonition, "Will the prophets live forever?"

This is a rather enigmatic question! What point is Zecharya making? The commentators differ in their interpretations. However, Malbim offers a simple explanation. Zecharya is bidding the nation farewell – on his own behalf and on behalf of the institution of prophecy. He is announcing that the era of the prophets has come to an end. All that is to be said by the prophets has been said. The prophets have delivered their warnings. Their admonitions were ignored and the foretold consequences came to pass. Now, it is the nation's responsibility to heed their often repeated message – return to Hashem.[26]

5. The mission of the prophets

Malbim is suggesting a solution to an oft asked question. The period of the prophets extended through the period of the first exile and then came to a conclusion. Latter generations were not admonished by their own prophets. Why did era of the prophets come to a sudden and absolute conclusion?

Malbim's response is that the prophets shared a primary mission. This mission was to communicate to and impress upon the nation that its fate is a direct consequence of its moral, ethical, and religious behavior. The geopolitical or economic forces that may drive the fates of other nations are not relevant to the destiny of Bnai Yisrael. The destiny of Bnai Yisrael is the product of providence and that providence is a response to the nation's behaviors and values.[27] Malbim is explaining that the prophets taught this lesson through constantly describing the events and experiences in the nation's life as the fulfillment of the promises outlined in the Torah.

The Books of the Prophets are the recorded account of the prophets' mission. Sefer Yehoshua begins this narrative. It describes the fulfillment of the historic promise made to the

---

[26] Rabbaynu Meir Libush (Malbim), *Commentary on Sefer Zecharya* 1:5.

[27] The intention here is not to imply that the Jewish people can or should disregard geopolitical and economic forces. Every human being is expected to care for himself and act responsibly. The same principle applies to the Jewish nation. We are not permitted to be idle in the face of danger and await Divine intervention. However, we must realize that the success of our efforts to secure our future is ultimately determined by providence.

patriarchs and recorded in the Torah that their descendants would possess the Land of Israel. This narrative continues through the last of the Books of the Prophets. Each of the books demonstrates the relationship between contemporary events and the promises of the Torah.

6. Sefer Yehoshua begins the account of the unfolding of the Torah's promises

Malbim's insight provides a possible alternative explanation for the opening of Sefer Yehoshua. The reference in the opening passages to Moshe's agreement with the shevatim of Reuven and Gad demonstrates that the Sefer is a continuation of the narrative of the Torah. It announces that the Navi begins at the exact point at which the Torah's account ended. The Torah's account outlined the blueprint for Bnai Yisrael's destiny. The Books of the Prophets describe the unfolding and fulfillment of that destiny. Reference to this event suggests the textual continuity between the Torah and the Prophets. The Torah's account of Moshe's final days serves as a segue linking the final episodes of the Torah to the opening scenes of the Navi.

And Hashem spoke to Moshe saying, "Command Bnai Yisrael and say to them: When you come into the Land of Cana'an, this is the land that will be yours as a portion – the Land of Canan'an and its boundaries." (BeMidbar 34:1-2)

1. The long journey described in Sefer BeMidbar

Parshat Massey concludes Sefer BeMidbar. It brings to a close the discussion of Bnai Yisrael's travels in the wilderness. The people entered this wilderness with anticipation, hopes, and dreams. They understood that Moshe would lead them back to the land of their forefathers. They would conquer the Land of Canaan and transform it into the promised Land of Israel. Moshe had described to them the beauty of the land and its wonderful fertility. They looked forward to an end of centuries of suffering and toil on behalf of cruel masters. They envisioned fashioning their own future under the shadow of Hashem.

But, Sefer BeMidbar's narrative continues to describe the shattering of this beautiful, inspiring vision. It tells the story of a squandered opportunity. Rather than seizing the opportunity to follow the cloud of Hashem into the land and to posses it through a swift, conclusive conquest, the nation was overwhelmed by fear and insecurity. The people refused to undertake the conquest. They were punished severely. They were condemned to wander for forty years in the barren wilderness. The generation that rejected the wonderful legacy of the Land of Israel would not enjoy its riches. Only their children – the next generation – would be granted the opportunity to possess the land promised to their patriarchs.

The final chapters of Sefer BeMidbar introduce the new generation that will be led into the Land of Israel and posses it. Parshat Chukat describes the conquest of the land bordering the eastern bank of the Jordan River. Parshat Pinchas describes the census taken of the nation. This census was conducted in anticipation of the possession of the land. The land will be apportioned among the *shevatim* – the tribes – and the families within the tribes based upon their numbers. Larger tribes and families will receive larger portions of the land.

In Parshat Massey the boundaries of the Land of Israel are defined. Further instructions are given to Moshe for the apportionment of the land among the *shevatim* – the tribes.

Sefer BeMidbar ends with the nations encamped on the eastern side of the Jordan River. The nation is prepared to embark upon the long awaited conquest of the land.

2. The sanctity of the Land of Israel and its meaning

The Land of Israel is endowed with sanctity. This sanctity is not an abstract or esoteric concept. It has concrete and practical implications. Many *mitzvot* of the Torah are tied to the Land of Israel and can only be observed upon the land that has this sanctity. For example, there are many commandments related to the agricultural cycle. When a field is harvested, a portion must be left to the poor. The Torah requires observance of this *mitzvah* in the Land of Israel and not in land that does not have the sanctity of the Land of Israel. *Shemitah* is only observed in the land endowed with the sanctity of the Land of Israel.

3. The basis of the land's sanctity

However, this sanctity is not bestowed upon all of the land that is within the borders described in the *parasha*. Instead, the land only became sanctified with its conquest. In other words, the Land that Yehoshua and the people conquered became endowed with sanctity. Any portion of the land – even if it were within the borders described by the Torah – did not acquire sanctity if it was not included in the conquest.

Maimonides explains that this sanctity was not permanent. It was created through conquest, and therefore, it could not survive the exile of the Bnai Yisrael from the land. When the people were forced into their first exile, the sanctity of the land which was dependent upon their conquest was annulled. Those *mitzvot* that are tied to this sanctity could no longer be fulfilled by the remnant of the people that remained in the Land of Israel. Seventy years later, the nation returned to the land. They came as subjects of a foreign nation and not as conquerors. They took possession of the land but not as sovereign rulers. Nonetheless, the land was again endowed with sanctity. But this sanctity was not founded upon conquest. It was founded upon the possession of the land and its settlement. This sanctity is permanent and continues to this day. Subsequent exile did not terminate it. We made the land ours – not though conquest –but by binding ourselves to it though its settlement and development.[28]

In short, the sanctity of the land is not a consequence of its inclusion within the borders described in the Torah. Sanctity was initially created through conquest and permanently renewed through the possession and settlement of the land. Do these boundaries have any role?

4. Living in the land and possessing the land

Let us first consider a different issue. Are we still obligated to posses the Land of Israel or is it adequate for a person to live in the land? We now have the opportunity to live in the State of Israel. The State of Israel represents the realization of an ancient dream that remained alive and vibrant throughout centuries of exile – the restoration of Jewish sovereignty in the land of our forefathers and ancestors. From the perspective of the Torah is there a distinction between living in Israel as a Jewish State and living in Israel during the time of Ottoman rule? Is there a difference between living in Israel today or during the British mandate?

Maimonides' treatment of this issue suggests that we have an obligation to live in Israel and that this obligation is very serious. Quoting the Sages, he compares one who lives outside of the Land of Israel to one who adopts idolatry. However, it is not clear from Maimonides' treatment of this obligation that he distinguishes between living in the land when it is under Jewish sovereignty or when it is controlled by of some other nation.[29]

---

[28] Rabbaynu Moshe ben Maimon (Rambam) *Mishne Torah*, Hilchot Terumot 1:2-5.

In contrast, Nachmanides acknowledges that there is an obligation to live in the Land of Israel. However, he explains that this obligation is subsumed within the commandment to take possession of the land and to assert our authority over it. According to Nachmanides this commandment has two essential components. First, we are obligated to posses the land and to settle it. Second, we are forbidden to allow any other nation to posses it or to allow the land to be desolate.[30]

According to Nachmanides, there is a fundamental difference between living in the Land of Israel under Ottoman control, or during the time of the mandate, and the opportunity that we have today. We do not fully observe the Torah's commandment by simply living in the land. The commandment requires that we have control and sovereignty over the land and that we do not allow some other nation to rule over it.

5. The significance of the boundaries described in the Torah

Now let us return to the original question. What is the significance of the boundaries outlined in the Torah? As we have explained, the boundaries do not define the sanctity of the land. According to Nachmanides these boundaries are very important. They define the land that we are required to posses and not leave in the control of another nation or people.

6. Personal reflections

My wife Shirley and I recently returned from Israel. During our two weeks in Israel, Arabs rioted in East Jerusalem and rockets pounded Israel from the Negev to Haifa. A number of people expressed surprise that we did not curtail our trip and return to the safety of the United States. We cannot claim uncommon bravery. Either as a result of our ignorance, or our confidence in the defense resources of the State of Israel, we felt safe. However, we also felt an obligation to remain in Israel. We explained that we had no intention of shortening our trip. A person does not leave one's home because a trespasser claims it as his. Staying in Israel was our way of expressing the message of Nachmanides. The Land of Israel is ours and no other nation may be allowed to seize it from us. The battle that has come upon us is not only about the security of our people. It is about our right and our divine duty to live in and posses the Land of Israel.

These are the commandments and regulations that Hashem commanded Bnai Yisrael through Moshe on the Plains of Moav, on the Yardain (Jordan River) opposite Yericho. (BeMidbar 36:13)

These are the commandments that Hashem commanded Moshe for Bnai Israel at Mount Sinai. (VaYikra 27:34)

The Role of Prophecy in Deciding the Law

1. The similar endings of Sefer VaYikra and Sefer BeMidbar

This first of the above passages is the final passage in Sefer BeMidbar. The passage is very similar to the second passage which is the final passage in Sefer VaYikra. The passage in

---

[29] Rabbaynu Moshe ben Maimon (Rambam) *Mishne Torah*, Hilchot Melachim 5:12.
[30] Rabbaynu Moshe ben Nachman (Ramban), *Critique on Maimonides' Sefer HaMitzvot* —
Positive Commands that Maimonides Neglected to Include.

Sefer VaYikra is the source of an important lesson. The Sages explain that the passage teaches us that a prophet is not authorized to add to the commandments of the Torah. Targum Yonatan Ben Uziel actually includes this lesson in his rendering of the passage. He renders the passage: These are the commandments that Hashem commanded Moshe and it is not possible to create within them any new element etc. Apparently, he maintains that the phrase "these are the laws" indicates that *these alone* are the laws and that no new laws can be attributed to revelation.

It is not clear why Sefer BeMidbar requires a similar closing. However, the comments of Malbim may be relevant to this issue. He explains that the passage in the end of Sefer BeMidbar refers to two categories of laws – *mitzvot* and *mishpatim* – that were taught to Bnai Yisrael on the Plains of Moav. Malbim explains that "*mitzvot*" refers to the various commandments that relate to our relationship with Hashem. "*Mishpatim*" refers to laws that govern our relationships with one another. In addition to the commandments that Moshe taught Bnai Yisrael when he descended from Sinai, Moshe expounded various laws of these two types on the Plains of Moav. Malbim further explains that our Sages dispute the origin of the laws taught to the people on the Plains of Moav. All of the authorities agree that these laws are rooted in the commandments that Moshe received at Sinai. However, they disagree over whether Moshe received the details related on the Plains of Moav at Sinai or whether he received the details on the Plains of Moav. However, it seems clear that Moshe did not teach these laws to the nation until they camped on the Plains of Moav, poised to enter the Land of Israel.

These comments suggest an explanation for why this passage is repeated at the end of Sefer BeMidbar. The passage at the end of Sefer VaYikra asserts that no prophet can add commandments or alter those that were revealed at Sinai. However, the laws that were expounded by Moshe on the Plains of Moav were not revealed to the nation at Sinai. They were first explained to the nation on the Plains of Moav. Therefore, the Torah explains that also these laws are not subject to a prophet's amendment or nullification.

In short, the message that emerges from these two passages is that the Torah is composed exclusively of the commandments that Moshe taught the nation – at Sinai or on the Plains of Moav. Hashem will not add to it or nullify any of its commandments. Any prophet claiming to have received a prophecy that alters the Torah is to be deemed an imposter and liar. This does not mean that the Sages are not entitled to interpret the Torah and to expound on its message. They have this authority. However, they must rely upon their own human knowledge and wisdom. They also have limited authority to create decrees, new institutions, and establish practices. But they may not claim that these new laws and practices are part of the Torah revealed at Sinai. They must identify these new laws as their own enactments and creations. They may not interpret the Torah or legislate on the basis of prophecy.

For the commandment that I command you today is not hidden from you and it is not distant from you. It is not in the heavens and not across the seas that you should say, "Who will cross the seas for us and take it for us and make it heard to us and we will perform it." (Devarim 30:12-13)

2. The Torah does not reside in the heavens

There is an additional passage in Sefer Devarim that is understood to communicate a similar message. Moshe exhorts Bnai Yisrael to observe the commandments. He tells them that the Torah is not in the heavens. The Sages of the Talmud explain that the message of this passage is that questions of *halachah* cannot be decided by referring them to the heavens. We cannot resort to prophesy to resolve such questions. Instead, we must rely upon our own wisdom and knowledge. In a famous discussion in the Talmud the Sages assert that even were we to receive an indication from the heavens – a miraculous wonder or a prophecy – regarding the proper solution to some halachic issue, the heavenly message is to be ignored and the issue must be decided on the basis of valid halachic debate and analysis.

This raises an interesting question. Apparently, the Talmud relies on two different passages for the identical message. The passages at the end of Sefer VaYikra and Sefer BeMidbar indicate that a prophecy cannot be used to amend or nullify any aspect of the Torah. This seems to be identical to the message of the passage from Sefer Devarim. Why are both sources required?

3. The two restrictions upon the prophet

Rav Yitzchak Zev Soloveitchik discusses this issue and explains that the passages deal with very different issues. The passages ending Sefer VaYikra and Sefer BeMidbar communicate that prophecy cannot add or subtract from the Torah. No new commandment can be added and no existing commandment can be revoked. The passage in Sefer Devarim is dealing with a different issue. It is discussing the appropriateness of deciding an issue in *halachah* based upon Divine messages. In such an instance the prophet is not adding or subtracting to the commandments. The prophet is seeking to resolve a difficulty within the detailed laws of the commandment based upon heavenly intervention.

An example will help illustrate this distinction. If a prophet were to suggest that Hashem no longer wishes for us to observe the Shabbat or that Hashem has commanded us to observe Shabbat for an additional day of the week, then he would violate the prohibition of adding or subtracting from the Torah's *mitzvot*. This is the prohibition associated with the passages at the end of Sefer VaYikra and Sefer BeMidbar. But what if the prophet merely claims that he received a prophecy regarding the number of meters in the Torah's measurement of a cubit. He is not claiming to have received a new commandment or to have received a message cancelling a *mitzvah*. He is merely saying that he has received a communication from Hashem resolving an issue debated among the authorities. He has not violated the prohibition derived from the final passages of Sefer VaYikra and Sefer BeMidbar. However, he has suggested a resolution of a problem in *halachah* based upon heavenly communication. His ruling will be discounted because of the restriction in Sefer Devarim. The Sages are charged with the responsibility of resolving problems in *halachah*. We cannot resort to signs or other communications from heaven.

Rav Soloveitchik's explanation is supported by Maimonides' treatment of the issue. In the opening chapters of his code – the Mishne Torah – Maimonides explains that prophecy may not be used to add to or subtract from the commandments of the Torah. In order to fully appreciate Maimonides' message it is helpful to consider its context. Maimonides begins the chapter by explaining that the Torah tells us that its commandments are permanent. They were reveled to Bnai Yisrael through Moshe for all generations. After stating this principle, Maimonides explains that any prophet attempting to alter the Torah is known to be false because he is contradicting the Torah itself – as revealed to us by Moshe. Maimonides then discusses other laws regarding the prophet. After that discussion he returns to the prophet's role in establishing Torah laws and explains that the prophet cannot decide issues of *halachah*. It is interesting that Maimonides divides into two sections his discussion of the prophet's exclusion from any role in establishing Torah laws. However, according to Rav Soloveitchik this is

238

completely understandable. Maimonides is dealing with two separate and distinct issues. First, he deals with the issue of creating new laws or nullifying laws based upon prophecy. Such prophecies are dismissed based upon the passages at the end of Sefer VaYikra and Sefer BeMidbar. Only later does Maimonides discuss the issue of resorting to heavenly arbitrations regarding questions that arise within the laws of the *mitzvot*. Relying on heavenly communication for such issues is inappropriate based upon the passage in Sefer Devarim.

4. A confusing discussion in the Talmud and its resolution

There is a mysterious discussion in Tractate Temurah regarding this issue. The Talmud explains that during the period that the nation mourned the death of Moshe 3,000 laws were forgotten. The nation turned to its new leader – Yehoshua – and asked him to restore the laws through prophecy. He responded that he could not do this and referred to the passage in Sefer Devarim. A latter generation appealed to the prophet Shmuel to restore these laws through prophecy and he refused. However, he based his response on the passages at the end of Sefer VaYikra and Sefer BeMidbar. Why did these two prophets refer to different passages in their responses?

Maharsha offers an interesting response to this question. He explains that Yehoshua and Shmuel were presented the same request. However, each faced different issues in determining their responses. Yehoshua had learned the entire Torah from Moshe. He had known all of its laws. However, he had forgotten a portion. The issue he faced was whether he could resort to prophecy in order to restore to himself information he had forgotten. If granted a response from Hashem, the prophecy would not be an addition to the Torah; it would be the restoration of the Torah that he had received from Moshe and forgotten. The passages at the end of Sefer VaYikra and Sefer BeMidbar were not relevant to this issue. Nonetheless, Yehoshua refused the request because of the passage in Sefer Devarim. Once given to Bnai Yisrael through Moshe, the Torah became our responsibility. The role of prophecy in *halachah* ended with Moshe.

When the same question was presented to Shmuel the situation had changed. Shmuel and his generation had not received the Torah from Moshe. The Torah they had received from their parents did not include the laws that were long ago lost. For Shmuel, these laws would be new and an addition to the Torah. Therefore, Shmuel responded that prophecy cannot add or subtract from the Torah and he referred to the passages ending Sefer VaYikra and BeMidbar.

Massay

"These are the journeys of Bnai Yisrael that went out from Egypt in their groups through Moshe and Ahron." (BeMidbar 33:1)

The final *parasha* of Sefer BeMidbar reviews the travels of Bnai Yisrael in the wilderness. The commentaries are concerned with the inclusion of this material in the Torah. The Torah is written very concisely. The recounting of the journeys in the wilderness seems superfluous.

Rashi explains that these journeys are recounted in order to communicate a key aspect of the wilderness experience. The Almighty had decreed that the nation should spend forty years wandering in the wilderness. Hashem did not constantly move Bnai Yisrael from one location to the next. The nation only traveled forty-two times during the forty years.[1]

This is a fitting conclusion for Sefer BeMidbar. The *sefer* recounts the changing of the relationship between the Almighty and His nation. This change was brought about by the nation's refusal to enter the land of Israel. Hashem decreed that Bnai Yisrael should wander in the wilderness for forty years. According to Rashi, these passages capture the nature of this decree.

Maimonides offers an alternative explanation for the description of the various journeys. He explains that the wilderness experience involved a great miracle. The nation was sustained for forty years in a land of complete desolation. The Almighty provided Bnai Yisrael with water, food and all other needs. The generation that experienced these wanderings could recognize the miracle of survival. However, future generations would not have the benefit of experiencing the forty years of wandering. These future generations might not appreciate the extent of this miracle. They might assume that the nation traveled near populated areas. They might believe that the path taken by Bnai Yisrael avoided arid areas. The Torah provides a detailed description of the journey. All of the stations at which the nation camped are enumerated. This route does not pass through populated areas. The path described in the *parasha* leads through an arid, desolate wilderness. With this information the reader can appreciate the miracles required for Bnai Yisrael's survival during these forty years.[2]

And you will drive out the dwellers of the land from before you. You should destroy their places of worship. You shall destroy their molten images, and all their high places you should destroy. (BeMidbar 33:52)

Clarifying Values, Part 2

The last edition of "Thoughts" discussed children who are abandoning observance. The discussion focused on the impact of our environment. The conclusion was that one must properly shape one's environment and the environment of one's children. This edition will continue the discussion. The focus will be on education. How can their education prepare our children for challenges to their commitment? How can their education prepare them for the doubts they may develop? How do we prepare them for the attacks upon the Torah and religion that they will inevitably encounter?

---

[1] Rabbaynu Shlomo ben Yitzchak (Rashi), *Commentary on Sefer BeMidbar* 33:1.
[2] Rabbaynu Moshe ben Maimon (Rambam) *Moreh Nevuchim*, volume 3, chapter 50.

1. Fundamentalism

Hashem directs Moshe to tell Bnai Yisrael that they will take possession of the Land of Israel. They are to drive out the idolators who dwell there. They are to destroy the idols in the land and the places in which they are worshiped.[3] We are required to remove from the land all elements of idolatry.

In 2015 ISIS seized control of Palmyra in Syria. Palmyra is the site of ancient temples and sculptures. It is designated as a World Heritage Site. ISIS demolished various sculptures and temples. Their destruction of these unreplaceable artifacts was decried by much of the world.

ISIS's actions were not vandalism. Its actions were motivated by religious doctrine. Islam condemns polytheism. Idols and temples of idolatry must be destroyed.

Soon after the destruction of these artifacts was reported, I was asked an important question. Much of the world has condemned ISIS for the destruction of these artifacts. But how should we, observant Jews, regard its actions? Is there a difference between their treatment of idolatry and the expectations that the Torah places upon us in the above passage?

This is one type of question for which our children must be prepared. We must demonstrate to them that there is a difference between the Torah's imperatives – especially those that seem inconsistent with contemporary liberal values – and radical fundamentalism. This preparation begins with how we present the Torah.

2. Torah as an objective truth

Let us begin our exploration with a fundamental question. Why do we believe in Hashem or the authenticity of the Torah? The popular perspective is that belief in Hashem and His Torah is the natural state of a healthy Jew. One who is not influenced by external forces will naturally embrace belief. One believes because it is one's nature to believe.[4] For many people, this may be an adequate basis for observance. However, it is also very dangerous!

This approach renders Judaism and Torah observance into a subjective choice. Hashem exists because one feels He exists. The Torah is true because it feels true. The message is that our faith has no basis other than one's subjective feelings. This provides the perfect excuse for the abandonment of observance. Belief in the Torah or its rejection is a personal choice. One choice is not more valid than the other.

But guard yourself and very intensely guard yourself lest you forget the things that your eyes saw and lest they turn from your heart all the days of your life. And make them known to your children and grandchildren – The day that you stood before Hashem, your L-rd, at Chorev, when Hashem said to me, "Assemble the nation and I will cause them to hear My words. [This is so that] they will learn to fear Me all the days that they live in the land and their children will learn. (Devarim 4:9-10)

---

[3] Bnai Yisrael is required to sue for peace before resorting to battle. We may not allow idolatry in the land. Also, we are not permitted to coerce conversion to Judaism. Those willing to abandon idolatry are permitted to remain in the land. Those who refuse are permitted to leave the land unharassed.

[4] For an extensive discussion of this issue see: "Dialogue for Torah Issues & Ideas", No. 7, Summer 5777/2017.

3. Teaching Revelation

What is the alternative? It has two components. The first component is to follow the directive of the Torah. In the above passages, we are told to not forget the Sinai revelation. We are to make it known to our children and grandchildren. Nachmanides – Ramban – explains that this is a commandment. We are required to understand that Revelation is not a mere tradition. We must establish for ourselves that it as a historical fact.[5] The proof of the historical factuality of the Sinai Revelation is discussed by Rabbaynu Yehudah HaLeyve in his Kuzari and by Rabbaynu Aharon HaLeyve in his introduction to Sefer HaChinuch.[6] Ramban makes it clear that we are required to study and master this argument and to make sure that it is taught to our children. Observing this commandment immediately replaces subjective belief with an objective foundation for Torah and observance.

And observe [them] and perform [them] for this is your wisdom and understanding in the eyes of the nations that will hear [of] these statutes and they will say, "Surely, this is a wise and understanding nation – this great nation. (Devarim 4:6)

4. Torah makes sense

The second component of our children's education is expressed in the above passage. We must demonstrate to them that the Torah is a system of wisdom. We must consistently present the Torah as sensible and reasonable. Inevitably, we will encounter material we cannot explain. We should not offer implausible or fantastic explanations. We should demonstrate humility, acknowledge the limits of our understanding, and admire the mystery of this element of the Torah.[7]

Unfortunately, sometimes the Torah is not taught in this manner. Difficult portions of the Torah or comments of the Sages are defended with explanations that are not rational. Halachah is also sometimes taught superficially. Its rulings seem arbitrary and its assumptions unrealistic. If our children perceive the Torah as an irrational and unreasonable set of religious doctrines and commandments, they have a ready rationale for abandoning it. When confronted with fundamental questions or confused by personal conflict they may seize upon this rationale.[8]

---

[5] Rabbaynu Moshe ben Nachman (Ramban), Critique on Maimonides' Sefer HaMitzvot -- Negative Commands that Maimonides Neglected to Include.

[6] These discussions are brief. For a more detailed development of the argument see: Lawrence Kelemen, Permission to Receive or Rav Yisrael Chait, "Torah from Sinai" available athttp://www.ybt.org/essays/rchait/torahsinai.html.

[7] It is important for a teacher to acknowledge to students the limits of his/her understanding. A scientist expects to encounter issues that s/he cannot comprehend. Aspects of the natural world defy human understanding. Hashem's Torah should not be presented as less profound than His natural world.

[8] Once, I listened to a presentation from a young man who had studied in a yeshiva for many years and remained engaged in serious Torah study. The topic was theological. The presentation made little sense. After the presentation, I asked the young man, "Is this the same reasoning you use in studying Talmud or halachah?"
He assured me that it was not. He explained, "The study of Talmud and halachah, requires precise reasoning."
I asked, "Why do some areas of Torah require precise reasoning and others do not?"

5. Setting priorities

In addition to these two components of our children's education, there is another issue that requires our attention. We need to prioritize. What is the most important outcome we hope our children to achieve through their education? Is our highest priority that our children be committed to Torah observance? Is our highest priority that they gain admission to a prestigious university? How we answer this question and how we communicate our position to our children will have an enormous impact on their attitudes. If we succeed in impressing upon them that Torah study and observance are the primary goals of their education, then we can hope that they will apply themselves to Torah study, come to appreciate the wisdom of the Torah, and move closer to a lifetime of commitment. If our children conclude that the primary goal of their education is to gain admission to the finest university, then they will distribute their energies and divide their attention accordingly. Torah studies will be an imposed burden that must be endured. Their attention and their focus will be on those studies and activities that most contribute to securing that admission.[9]

6. Closing vignette

A set of parents asked me how to respond to their teenage children who were moving away from observance. In the course of our discussion, I asked these parents – both had become observant as adults – whether they had shared with their children their reason for adopting an observant lifestyle. The parents responded that they had not. I suggested that their experience might be meaningful to their children and that they should consider sharing it.

I was encouraging dialogue between parents and children. The Torah provides us with a wonderful lifestyle. Sometimes, we need to remind ourselves how Torah observance has impacted and enriched our lives. Also, we need to share our experiences with our children.

Are the attitudes of a Torah observant person different from those of ISIS? Discussion of that question with our children is an excellent opportunity to apply the educational model discussed above.[10,11]

He responded, "We cannot understand some areas. They are not accessible to human reasoning." This is a dangerous assertion to make to our children.

[9] In recent years the impact of this issue has increased. The competition for acceptance into the most prestigious universities is intense. Students determined to be accepted sometimes allow this consideration to guide many of their decisions. The courses they take in high school, their athletics and extra-curriculars, and even their summer plans are decided based on how these choices will look on their college application. These students are not likely to give Torah studies the same attention as their secular studies. They may give them very little attention.

[10] How should we deal with belief in Hashem? Should we provide students with proof of His existence? We need to be prepared to respond to the student who has doubts. We will not convince this student of Hashem's existence by asserting that this is one our beliefs as Torah committed Jews. Rav Yehudah HaLeyve contends that through proving the historical factuality of Divine Revelation we implicitly establish that there is a Divine Being Who revealed the Torah. Some students may need more direct evidence. Teachers and parents must be prepared for these students. For an introduction to this discussion see: Rabbi Netanel Wiederblank, "Jewish Action" Vol. 79, No. 4, Summer 5779/2019, "The State of Orthodox Belief" pp 59-60.

[11] Thank you to Rabbi Chaim Weiss for his review of much of this material and his excellent

"Command Bnai Yisrael and say to them, "When you come to the land of Canaan, this is the land within the borders of the land of Canaan that shall be your hereditary territory." (BeMidbar 34:2)

Hashem describes to Moshe the borders of the land of Israel. This land will be divided into portions and distributed among the tribes. Rashi explains that these boundaries are very important in *halacha*. Various *mitzvot* only apply in the land of Israel. Therefore, any territory outside of the borders is exempt from these commandments.[12]

It must be noted this description of the boundaries indicates that the eastern border is the Jordan River. This is difficult to explain. The tribes of Reuven, Gad, and half of the tribe of Menashe settled in the territory conquered from Sichon and Og. In general, any land conquered by the nation is considered, in *halacha*, to be part of the land of Israel.[13] This land was situated on the eastern side of the Jordan. The proper eastern border should be the eastern boundary of this territory!

Rav Moshe Feinstein *Ztl* explains that there is a basic difference between the land of Israel west of the Jordan and the territory to the east. The land to the west was promised to Avraham and the forefathers. It was destined to be conquered and become the land of Israel. The land of Sichon and Og was not included in this covenant. It was not predetermined that this land should become part of the land of Israel.[14]

This distinction can provide a possible answer to our question. Moshe had awarded the land of Sichon and Og to Reuven, Gad, and half of Menashe. However, he had stipulated a condition. This land would become their portion after they had conquered the territory west of the Jordan. Moshe had required that first the land of the covenant must be captured. Then, this additional land could become part of the land of Israel. The sanctity of the land of Sichon and Og was suspended until the land of the covenant was possessed.

Now, the description of the boundaries can be explained. Hashem specifically described the borders of the land of the covenant. This is the land that must first be sanctified. Once this is accomplished, the land of Sichon and Og can be possessed and sanctified.

And Hashem spoke to Moshe saying: Command Bnai Yisrael and say to them, "Behold, you come to the Land of Cana'an. This is the land that shall fall to you as a legacy – the Land of Cana'an according to its borders." (BeMidbar 34:1-2)

The True Meaning of Exile

1. The theme of the parasha

Parshat Massay deals primarily with issues related to the forthcoming conquest of the Land of Israel. In this parasha, the Torah admonishes Bnai Yisrael to remove all remnants of idolatry from the land and to not enter into inappropriate treaties with the land's inhabitants. It

---

suggestions.
[12] Rabbaynu Shlomo ben Yitzchak (Rashi), *Commentary on Sefer BeMidbar* 34:2
[13] Rabbaynu Moshe ben Maimon (Rambam) *Mishne Torah*, Hilchot Terumot 1:2.
[14] Rav Moshe Feinstein, *Derash Moshe*, Sefer BeMidbar 32:29.

describes the boundaries of the land. A brief set of directions is provided for dividing the land among the tribes. Shevet Leyve – the tribe of Leyve – is not to receive an equal portion with the other tribes. Instead, the tribes are commanded to set aside cities for members of Shevet Leyve within their individual territories. Also, cities of refuge are to be designated. A person who takes a life unintentionally is to be exiled to one of these cities. The parasha ends with a directive requiring a woman who has inherited a portion of Land of Israel from her father to marry within her own shevet – tribe. This marriage restriction assures that the land she inherited from her father will remain within the tribe.

The above passages introduce the Torah's description of the boundaries of the Land of Israel. The description begins with the southeast corner and proceeds clockwise.

And this shall be your north border: from the Great Sea you should turn your line unto Mount Hor. From Mount Hor you shall turn a line unto the entrance to Hamat; and its extension should be to Tzedad. And the border shall proceed to Ziphron, and its extension to Chatzar-enan. This shall be your north border. (BeMidbar 34:7-9, according to Rashi)

And this shall be your north border: from the Great Sea you should set as your boundary Mount Hor. From Mount Hor you shall extend the boundary to the entrance to Hamat; and its extension should be to Tzedad. And the border shall directly proceed to Ziphron, and its extension to Chatzar-enan. This shall be your north border. (BeMidbar 34:7-9, according to Rashbam)

2. Two interpretations of the Torah's description of the borders of the Land of Israel

The above passages describe the northern border of the Land of Israel. The passages are first translated in conformity to Rashi's understanding of their meaning.[15] The passages explain that the western border which is the Great Sea – the Mediterranean – proceeds north to Mount Hor. The border turns east from Mount Hor and proceeds eastward toward the entrance to Hamat. The northern border passes through Tzedad and Ziphron and reaches its eastern extreme at Chatzar-enan. According to this translation, the border is described as a continuous line. The passages describe this line as extending along the length of the Great Sea until Mount Hor, then turning eastward and extending until Chatzar-enan before turning south to form the eastern border. Considered in their totality, the Torah's description is of a closed figure surrounding the territory of the Land of Israel.

The second translation of the passages is suggested by Rashbam.[16] According to his translation, the Torah describes the northern border from its western terminus to its eastern terminus. It does not describe the northern border as a part of a continuous border. Rashbam actually emphasizes this distinction between his understanding of the Torah's description of the borders and Rashi's interpretation. Rashbam explains that the Torah describes the borders as four distinct boundaries.[17]

In short, according to Rashi, the Torah describes the border as a continuous line forming a closed figure. It describes the location of this border line on all sides of the Land of Israel. Rashbam does not agree that the border is described as a continuous line. Instead, he suggests

---

[15] Rabbaynu Shlomo ben Yitzchak (Rashi), Commentary on Sefer BeMidbar 34:7.

[16] Rabbaynu Shemuel ben Meir (Rashbam) Commentary on Sefer BeMidbar 34:7.

[17] Rabbaynu Shemuel ben Meir (Rashbam) Commentary on Sefer BeMidbar 34:2.

that the Torah describes four discrete boundaries – one boundary for each direction. This seems like an odd dispute. What is its basis?

And your southern side will be from the Wilderness of Tzin adjacent to Edon. And your southern border will be from the edge of the Salt Sea on the east. And the border will bend from the south toward Ma'alai Akrabim and pass toward Tzin. And its extension will be to the south – to Kadesh Barnea. And it will continue to Chatzar Adar and pass toward Atzmon. And the border will bend from Atzmon toward Nachlah Mitzrayim and its extension will be to the sea.
(BeMidbar 34:3-5)

3. A second dispute regarding the description of the borders

Rashi and Rashbam also differ over the meaning of the above passages. The passages are translated according to Rashi's understanding of their meaning.[18] They describe the southern portion of the border. The border is described from its eastern extreme to its western extreme. In this description, this segment of the border is described as bending. In other words, the passages explain that the border does not proceed from east to west in a straight line. Instead, at two points, the border is described as deviating from its westward path.[19]

Rashbam suggests a slightly different translation of the passages. He explains that the passages do not describe the border as bending, but as protruding.[20] In other words, according to his understanding of the passages, at two points along the southern boundary, there are protrusions that increase the territory encompassed by the borders.

4. The foundation of the dispute between Rashi and Rashbam

An important difference between the interpretations of Rashi and Rashbam is the geographic perspective implicit in the description of the border. In Rashi's interpretation, the border is described in a very objective, geometric manner. There is no specific geographic perspective implicit in the description. In other words, the description would be accurate whether provided by a speaker located outside the borders or by a speaker located within the borders. This is not true of Rashbam's understanding of the description. The term "protrusion" implies a geographic perspective. The southern border's deviation from its east to west path can only be described as a protrusion from the geographic perspective of a speaker located within the boundaries of the land.

This same distinction underlies the first dispute between Rashi and Rashbam. According to Rashi, the Torah describes the borders of the Land of Israel as a continuous line. The account begins from the southeast corner and describes the progression of the line towards the west, then along the Mediterranean coast northward, then from the northwest on a westward path, and finally from the northwest to the southwest. According to Rashbam, the Torah does not describe the border as a continuous line. Instead, it describes the boundaries of the Land of Israel in each direction. In other words, it describes four intersecting lines. In this manner, it describes the point to which the territory of the land extends in each direction. Again, these two descriptions reflect

---

[18] Rabbaynu Shlomo ben Yitzchak (Rashi), Commentary on Sefer BeMidbar 34:4.
[19] Rashi's comments are not easily understood and are difficult to reconcile with the actual geography of the area described. However, the above is adequately accurate for the purposes of this analysis.
[20] Rabbaynu Shemuel ben Meir (Rashbam) Commentary on Sefer BeMidbar 34:4.

alternative geographic perspectives. Rashi understands the Torah's description of the borders as objective. The formulation of the description does not reflect the geographic perspective of the speaker. The description merely defines the continuous line or closed figure that separates the space or territory within from the territory without. Rashbam's understanding of the Torah's description does imply a geographic perspective. It is formulated as a description of boundaries or limits. The Torah describes how far the territory of the Land of Israel extends in each direction. This formulation implies that the speaker's geographic perspective is from within the territory.

5. The problem with Rashbam's interpretation

Rashi's interpretation of the passages is consistent with their context. Hashem is speaking to Moshe and describing the borders of the land that will be captured. At the point in time at which the communication takes place, the nation is encamped on the eastern bank of the Jordan. The Land of Cana'an is before Bnai Yisrael. They are situated outside of its borders. Therefore, it is reasonable to describe the borders in a manner consistent with this context. According to Rashi, this is exactly what occurs in the passages. The borders are described objectively. The description is not reflective of the speaker's geographical location or perspective.

However, Rashbam's position is more difficult to understand. The description of the boundaries implies that the speaker is describing the land from the geographic perspective of one standing within the territory being described. This is not consistent with the context of the passages. The nation with Moshe stood outside of the land.

And Bnai Yisrael traveled and camped upon the plains of Moav on the far-side of the Jordan.
(BeMidbar 24:1)

6. Rashbam's understanding of the Torah's literary style

The above passage is found at the end of Parshat Chukat. Bnai Yisrael has conquered the territories of Sichon and Og. The nation is encamped on the eastern bank of the Jordan River. Rashbam notes that the location of Bnai Yisrael's encampment is described as the far-side of the Jordan. This description is only appropriate from the geographical perspective of a speaker on the opposite – western bank – of the Jordan.[21] Rashbam's point seems to be that although the Torah is describing events that took place before the nation entered the land, the events and their locale are described from the geographical perspective of a speaker located within the Land of Israel.

Now, Rashbam's understanding of the Torah's description of the boundaries of the Land of Israel is more readily understood. The description is written from the geographical perspective of a person within the territory of the Land of Israel. This is consistent with the overall literary style of the Torah. The Torah consistently adopts this perspective, not only in describing the boundaries of the Land of Israel.

Rashbam does not present an explanation for this phenomenon. However, the apparent explanation is that although the Torah was given outside of the Land of Israel, it is intended to be observed within the Land. Therefore, it speaks to the generation that entered and conquered the Land and their descendents.

7. The significance of exile

---

[21] Rabbaynu Shemuel ben Meir (Rashbam) Commentary on Sefer BeMidbar 24:1.

The period between the 17th of Tamuz and the 9th of Av is designated as a period of mourning. This mourning is a response to the destruction of the Bait HaMikdash and the subsequent exile from the Land of Israel. Rashbam's comments and his outlook provide an important perspective upon these tragedies. The destruction of the Temple and the exile do not merely represent a national and material disaster. They reflect a spiritual tragedy of enormous proportion. The Torah is designed as a directive for life in the Land of Israel. Exile is not merely a material, national, and geopolitical phenomenon. It is essentially a spiritual state. It is a state of estrangement from Torah observance in its fullest state. This observance can only take place in the Land of Israel and with the Bait HaMikdash.

And the cities that you should give to the Leveyim – the six cities of refuge that you will give so that the murderer may flee there and in addition to them, forty-two cities. (BeMidbar 35:6)

The Role of the Mesorah in Determining the Correct text of TaNaCh

The Torah explains that the Land of Israel was to be divided among the tribes of Israel. Each *shevet* – tribe – was to receive a portion in the land. However, Shevet Leyve – the tribe of Leyve – was not to receive a typical portion. Instead, each of the other tribes was instructed to designate cities within its portion for the Leveyim to live in. Tribes that received a larger portion would be required to provide a greater number of cities. Tribes that received a smaller portion would apportion a lesser number of cities to the Leveyim. These cities – *arey migrash* – were to serve as the settlements of the Leveyim.

In addition to these cities, the Leveyim were also assigned the cities of refuge. These cities of refuge are also discussed in our *parasha*. A person who accidentally takes another's life is exiled to one of these cities of refuge. The portion of the Leveyim also included these cities of refuge. In addition to the *arey migrash,* the Leveyim lived in these cities.

Our *pasuk* explains that the Leveyim were to be given forty-two *arey migrash* and an additional six cities of refuge as their portion in the Land of Israel. Of course, these instructions could only be carried out once the Land of Israel was captured and occupied. Therefore, it would be Yehoshua's – Moshe's successor – responsibility to carry out these instructions.

Sefer Yehoshua outlines the process by which these cities were assigned to Shevet Leyve. The Navi provides a detailed account. It enumerates the number of cities contributed by each tribe, lists the specific cities, and identifies the family within the Shevet Leyve that received each city. As required by the Torah, forty-eight cities were assigned to the Leveyim – forty-two *arey migrash* and an additional six cities of refuge.

There is an interesting problem in the account in Sefer Yehoshua. In order to fully appreciate this problem, it is helpful to begin with an outline of the account in Sefer Yehoshua. The account is highly structured. The account has two parts. In the first portion of the account, each family within the Shevet Leyve is identified and the tribes within Bnai Yisrael that contributed cities to this family are listed. This portion of the account ends by indicating the total number of cities provided to each family by the tribes. The second portion of the account again identifies each of the families and the tribes that contributed cities for this family. However, in this portion of the account the names of the specific cities contributed by each tribe are listed.

Like the prior portion of the account, this portion of the account ends by providing the number of cities contributed to the family.

In the Navi's account of the cities to be given to the family of Merari there is a problem. In the first portion of the account, the Navi explains that twelve cities were assigned to the family of Merari. These cities were contributed by the tribes of Reuven, Gad and Zevulun.[22] In the second portion of the account the Navi provides a detailed enumeration of the cities contributed by each of these tribes. The Navi lists the four cities contributed by Shevet Zevulun and the four from Shevet Gad. The accounting ends by repeating that the family of Merari received a total of twelve cities.[23] The problem with this account is obvious. The Navi only list eight cities – those contributed by Shevet Zevulun and Shevet Gad. Missing are the four cities assigned to Merari from the portion of Shevet Reuven.

Rabbaynu David Kimchi – RaDaK – discusses this problem. He begins by noting the discrepancy. The family of Merari was to receive twelve cities from the tribes of Zevulun, Gad and Reuven. However, the detailed enumeration of these cities only accounts for eight cities. The four to be provided by Shevet Reuven are not listed. RaDaK comments that he has seen alternate versions of Sefer Yehoshua that "correct" this apparent omission in the text. In these versions, a list is provided of the four cities contributed by Shevet Reuven. This list does correspond with a list provided in Divrei HaYamim. RaDaK explains that in his research of carefully copied versions of the text he has never seen this correction. Therefore, he rejects the suggested correction. RaDaK adds that it is apparent from the writings of Rav Hai that he too was aware of the problem in our text but nonetheless insisted that the text is accurate.[24]

There are three difficulties with RaDaK's comments. First, although RaDaK rejects the alternate version of the text, he seems to concede that these alternate versions are more reasonable and do solve the problem in the text. Second, RaDaK rejects these alternate versions of the text. However, this leaves a problem. There is an inconsistency in the narrative. The cities contributed by Shevet Reuven are omitted. RaDaK does not make any effort to explain the inconsistency! It seems strange that RaDaK rejects the more reasonable version of the text and accepts the more traditional version without offering any explanation for the clear inconsistency in our version. Finally, RaDaK supports his conclusion by referring to Rav Hai. He notes that Rav Hai was aware of the problem in the text but insisted that nonetheless, the text should not be altered. What is RaDaK adding to his analysis through referring to Rav Hai? RaDaK has already concluded that the more ancient versions of the text that he examined do not enumerate cities contributed by Shevet Reuven.

In order to understand RaDaK's position, it is important to appreciate the fundamental issue that he faced. RaDaK was confronted with a clear inconsistency in the text of the Navi. On the one hand, alternate versions of the text resolved this issue by adding a verse. These alternate versions are more consistent than our text. From an analytical, scholarly perspective these alternate texts seem to be more reasonable than our text. On the other hand, all of the ancient versions of the text that RaDaK could authenticate were identical to our text and contained the

---

[22] Sefer Yehoshua 21:7.
[23] Sefer Yehoshua 21:34-38.
[24] Rabbaynu David Kimchi (RaDaK), *Commentary on Sefer Yehoshua* 21:7.

inconsistency. RaDaK was faced with the dilemma of choosing between unauthenticated alternate texts – that make sense – and more a more traditional text – that is clearly problematic.

In other words, the issue can be reduced to a simple question. How do we determine the proper text? Do we establish the text through analytic scholarship or through tradition? RaDaK maintains that the actual text is determined by *mesorah* – tradition. This is an important conclusion. In determining the text of TaNaCh, we are not permitted to decide issues based on analytic scholarship alone. We can use this method as a guide in choosing between authenticated alternates. But we cannot establish the text on the basis of analytic scholarship alone. Instead, the *mesorah* establishes the text.

But there is another element to RaDaK's analysis. RaDaK does not attempt to explain the inconsistency in our text. Apparently, he maintains that providing an explanation is not fundamental to his decision to accept the ancient texts. In other words, even if the text suggested by *mesorah* is obviously problematic it must be accepted. This implies that – in establishing the text of TaNaCh – *mesorah* is not just more important than analytic scholarship. It actually defines the text. In other words, the key issue is not to determine the actual text created by the author. *Halachah* requires that the valid text is the one indicated by *mesorah*.

An illustration will help clarify this point. Let us assume we discovered that the text of Sefer Yehoshua contained in the Dead Sea Scrolls corresponds with the alternate text that RaDaK had seen. The Dead Sea Scrolls predate Rav Hai. Would this discovery suggest that the alternate text should be accepted? Could it not be argued that these ancient documents are more accurate and less subject to errors and omission that may have slipped into the text with the passage of time? The implication from RaDaK's comments is that we would still reject the alternate text! How is this implied? RaDaK seems completely willing to concede that the alternate text is more consistent than our text. In turn, this implies that RaDaK is not primarily concerned with determining the actual original text. Instead, he focuses on the text established through *mesorah*. *Mesorah* determines the proper and accepted text. In other words, the accepted text is not necessarily the one that most closely corresponds with the original document. The accepted text is the text indicated by *mesorah*. We cannot establish a continuous chain of *mesorah* leading to the Dead Sea Scrolls. Therefore, in regards to determining the *mesorah* text, these scrolls are irrelevant.

It should also be noted that RaDaK's approach seems to be the only reasonable course to be taken by *halachah*. How can we ever determine the exact wording of the original text? Let us return to our example of the Dead Sea Scrolls. Our discovery would prove only that the alternate text existed at the time at which these scrolls were created. We cannot know if the text in the Dead Sea Scrolls was the only text in existence at that time. It is possible that our text also existed at that time! Therefore, *halachah* requires that these issues be resolved on the only basis that is practical. *Mesorah* defines the proper text.

Now, we can appreciate RaDaK's reference to Rav Hai. RaDaK's point – in making this reference – is that Rav Hai's version of the text was the same as ours. Because RaDaK maintains that *mesorah* actually establishes the text, this is a relevant observation. Rav Hai was his generation's transmitter of the *mesorah*. His comments indicate that there is a strong and established *mesorah* regarding our text. Based on the criteria he has established for determining the proper text, this indication of the *mesorah* is fundamental to his conclusions.

Made in the USA
Middletown, DE
03 May 2022